Mrs. Adams in Winter

Mrs. Adams

❧ IN ❧

Winter

A

JOURNEY IN

THE LAST DAYS OF

NAPOLEON

·

MICHAEL O'BRIEN

Farrar, Straus and Giroux

NEW YORK

Farrar, Straus and Giroux
18 West 18th Street, New York 10011

Distributed in Canada by D&M Publishers, Inc.
Printed in the United States of America
First edition, 2010

Map on pages x–xi copyright © 2010 by Jeffrey L. Ward

Library of Congress Cataloging-in-Publication Data
O'Brien, Michael, [date]
    Mrs. Adams in winter : a journey in the last days of Napoleon /
Michael O'Brien.—1st ed.
        p.   cm.
    Includes bibliographical references and index.
    ISBN 978-0-374-21581-1 (hardcover : alk. paper)
    1. Europe—Description and travel.   2. Europe—History—1789–1815.
3. Adams, Louisa Catherine, 1775–1852—Travel—Europe.   4. Adams, John Quincy,
1767–1848—Family.   5. Coaching (Transportation)—Europe—History—19th century.
6. Russia—Description and travel.   7. Baltic States—Description and travel.
8. Germany—Description and travel.   9. France—Description and travel.   I. Title.

D919.O27 2010
940.2'7092—dc22
[B]

2009025437

Designed by Abby Kagan

www.fsgbooks.com

1   3   5   7   9   10   8   6   4   2

Frontispiece: *View of the Moika and Palace Bridge* by Michel François Damame-Demartrais
(1812), © 2009, State Russian Museum, St. Petersburg

For
Heather and Ross
and
in memory of Brian

CONTENTS

LIST OF ILLUSTRATIONS   viii

MAP   x

PREFACE   xiii

1. SAINT PETERSBURG   3

2. FROM SAINT PETERSBURG TO RIGA   44

3. FROM RIGA TO BERLIN   96

4. FROM BERLIN TO EISENACH   138

5. FROM EISENACH TO FRANKFURT   191

6. FROM FRANKFURT TO PARIS   262

APPENDIX: PLACES   297

NOTES   305

ACKNOWLEDGMENTS   351

INDEX   353

ILLUSTRATIONS

Michel François Damame-Demartrais,
  View of the Moika and Palace Bridge (1812)   Frontispiece
Map: Louisa Catherine Adams's Route, Saint Petersburg
  to Paris, February 12–March 23, 1815   x
Charles Robert Leslie, *Louisa Catherine Adams* (1816);
  engraving by G. F. Storm (ca. 1839)   2
Carriage on Runners   43
Louisa Catherine Adams, "Narrative of a Journey
  from Russia to France 1815"   48
Itinerary from Riga to Saint Petersburg   52
Berline carriage   57
Kibitka   58
Map: Saint Petersburg to Narva   61
Johann Christoph Brotze, *Taproom in Inn* (1795)   63
Narva   67
Map: Narva to Dorpat   79
Johann Christoph Brotze, *The Dorpat Stone Bridge* (1800)   82
Map: Dorpat to Riga   88
Map: Riga to Memel   97
Johann Christoph Brotze, *Peasant Wagons in Estland* (undated) 99

Memel Lighthouse (1838)   116

Karl Wilhelm Wach, *Queen Luise as Hebe in Front
of the Brandenburg Gate* (1812)   120

Map: Memel to Brandenburg   122

Map: Braunsberg to Graudenz   125

Map: Graudenz to Schönlanke   130

Map: Schönlanke to Berlin   133

Edward Savage, *Louisa Catherine Johnson* (ca. 1793)   139

J. D. Laurens and F. C. Dietrich after F. A. Calau,
Mausoleum of Queen Luise (1818)   164

E. Malcom, *Water Color of the Old Adams House, Quincy* (1798)   171

Map: Berlin to Leipzig   179

Map: Leipzig to Eisenach   186

Eisenach and Wartburg (ca. 1700)   190

Map: Eisenach to Frankfurt   196

Alexander Keith Johnston, *The Battle of Hanau*   198

Johann Jakob de Lose, *Simon Moritz von Bethmann* (1812)   203

C.J.M. Whichelo, *South East View of All Hallows Barking
(by the Tower)* (1803)   206

John Singleton Copley, *John Quincy Adams* (1796)   217

Map: Frankfurt to Kehl   263

Map: Strasbourg to Châlons-sur-Marne   274

Map: Châlons-sur-Marne to Paris   279

George Lewis, *Beggars Surrounding a Carriage, Epernay* (1823)   281

B. de Belport, *Claude Étienne Michel* (1826)   283

Port-à-Binson in 1815   286

Post station, Port-à-Binson   289

William James Hubbard, *Louisa Catherine Adams* (1828)   294

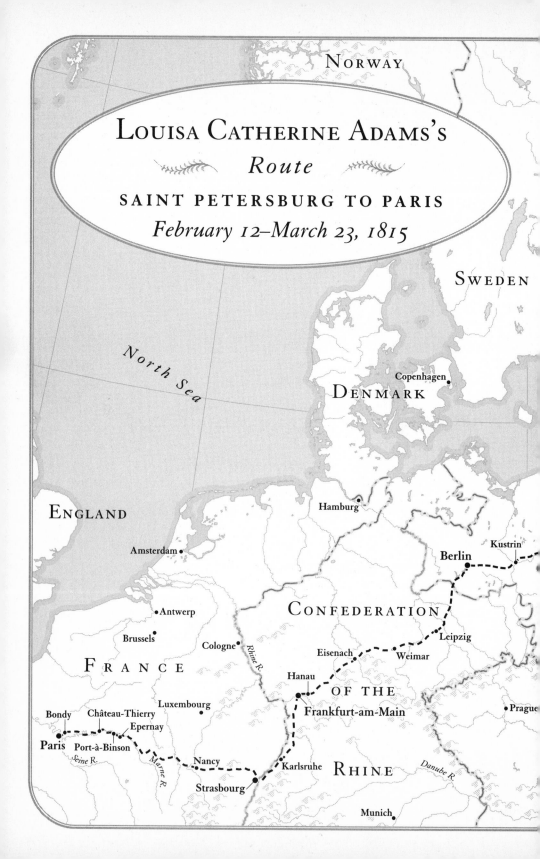

PREFACE

As many stories do, this one started within the family. The tale was first told in a Paris hotel in the spring of 1815, when a very tired Louisa Catherine Adams was reunited with her husband, John Quincy Adams, and explained what had happened to her. Beginning in winter, for forty days she and her very young son had been traveling across Europe in a heavy Russian carriage from Saint Petersburg, through the Baltic states, across Germany, and into France. It had been a difficult journey. This was Napoleonic Europe and there had been danger, battlefields, and fear. At first, she herself was inclined to understate what she had done, but eventually she saw that there might be significance in her journey. She became shyly proud of the accomplishment, as did members of her family, who began to speak of it in conversation and eventually in print. By 1836, Louisa Adams thought enough of her 1815 experience to write a memoir of it. By then, she had lived in the White House as the wife of an American president and was known for belonging to a great political dynasty, the Adamses of Quincy, Massachusetts. Later, she was known not only as the wife of John Quincy Adams and the daughter-in-law of John Adams, but as the daughter-in-law of Abigail Adams, because Abigail's fame as an American revolutionary and a woman began to spread, after her letters were first published in

1840. Later still, Louisa Catherine Adams would be known for being the grandmother of Henry Adams, the great historian and autobiographer, who would make her a significant character in his own story.

Living among the Adamses had a way of defining you. You were the wife of this Adams, the daughter-in-law of another Adams, the mother of yet another Adams. Apart from Abigail, they were mostly men, important men who helped to invent the United States, redefine its foreign policy, save the Union, and rewrite American and world history. They were men who not only deserved fame, but had been trained to earn it. But if you were a woman and an in-law, this was not an easy business, all this ambition and accomplishment. It came at a price. Louisa Catherine Adams, née Johnson, paid this price with much reluctance and, in the various memoirs she wrote late in life, tried to reason out how it had happened, what life had done to her, and how she had passed from living as a child in London to the places her husband had taken her: an apartment over the Brandenburg Gate in Berlin, an old homestead in Quincy, a dacha near Saint Petersburg, a mansion in Washington—these and many more places. Among these memories, her journey from Saint Petersburg to Paris acquired an iconic significance, as the moment when she had proved herself, not only as Louisa Catherine Adams, but as a woman acting in the name of other women.

She was right to think the journey could yield meanings, and this book attempts to reconstruct some of them. First, since this is a story about a woman traveling, it must be a biography of that woman, at least up to 1815. (Later is a different story, only a little told here.) A life can have meanings opaque to the person living it, but Mrs. Adams herself was most self-conscious about family, identity, and gender. For her, family meant two things: growing up a Johnson and becoming an Adams. She liked to remember the first as easy and the latter as hard, but she was notable for trying to hold on to being a Johnson, even when being swallowed up by the Adamses. The incompleteness of her transition from Johnson to Adams was partly explained by the richly complicated relationship that was her marriage, since John Quincy Adams was often difficult, sometimes kind, usually fascinating, and always stubborn. She never really knew whether her marriage had been a success, if she closely weighed the pain and the happiness, as she often did. As a wife, she was obliged to face many demands, for the partner of a diplomat and politician was a chess piece in several great games. As a First Lady, she had to endure what many such women had to endure: the sacrificing for a husband's early career and the splendid miseries attendant upon its later, always mixed success. But for Louisa Adams, being a mother was almost harder than being a wife, because she had a debilitating succession of miscarriages and one stillbirth, and, of the four children she bore, only one was to survive her. Because of this, she was only fragilely knitted into the succession of generations and never quite became a matriarch, which was what her culture said a woman should be.

In her mind, this sense of being an outsider was much tangled up with the worrisome business of identity. She had been born in England of a colonial American father and an English mother, had spent the impressionable years of her girlhood both in France and England, and then married an American who immediately took her to live in Prussia. She was twenty-six before she set foot on American soil and only eight years older when she left again, this time for six years in Russia and two back in London. She did not become a permanent resident of her husband's country until she was forty-two and, by then, had lived in Europe for thirty-four years. She remains the only First Lady to have been born outside the United States, a fact that John Quincy Adams's political opponents liked to mention as evidence of her disloyalty and probably his, too. If she were living now, it would be easy to find words to describe her—migrant, transnational, bicultural, bilingual, hybrid. Many a modern novel, history, and sociological treatise has sympathetic portraits of such women. But 1815 did not have the same words and sometimes had less sympathy. What it meant even to be an American was unclear then, though the Adams family was working at a clarification, and Louisa Adams spent the first half of her life among a cosmopolitan elite, which administered countries but did not always identify with them. Political and cultural nationalism was a new thing, more important to her husband and in-laws than to her. Yet she felt this cultural pressure acutely and was more than a little lost, because she never wanted to call herself English and, though she often proclaimed herself an American, she was less sure that others acknowledged her right to do so.

What she did know was that she was a woman and a lady. As a woman of high social standing in the late eighteenth and early nineteenth centuries, she could not have an independent career. She wrote, but she was not an author. She performed diplomatic tasks, but she was not a diplomat. She worked at politics, but she was not a politician. When her husband left home for the U.S. Senate or the office of the Russian foreign minister, she spent her time among other women, similarly situated—the wives and relatives of politicians, diplomats, merchants, aristocrats, and royalty. She inhabited these circles of women wherever she came to live. So this book is also a portrait of ladies, for they formed much of Louisa Adams's world. She herself observed them, lovingly, spitefully, or dispassionately. For her, they could be models of social or domestic success, though sometimes they offered warnings of sexual danger. They were remarkable people, some still famous (Abigail Adams, Queen Luise of Prussia), many now obscure (Condesa Colombi, Pauline Néale), but all important to Louisa Adams. Their significance was evident even as she crossed the European continent in 1815. For it seemed that to get from Saint Petersburg to Paris, she was obliged to navigate between islands of welcoming women by avoiding crosscurrents of difficult men. Much of her life seemed like this, too.

At its simplest level, *Mrs. Adams in Winter* tells the story of this journey, which has never been told in full. Her 1836 memoir was brief, written twenty-one years after the fact, and (as she admitted) often confused about details, because she set down her memories spontaneously and rapidly. For the most part, later historians have taken her at her word, seen the journey as a minor anecdote, and transcribed the confusions. By collating her memoir with contemporary travel accounts, guides, maps, and later histories, it is possible to straighten out some of the confusions, though not all, and offer a reconstruction of what certainly or probably happened. So this is, among other things, a book about the experience of traveling across Europe in the latter days of Napoleon: how it was done, what it cost, where you stayed, what you saw, and which cultures you encountered. As such, it begins with a departure.

Mrs. Adams in Winter

Charles Robert Leslie, *Louisa Catherine Adams* (1816);
engraving by G. F. Storm (ca. 1839)

·*1*·

SAINT PETERSBURG

S HE WAS IN A HURRY, because anxious. And she disliked partings, all the business of embraces, regrets, and promises. So she began the journey and left the city without ceremony, while her friends were distracted at Sunday dinner, which in Saint Petersburg occurred at five o'clock. The Moika Canal sat frozen close to her small, leaking apartment, and the deep snow and the hour deadened sound.[1] The unsteadiness of the horses, the ordering of the servants, the instructing of the postilions, the care of a small boy, the disposition of a heavy carriage on runners and a sled behind, the noise of three languages, the heaving of luggage, and the storing of provisions made a muffled confusion in the dusk.

She was right to be anxious, because she was committing herself mostly to strangers. Though she knew her servant John Fulling, the postilions were anonymous and she barely knew the French nurse, Madame Babet, who had only been employed that day. And there was a rough soldier called Baptiste, a prisoner of war she had agreed to take westward in exchange for his services. Baptiste worried her.[2]

To be sure, she had pieces of paper that were reassuring. There was a Russian passport from the State Board of Foreign Affairs, which had been issued five days before. Written in German, "in pursuance

of the edict of His Majesty, the Sovereign Emperor Alexander Pav-
lovich, Ruler of all the Russias, etc., etc., etc," it gave her leave of absence and free passage from his empire. The minister of the interior,
Osip Petrovich Kozodavlev, had given her the obligatory *padarojna*,
or order for post-horses, and sent commands that she should be well
treated by all the postmasters on the road "on pain of punishment."[3]
(Punishment from such a man was not something to contemplate
lightly, for he was the tsar's spymaster and prison warden.) There was
her French passport, signed in the name of the French ambassador by
his secretary, but *"au Nom du Roi,"* the restored Louis XVIII. The
Prussian ambassador had given her yet another passport *"im Namen
seiner Majestät des Konigs von Preussen,"* which had a comforting ring,
since she knew the Prussian king well, had danced with him, and
trusted to his protective kindness. Then, too, she had hidden bags of
gold and silver, as well as letters of credit to bankers along her way.
For she was a fine lady of lofty rank, someone of fur and turquoise
rings, someone who knew the tsar, the tsarina, a king or two, and
aristocrats beyond number and often beyond remembrance. In crude
post stations, in flea-bitten inns, she would be someone who might
elicit deference, even fear. She would manipulate this response.

To her surprise, she was a little sorry to leave. For most of her time
there, she had disliked the place, with its biting cold winters and hu-
mid listless summers, and she disliked the "gaudy loneliness" of being almost the only woman of her kind in the city.[4] In Saint Petersburg,
she had found few friends and little comfort. On that twelfth of
February—as it happened, her fortieth birthday—she entered her
carriage with trepidation. All her life, she had lacked confidence and
seen the world as a challenge she could not meet. This journey would
be a test, or so she came to think.

Being only seven, the boy had as yet little history that anyone cared
to record. He was known as a child of quick passions, so wild that his
mother could find him difficult to manage. But he was sweet and
needy, someone who tried hard. He had lived almost all his short life
in Saint Petersburg and there acquired an unstable mix of cultures.
He was formed by a German nursemaid, parents who often spoke

French, and servants who were Russian. English was only his third language, and he wrote letters in it blunderingly, with a pained sense of inadequacy. The city had made him grow up faster than was usual, for the Russians were uninterested in the innocence of childhood, and treated children like him as small adults. When not yet three, he had attended in fancy dress the palace of the French ambassador and opened a ball by leading out the ambassador's illegitimate daughter (at three and a half, his senior by about six months). Afterward there had been an "elegant supper" with "oceans of Champaign for the little people." For this hothouse growth his mother had been grateful in this last year, for he had discerned that she needed reassurance and had offered her "little tender assiduities; attentions gentle and affectionate" beyond his years.[5]

Being middle-aged and having hair streaked with gray, the boy's mother had a longer history. In appearance, she was petite and slim, though many years of a grueling social life—balls, dinners, fêtes, conversazioni—had added some weight. She was not sure this was a bad thing. ("At our time of life fat is very becoming.")[6] She dressed fashionably, but she had never been a belle. She stopped no conversations when she entered a room, nor did she occasion pitiful stares. She was the middling sort, a girl and then a woman usually thought very pretty with her "heavenly blue-eyes," though her prettiness arose as much from her personality and what she did with words as from her form. She came from a family that had been acutely aware of physical appearance and had good reason to be. Her own mother had been "very lovely," "exquisitely delicate, and very finely proportioned." Her father was "the handsomest man" she ever saw, and this opinion had more basis than daughterly prejudice. Her eldest sister had an easy and graceful deportment, a fair complexion, auburn hair, a dimpled mouth, beautiful teeth, and hazel eyes with an "expression it is impossible to describe, for their brilliant gaiety seemed to call on those she looked on to be as gay and as happy as herself." Among such riches, she had felt herself inadequate, less attractive.[7]

Her wit had been too sharp to encourage brainless young men in drawing rooms, but people of urbanity thought of her as a peer, though only eventually. When young, she had been as "timid as a hare," had disliked to go into society, and had been a wallflower when forced into assembly rooms.[8] Over time, painfully, she had acquired the knack of sociability. But she had a persistent sense that she entered society as an alien, scrutinized with skepticism by those who belonged. This anxiety meant that she made herself a close student of how society worked, of its rules and regulations, those plain and those implied. She was a closer student of those who inhabited society, for studying them helped her survive. She was sharply aware of glances, the placement of a jewel, the lifted eyebrow, the snigger in the corner, the candid smile. She warmed at kindliness, shrank from cynicism, and was offended by hypocrisy. She was not a natural inhabitant of an eighteenth-century or Regency salon, though there was nowhere else for her to live.

She thought of herself as proud and haughty, a trait that went back to her childhood, when she used to stand aside from schoolgirl cliques and so had been mistrusted. In fact, she needed to connect, for she was sentimental, readily amused, and liked parties where there were gossip, smiles, English country dances, and a lingering past midnight. But she preferred a society of those she knew and trusted. She did not need to be the center of attention, but she disliked being ignored, too, and she knew the entitlements of her rank. This delicate balance was not easy to accomplish, especially for those who had to deal with her. Her emotions lay very close to the surface. Anger, happiness, and fear registered on her face and in her movements quickly, and as quickly changed. This led some to think her shallow, even insincere, but it was not so. With her, emotions ran deep, too deep. She was less sure whether her reason ran as deep. Over the years, her greatest problem was a body that seemed always to betray her, and she was never sure where body ended and mind began. So fevers and aches, nerves and agitation, were hard to disentangle. Had her body given way because her mind was weak, as she feared that people thought? Or had her mind given way because her body was weak? She did not know.

Her last days in the city had been frantic, because the decision to leave had been unexpected and abrupt. For nearly a year, she had been alone and drifting, unsure about what would happen next. Her taste for independence had been modest, but being "dreadfully isolated . . . in this *great City*" had fed the taste. Over that time, she had grown used to running her own life. Apartments had been rented and changed, the city abandoned in summer for a rural dacha, horses and carriages bought and sold, drunken servants dismissed and replacements employed, unwonted duties assumed, all upon her own authority. To the skeptical, she had pleaded necessity. "I have been obliged to do many things," she said. Often her mood had been bad. She had been "sick and cross," and restless about the sacrifices she was being asked to make. On the other hand, there had been pleasure in this moment of detachment. She had always been forced into care with money, because someone else had kept the books, the margins had been slim, and wearying homilies about thrift had been commonplace. Now, unmonitored, she felt freer to buy a new carriage and new clothes—"I have been under the necessity of expending [more] for my toilet than usual on account of the fetes"—and there was little conviction in her remark that "I am very sorry for it but I could not withstand the temptation and indulged myself."[9] She was not really sorry.

A letter had come only three weeks before and had precipitated her going. It had invited her to Paris. It had advised breaking up her establishment, selling whatever furniture she did not wish to keep, packing up the rest, and leaving it to be forwarded to a destination as yet obscure. If she wished, she could leave as soon as possible or wait until spring. But, in either case, the letter suggested traveling with a "good man, and woman servant," and perhaps "some Lady or person of your acquaintance." If she left promptly, when it was still deep winter, the letter recommended using only a kibitka, a large sled, in which she would need to wrap up warm against the chill. The roads would furnish "very tolerable lodging for the night, at any of the Post houses," the letter said.[10]

Her first reaction had been astonishment, then confusion, then exhilaration, then action. ("I am turned woman of business.") She had instantly decided to go as quickly as possible. Tsarina Elizabeth Alexievna was to remark, with that sad kindness for which she was known, that "joy sparkled" in the prospective traveler's eyes and that "she had never seen a Woman so alter'd in her life for the better." The traveler had quickly decided, too, to stop on the way in Berlin, to pay her respects to old friends.[11] But there had been much to do. It was necessary to put a notice in the imperial gazette, weekly for three weeks, to announce her name and age, her intention to depart, and her freedom from debts, to give creditors an opportunity to come calling if the last assertion was an untruth.[12] She had to see her bankers, John Christoph Meyer and George Augustus Bruxner, who closed her account, agreed to look after some trunks, and gave her letters of credit. To Messrs. Schwink and Koch in Königsberg, they wrote with brief, formulaic, but delicate courtesy: "We do ourselves the Honour to introduce to you by the present Her Excellency . . . who passes your Place on her Tour to Paris, to request you would advance her against her Receipt, what money she may want . . . any Civilities & Services you may render Her Excellency will confer on us a particular Obligation." The practicalities of the household were harder. Furniture and goods proved difficult to sell, but expensive to keep and ship onward. Few had "ready money," though one gentleman offered her diamonds or pearls in lieu of cash, and she had been tempted to accept.[13] No easier were the elaborate bureaucratic procedures. The Russian Empire was a police state and did not permit people to come and go readily.

Her French passport was dated February 7, 1815, according to the Gregorian calendar, and January 26 according to the Julian calendar by which the Russians kept time. On it, her party was described as *"Madame Louise Catherine Adams et Monsieur Charles Francois Adams son fils, se rendant à Paris avec leur domestiques."* It did not explain why Louisa Catherine Adams and her son Charles Francis Adams needed to make their way by road to Paris in the depth of winter and alone, save for the servants.

On its surface, the reason was simple. Her husband, John Quincy Adams, was two thousand miles away in France and they were to join him. They had been apart for nearly a year. He had been commissioned by his government to intermit his office as American minister plenipotentiary to the court of Tsar Alexander I and to join the commission charged with negotiating a peace treaty between the United States and Great Britain to end the war that had been waged halfheartedly since 1812. So he had left her in Saint Petersburg in April 1814 and followed a meandering route from Russia, to Sweden, to Denmark, and on to Ghent in the Netherlands, where the treaty was concluded in the last days of that same year. By way of reward for his labors, partly at her urging, he had gone on to Paris. There he waited, reluctant to return to the cul-de-sac that was Saint Petersburg, a place that had come close to burying his career. Poised and hopeful of better things, easier to imagine in a Parisian spring than a Russian winter, he waited, partly for her.

She was leaving with many memories, some of which she had already set down in diaries, some of which she was to drag up from the back of her mind much later, when it seemed important to remember. They were not simple memories. There was little nostalgia, at least not for Russia.

She remembered how she had come. On August 5, 1809, she had left her house at the corner of Boylston and Nassau Streets in Boston, gone north to cross the Charles River bridge to William Gray's wharf in Charlestown, and there embarked on the *Horace*, which was to sail directly to Kronstadt, the port of Saint Petersburg. She was in a motley party. There had been nine of them. There was herself, her husband, and their third son. There was her young sister Catherine, pretty, flirtatious, indiscreet, and witty, "without one sixpence in the world [and] not even clothed properly." There was John Quincy Adams's disreputable, silent, and gentlemanly nephew William Steuben Smith, who was to be his private secretary, and two other young New Englanders (Alexander Everett, Francis C. Gray) who were coming as diplomatic attachés, for the experience. There was Martha Godfrey, who had for a year been Louisa Adams's cook and chambermaid, and "a black man-servant named Nelson," who was from Trinidad. The ship's crew had numbered nineteen: Benjamin Beckford, the captain; Nathan Poland, his mate; George Louder, the second mate; John Laighton, the clerk; Noah Jewett, the carpenter; William Cooper, the ship's boy; John Johnson, the steward; and twelve seamen. Some of these were never to return from Russia, because in Kronstadt, cholera was waiting.[14]

The voyage had taken a slow eighty days. On it, the young male travelers had begun jealously to quarrel, which Mrs. Adams had noticed. She took it as an ill omen, for it was possible they would be years together, cooped up during long, claustrophobic winters in Saint Petersburg lodgings, where the young men would encircle her sister.[15]

She was traveling toward a Europe that had been irregularly at war for nearly twenty years. In the mid 1790s, conservative powers, including Austria, Prussia, Britain, the Netherlands, and Spain, had tried to defeat the republican regime that had emerged from the French Revolution, but failed. Thereafter, especially after Napoleon's accession to power as first consul in 1799 and as emperor in 1804, this sequence of attempted containment and failure remained the pattern. Between 1793 and 1807, four coalitions of monarchical regimes tried unsuccessfully to roll back French power, only to be forced into yet more concessions. When Mrs. Adams left for Russia, Napoleon's power was at its zenith, for then he was both emperor of France and king of Italy (at least of its northeastern provinces), and France had incorporated Belgium, the Netherlands, parts of northwestern Germany, Corsica, much of northwestern and central Italy (including Rome), Slovenia, Croatia, and Dalmatia directly into the French Empire. Then there was a series of French satellite states that encompassed Switzerland, the rest of Italy as far as the Strait of Messina, the newly established Confederation of the Rhine, Spain, and the duchy of Warsaw. Further, France had alliances with Austria, Prussia, Russia, Sweden, and the kingdom of Denmark and Norway. In 1809, only the British remained as an active enemy. Over the years, save for a single truce, British opposition to France had remained implacable, but other powers had drifted in and out of opposition, in and out of alliance, as opportunism and the fortunes of war dictated. The Russians had stood aside for most of the 1790s, joined the Second Coalition against France briefly in 1799, founded the Third Coalition with Britain in 1805, but was forced to sue for peace at Tilsit in 1807, after Napoleon's comprehensive defeat of Prussia. In 1809, the Russians were uneasy partners of France and obligated by treaty to honor Napoleon's Continental System, intended to prevent the British from trading with mainland Europe. In retaliation, the British, too, were waging economic warfare and used their own greater naval power to interdict ships bound for ports sympathetic to France. As Mrs. Adams was to discover, the seas over which she passed were theaters of war.

It took six weeks for the *Horace* to sight the Orkneys in the north of Scotland, though the voyage across the North Sea was more brisk. Then there were five weeks of delay in the Baltic Sea, because of very bad weather and the British blockade of Danish ports. Off Norway, they had been stopped by a British brig of eighteen guns, then by another disguised under Danish colors, then by a Danish two-mast boat with fifteen armed men who ventured to board. They would be forced to stop eleven times in all, by either Danish or British ships. They had landed at Kristiansand on the southern tip of Norway and there found thirty American merchant ships, brought in by privateers and imprisoned. But the progress of the *Horace* was helped by diplomatic passports and the absence of a merchant cargo, though squalls and gales ("the heaviest that I ever witnessed," one experienced passenger said) slowed her exasperatingly. A battery placed upon "three sunken seventy-four-gun ships" near Copenhagen had opened fire on them, a cannonball had struck just before the prow, and they had been forced to come to for yet another examination of their papers. Thereafter, with adverse winds, biting cold, low provisions, and lower morale, there had been a slow, zigzagging "dismal course" from Baltic island to Baltic island before they reached Kronstadt. Perhaps this experience explains why, six years later, she preferred not to wait until spring and hazard sailing, but to leave in winter and trust to land. For she sharply remembered the "tedious, and dangerous passage, of eleven weeks; during which I suffered considerably, both fear and sickness."[16]

After fear came anxiety, the trepidation of entering an alien world. Soon after reaching Saint Petersburg, she had to be introduced to the imperial court, for without an introduction she would be a nonperson. The process had not begun well. She had been given advice on etiquette but it was incorrect, and she knew enough about courts to know that punctilious etiquette was of their essence. A misstep would be long remembered and little forgiven. Then the imperial master of ceremonies had called on her to outline the right procedure. Fortunately, the Commandeur de Maisonneuve was an old acquaintance and "a most delightful old man," so this visit was reassuring.[17] She was instructed to write to the foreign minister, Nikolai Petrovich Rumiantsev, and request an audience with the empress mother, Maria Federovna, and Tsarina Elizabeth Alexievna.

Maisonneuve further advised that, on the next Saturday evening, Mrs. Adams ought to call on Ekaterina Vassilievna, Countess Litta, who would give more detailed information about the niceties of ceremony, for she was the grand mistress of the court. A British diplomat's wife, Lady Sarah Lyttelton, was to make the same visit, for the same information, four years later and found herself in the company of "a great fat woman, sitting in a fine room, dressed in a cambric gown and great mob cap, very dowdy, but with a most splendid scarlet shawl of immense price, which is to say 200 pounds sterling, for they make nothing of giving that for shawls." The countess was certainly very rich, mostly from being the niece and heiress of Prince Grigori Alexandrovitch Potemkin, perhaps the greatest of Catherine the Great's lovers, ministers, and favorites, and one of the builders of the Russian Empire to the east. Like her four sisters, Ekaterina had been not only Potemkin's niece but his lover. (Most of the family was unfussy about incest, though Grandmother had been upset.) Ekaterina had been Potemkin's blond "Katinka" or "Kitten," who when young "had yielded to his passion more out of pity than out of reciprocity." In her youth, she had been ill educated and passive, a woman who in

Naples had liked to spend all day stretched on a sofa, there "enveloped in a big black fur coat without a corset." Now, however, she was approaching fifty, with traces of her former beauty still discernible amid the folds of skin. She had been married twice. First, there had been the sometime Russian ambassador to Naples, Count Paul Martinovitch Skavronsky of Livonia, a descendant of Peter the Great's wife, a clumsy man widely thought "a tolerant buffoon" whose obsession had been music, which he wrote with little-surpassed incompetence. He used to compel his servants to speak in recitative "according to exact pitch," and requested his visitors to converse in "musical improvisations." Second, in 1798 Ekaterina had married, with more happiness, Count Giulio Renato de Litta, a large and talkative Milanese whom she had met in Naples but who had been in the Russian navy under Catherine the Great and later served as the diplomatic representative of the Knights of Malta in Saint Petersburg.[18]

Sunday, November 12, 1809, was to be the presentation of Mrs. Adams at Court.[19] Just before eleven, the American consul in Saint Petersburg came to her hotel apartments. He and her husband were to leave promptly for a Te Deum to mark the conclusion of peace between Austria and France, before John Quincy Adams's own presentation to the empress mother. (He had met the tsar a week earlier.) Just as the two men were going, a note came from Rumiantsev marked *tres pressée*. This postponed her presentation to 2:30 that afternoon. The delay left her "*quite* alone," with three and a half hours to wait. For the men, there was a sonorous ceremony in the Great Church of the Winter Palace. The diplomatic corps filed in and afterward the imperial family. All stood as the inexorable liturgy of the Russian Orthodox Church was followed and the choir chanted. The tsar advanced to the railing that separated clergy from congregation to kiss the crucifix presented by Ambrose, the metropolitan of Saint Petersburg and Novgorod, and then Maria Federovna and Elizabeth Alexievna followed. At the moment this service began, at noon, celebratory cannon were fired from the Admiralty Building and the sound reached Mrs. Adams, waiting doubtfully in her hotel room at the corner of the Nevsky Prospect and Admiralty Square.

In time, she received a second note, carried by a messenger from the Department of Ceremonies, to say that her presentation would be earlier, at two o'clock. So she adjusted her anxious expectations and continued to wait, still "left alone to go through all the fears and frights of the Presentation perfectly alone at the most magnificent Court in Europe." Then yet another note came. It was now to be 1:30. So she fretted more, about etiquette, about her inadequacy, and about her appearance, though she had taken as much care as her taste and limited means allowed. Her hair was "simply arranged and ornamented with a small diamond arrow." She wore a silver tissue skirt with no hoop, white satin gloves and shoes, a "heavy crimson Velvet Robe with a very long train lined with White body and sleeves trimmed with a quantity of Blond." Thrown over it was a fur cloak to keep out the chill as, in a carriage attended by two footmen, she crossed the western edge of the square and turned right down the Neva embankment to a northern entrance of the Winter Palace.[20]

She was to remember descending from the carriage with difficulty, because her clothes got in a tangle. But she arranged herself and was met by a court official. Then she walked into the palace and ahead, to the south, saw another entrance, which led to the palace's courtyard and an entrance reserved to the imperial family. But she had turned to her left and passed eastward along the Jordan Gallery, so called because it was along this wide passageway that the imperial family went at Epiphany to undertake the ceremony of the Blessing of the Waters, a ritual that recalled the river Jordan and mimicked how Venetian doges went to bless the Adriatic. All around Mrs. Adams were the baroque imaginings of Francesco Bartolemeo Rastrelli, who had reconstructed the palace from 1754 to 1762. She passed through an arch and mounted the lower flight of the wide Ambassadors' Staircase, finished in white and pink marble, with low steps not easy to mount gracefully. Ahead of her, in an alcove, was a white marble statue of a woman representing justice. Everywhere were allegorical statues (Loyalty, Wisdom, Majesty, Law, Abundance) and everywhere gilt, caryatids, and candelabras. Above her was a billowing fresco of Mount Olympus, painted by Gaspare Diziani in the

1750s. At the top of the stairs, she passed westward between blue marble columns, topped with gilt Ionic volutes, and to her right were tall windows that gave a glistening view of the frozen river and, across it, the Peter and Paul Fortress. Ahead of her lay the Neva Enfilade, the great suite of state rooms that Rastrelli's successor, Giacomo Quarenghi, had reconstructed in the 1790s. In 1809, the Enfilade consisted of three successive rooms—the Fore-Hall, the Great Gallery, and the Concert Hall.[21]

She was met in the Fore-Hall by Countess Litta, "superbly dressed and covered with diamonds." The countess explained that the first presentation was to the tsarina, that Mrs. Adams should stand in the middle of the hall and face westward toward the folding doors, through which the tsarina would enter. The debutante was to stand unmoved until Her Imperial Majesty reached her and then remove her glove in preparation for kissing the tsarina's hand, though the kiss would not be permitted.[22] She would be expected to bow and, in rising, she was to be careful not to touch the imperial body. This said, the countess retired "to the embrasure of a window," and perhaps looked out on the river to pass a time that was for her a little tedious, but which for the trembling Louisa Adams was consumingly anxious, as she stood alone in her satin, crimson, and velvet, with her modest diamond arrow in her simple hair, and awaited she knew not quite what, except that it was unlikely to be simple.

At the doors before her were stationed two black Africans in Turkish costume, each holding a drawn saber with a gold-tipped handle. As the doors opened, she saw that at each successive set of doors leading to the Great Gallery and the Concert Hall were duplicate pairs of Africans. More pressingly, she saw not only the tsarina in court dress, but also the tsar in military uniform, both moving in her direction.

Alexander I was then thirty-two years old and had been tsar since 1801. He had been the favorite grandson of Catherine the Great, who had planned that the succession should fall upon Alexander and not his father, Paul, whom she rationally mistrusted. In the event, Paul did become tsar in 1796 and had a brief reign marked by such paranoia and autocratic severity that his assassination, upon which his son conferred a reticent and guilty blessing, was widely viewed as a deliverance. (The Romanovs seldom hesitated to kill a relative, if power was at stake.) As tsar, Alexander had a mixed record. He had toyed with liberal reform, to little purpose, and was regarded by some as little better than "a frenchified innovator." He had wavered in his foreign policy between the British and the French until he had taken the side of Prussia in 1806, shared in its military defeat, and then abandoned Frederick William III at Tilsit and forged an uneasy understanding with Napoleon. By 1809, most foreigners regarded him as marginal to the European political scene and ineffectual. That he had charisma, however, few doubted. He was tall, handsome, and blue-eyed, with a slightly receding hairline. He was somewhat deaf in his left ear and shortsighted, and this contributed to the impression that, when turning his head to the right and leaning toward those he met, he was winningly interested in what was being said to him. He thought of himself as accessible and open, comradely and friendly, though this tone was easier for him to maintain if his interlocutor agreed with him. Considering that Alexander was an autocrat, most did. Women were usually charmed by him, at least at first, and he was a constant flirt. (A better flirt than a lover, the malicious said, for his flirtations were "seldom dangerous to the objects of his attentions.") He had once been slim, but was now beginning to be stout. In his youth, he had been well educated by a learned Swiss republican and spoke five languages, including English, though he was not an intellectual, hardly ever finished a book, tended to garble what was complicated, and often used phrases in lieu of ideas. But almost everyone agreed that he usually meant well. Especially around women, he seemed to convey a delicate sense that he was imprisoned by being tsar and needed a sympathetic rescuer.[23]

The woman next to him, who moved lightly with a graceful step, would have liked to have been that rescuer, but the tsarina had long since been disappointed in her love for him, and she was one of the few women to whom Alexander could be pointedly rude. That she had failed to give him an heir—she had borne only two daughters, who died within eighteen months of birth—was part of the explanation for his coldness, as was the possibility that the first of the infants was not his child, but that of her lover, Prince Adam Czartoryski. She had, to be sure, been provoked into infidelity and it was not habitual, and she had clung tearfully to a hope of loving reconciliation, long past the point when anyone else at court thought it possible. This was a source of regret for many, for few found this tall, slim, and elegant woman anything other than sympathetic, kind, and gracious. Elizabeth Alexievna had a dignified air of exquisite melancholy that appealed to a Romantic age, and she certainly came to appeal to Mrs. Adams, who shared the sense that "a touch of suffering in her eyes and in her voice only increases her charm."[24]

Behind this unhappy couple followed the grand marshal and a swirling train of courtiers (grand dukes, princesses, counts) who had come from the Te Deum and the many quarters of the immense palace to attend their sovereign. Mrs. Adams stood alone trying to be still, as Countess Litta watched critically, as the grand marshal and the courtiers paused, and as the doors were half closed behind Their Imperial Majesties, who left the Great Gallery, entered the Fore-Hall, and approached. Louisa did as she was instructed: making the bow, aborting the kiss, keeping her distance. The tsarina was affable but said little, and the tsar did most of the talking for the fifteen minutes the audience lasted. The doors were reopened, they returned whence they came, and Louisa was left alone again, in the middle of the great room.

The countess abandoned her window and said that all had gone well, and that now Mrs. Adams must proceed to meet the empress mother in her private "superb but not so elaborate" apartments, with rich marquetry floors, pastel doors, tapestries, and amiable putti looking down.[25] These rooms required a considerable walk to reach, for they were in what was known as the Palace Enfilade, in the southern part of the building, where they overlooked the square. This audience was a less nerve-racking venture, partly for being in private and not public rooms, partly because Mrs. Adams was now a little seasoned in imperial encounters. However, the former Princess Sophie

Marie Dorothea Auguste Louise of Württemberg was a more prickly character than her daughter-in-law, the former Princess Louise Maria Auguste of Baden. Elizabeth Alexievna was sad, childless, and defeated, and her defeat had partly been arranged by her mother-in-law. Maria Federovna was indomitable, sharp-tongued, and the mother of ten children, two of whom became tsars, one a viceroy of Poland, another a queen of Württemberg, and yet another a queen of the Netherlands. While the tsar liked to play at simplicity and his wife had to respect this preference, the empress mother saw no reason to stint, which led the tsarina to speak of her mother-in-law's "colossal vanity." The tsar would walk alone on the Admiralty Embankment and was frequently seen "wrapped up in his regimental cloak, riding about the capital alone, upon a little common [troika]" or, more extravagantly, "in a chariot, perfectly plain, of a dark olive, drawn by four horses, driven by a bearded coachman, a common little postillion, and attended by a single footman." But his mother required a carriage and six horses, with an escort of hussars, and she liked to wear military uniforms, as had her mother-in-law, Catherine the Great. Maria Federovna ran her own court, which it was wise for all to attend frequently. Partly out of guilt for having acquiesced in the murder of his father (her husband), Alexander paid her far more deference than he did his own wife, would sometimes dine with her three times a week, and occasionally would sleep in her apartments. A French general once explained to Talleyrand, the French foreign minister: "The Empress Mother is the one who displays her imperial state . . . In public ceremonies, Maria Feodorovna often takes the Emperor's arm; the Empress Elizabeth walks behind, and alone. I have seen troops under arms and the Tsar on horseback waiting for his mother to arrive. Not a favor is granted in Russia, not a single appointment is made, but the beneficiary goes to pay his respects and to kiss her hand in thanks without her having taken the least part in attaining the favor; but he does not go to say anything to the Empress Elizabeth."[26] So Mrs. Adams, passing from one to the other, was passing from one enemy camp to another, though she is unlikely to have known that, not then.

This audience lasted twenty minutes. In appearance, the empress mother had a fine complexion, hazel eyes, and, though now "somewhat corpulent," she gave evidence that once she had been beautiful. When she tried, she could have manners "in a peculiar degree soft, benign and captivating."[27] But she liked newcomers to be impressed with her imperial city and habitually asked questions intended to elicit their sense of wonder. Mrs. Adams duly expressed her admiration, but also mentioned that she had seen London, Paris, Berlin, and Dresden, and, even so, would give the palm to Saint Petersburg. "My God, you have seen everything!" Maria Federovna exclaimed in French, and was not pleased. She had been told to expect an American lady, an untutored "savage," and not a seasoned cosmopolitan. For all that, the old lady was "wonderfully gracious," not something she always felt it necessary to sustain over the years in which they were to meet.[28]

At this point, Countess Litta left Mrs. Adams, because the next, very brief audience was only with a grand duchess and did not require the lofty superintendence of a "Madame Field Marshall." Instead, control of the protocol passed to Countess Charlotte von Lieven, then sixty-seven and a widow, who was scarcely less important in court circles. She had served as governess to the children of Tsar Paul, and, in that capacity, had helped to bring up Tsar Alexander himself. She had long worked unsuccessfully to quieten a turbulent court and had often been charged with difficult missions, not least when she had had to break the news to Maria Federovna that her husband had been strangled, after a heavy snuffbox had been smashed into his left temple. Louisa Adams remembered the countess as "an elegant presence," but as possessing no traces of beauty. The German author Johann Seume four years earlier had observed of her: "I found her possessed of so much pure, friendly, affable, female character, that I almost forgot her connection with the court, and only fancied myself in the society of a worthy matron." As the governess, she would introduce Mrs. Adams to Alexander's youngest sister, Grand Duchess Anna Pavlovna, then only fourteen, though even so she had only recently been delivered from having to accept Napoleon's offer of marriage.[29]

This had been Louisa Adams's introduction to the court, which dominated the life of the city. Over the years, she would spend much time there. She came to regard the experience with a mix of wonderment, anxiety, boredom, and exhaustion. There were ceremonials that might have an attendance of four thousand people; there were operas and plays in the Hermitage Theater; there were fêtes at Peterhof and Pavlovsk, with pavilions decked in roses; and everywhere there was a "luxury of dress [exceeding] any thing you can form an idea of." During the winter, there were balls beyond counting— ordinary balls, masked balls, balls for children, balls at court, balls given by the diplomatic corps, balls in aristocratic palaces, balls to mark birthdays, balls to celebrate a marriage, balls for military victories. They usually started late, often went through the night, and ended with carriage rides home at four or six in the morning. The Adamses often did not get out of bed with sore heads and dry throats until early in the afternoon. This exquisite treadmill, this parade of velvet and diamonds amid a "mass of burnished gold, painting, and carving," was mandatory for a diplomatic couple. At first, Louisa Adams had reveled in "gentlemen wearing black Venetian hats with large Plumes of Feathers and Cloaks," in ladies' "rich dresses of the most splendid style," and in illuminations outside the Winter Palace that exceeded "all description," such that a bewildered brain floated in "gay delight." For her, this was "too much like a fairy tale." Over the years, the emphasis came to rest less on the fairy tale and more on the "too much," more on this being a "killing life." And over those same years, she noticed the diamonds less and the courtiers more. She saw past the glitter to the fallibility of the people who danced their polonaises, gossiped over their schnapps and reindeer's tongues, smilingly damned an enemy or a friend, and maneuvered to possess what a court had in abundance, money and power.[30]

In the imperial family itself, Mrs. Adams encountered a mixed group. She always found the tsarina to be sympathetic, someone willing to spend an hour entertaining her son Charles Francis, and even willing to get down on her knees to look at prints with the boy. Like everyone else, Louisa pitied the tsarina and could not forget what all knew, that Elizabeth spent much time alone, sad, humiliated, and in tears. Later Mrs. Adams was to write: "I have seen an Empress in the midst of splendour . . . pine for that greatest of all blessings her husbands love, and confidence, insulted by his neglect; affronted by his Mistress while under her eye; and she, obliged to wear the specious mask of courtesy, while every natural feeling of virtuous indignation, was closely concealed in her heart of hearts, to add to the bitter anguish of her wounded spirit."[31]

The empress mother, on the other hand, was censorious and demanding. On one occasion, when the tsar gave a ball to mark his mother's birthday, Mrs. Adams decided to decline, because she did not have a new dress to wear. She sent an excuse of ill health and went instead to a friend's for tea. Maria Federovna, hearing of this subterfuge, sent word that this should not happen again or Mrs. Adams would find herself excluded. It was said that the old lady had once tartly remarked to a courtier, who had had the temerity to wear the same dress twice, that she "wished that she . . . would get another for that she was tired of seeing the same colour so often." There was always a sense that her eagle eye was being cast around the salon, to see who had come, who was missing, who was adequately respectful. But, if you toed the line, she would look after you. During 1814, when Mrs. Adams was alone in Saint Petersburg, it was the empress mother who was her "protectrice," and it was to Maria Federovna that she last went to say goodbye.[32]

The tsar was a more complicated matter. Mrs. Adams was charmed by him, even attracted, and came to see him as the beau ideal of statesmanship, especially for his role in sustaining Russia during the Napoleonic invasion. He would talk amiably to her at balls, usually in French, and made sure she was offered courtesies, even those a little beyond the norm. He would even permit her the gentlest of impertinences. He once suggested that she go and sit with the tsarina "on an elevated Seat attended by her Ladies," and Mrs. Adams had declined. "Don't you know that no one says Nay to the Emperor?" he had said. She had laughed and replied, "But *I* am a republican." At this, "he smiled and went on his way."[33]

But there was a problem, if not two. The tsar decided to take an interest in Louisa's sister Catherine, of whom he became aware during his daily walks along the Admiralty Embankment or the Nevsky Prospect. On these, he encountered sundry people with whom he liked to stop and converse about the weather or the times. Mrs. Adams and her sister, too, chose to take walks and the three started to run into one another. The tsar admired what he saw and came to expect these meetings. But the young American attachés, who had their own interest in Catherine Johnson and were well apprised what these imperial attentions might mean, began to tease both sisters, so they stopped their walks to save themselves vexation. But then the weather improved and they resumed, only to encounter the tsar again. He signaled cold displeasure at the interruption. He told Mrs. Adams that walking was good for her and then, looking straight at Catherine, said that he expected to meet them every day. With this "real Imperial command in its tone and manner," he tipped his hat and walked on. No one doubted the meaning of this, not the silent American minister, not the garrulous young attachés, not Mrs. Adams.[34]

Very soon after came an invitation to a birthday ball given by the tsar for the empress mother, and Catherine Johnson was included. This was odd, because she had never been presented at court, so she had no standing and ought never to have been asked. Inquiries were made with the arbiters of etiquette, and the master of ceremonies said that he had been "ordered by the Imperial Family to say that Miss Johnson would be [regarded] as already presented and be privileged to attend on all occasions when notified." The tsar had decided to quicken the pace and the pressure. The Adamses were told that, with Miss Johnson, they might enter the Winter Palace by an entrance usually reserved for the imperial family; that they would be shown into a private receiving room, where the tsar, the tsarina, and the empress mother would greet them; and that then the imperial family would proceed into the public room escorted by military officers and the Americans would follow after. And so it happened, the privilege and the risk.[35]

In the spring of 1810, at a ball given by the French ambassador to mark the marriage of Napoleon and Marie Louise of Austria, the tsar made his purposes plain. He asked Louisa Adams where, in the swirling company, he could find Miss Johnson. Mrs. Adams volunteered to seek her out, but the tsar said he could do it himself and wandered away. He found Catherine, brought her back, and danced a polonaise with her. All things considered, she was unusually relaxed. She treated him like an American, not a tsar: she laughed and she spoke before she was spoken to, contrary to etiquette. But the tsar liked the impertinence, wanted it to go on, and insisted that the music be prolonged, even though this postponed the ambassador's supper by twenty minutes. This scandalized the court, astonished the diplomatic corps, and offered amusement to Mrs. Adams. But she knew that she was being used as "a passport to the act" of deepening the entanglement, whereas she was supposed to be the duenna, the custodian of her sister's honor. She needed to fend off these attentions without occasioning offense, and this she managed to do. She was helped by the fact that, in such matters, the tsar had a short attention span. The streets of Saint Petersburg and the salons of the Winter Palace presented him too regularly with pretty young women for Catherine Johnson to linger long in his mind. And Catherine was to find her own distractions. She was to have an affair with William Steuben Smith, Mr. Adams's nephew and secretary, and got herself pregnant. They were forced abruptly into a marriage that, in later years, was to be unhappy, because Smith drank, was haunted by bailiffs, and ended up often in debtors' prison.[36]

Louisa Adams's other problem with the tsar was that, because he presided over a police state and because he was vain, he liked to read other people's letters, in the hope of catching a compliment or noticing a resistance. In this prying, he was pleased to see that Mrs. Adams's letters praised him, though displeased that her servant Martha Godfrey was less complimentary, both to himself and to his brother the Grand Duke Constantine. In truth, hardly anyone had a good word to say for Constantine, habitually viewed as a brute and an "empty-headed braggart." If the tsar read his own wife's correspondence, as he probably did, he long ago saw her write of "the full baseness of [Constantine's] character." The tsar became curious to meet Miss Godfrey as someone inexplicably impervious to his imperial accomplishment and personal charm, so he summoned her, upon the pretext of wanting to meet Charles Francis Adams. The tsar was reassured to find that she was not handsome. It made sense to him that ugliness would reproach beauty. The experience was less reassuring for Mrs. Adams.[37]

The imperial court was a world Louisa Adams frequented more than a world she inhabited. Her real world had been Saint Petersburg, the city she prepared to leave in 1815 with such mixed feelings.

Least mixed had been her despairing response to the city's climate, with its interminable winters, its brief and erratic summers. By late October, the Neva began to freeze and the temporary pontoon bridges were removed before they were swept away by jarring sheets of ice drifting down from Lake Ladoga. The city's inhabitants would begin to take their carriages down the slipways placed on the banks and cross the river upon the packed ice, with their roadways delineated by the placement of fir trees. This freeze continued to at least late March and not infrequently to early May, so winter would last a minimum of six months, but could extend to eight. Near the winter solstice, there was daylight only from ten in the morning to two in the afternoon, and, since the sun seldom shone, this was but "a gloomy half-darkness." In this darkened period, though there were outdoor amusements—sleigh rides and sliding down great ice hills—Mrs. Adams was trapped inside buildings, usually deemed "not so elegant within" as without. "There is great show, but no comfort," one American visitor observed in 1812. Double windows were hermetically sealed against temperatures that regularly fell below zero degrees Fahrenheit, and rooms were kept too warm by tiled brick stoves, which might reach to the ceiling and were stoked with firewood, whose purchase was an integral part of the negotiations with any landlord. Rooms were often claustrophobic, "close and sultry," such that colds and infections multiplied, and everyone was more or less ill for months on end.[38]

As Louisa came to realize with a sickening sense of entrapment, Saint Petersburg was immensely expensive. This was noticed by all visitors and endured by most residents. Even the elegant and careless Joseph Allen Smith of Pennsylvania, who did not lack for means, noticed in 1802 that "at Petersburgh living is very dear." Louisa Adams had to grapple with the fact that "a plain Leghorn Hat with a simple Ribbon to tye it" cost four and a half guineas, then the equivalent of about thirty dollars. And prices might fluctuate wildly—lower when the tsar was absent from the city, higher when his return precipitated more balls, more suppers, more ladies needing more dresses. In 1814, Louisa had gone to buy a gown and been told that it would cost seven hundred roubles; a few months later it was fifteen hundred.[39]

This expense was not accidental. The new city had been purposefully designed by Peter the Great and his heirs for munificent display. This had been done partly to impress the outside world that Russia was now the equal of other European monarchies, that Saint Petersburg was a match for Paris, Peter the peer of Louis XIV, the Winter Palace and Peterhof equal to the Tuileries and Versailles. For a century and more, the city had been crowded with new buildings, often on the site of scarcely old ones ripped down. Along the southern shore of the Neva River, a Winter Palace had been built and then replaced three times, and each time it grew. On its eastern end was added a small Hermitage, then a larger Hermitage, in which was nestled a small and exquisite theater. Catherine the Great famously accumulated fine art on a prodigious scale, such that the Hermitage expanded incomprehensibly to contain what came to seem a goodly proportion of the aesthetic production of civilized Europe for centuries. By 1790, works by Michelangelo, Veronese, Titian, and Rembrandt were to be found among the 4,000 Old Masters, 38,000 books, 10,000 engraved gems, and 1,600 coins and medals, which came to be placed in multiplying rooms of exhausting opulence.[40]

But munificence had not been intended only to impress the world beyond Russia, or to be an imperial monopoly. Tsars and tsarinas presumed that their glory was the greater for being surrounded by those who, though less glorious, were nonetheless glittering. Peter had required that the aristocrats who attached themselves to his court and moved from Moscow, the old capital, as well as the nobles whom his laws profligately created, should build residences on a grand scale. Thereby all would embody and confirm the heroic pretensions of the city Peter had, by an inexorable act of brutal will, built on malodorous marshland, at the expense of uncounted squandered lives. But Peter was also a practical man, an artisan manqué, and he knew that his city was expensive. So, as an allowance toward ostentation, he doubled the salary of any state employee who served in Saint Petersburg. Along the canals that he had made in imitation of Venice and Amsterdam, next to the waterways that Catherine perfected with granite walls and wrought-iron railings, came to be great palaces, deficient in originality but consistent in style. The palaces had been designed mostly by Italian architects, careless of expense and free with baroque elaborations. The city became an education in allusiveness. Most things were reminiscent of something else—a street in Paris, a bridge in Delft, a palazzo in Florence, an arcade in Milan, a church from anywhere but Moscow. Much was imported: granite from Finland, marble from Italy, porphyry from Sweden, sandstone from Poland.[41] The streets were broad, the pavements wide, the buildings tall, the colors vivid, and the acquisitiveness overflowing, for (as was familiarly observed) Saint Petersburg was a theater, where the costumes and the staging were intended to dazzle and almost everyone trod the boards.[42]

A case in point was the Stroganoff Palace, which sat on the southwest corner of the intersection of the Moika Canal and the Nevsky Prospect. There Louisa Adams became a familiar and there, invited to dine or to dance, she entered a complex of buildings packed with the reassuring treasures procured by immense family wealth accrued since the sixteenth century from salt works, iron mines, and land farmed by thousands of serfs. In high salons of marble, on exquisite wooden floors, amid glittering gilt, under frescoed ceilings, and on intricate French furniture, she encountered Etruscan bronzes, Greek and Chinese vases, late antique silverware, a Mexican jade mask from Teotihuacán, icons by great Russian masters, and paintings by Botticelli, Van Dyck, Lorrain, Poussin, and Watteau. On the walls sat contemporary portraits by the French artist Élisabeth Vigée Le Brun, who in the 1790s had become the favored portraitist of the Russian aristocracy and, with gentle flattery, had furnished them with faces transformed by her kindly and diplomatic humanity.[43]

A diplomat was a courtier, and Mrs. Adams's husband was expected, if not to match, at least to approximate an aristocratic lifestyle. For some diplomats, from countries rich and ostentatious, this was a demand easier to meet. For a French ambassador, who was given a palace by the tsar as a courtesy and half a million dollars annually by his government to cover expenses, it was much easier, the more so as such an ambassador was a man of personal wealth and sometimes of "refined elegance," with a sweeping name and sonorous titles. In 1809, this was Armand Augustine Louis de Caulaincourt, *général*, *grand écuyer de France*, *ambassadeur extraordinaire*, and duc de Vicenza. Such an ambassador gave balls for 40 people, or 130, or 500, and furnished elegant suppers, cooked by his renowned chef Tardif. These the tsar himself would attend and there be presented with sweet-tasting pears in "a gorgeously ornamented Boat of wrought gold." Such a diplomat could put on theatrical performances and operas in his town palace and summer fêtes at his two country estates, and pleasantly display his mistress everywhere. Even so, Caulaincourt ran up debts and inquired of his imperial master, "Must I sell my shirt?"[44]

For an American minister, who was no more than a "mister" and given a mere nine thousand dollars a year by a government that believed in frugality and thought ostentation an offense to republican virtue, the path to shirtlessness was more direct. Coming so far, the Adamses came with little more than clothes, books, and a few pieces of jewelry. To make their way, they needed to find a suite of apartments, furniture, a carriage, horses, servants, and apparel that would not make people laugh. John Quincy Adams was to lament that "not a particle of the clothing I brought with me have I been able to present myself in." Mrs. Adams had noticed the problem more quickly.

Her first memory was of reaching Kronstadt and feeling immediately out of place. En route, she and her sister Catherine had bought new hats in Copenhagen so "that we might appear fashionable." On landing, they were taken to an admiral's house and ushered into a salon "full of elegantly dressed Ladies and Gentlemen," whose sophistication set an unexpected standard. Their brown beaver hats seemed suddenly too large, too vulgar. They noticed this beau monde "with extreme difficulty restraining [its] risibility" and worried that they were destined to be comic figures.[45]

Louisa Adams's life in the city proved to be migrant, as she had been for almost all her adult life, and as she would continue to be. In six years, she lived in two hotels and three sets of apartments, and had three spells in rural dachas during various summers. At first, as many newcomers did, she went to the Hotel de Londres at the northern end of the Nevsky Prospect on Admiralty Square, diagonally across the parade ground that stood in front of the Winter Palace. The hotel was owned by an emigré Frenchman called Demuth, who also owned another establishment on the Moika Canal, a man who knew "how to charge" and who delegated the running of the Hotel de Londres to a concierge. A later traveler thought that even the best Saint Petersburg hotels were "deficient in every respect, all equally dirty, ill-furnished, and ill-attended." Louisa's opinion of her "five indifferent chambers" was as severe. The place was "horrid," with its stone passageways, stone chambers, fetid water, and rats that dragged bread from her bedside table and seemed to threaten her son Charles, then only two. The rats were not an aberration. In such places it was usual for there to be scanty furniture, no carpets, no curtains, and no bed hangings, "because they would form too many depots for vermin to lodge their stores."[46]

Thus discontentedly lodged, the Adamses looked for better quarters. But everything was too expensive or, if cheaper, unavailable. There were few rented lodgings in the city and they fetched high prices. So, after a few weeks, they moved to the Hotel de la Ville de Bourdeaux, which faced the Moika Canal, and there they stayed for seven months. In June 1810 they migrated again into expensive, "small and inconvenient" apartments overlooking the street, at the corner of the same canal and New Street. This involved signing a lease for two years, at six thousand roubles a year. In fact, the arrangement was to last for barely a year, because the tsar decided to buy the property and so the lease was summarily terminated. In early July 1811, the family took a summer dacha on the northwest corner of Apothecary's Island and stayed there until early October, when they removed to apartments on the corner of Voznesensky Prospect and Little Officer's Street, "within five minutes walk of the house where [they] formerly resided," a little to its south and west. These lodgings cost five thousand roubles annually and were retained until March 1814, though several months in the summer of 1812 were spent at a dacha in Octa, to the northeast of the city. After her husband left in the spring of 1814, Mrs. Adams gave up the apartment and returned to a dacha by the banks of the Neva. Only in the autumn did she return to a different (and small) city apartment, where she was to stay until her own departure in 1815.[47]

Money was a persistent problem, in part because currency exchange rates fluctuated, sometimes wildly during wartime, so much so that it was hard to keep track.[48] But an annual rent of six thousand roubles came roughly to £425, or about $1,900, more than a fifth of her husband's salary.[49] And rent was only the beginning. Furnishing their first apartment required about ten thousand dollars, more than his salary, and their household was large, about three times a Bostonian norm. Sustaining seven resident Americans required fifteen servants: a steward, a cook, two scullions, a porter, two footmen, a mujik (peasant) to light fires, a coachman, a postilion, a valet, a maid, a *femme de chambre*, a housemaid, and a laundry maid. Many of these lived in and some—the porter, the cook, the housemaid, the laundry maid—had spouses. Further, there were three children (the steward's two, the washerwoman's one). So, at a minimum, the household of servants consisted of twenty-one people.

All these had to be fed, so there were endless bills from the baker, the milkman, the butcher, the greengrocer, the poulterer, the fishmonger, the grocer, the vintner. The accounts of the cook Jean Pierre

Quinzard—the best of an indifferent series—show monthly expenses for food and wine of 650 roubles and an annual expenditure of about $2,100, or nearly a quarter of the available salary. There was, inevitably, the money that disappeared for services never received. It was customary for the steward and the cook to enforce a tariff on each purchase and, along with others, to help themselves to whatever comestibles took their fancy and might go unnoticed. It is "the law of nature between master and servant that the servant shall spoil or plunder the master," John Quincy Adams was to observe. Knowing this maxim, he could aspire only to contain but never to expunge this thievery, though not infrequently rampant pilferers were summarily dismissed. Among the expenses were horses, four of them that needed to be stabled, for it was obligatory in Saint Petersburg to ride in carriages; the streets were alive, as the American traveler Joel Poinsett had observed in the deep winter of 1807, "with carriages of every description dashing along, some on wheels with four horses, some on runners with two, one horse in the shafts drawing the vehicle while the other, with long tail and main touching the ground, prances and curvets on one side them." Pushkin put it better in *The Queen of Spades* (1833): "The street was crowded with carriages; one equipage after another rolled up to the lighted entrance. Now a young beauty's shapely leg, now a clinking riding boot, now a striped stocking and a diplomat's shoe emerged from the carriages."[50]

To the Adamses, this expense seemed insupportable. But they were living on a Bostonian salary in a very un-Bostonian place. It was traditional for Russian households to be large. The Sheremetev Palace, or "Fountain House," on the Fontanka River, was at the extreme end of this extravagance, for it had 340 servants to care for a family richer than almost any other.[51] But fifty or a hundred servants were commonplace in run-of-the-mill palaces. Hence, by aristocratic standards, with only fifteen servants the Adamses lived in lonely, untended isolation. But in truth, though they were highly placed in the rigid protocols that decided where one should stand in a procession at Kazan Cathedral or where one should sit in the Hermitage theater, at home the Adamses lived like merchants, and modest merchants at that.

This placed them strangely in a city with a peculiar demography. In 1800, Saint Petersburg had 222,000 inhabitants, but men outnumbered women by nearly two to one, because there were so many soldiers to satisfy the needs of a militaristic regime, and so many migrant workers to dig the canals, construct the buildings, and swell the household retinues, especially in the summer, when male peasants would come from the countryside to seek employment. The aristocracy was unusually large, for rank adhered to positions in the military and civil service, a system that had been lovingly defined in 1722 by Peter in a "Table of Ranks," which had reinvented the Russian aristocracy. He had defined fourteen such ranks, with titles specific to the civil service, army, and navy. In the first rank were chancellors, field marshals, and general admirals; in the second, privy councillors, generals, and admirals; in the third, procurator generals, lieutenant generals, and vice admirals; and so on, down to the fourteenth rank, where there were the modest likes of collegiate commissars and ensigns. Anyone in the top eight ranks acquired hereditary titles. In general, military titles were more prestigious than civil ones, but everyone had a uniform specific to his rank, so black trousers denoted superiority over white, blue ribbons over red, gold thread over silver. This system existed in parallel to the more traditional structure of the nobility, which consisted of princes, counts, and barons, titles that might or might not bear a relationship to landed property and that were usually hereditary but need not be, and which were conferred by the "Empereur et Autocrateur des toutes les Russies, &c, &c, &c." The existence of so many ranks, so many duties, so many regulations to be enforced by a state machinery of paranoid vigilance, created a neatly coiffured and self-conscious body of aristocrats who ran into thousands in the city, men who swarmed through the streets in their sleighs, who carefully stood in line to be received, and who gazed at their epaulets in mirrors. Mrs. Adams would later remember, with dry amusement, some of the cogs in this apparatus, "the Russian officers at St Petersburg; who were always denominated Waltzing Machines, and ready at the bidding of any grandee, to spin round the Hall with the partner selected."[52]

In the city, aristocrats far outnumbered merchants. By 1790 there were seven thousand of the latter, many of them foreign; mostly German, sometimes English, very rarely Jewish. Saint Petersburg was an administrative and military capital in the manner of Washington, D.C., but it and Kronstadt together formed an entrepôt, which exported "iron, leather goods, linen and flax, canvas, rope, hemp, and lard," and imported English woolens, South American coffee, Jamaican sugar, Batavian spices, and French wines. All these consumer goods were richly on display in the Gostiny Dvor, "the great bee-hive of the city," a neoclassical shopping mall on the Nevsky Prospect that Catherine the Great had completed.[53] The empress had understood the necessity of such a place, because she had been a ferocious shopper on an imperial scale.

It was among expatriate merchants and professionals that Louisa Adams mostly lived. Prominent among them were the Krehmers. Mrs. Adams remembered the banker Sebastian Krehmer as Swedish, but he was a Baltic German from Narva, and his "particularly kind" wife, Anna Dorothea (known as Annette), came from an Anglo-Russian merchant family called Smith. Both made a habit of befriending visiting British and Americans. With these, the Krehmers could speak freely, since the habitual language of their own household was English and they had an adopted Russian daughter, Helen Gregorofskii, who was to marry in 1813, by the tsar's special consent, a Philadelphia merchant called Miers Fisher Jr. (He died a scant forty hours after their nuptials.)[54] One of the Krehmers' daughters, Sarah, was in 1814 to marry an Englishman named Thomas John Gisborne, who worked for the British Embassy, was later an agent for Lloyd's underwriters, and was the son of Thomas Gisborne, an English moral philosopher and opponent of the slave trade.[55] These facts help to explain why, almost as soon as Mrs. Adams reached the city and was grimly lodged in the Hotel de Londres, Annette Krehmer came to call, took a great interest in Charles Francis, sitting prettily on his mother's knee, and went away to dispatch "every requisite for our toilet . . . sent with a Note" expressing "a wish that we would make a free use of the Articles as long as they could be convenient with a large supply for the Child she having one of the same age." A few days later, Mrs. Adams and Catherine Johnson returned this call and went with Mrs. Krehmer to milliners, mantua-makers, and furniture shops. Over the years, they became if not intimate then very friendly, and frequently Mrs. Adams visited the Krehmers' country residence in Octa, which was in the Vibourg district, about four miles from the city. They were also habitués of the Krehmers' large town residence, where an evening party of fifty might be thought small. It was from an apartment owned by Sebastian Krehmer and recently inhabited by Thomas John Gisborne that Mrs. Adams left for Paris in 1815.[56]

However, Louisa Adams became closest to Condesa Marie de Bode-Kynnersley de Colombi, since 1807 the wife and after 1811 the widow of the Spanish consul general, Conde Antonio Colombi y Payet, a man "grave and portly" and a husband jealous of a "young and lively Wife" thirty-three years his junior. Countess Colombi, as Mrs. Adams usually called her, came from an extraordinary family, which had taken a strange route to Russia. Marie's mother, Mary Kynnersley, had been born into the English squirearchy in Staffordshire in 1747 and, when young, had traveled to France, where she had met and married Charles Auguste Louis Frederick de Bode, baron de Bode, then in the army of Louis XVI. They had knocked around for some years on the borderlands of Germany and France, not affluent but well connected with assorted princes, landgravines, and electors. They had had many children, Clement being the eldest and Marie being born in 1782. Eventually, in 1788 the baron had extracted from the obese but amiable elector-bishop of Cologne for a payment of eight thousand guineas the rich fiefdom of Soultz in Alsace. As the baroness complacently told her English relatives, "If God has sent us a quantity of children, he has also sent us plentifully to provide for them!"[57]

But 1788 was not a good moment to acquire a fiefdom, for the French Revolution abolished feudalism and the baron came to be threatened by mobs. At first he showed defiance, but then prudently retreated across the Rhine, where the family was reduced to émigré penury. But the baroness was an enterprising woman and saw an account in an aged newspaper, to the effect that Catherine the Great had offered to the Prince de Condé "a Southern part of Russia which he should take as a fief." Had not the Bodes lost a fief, and might not the good tsarina help them, too? So the baroness took what even her husband regarded as a "violent step," and set out in 1794 with her flock of children for Saint Petersburg, though first she took care to tour German courts to accumulate affidavits, presentable to a German-born tsarina. Improbably, in 1795 the Bodes were granted money, a pension, and in the Ukraine near Ekaterinoslow "an immense do-main called Krameroff, situated on that Dnieper, consisting of great lake and forest districts." They were promised an estate in the Crimea in due course. This was well and good, the cattle being "very fine," the "rivers, lakes, and pools . . . charming," and the Tartar peasants a "very good sort of people," if too prone to amiable drunkenness. But the estate had no house, the pension never appeared, the winter was biting cold, and Catherine the Great died. So husband and wife set off in 1796 to persuade the new tsar, Paul, a man not known for kind-liness, to furnish another estate. They were successful and Ropsha, near Narva, came with two hundred serfs, six villages, and forests full of wolves and bears. The baron was sent back to the Ukraine to sell Krameroff and pick up the children, but there died of a fever. The children, too, became ill and endured their convalescence "lodged part under a tent and part in a cottage consisting of one poor little room," with an earthen floor and a thatched roof. So the baroness went herself and, after sundry vexations, led toward Narva a caravan of "eight carriages, kibitkas, and wagons, with twenty-two horses and six oxen." Thereafter matters settled down, the children were set to a Russian education, and all entered society.[58]

So, against the odds, the baroness's daughter Marie de Bode-Kynnersley grew into a young and vivacious woman with "not very regular features," an open and expressive countenance, and easy and graceful manners, all displayed at agreeable parties, at which she might play the harp. Mrs. Adams was to find in her a sensible and attractive woman, so much so that it was "impossible to know her without loving her." It is likely that they came to know each other partly because the baroness, when first traveling to Russia, had dallied in Berlin and there knew a doctor and a countess whom Mrs. Adams, too, had known well. But, more broadly, it was the case that like attracted like. Though the baroness's adventures had been most exotic, she, her daughter, and Louisa Adams were of a kind: enterprising women who married foreigners, had their fortunes cast in foreign lands, and were forced to cope. Marie long lingered in the memory of Louisa, who habitually wore a turquoise ring given by the countess and "almost the only Russian Memento which I bore away as a gift from that Country."[59]

There were other expatriates in Mrs. Adams's circle. There was General Augustin de Bétancourt, a Spanish military engineer who ran an engineering school, was responsible for all the city's public buildings, and came to be deeply involved in the rebuilding of Moscow after 1812. He was notable for a "strong mind and indefatigable industry," while his English wife was (as Louisa thought) very kind and very hospitable, but also "very illiterate" and "very ambitious." The family had not been in Saint Petersburg for very long when the Adamses arrived, for Bétancourt was a political refugee from Madrid who had been banished by the Godoy regime in 1807. Understandably, the family observed Spanish customs. At parties, their three daughters, one of whom was "a great beauty," would dance the bolero with castanets. And in 1812, the girls were to embroider a standard for a Spanish regiment, outfitted by the tsar and made up of prisoners of war sent back to Spain to fight Napoleon.[60]

For the rest, Mrs. Adams mixed much with the English and American merchant community. She attended the Anglican church, commonly called the "English Factory Chapel," which lay on the English Embankment to the west of the Bronze Horseman on Admiralty Square. She sometimes frequented the balls given by the English Club. She played hostess to any and all Americans of genteel standing, either resident or visiting. Most prominent among the American residents was the consul Levett Harris, a neat and fastidious Quaker from Philadelphia, "a very genteel man" known for amiability and polished manners. At first, the Adamses' relations with him were cordial. When they had landed, he had met them and explained how things worked. There was advice on how frequently to bow, the desirability of light banter ("as the Russians must be amused"), and the necessity of a carriage ("for the fact was that in St Petersburg 'Il faut rouler,'" one had to roll along). But from the first, they had noticed that he was lavish with presents, including an "elegant Turkish shawl" for Mrs. Adams, and this was a propensity that worried John Quincy Adams, alert to the possibility of corruption. Over time, Louisa was to find Harris's pedantic fussiness irritating and she came to see him as "a petit Maitre," whose household, furniture, equipage, and person were elegant and tasteful, but to the point of "effeminacy."[61]

By tradition, to speak of "effeminacy" in a man was to imply homosexuality. This may explain her anecdote about Harris too-elaborately instructing her on how to behave, on an occasion when he was to be her escort. On climbing the stairs, he said, she might take his arm, but then he would have to leave her and she "must walk up to the Lady or Gentleman of the house alone." Otherwise, they might seem too familiar and there would be a suspicion of impropriety, even of their having a liaison. As she remembered it, "This was quite too much for my gravity and I laughed in his face assuring him that whatever fears he might have for *his* reputation I had none whatever for my own." It may also explain why she spoke of him as associating with "men of corrupt habits."[62]

But an allusion to corrupt habits may only have meant that Harris took bribes, as it seems clear he did. On several occasions, accusations to this effect were brought to the American minister's attention and, almost always, the minister declined to notice them, perhaps because he knew that the tsar and the foreign minister thought very well of Harris and may have known that in 1807 they had signaled that Harris's promotion from consul to minister would have occasioned "great satisfaction."[63] It became customary for the Adamses to speak of "the Count *Harris Levity* as they called him in Russia" with a dry skepticism, as "our little great man." Certainly he lived suspiciously well for a consul, indeed better than the minister. An American visited Harris's apartments in 1813 and found them "very handsome," "very tasty and expensive," with walls covered in crimson damask and furniture to match. In the dining room was a "very brilliant chandelier which cost 2000 rubles." In 1814, the American vice-consul in Riga, Christian Rodde, was to submit a deposition that claimed that, over the years, Harris had received about 320,000 roubles in bribes and that "in many instances, Mr. Harris received large sums of money from me for admitting vessels to entry whose papers were notoriously false." Later, in 1821, there was a libel suit in Philadelphia, in which Harris sued an American merchant called W. D. Lewis, with whom he had had business in Saint Petersburg. Lewis and his brother had gone around accusing Harris of "having prostituted his office for personal gain." In the trial, John Quincy Adams, then secretary of state, submitted a deposition by no means friendly to Harris and, in due course, the jury awarded the plaintiff token damages of one hundred dollars. Considering that Harris had demanded $50,000, this was a verdict of guilty.[64]

Of these two matters—homosexuality, venality—it was the latter that was more likely to have concerned Louisa Adams, who was relaxed about the sexual impropriety everywhere about her. She could not be too prim, for she would have spent her life in a torment of indignation, as marital fidelity was an eccentric foible in imperial and aristocratic circles. In her world, all women were on display to win a husband, to keep a husband, to lose a husband, or to find a lover. The sensual was a demand of the salon, the dance floor, and the dining table. Diamond, velvet, rouge, and silk all worked to drape, improve, and disguise bodies, which the Empire style strove to expose.

The tsar had a long-term mistress, Maria Dmitrievna Naryshkina, a black-haired Polish countess who was voluptuous and sultry, vivacious and brazen, a woman whose beauty was thought "supernatural." Alexander was intermittently guilty about this liaison, but she gave him three children, whose existence was reassuring to his manhood. The tsarina was deeply troubled by this betrayal, but the empress mother, who had treated her own husband's courtesans as "personal friends and companions," was unconcerned that her son had acquired an extra bedmate. "He had sacrificed his Wifes peace of

mind, and happiness" was Louisa Adams's view, but she also understood that the Polish woman was but the tsar's "favorite Mistress," for
he had a roving eye and, after all, Louisa had seen it rove over Catherine Johnson. In fact, it was difficult to keep track of all the tsar's
rovings. Years earlier, there had been Anna Lopukhina (later Princess Gagarina), a French singer called Mademoiselle Phillis, and a
French artist named Madame Chevallier. Later, when visiting western Europe and attending the Congress of Vienna, there was Princess
Bagration and perhaps Countess Esterhazy-Roisin, and many others,
including Viennese merchants' wives. He did not even mind paying
for his amusements, for it was said that he was furnished with Viennese prostitutes. There were even whispers about his sister Grand
Duchess Catherine, to whom he could write, "I hope to take delicious
rest in your arms."[65]

The diplomatic corps furnished its own supply of roués and rep-
robates. It was rare that an ambassador brought his wife to so remote
a place, and this isolation alone made dalliance probable. Baron Otto
Blome, the Danish minister, was "the very pink of elegance," a bachelor with "a great reputation for gallantry." Count Saint Julien, the
Austrian ambassador, was "an old Rake," though one "whose desire
has long since outlived his performance." Caulaincourt, the French
ambassador, had a mistress, Madame de Vlodeck, and thought that
Louisa Adams herself might join in a little more. At dinner, he once
told her that she "was too serious for a pretty woman" and that, when
in Rome, she ought to do as the Romans did. She replied, "If I should
go to Rome perhaps I might."[66]

This meant that the diplomatic corps provided Mrs. Adams with
only intermittent female company. In the beginning, there was the
wife of the Bavarian minister François Gabriel Bray, comte de Bray.
She was a woman "young and very pretty," the daughter of German
aristocrats near Narva. Louisa found the count "full of Bonhommie
displayed altogether in the German style," though in fact he was
French and from an old Norman family. An impoverished émigré
from 1792, he had roamed central Europe and England, mostly
working for the Order of Malta, until the Bavarians employed him as

a diplomat and sent him in 1809 for four years to Saint Petersburg.[67] Pinched means and cosmopolitanism, or so Louisa thought, tended to strip him of social pretensions and he had a gift for making people feel at home. The Bray residence was a social focus for the diplomats, "who in Petersburg live much together." He was cleverer than he looked and was to appear in light disguise in a foundational text for European conservatives, the *St. Petersburg Dialogues* of Joseph de Maistre, the Sardinian ambassador to Russia. In the dialogues, Bray appears as a more or less worthy foil to Maistre's delicately complicated meditations on the nature of society and God's purposes. Offering a counterpoint to Maistre's conservative Catholicism was apt, since Bray was bored by church services, and he once struck John Quincy Adams as being inadequately acquainted with the Holy Scriptures.[68] In secular knowledge, however, Bray was a learned man, much interested in medieval history, and an author, most notably of the three-volume *Essai critique sur l'histoire de la livonie* (1817); later still, he wrote memoirs and works on botany, and recounted his picturesque travels in the Tyrolean Alps.[69]

Most formal events at court were for the male diplomats alone, though occasionally diplomatic wives were included. But though the boundary between public and private worlds was unclear, unofficial society during the season was amiable enough. The Adamses gave dinner parties, which were reciprocated, and diplomats would call casually and mingle with the likes of the Krehmers, the Bétancourts, and the Colombis. The French ambassador was too grand for such informality, but the rest of the *corps diplomatique*—suave, eccentric, bored—offered the approximation of a social world. Among them, Mr. Adams was an oddity for being a committed nationalist, a man for whom service to a foreign country would be political and moral treason. But Saint Petersburg was an ancien régime city, and its diplomats were men hired as agents by governments for their knowledge, their command of French, their worldliness, and their politesse, men for whom political commitment was a game and a job.

They were often bored, because diplomacy was a desultory occupation. That an envoy expressed the cordiality of one state to another, as well as the standing of a country in the community of nations, was usually more important than any technical issues of bilateral relations. There was little that embroiled Sardinia and the Russian Empire, little that might keep Joseph de Maistre busy, and so he spent his time on philosophical meditations and finding still more ingenious reasons why the French Revolution had been a mistake. Similarly, Russia and the United States shared no borders, stood little chance of coming into serious conflict, and regarded each other's political systems with diffident contempt. Russian diplomats in Washington often had occasion to complain of such indifference. In 1811, one observed a silence about Russia in the president's annual message and was outraged: "Feelings of justice and gratitude ought to have led the American government to give more plausible indications of the importance which it attaches to the friendship of Russia and to the unique reception which American commerce enjoys in her ports, as well as of the opinion they have of the deference of our magnanimous Emperor toward the young American nation. They still have not expressed themselves on the subject in a manner that would indicate adequately their capacity and eagerness to appreciate the good will of a power such as Russia." It was all very puzzling. One could only conclude that the Americans were "confused."[70]

Louisa Adams found herself in Russia because over the preceding twenty-five years the Russian government had reluctantly concluded that the United States had a right to exist and might even have a marginal use. In 1781, the Continental Congress had sent Francis Dana to Russia as minister plenipotentiary in the hope of gaining Catherine the Great's diplomatic recognition of American independence. John Quincy Adams, then only thirteen, had left his father in the Netherlands and gone along as Dana's secretary. The venture was ill-fated. When John Adams sent from The Hague to Saint Petersburg a miniature portrait of George Washington, it was returned with the annotation: "Her Imperial Majesty has been most pleased to order that the portrait of the American Washington, enclosed with this letter and addressed to Dana, an American gentleman whom Her Majesty does not know, be returned to that very place where the courier re-

ceived it." In time, the Russians relented. By 1806, the tsar was willing to receive a copy of John Marshall's four-volume biography of the
same George Washington and politely express his "pleasure [at] becoming more particularly acquainted with the hero of a country in
whose well-being I shall not cease to take the most lively interest." It
had taken until 1803 for diplomatic relations to be established, when
an American consul was appointed to Saint Petersburg, and it was
1808 before Alexander I and President Jefferson agreed that something more was needed, though what was unclear. The Russian Empire received ambassadors from commensurately mighty powers like
France, Britain, and Austria, and such envoys had the privilege of
negotiating directly with the tsar. For mere Americans, a minister
plenipotentiary who was confined to talks with the Russian foreign
minister seemed more fitting.[71] In that spirit, at first the Russians sent
across the Atlantic only a chargé d'affaires, who doubled as the consul general in Philadelphia, and only in 1810 was this position elevated to that of a minister.

Most at stake between the two countries was trade. The Russians,
who had a very small merchant marine and a smaller navy, were
overly reliant on British traders and had an interest in encouraging
alternatives, among whom the Americans were prominent, considering their eager Yankee ships. As Rumiantsev candidly told John
Quincy Adams in 1811, "It was the interest of Russia to encourage
and strengthen and multiply commercial powers which might be rivals of England, to form a balance to her overbearing power." The
tsar had been still more blunt in 1810, when writing to Fedor Pahlen,
the new Russian minister in Washington: "I seek in the United States
a sort of rival to England." By 1811, a tenth of American exports arrived in Russia and American ships entered the Baltic to sell tobacco
and beaver and otter skins, and to buy hemp, iron, and flax. So John
Quincy Adams and Levett Harris spent most of their time dealing
with sailors, captains, and merchants, especially in helping them to
understand the complicated and authoritarian Russian bureaucracy.
But this was more the consul's business than the minister's. Harris,
who got no salary from the Americans, formally made his living by

taking a percentage of each cargo's value for his services as a middle-man.[72] It is doubtful that Mr. Adams himself needed to spend more than a few hours a day on such matters. More time was spent on long dispatches to the secretary of state, James Monroe, a world and several seas distant. A diplomat was supposed to gather information, pass on gossip, and offer advice to his masters, and Mr. Adams was good at two of these tasks at least. He would have long and grave conversations with the Russian foreign minister and more informal talks with his fellow diplomats, indeed with anyone else who came his way in salons or on the street who might have a fact or a thought about what the Swedish government might be planning to do, or how many American ships were marooned by ice in Archangel, or if the commerce from Novgorod was faltering. This was sometimes useful to an American secretary of state, but mostly not. It might take three months or more for such a dispatch to wind its way from Adams's study on the Moika Canal to the State Department. Events would have moved on, though how they had moved might be as unclear to James Monroe in retrospect as it had been to John Quincy Adams in prospect. So what mattered for an American diplomat, so remote from the American shore, so marginal to European affairs, was mere existence. A minister plenipotentiary's role was more a matter of being, less a matter of doing.

It is little wonder that Mrs. Adams did not always see the point and was grateful for an ending, the more so because a quasi-pointless existence had been very draining to her husband, who had been worn down by this listless existence and by the climate, and who, as she put it to him, had sunk into a "state of inanity."[73] She herself had experienced so many mixed emotions in Saint Petersburg—resentment, amusement, anxiety, vulnerability—that the exhilaration of leaving came as a relief.

So, on February 12, 1815, at five o'clock, she committed herself to the open and unfamiliar road, which stretched ahead for nearly two thousand miles. To complete such a journey, she would need to pass through about 160 post stations, be pulled by as many as 960 horses, and deal with perhaps 320 postilions. She would need to hazard a

Carriage on Runners

(Detail from *Imperial Bolshoi Theatre in St. Petersburg* by Benjamin Paterssen [1806],
© 2009, State Russian Museum, St. Petersburg)

Europe crowded with battle-weary soldiers poised to renew war or enforce peace, and populated with nervous inhabitants unsure about strangers. In truth, she had little idea what she might face when she stepped into her carriage, settled into her seat, made sure she was warm enough, looked at her son, and glanced out the windows at the darkening and unlighted streets disappearing from her sight for the last time. She crossed the Moika Canal and the Fontanka River, passed through the granite triumphal arch of the Riga Gate, and went on to the first post station at Strelna.[74]

2

FROM SAINT PETERSBURG TO RIGA

F OR THOSE FAR AWAY, her journey seemed exotic and dangerous, as though she were choosing to enter a dark forest without guides. This perspective was the more common because she was starting out from eastern Europe, which most western Europeans and Americans regarded with deep suspicion as a desolate place of barbarism, lurking danger, and irrational backwardness. For those who traveled from west to east, especially if they were French and philosophical, it seemed as though they moved back in time. Gradually the lights of civilization began to dim and go out and, in the darkness, anything might be possible. In the year Mrs. Adams set out, English schoolchildren, asked to travel in their imaginations, were confidently informed that in eastern Europe "the places and the people are less cultivated and enlightened," and that Russians were especially marked by "ignorance and barbarism." So some thought (and told her) that the accomplishment of such a journey made her a heroine even if, moving westward, she was moving from darkness into light. She had lived long enough in the east to know better than that and she was to deny this flattering characterization. It was, to be sure, very unusual for a woman to travel without a male companion of her own rank, and few covered as many miles as she did, so quickly and at so uncertain a moment. But she was proposing to follow established routes and would not have thought to venture forth but for the knowledge that it was something often done, indeed done by those she knew well. With amiable hyperbole, the German playwright August von Kotzebue had observed a few years earlier, "Our ancestors . . . if obliged to undertake a journey of twenty miles . . . took leave of their relations and friends in a solemn manner, shed tears, and would not infrequently make their wills. Now, however, on the very next day after our determination is formed we set out full speed for Paris or for Rome; we step into our travelling carriages as unconcernedly as our ancestors inclosed themselves in a sedan chair, to be carried, for their afternoon nap, to the next church."[1]

She was traveling during an era that was informed about the practicalities of travel, though little was systematic. This information took two forms: travel accounts and travel guides. The former were narratives of personal experience, which described how an author set out from home, observed an alien culture, and circled back, usually with a sense of having returned to a better place. Such accounts were venturing what a later era would call ethnography, lightly informed by a historical sensibility, and were often conscious that the commerce of the modern world was bringing cultures into conversation. By 1815, a number of these narratives described traveling to and from Russia. Some were by English travelers, whose books were in the Adams family library in Saint Petersburg and discussed within the family. Notable among these were John Carr's *A Northern Summer* (1805) and Robert Ker Porter's *Travelling Sketches in Russia and Sweden* (1809).[2] But there were also German and French accounts, such as Johann Gottfried Seume's *A Tour Through Part of Germany, Poland, Russia, Sweden, Denmark, &c. During the Summer of 1805* (1807), and the comte de Messelière's *Voyage à Pétersbourg* (1803). Reversing the flow was the narrative of a Russian going abroad, the historian Nikolai Karamzin's *Travels from Moscow* (1803).

In these and other works, Mrs. Adams could find accounts of the road she would take. With one minor deviation, the English lawyer and semiprofessional travel writer John Carr (mocked as "the jaunting car") had followed the route she would take as far as Marienburg in East Prussia, and George Green's *Original Journal from London to St. Petersburgh* (1813) was still more exact, describing the road she would take as far as Berlin. In these works, she could find descriptions of post stations, bridges, towns, and people. Interfused were scattered pieces of practical advice. As Carr put it, "Whilst I wish to amuse, I am desirous to facilitate those who may follow me, by giving the detail of coins, and post charges, and some little forms which are necessary to be observed in a northern tour." But these details were given episodically, for such works were stories written by gentlemen for other gentlemen, and so tended to the lofty generalization, the picturesque image, and the telling anecdote. Carr's *Northern Summer* was prefaced by an "agreement" with the reader, that the latter should "support without disappointment those vicissitudes of amusement and languor, that seldom fail to diversify all the roads both of literature and life."[3]

These were male travel accounts, not female. A man portrayed himself as in a place and on a road because he had chosen this journey and was amused or instructed by what he saw, and casually offered to others what he had learned. Female accounts were different, not least for being more rare. In 1815, there were far fewer travel accounts about eastern and northeastern Europe by women. Among them, most notably, was Mary Wollstonecraft's *Letters Written During a Short Residence in Sweden, Norway, and Denmark* (1796). But there were almost none about Russia until after Mrs. Adams's time, when they would begin to appear, though only occasionally. Women tended to be travelers out of necessity: usually the need to follow a husband, sometimes the need if unmarried to seek employment, occasionally the obligation to visit relatives.[4] As the wife of a diplomat, Mrs. Adams belonged to the largest group of such female travelers, at least before the middle of the nineteenth century, when the categories began to multiply and Victorian ladies started to venture forth as missionaries, explorers, and professional authors in search of a remunerative experience. A diplomat's wife, by contrast, was in an alien place because a government had decided her husband should go somewhere and, willingly or not, the wife ended up on a ship, in a strange hotel, in a puzzling salon, with unexpected servants to administer and lost children at home in boarding schools, to whom she would send admonishing or sympathetic letters. The most famous earlier member of this club was Lady Mary Wortley Montagu, whose husband had been the British ambassador in Istanbul in the early eighteenth century. But Abigail Adams herself belonged to the sorority and had kept a travel journal when she had gone to join John Adams during his diplomatic postings in Paris and London in the 1780s. Like her daughter-in-law, she never published what she had written of her travels, and this was characteristic. For the wives of diplomats were usually of high social standing and often felt themselves to be above the vulgar business of bookmaking. The letters of Anne Disbrowe, for example, whose husband was the British ambassador to Russia in the 1820s, were only published posthumously by her daughter in the 1870s.[5]

Louisa Adams came late to composition. When young, she had disliked even writing letters, but did keep episodic diaries after her marriage and wrote scraps of verse. When her husband became secretary of state, she began to write long letters to Abigail Adams about Washington political and social affairs, letters that took the form of a journal. When Abigail died, she continued the same practice with John Adams. Though Louisa also kept more conventional diaries, for the rest of her life she dabbled in this form (the epistolary diary), which had been common in the eighteenth century. In 1825, soon after entering the White House, she wrote an eighty-six-page memoir of her childhood, marriage, and early days in Berlin, when her husband had been the American minister to Prussia: this she entitled "Record of a Life or My Story." Then she started experimenting with other forms: more poetry, plays, a roman à clef, and eventually theology. In 1836, she wrote "Narrative of a Journey from Russia to France 1815," which was subsequently copied out and slightly revised. In 1840, she resumed the task of autobiography by starting "The Adventures of a Nobody," which briefly recapitulated her childhood, completed her narrative of the Berlin years, and carried on her story during her first American

Louisa Catherine Adams, "Narrative of a Journey from Russia to France 1815"
(Courtesy of Massachusetts Historical Society, Boston)

years and the Russian experience as far as 1812. Both "My Story" and
"The Adventures of a Nobody," but especially the second, were a
curious mix of conventional autobiographical narrative and diary entries, evidently from journals mostly no longer extant; these original
entries seem sometimes to have been elaborated from memory, but
often were simple transcriptions. It seems probable that, on occasion,
she prompted her memory by looking at her husband's diary. Almost
none of this was ever published, except occasional pieces of verse
never attributed to her and a short autobiography written in the third
person. The latter was published anonymously in 1827 in a newspaper, in order to refute assorted political slanders against her, especially the accusation that she was inadequately American.[6]

These many writings, but especially the memoirs, were preemi-
nently attempts to understand where she had come from and where
she had ended up, and how she had felt pain and pleasure. Her writing mapped a landscape of people with feelings, thoughts, and stories. So when she wrote about her many travels, she did not write as
men usually did, for she was little interested in ethnography. Only
occasionally did she reach for cultural generalizations, and she scarcely
noticed landscape and what she called "the ornaments of picturesque
taste."[7] For male travel writers, a waterfall, a mountain, and a ruined
castle provoked warm sentiment and, thereby, modified cold rationality. For Louisa Adams, a river was not something whose tumbling
beauties she paused to contemplate, but a barrier she needed to cross,
something threatening to her and her own. Rather, her 1815 travel
narrative was a story about moving through a landscape of people,
but especially of women. Mrs. Adams thought more than was usual
about what it meant to be a woman, about how women were viewed
by men, and about how women dealt with men. In her writings,
women were incomparably more important than men. Her story of
1815 was self-consciously fashioned as a metaphor for how a woman
could manage the difficult business of life, by fighting off the violent
brutalities of men and enlisting the intelligent sympathies of women.

In retrospect, when in June 1836 she had sat down in Washington,
opened her notebook, and dashed off "Narrative of a Journey from

Russia to France 1815," she was only a little interested in remembering practical details. She laughingly mocked her own incapacity for recalling the details of her itinerary. It only mattered to her that she recover the feel of things and establish a rough trajectory of getting from there to here. Nonetheless, she did experience things that, though they were to fade in her memory, were inescapably real.

For anticipating practicalities, the narratives found in books like Carr's *Northern Summer* were less useful for travelers than guidebooks. Such guides were not then what became available to travelers a few decades later, when John Murray in London began to publish handbooks for travelers, and a little later Karl Baedeker in Koblenz did likewise in volumes notable for their researched attention to the details of hotels, restaurants, cultural sights, and travel arrangements. In 1815, there were more fragmentary books known as *guides des voyageurs*. The pioneer of these was a court official in Saxe-Gotha called Heinrich August Ottokar Reichard, who in 1784 at Leipzig had published in German a guide for European travelers, a work that then met with little success. In 1793, it was translated into French as *Guide du voyageur en Europe*, was published in Weimar, and was subsequently broken down into smaller volumes—*Guide d'Espagne et du Portugal*, *Guide d'Allemagne*, and so forth, including even *Guide de la Russie et de Constantinople*. These met with a wider acceptance and thereafter were industriously marketed, often abridged, and freely plagiarized, even by official state publications. By 1816, Samuel Leigh in London, who had already ventured travel guides by others, began to publish English translations of Reichard.[8]

These books had standard elements. There was a brief introduction, which gave general advice about *le manière de voyager*. One was told to plan carefully, acquire maps, collect letters of introduction, and arrange for correspondence to be delivered poste restante along your route. One was advised to be careful with strangers, to try to learn French, and to make sure you knew customs regulations and methods for exchanging money. It was urged that one should stay away from political discussions and overt criticism of local customs, and, if possible, travel with friends or family. There was elaborate advice on what sort of pistols to carry, how to hold them, and when to use them.[9] Beyond these generalities, other sections detailed passport regulations, customs duties, what to expect at a hotel or inn, what sort of food was served, and how to employ servants. It was common to furnish tables that detailed exchange rates between currencies, and that explained local systems of weights, measures, and distance. There might be a brief description of a country: its history, political system, manufactures, and landscape. Commonly a short gazetteer listed prominent towns, notable buildings, populations, and the names of chief hostelries. In general, all these elements were rapid, cursory, and incurious.

At the heart of any such book was a description of the post road system, a listing of itineraries between cities, and sometimes a map, which might be published separately. This description would explain the regulations for traveling on public diligences or in private carriages, and how much one was obliged to pay for each stage of a journey for postilions and horses. Then the itineraries were listed, beginning with the routes that radiated from a capital city: Paris to Calais, Berlin to Königsberg, Saint Petersburg to Moscow. Thereafter the lists descended to cross-country routes that did not involve a capital, or to routes that passed beyond a frontier. These itineraries could take two forms: the first listed the names of the towns and post stations through which a traveler would pass, the distance between each stage, and the total length of a journey; the second would be a more leisurely itinerary, which would pause to give brief descriptions of a place, and, in effect, enfold the gazetteer into the itinerary. In earlier versions of these guides, this gazetteer element tended uncritically to characterize what was worthy of praise. So this inn was a *"bonne auberge,"* this town *"un jolie ville,"* that region "famed for its wines." It was only later that a principle of discrimination began to creep in and one might be advised that in Troyes "the water . . . is scarcely drinkable."[10]

It is not known which of these guides Mrs. Adams used, but it is difficult to think she went without. Certainly her husband used them. As it happened, the route she was to follow was almost identical to that recommended in the *État général des postes du royaume de France,*

e) De Riga à Pétersbourg.

Werstes.		Werstes.	
De Riga à		Klein - Pungern	24
Neuenmühlen	11	(Ici l'on quitte le lac Peï-	
Hilkensfehr	15	pous.)	
(Passage de l'Aa.)		Jewe,	20
Engelhardshof	19	(On découvre le golfe de	
Roop	21	Finlande.)	
*) Lenzenhof	22	Fokenhof ou Kudley	11
Wolmar	18	(On arrive aux bords du	
Stakeln	18	golfe.)	
Gulben	21	Waiwara	17
(Passage de l'Embach.)		Narwa	22
Teilitz	18	Jambourg	22
Kuikatz	22	(Passage de la Narowa.)	
Uddern	24	Apolie	15
Dorpat	25	Czierkowitz	25½
Iggafer	23	Kaskowa	22
Torma	23	Kiepena	19
(On arrive ici au Lac Peï-		Strelna	25
pous.)		St. Pétersbourg	17
Nennal	25		
Rana - Pungern	14		
		561 W.	

Par conséquent toute la route de Leipsick à St. Pétersbourg fait

1) Par Berlin et Königsberg   252½ M.
2) Par Dresde et Varsovie   304½ M.
3) En droiture de Leipsick par Königsberg 249½ M.

*) Wenden, non loin de Lenzenhof, est le séjour du sieur Reichel, auteur d'une carte itinéraire très-detaillée de la route de Riga à St. Pétersbourg. On peut se procurer chez lui des exemplaires de cette carte, qu'il avait eu l'honneur de présenter à Paul I.

Itinerary from Riga to Saint Petersburg

(From H.A.O. Reichard, *Guide des voyageurs en Europe*, 3 vols.

[Weimar: Bureau d'Industrie, 1805], 3:541)

avec les routes qui conduisent aux principales villes de l'Europe, dressé par ordre du Conseil d'Administration, pour l'an 1814, an annual publication of the French government.[11] (It is doubtful that the 1815 edition would have been available in Saint Petersburg by early February.) But, in truth, there were so many versions of Reichard, some by him, some plagiarized from him, that she could have planned her journey from any number of published sources.

John Quincy Adams's claim that his wife's journey would be straightforward was conveniently optimistic. He had, in fact, taken care to draw her attention to his will when he had left Saint Petersburg in 1814. But the claim was not implausible. The system of post roads was an ancient one, which in western Europe stretched back to the time of the Roman Empire, but had been inconsistently improved in the eighteenth century, mainly in France and southern Germany. The network was controlled by states, less for the sake of travelers than for the sake of the postal system and its couriers. Power rested on knowledge. News of wars, dynastic changes, and commercial activity was urgently needed by governments, and the advantage of a day, a few days, a week in knowing something might save a throne, make a fortune, or ruin an enemy. But news traveled at two paces: on a courier's horse or in carriages. It might take forty days and more for a traveler to go from Saint Petersburg to Paris, but Mrs. Adams had been in the habit of receiving letters from western Europe more quickly. The letter advising her to come to Paris had been written on December 27, 1814, and she had replied to it on January 20.

To travel from Russia to France was to receive an education in ancien régime Europe and the stubborn idiosyncrasies that the impulse toward regularity preferred by French revolutionaries, Napoleon, and John Quincy Adams had little succeeded in erasing. Difference took many forms. There were differing forms of administration: in the Russian Empire matters were structured by imperial ukase, in Prussia by royal commands administered by the post office, in France by legislation regularly amended. Units of distance differed: in Russia they used the verst, equivalent to about two-thirds of an English mile; in central Europe, the German mile or four and two-thirds English miles; in France, both the kilometer and (for the post system) the league, about two and a half English miles. There were immensely varying forms of currency, though the Dutch ducat informally served as a pan-European currency. There were even different rules about the width of a carriage's axle, just as in later days national railways would have different gauges: in Russia, it was as wide as 4.5 feet, in Prussia as narrow as 3.26. This was because carriages bumped along in ruts caused by other carriages, and it simplified a postilion's life if a carriage fitted into these ruts. Further, how horses were arranged and where postilions sat differed: in Russia, if there were six horses, they were usually arranged two abreast in front, four abreast behind, and the postilion sat on the second left-hand horse in the rear row. Elsewhere there might be six horses arranged in three rows of two, but this by no means exhausted the possibilities.[12]

But the manner in which the system worked was broadly similar everywhere. A road was divided into posts, which was not necessarily the distance between two post stations, but was a unit for calculating the charges levied on a traveler. So the first post station east of Paris when traveling toward central Germany was Bondy. But the distance between Paris and Bondy was such that it counted as one and a half posts, and the next stretch (Bondy to Claye) as two. According to the *État général des postes du royaume de France* (1814), when Mrs. Adams traveled from Frankfurt to Paris, she passed through fifty-one towns and post stations, but seventy-five posts. The location of stations roughly depended on the ease or severity of the terrain, but stations tended to be placed about every six to twelve miles, but might be farther apart in less populated areas.[13]

A stage might be covered in an hour; indeed the French regulations required this speed under ordinary conditions. But it could take twice as long or more if the conditions (the road, the weather, the intercession of a river) were out of the ordinary. Four miles an hour was slow, six a good pace, nine very fast, in fact so rapid that it required the horses to gallop and put passengers in fear of an upset. It was common to think that Russian postilions went very quickly,

Livonians a little slower, Prussians very slowly, and the French briskly without being breakneck. At a post station, a quick turnaround was half an hour, but an hour was more common. Sometimes the carriage wheels had to be greased, and minor or major repairs effected. The horses, hitched at the previous station, had to be changed for new ones, and likewise changed were the postilions, local men who knew the roads and could find their way. Often this involved three-way negotiations between traveler, postmaster, and postilions, and often required a wait for horses to be available.[14]

Mrs. Adams was to travel nearly two thousand miles in forty days, but she was not traveling for nine of those days. So she was to average about sixty-four miles a day, which required (if she went at an average of six miles an hour) over ten hours a day on the road, plus stops at post stations of perhaps another three hours, if she was lucky. However, she sometimes traveled through the night, so it was not always a matter of starting at eight in the morning and stopping at nine at night.

A post station served as both a stable and an inn, which might furnish a bed for the night, food, drink, and perhaps latrines. In rural areas, often the station was the only place where one might pause. But in towns and cities, a traveler would usually proceed from the station to a hotel. The merchant William Jacob, for example, observed in 1820: "In travelling through the Prussian states, it is necessary to be apprised, that the post-houses are generally the worst inns; and if a traveler intends to spend the night in a town, he should go to some other."[15]

In theory, official regulations fixed charges. It was usual to post these mandates on the wall of the post station; these specified the cost for units of distance, postilions, and horses, the rates varying in proportion to the size of the carriage and, in some jurisdictions, even the time of year, for the season affected the ease or difficulty of travel. With experienced logic, the Russians calculated that traveling was easiest in the deepest winter (when the roads were frozen) and high summer (when the roads were baked), but hardest in spring and autumn (when there were thaws and rains). Hence they divided the year into December 15–March 15 (cheaper), March 16–May 14 (expensive), May 15–September 15 (cheaper again), September 16–December 14 (expensive). In general, posting in Russia was cheap, though in the province of Kurland it was twice as expensive. When in the spring of 1814, John Quincy Adams was using his own carriage to go along the Baltic coast from Saint Petersburg to Reval (now Tallinn, Estonia), he paid thirty kopecks a verst; four horses at five kopecks apiece, a postilion at five, and five more to earn goodwill. As Alexander Everett, who traveled from Saint Petersburg to Moscow in 1810, observed, "The dexterous application of a small number of kopecks [makes] everything very easy." In fact, Adams ought to have paid more, because he had a two-seater coach with trunks, and the regulations specified that in spring such a carriage required six horses, not four.[16]

French regulations differed. For each relay, a traveler had to pay one and a half francs for each horse, and seventy-five centimes for each postilion. How many horses and postilions one was obliged to have depended on the size of the carriage and the number of passengers. Carriages were divided into three categories: small (cabriolets), middling (limonières), and large (berlines). Cabriolets and limonières needed only one postilion, but the number of horses varied with the number of passengers. A cabriolet with one or two passengers required two horses, but three or four passengers added a third horse. A limonière always required three horses. A berline needed two postilions and four horses for up to three passengers, and six horses for more passengers. All this was payable in advance, before the carriage left the post station. In general, the French were meticulous about proprieties. A *maître de la poste* had to be resident in his station, was mandated to keep good order (no cheating, no complaining, no insubordination to travelers), and had to ensure that there was an adequate supply both of postilions and horses. Postilions had to be registered with the local municipality, had to be at least sixteen years of age, were required to act as porters for luggage, and were supposed to wear numbered badges bearing the royal or imperial arms and indicating the station to which they were attached. Further, postilions were responsible for the exchange of horses, were forbidden to abuse them, and were subject to various punishments (suspension, fines) for any infractions.[17]

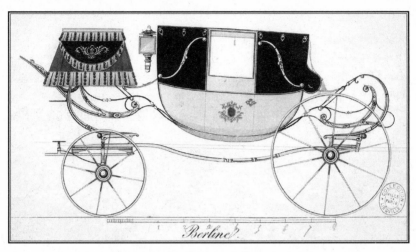

Berline carriage
(Courtesy of Musée Carnavalet/Roger-Viollet/The Image Works)

Louisa Adams was traveling in a berline, a large enclosed carriage with four wheels, the rear wheels larger than the front.[18] The cabin had four seats, glass windows, and external lamps for traveling at night. There was a high driver's seat in front and usually a space behind for storing luggage. What most defined a berline was its distinctive suspension system of springs, which passed under the cabin, restrained lateral sway, and made for a less bumpy ride. If she did what most did, she would have bought her vehicle in the Yemskoi district of Saint Petersburg, where builders produced "all sorts of carriages, some of them very neat, some of them very heavy, but none very lasting." She herself described her carriage as "heavy" and "Russian," indeed so evidently Russian that later in the journey she would be exposed to danger from those who recognized what was Russian and disliked the quality. As a very large carriage, it was liable for the heaviest fees (six horses, two postilions), which partly explains why she was later to speak of "travelling at great expence," and in 1815 of an "expence which has already frightened me." Her kibitka, which the servants were to use until Riga, was a much simpler and cheaper affair. It was a hooded sledge, with a driver perched close to the horses' tails, and behind him a beech or birch cradle, rounded at the bottom (its passenger semiprotected by a roof like a Quaker bonnet), but strong enough to have luggage strapped to it. It might have two or three horses, rarely more.[19]

Kibitka

(Detail from *Imperial Bolshoi Theatre in St. Petersburg* by Benjamin Paterssen [1806], © 2009, State Russian Museum, St. Petersburg)

Her frightening expenses began with the berline itself, which cost 1,650 roubles, or $330. To be sure, this was more than offset by her sale of the family furniture, which had brought in $1,693. But the overall cost of the journey came, according to her husband's bookkeeping, to $1,984.99: $330 for the carriage, $48.61 for initial provisions, and $1,606.38 for traveling expenses. Translated into today's values, this comes to about $28,000.[20]

She never gave an inventory of what she took with her, but it was usual to carry a formidable array of serviceable items, some of which were stored in elegant and ingenious boxes.[21] There needed to be food and drink, not only because the provisions at post stations were unpredictable, but for the probable contingencies of accident and getting lost in places beyond sustenance. These required their accoutrements: knives and forks, plates, glasses, a coffee- or teapot. Letters might need to be written en route, so there had to be pen and ink, with possibly a small slope on which to rest the paper. There would be a compass, with perhaps a barometer and a telescope. There had to be a map of the post roads, plus books to while away the long hours, if a landscape proved tedious. Since she would often travel through the night and it was winter, Louisa needed blankets and pillows, which might double as cushions to soften the jarring of the roads, as well as lanterns and candles. Clothes often needed repair, so there had to be needles, thread, tape, and pins. Though a traveling lady dressed plainly, she had to anticipate being invited into local society along the way—certainly Mrs. Adams knew that she would be—so she needed fancier dresses, jewelry, bonnets, ribands, combs, and perfumes. Washing regularly was not easy, so perfumes had a double purpose. Since roads were dangerous places, servants needed to carry pistols, gunpowder, shot, and knives. It was useful to have a strongbox for valuables and hence locks and keys.

Then there were medicines, which Mrs. Adams was unlikely to have forgotten, for ill health was her constant companion and she had care of a son, also prone to illness. Traveling medicine chests came stuffed with all manner of implements (a thermometer, a pestle and mortar, a drop measure, toothbrushes) and many potions to guard against many ailments, which it was usual to presume foreign lands transmitted. The English traveler Mariana Starke, who turned her experiences into one of the earliest guidebooks in 1820, advised that the following medicines be to hand: "Iceland moss—James's powder—bark—sal volatile—aether—sulphuric acid—pure opium—liquid laudanum—paregoric elixir—ipecacuanha—emetic tartar—prepared calomel—diluted vitriolic acid—essential oil of lavender—spirit of lavender—sweet spirit of nitre—antimonial wine—super-carbonated kali—Epsom-salts—court-plaster and lint." The carriage itself needed a range of tools, for it was routine to break down between post stations: there had to be hammers, nails, grease, bolts, extra linchpins, ropes, leather straps, and reins. There especially needed to be a drag chain, to prevent a heavy carriage outrunning the horses when going down a steep hill.[22] Hence the carriage that left Saint Petersburg was a miniature household, traveling through but also fortified against the world.

The first few miles of the journey took her along the southern shore of the Neva and the Gulf of Finland. This was "gently rolling ground, studded with groves of birch and fir." She passed a chain of elaborate wooden dachas belonging to wealthy merchants, with newfangled and fashionable English lawns, vases and statues under snow, and Italianate designs hidden in the dark.[23] If anyone was in them, and there could have been very few but servants in deep winter, they would have heard her pass, because her horses were required to have bells, sounding so that the unwary would not be surprised by the near silence of a carriage on runners. After twelve miles, she reached Strelna, a town that for many years had been alternately built up and neglected. The year 1815 was one of its better moments. She had been there before. On April 28, 1814, she and Charles Francis had accompanied John Quincy Adams on his departure for his diplomatic mission, by way of postponing their separation. There the three of them had dined at the handsome two-story post station, which sat opposite the scarcely completed palace of the tsar's brother Constantine. After dinner, when the carriage had driven off with his father inexplicably in it, Charles Francis had "shed some bitter tears" and "his little heart [had] swelled with indignation," the more so because he had seen his mother crying.[24]

It is likely that, as before, she dined at Strelna. She then pressed on through the night. Except to change horses, she was not to stop until she reached Narva. If she traveled as fast as her husband in 1814, she would have been on the road for twenty-one hours and reached Narva late on Monday, February 13.[25] After Strelna, the road turned southwest, inland, and passed a few miles to the west of the imperial

Saint Petersburg to Narva

(From Aaron Arrowsmith, *Map Exhibiting the Great Post Roads,*
Physical and Political Divisions of Europe [London: A. Arrowsmith, 1810])

palace at Pavlovsk, a place of many memories for her. Then she proceeded westward through a series of small villages (Kiepena, Koskova,
Cherkovitza, Opolie) before reaching Yamburg, which was larger.
This was flat country, scattered with trees, with occasional very low
hills visible to the south. It was a landscape often deemed "monotonous" and "barren" by travelers missing amusement, though the English aristocrat who spoke of a "hideous, monstrous country: bound-
less marshy plains, no cultivation" was too severe. It was true that the
land was little populated, though here and there were onion-domed
churches, small windmills, and dachas with porches and sometimes
chimneys, though a hole in a thatched roof was usual. The road,
however, would not have been empty, for it was shared with the local
wolves, who "continually crossed . . . between the sledges with as-
tonishing boldness and *nonchalance*." As winter was the easiest time
for getting about, "well-to-do families . . . accompanied by their ser-

vants, regularly travelled in convoys of sledges to visit friends and relatives in the countryside." These convoys did not pass each other serenely. Rough terrain and disruptions occasioned by wind, drifting snow, and runners created "uneven hillocks and holes." As a consequence, "the sledges [danced] upon these eccentric roads like ships upon the waves, and many passengers became regularly seasick." Such nautical imagery was commonplace among literary travelers. In December 1827, the Italian doctor Augustus Bozzi Granville was to cover this same terrain in a carriage on runners and wrote of it: "The roads were so uneven from the drifts of snow, hardened by the frost, that we . . . tossed about as in a rough sea, rolling and pitching, and frequently in danger of upsetting."[26]

The post stations Mrs. Adams encountered varied widely. In the Russian Baltic lands, a station of the older sort was a large barn, built parallel to the road, and perhaps a hundred feet long and forty feet wide. The carriage stopped before an "immense door," the coachman dismounted and knocked, and the door was opened so that the carriage could drive into a noisy, dark, and oblong hall, crowded with equipages, postilions mending tackle, scattered bales of hay, feeding horses, and fluttering chickens. One exited by a similar door at the other end. A side entrance opened into the inn, which had a suite of three or four rooms. If unlucky, you encountered there such "filth and stench" that "no stranger would dare to enter," and you slept in your own carriage in preference to "little dirty rooms only parted by boards half-way up, upper part like a hen-coop on board ship." If lucky, you found chairs and tables made of birch "brilliantly polished," the usual suffocating warmth from a stove, and even in winter flowers on the sills of the double windows. Privacy was not an option, for each bedroom had three or four narrow beds and, since the station was also the local hostelry, it was common to share the eating and drinking area with the local peasants, who might keep travelers awake with their "simple and mournful" songs. These, at least, were the adjectives to which travelers were drawn. It was usual to infer melancholy and simplicity when in northeastern Europe. As Alexander I's former tutor, Jean François de la Harpe, observed in

1805, the north was perceived as "a remote and dismal region where the mountain mists, the monotonous sound of the sea, and the soughing of the wind among the crags, inspire the mind with a contemplative sadness which becomes habitual."[27]

Johann Christoph Brotze, *Taproom in Inn* (1795)
(Latvian Academic Library, Riga)

But there might be no chairs and flowers, only trestle tables and benches shoved close to the wall. And at busy times there would be no comfort, especially for men who might end up sleeping on the floor. A year earlier, also in driving snow, James Bayard (one of the American diplomats commissioned to negotiate a peace treaty with Britain) had traversed Mrs. Adams's route from Saint Petersburg to Narva and found the inn at Cherkovitza to be a crowded and "most wretched Hovel," where he was obliged to sleep in the family's kitchen, a room "covered with filthy articles and being a hot close stove room, stinking almost intolerably of the fumes of the pipe." Better was Yamburg, where one was lodged in an "ancient château of considerable extent, in the form of a semicircle," a stop deemed "a good inn, with good beds," which came regularly recommended.[28]

In these places, there was a characteristic ritual. Arriving and dismounting, the traveler would be surrounded by Russian postilions, "every one requesting to be employed, yet as constantly refusing." But a traveler had first to present to the postmaster her *padarojna*, which stated her name, her points of origin and destination, and the number of horses for which she had already paid a share of the post money. These details were entered into an official book. Initially, the postmaster—who was a government official, usually with a rank equivalent to that of a lieutenant—would look uninterested and say that no horses were available, or they were being reserved for more important people, and the traveler would need to wait until horses arrived. (Alexander Pushkin was to observe in a short story that "ranks in Russia are a necessity, if only for the sake of post stations where you cannot get a horse unless you have rank.") This prevarication need not always have been a ploy, for a postmaster was supposed to reserve ten horses for the service of the crown, but it usually was. So a modest bribe was then offered to remedy this dilatoriness. Resistance to this exaction was seldom efficacious. The English sailor George Jones, traveling these same roads in February 1823, was to remember: "At some stations we found tolerably good accommodations, at others none, but at all we experienced an extraordinary attempt at extortion; for example, demanding six rubles for a cup of coffee; we generally gave half, but at one station, upon our refusing to pay the whole, they very coolly took the horses back to the stable, and we were obliged to accede to their terms." As Pushkin was to add elsewhere, in a story intended to remind a reader that even postmasters were human and endured profligate abuse, not always deserved, from travelers: "Who has not cursed stationmasters?—who has not quarreled with them frequently? Who has not demanded the fateful book from them in moments of anger, in order to enter in it a useless complaint against their highhandedness, rudeness, and negligence?"[29]

But if adequate sums changed hands, the postmaster moved to hire the horses, which might be immediately available or might need to be fetched from distant fields. Once the horses were found, their owner became the postilion. But it was usual for there to be loud arguments about who should be hired, and sometimes a cudgel was necessary to settle the dispute. A postilion did not get much money, but the position had advantages, including exemption from the poll tax and military service. (Considering that the term of such service was twenty-five years, this was no small inducement.) When hired, the man would remove a bell from his belt, attach it to the carriage or horse, say a brief prayer with many crossings, and set off. It was customary when another postilion was encountered on the road for oilskin hats to be doffed, and as customary for the carriage to stop when there was a church by the side of the road, so that the postilion could pray further, for traveling was hazardous and divine intervention thought useful.[30]

Leaving Yamburg, Mrs. Adams encountered the steep and rocky banks of the river Luga, which she crossed on a "flying bridge." Such bridges could take several forms, but usually consisted of two barges lashed together, with planking overlaid so that carriages and foot passengers could drive and walk on. On these barges were erected two masts, connected at their top by a crossbar, from which ran a cable, connected to a boat stringently anchored upstream. When all were aboard, the barges were untethered and, impelled by the force of the stream and guided by a rudder, the device pivoted on the fulcrum of the anchored boat and swung to the farther shore "like the pendulum of a clock."[31] At this particular flying bridge, Mrs. Adams may have boarded past sentinels, for they often stood with trumpets to make "signals in stormy weather," though also to summon the bridge from the opposite shore. If the experience of Abbé Georgel in 1799 is a guide, she would have been handsomely overcharged for crossing the Luga, though this was a dangerous passage, especially in winter.[32]

From the river, she climbed a steep hill and then proceeded along a plateau "in a straight line, and fine as a turnpike" until there appeared before her the two citadels of Ivangorod and Narva, facing each other across the Narva River, which marked the boundary between Russia and its western empire. They were the first great buildings she had seen since Constantine's palace at Strelna. Of the two castles, that of Ivangorod (built in 1494 by Ivan III) was the larger, with eight towers jutting from ramparts, reminiscent of the grim stone bastions found in the Welsh marches. But in 1815 the castle was little more than "majestic ruins," dilapidated because its ancient role of defending Russia from the Germans and Swedes had long since lapsed. The older fourteenth-century castle at Narva (first built by the Livonian Order of Teutonic Knights) was, by contrast, still garrisoned by the Russians and spruce. Its square tower, surrounded near its roof by a wooden balcony, faced Mrs. Adams to her left as she crossed a long, wooden bridge.[33]

Of "the famous town of Narva," as James Bayard conventionally called it, Mrs. Adams would have heard much. Her friends the Bodes had an estate nearby, as did the father-in-law of the chevalier de Bray. (The chevalier would call on her when she reached the town.) Saint Petersburg merchants came there often, as did the Russian aristocrats who spent summers on the Baltic coast and passed through on their way to Reval. The town's fame rested mostly on the battle fought there in 1700 during the Great Northern War, an engagement lost by the Russians to the Swedes, even though Peter the Great had thirty thousand men to Charles XII's barely ten thousand. Matters had been decided when a shifting wind and a blizzard, blinding the Russians' eyes, persuaded Charles to effect a surprise attack. This led to casualties of less than seven hundred on his own side but more than fifteen thousand among the Russians, many of whom perished in the freezing waters of the Narva River as they had been driven back. But the victory proved costly, because it drew the Swedes into an invasion of Russia, led to their 1709 defeat at Poltava in the Ukraine, and lost them the lands they had held for several centuries in the southern Baltic. So the battle of Narva was one reason why Mrs. Adams would, for many miles yet, remain within the Russian empire.[34]

But Narva was also known for its beauty, which came unexpectedly upon those who, traveling westward, had been dulled by a mostly flat scenery. The river was very wide, with high banks and a swiftly flowing stream, and about a mile to the south was a cataract, a sight that excited wonder in people of willing sensibility. "Magnificent! I've never seen anything so beautiful," the amiably licentious and enthusiastic Livonian soldier Baron Boris Uxkull exclaimed of it in 1812. Even reticent English visitors were struck by the fine mist that, through the trees, could be seen to hang over a falls that, though descending a very

Narva

(From John Carr, *A Northern Summer; or, Travels Round the Baltic, Through Denmark, Sweden,*
Russia, Prussia, and Part of Germany, in the Year 1804 [London: Richard Phillips, 1805], facing 419)

little distance, was three hundred yards wide and impressive for the complexity of torrent that battled past hundreds of boulders.[35] Mrs. Adams would not have diverted for the sight, but she would have heard the noise of waters as she turned right after the bridge and climbed through Narva's narrow medieval streets, nestled behind the city walls.

She stopped not at the post station (which was outside the town) but at "the best Inn in the place," which George Green a few years earlier found to be "tolerably good." She had scarcely settled when in her room appeared an emissary from the commandant of the garrison, who had been apprised by the Russian minister of the interior that she would be coming and by the guards at the city walls that she had arrived. (At such places, one's passport had to be shown.) She was told that an apartment was prepared for her at the commandant's house, that she was politely and urgently invited to stay, and that she would be entertained as an important person. This was flattering, but she declined. She had already ordered horses for the onward journey and she was in a hurry, indeed would always feel in a hurry. This response was passed back to the commandant, who then appeared in person, repeated his courtesy, and was again refused. These exchanges were in German, the commandant's language. Mrs. Adams did not speak German except in a very patchy way, so the exchange was halting. In Saint Petersburg this deficiency had not mattered, because there French was the language of the court and in French she was fluent. As a very small girl, she and her parents had lived for a few years in Nantes, and there she had gone to a French convent school and learned the language far better than she then knew English. But though she had also lived in Prussia when a young woman, she had never learned German. In the late 1790s, it was not a language that civilized people thought it necessary to know. She had a few words, a few phrases, but little more. This ignorance would matter more as she moved westward, for the road from Narva to Riga was sometimes called the German Post, "because the Post-Commissaries at all the stations are Germans."[36]

Narva would have seemed both familiar and unfamiliar, the latter because it was the first medieval city she had visited—apart from a brief visit to Elsinore on her way to Russia in 1809—since she had been in Germany in the late 1790s. Medievalism did not appeal to her. Hamburg, she wrote in 1797, "is a dreary looking City the Streets very narrow and the houses like those described by travelers in Edinburg of many stories high—They are dirty and gloomy and the narrow canals which intersect some of the streets have a dirty gloomy and disagreeable appearance." Her taste had been differently formed. She had spent much of her adult life in modern cities, newly designed by newfangled architects, fond of symmetry. Berlin, Washington, and Saint Petersburg distinguished themselves by a refusal of what was old and tortuous. These cities had broad avenues, lines of carefully planted trees, space in which to imagine that new worlds were possible. Narva was what she had known as a child, in London and Nantes. Half-timbered houses, city walls, tangled streets, alleyways, a confusion of medieval buildings jostling with baroque intrusions, in this case mostly Swedish. The city's architecture mirrored the cosmopolitan character of its inhabitants and history. Though the city's maritime trade was much declined from its seventeenth-century heyday, when it had plied its prosperous trade just beyond the magic circle of the Hanseatic League, Swedish merchants were still important in Narva, but so were their Dutch, Russian, and English counterparts, the last of whom had their own Anglican clergy.[37] The Lutherans were predominant, however, as they would be for many miles to come. Both Swedes and Germans hereabouts had embraced the Reformation and then worked hard for centuries to wrest the indigenous population from their commitment to a quasi-animist version of Roman Catholicism.

Mrs. Adams in reaching Narva had crossed not only a bridge but a cultural divide, for Narva was a "frontier town." Francis Gray, one of the young American attachés who had lived with her in Saint Petersburg, crossed the same bridge in 1811 and noticed this divide, if unsympathetically: "We found that we had left every thing Russian behind and the change was not for the better excepting in the face of the country. The people are dirtier and less civilized than the muzicks their dress an odd mixture of German and Russian." John Carr felt much the same: "Here the Russ character began to subside; most of the boors speak German." Matters were more complicated than this, though Gray and Carr both grasped that the three provinces of the Russian Baltic empire were places that mingled cultures, and that the German was, at least for a rapid traveler, the most visible. It was common to observe that, suddenly, the men lacked long beards, no longer smelled of garlic, and smoked pipes, and in the sweet-smelling wreaths they exhaled one could dimly discern new cultural shapes.[38]

From north to south, these three provinces were Estland, Livland, and Kurland, the first two having been Russian since the Great Northern War, the last having been annexed in 1795, when Poland was partitioned and the duchy of Kurland, technically a vassal state of the Polish-Lithuanian commonwealth, had disappeared. These were places with tense layers of ethnicity, language, and power. At the bottom were the indigenous rural peoples, who would come to be called the Estonians, Latvians, and Lithuanians, with their own languages and customs. These were subdivided into more local groupings. In what would become Latvia, for example, there were Lettgallians, Selonians, Semigallians, and Couronians. But when Mrs. Adams passed through, any sense of linguistic and national identity was still many decades from emerging. In the eighteenth century, the Estonians called themselves not *eestlased* (the modern word for "Estonian") but *maamees* and *maarahvas*, which meant people of the land.[39]

Above these peasants were three sorts of governing classes. The oldest of these, and still dominant, were the German aristocrats and merchants whose ancestors had in the thirteenth century colonized the region. This venture had been spearheaded by the Livonian Brothers of the Sword, later habitually and chillingly known as the Sword Brethren. With their brotherly swords, these had imposed Christianity on skeptical pagans, had founded cities, built castles, divided land into manors, and come to control almost all local power and wealth. But the Germans had not been the only invaders. From the early Middle Ages onward, the region had been regularly invaded and sometimes governed by Vikings, Finns, Danes, Swedes, Russians, and Poles, for this was one of the cockpits of Europe. Of these, the Swedish and Russian invasions were most significant. In the early seventeenth century, the Swedes had perfected their control of what would become, in the twentieth century, Estonia and northern Latvia, but they had carefully respected the prerogatives of the local German elite, a policy followed with more reluctance by the Russians in the eighteenth century. In fact, not only did the Russians exercise relatively little power in their western empire, German Balts supplied a disproportionate share of the Russian army and bureaucracy, which is why Mrs. Adams knew so many of them in Saint Petersburg. Some Russians wondered who had conquered whom. But this was not a question that Alexander I, the husband, son, and grandson of a German, was likely to ask.[40]

Deeper into this tangled world Mrs. Adams ventured. From Narva her road went westward over a "barren common, on the surface of which . . . [were] primitive blocks or boulder-stones." Here she was out of sight of the sea but close enough to hear "a faint sound of waves." She went past Vaivara until she came within a mile of the Baltic at a town called by the locals "Tschudelei." Properly, this was Chudleigh and it shared its name with a small English town in Devon, for reasons which would have been familiar to Mrs. Adams, for its story was part of the lore of Saint Petersburg.[41] Her father-in-law had known part of the story and her husband knew enough, when passing through in 1814, to complain that the name was "grossly misspelt" in books and on the post map, though correctly painted on the door of the posthouse.[42] Louisa Adams liked the gossip of a scandal and few were more deliciously scandalous than the founder of Chudleigh, known to later fame succinctly as a "courtier and bigamist."[43] The courtier's story is pertinent, because the world out of which she had come was the world Mrs. Adams had known as a child and a young woman, a world uneasily relevant to the person Louisa Johnson was and became.

The courtier's maiden name had been Elizabeth Chudleigh. She had been born in 1720 to the lieutenant governor of the Chelsea Hospital, which catered to English veteran soldiers. He had lost his fortune in the South Sea Bubble. Impoverished as a teenager, she had used her voluptuous charms to become the mistress of assorted notables (perhaps the Earl of Bath, probably the Duke of Hamilton) who gave her patronage, most significantly as maid of honor to Augusta, Princess of Wales. In 1744, Elizabeth secretly married an aristocratic sailor, Lieutenant Augustus Hervey—secretly because maids of honor were not supposed to marry. He conveniently went away to sea and then inconveniently returned to find himself a cuckold. They quarreled, reconciled, quarreled again, and then parted without bothering to divorce.

Intent on making a splash, in 1749 she appeared at a "subscription masquerade" at the King's Theatre, Haymarket, as Iphigenia dressed—or undressed—for sacrifice. Rumor had it that she had only some foliage casually distributed around her middle and a transparent gauze everywhere else, though it is probable that rumor exaggerated. Nonetheless Charles Churchill was to observe that "her costume 'showed at once the graces of her person and the disposition of her mind.'" The Princess of Wales attempted to effect decency with a veil and the other maids of honor would not speak to her, even though (as Mrs. Elizabeth Montague noticed) they were "not of maids the strictest." But George II "asked if he might touch Miss Chudleigh's breasts." To this she replied, "Your Majesty, I can put it to a far softer place." This was promising for him, but she mischievously and riskily guided the king's hand to his own forehead. He was amused, gave her gifts, and in time made her mother a housekeeper at Windsor.[44]

The occasion was to became famous, for the newspapers wrote of it, the gossips were enthralled, and there came to be engravings for the innumerable voyeurs of eighteenth-century England. From this salacious triumph, Elizabeth moved on to fresh conquests, probably not including the king, though they were flirtatious. Most notably, she became the permanent mistress of Evelyn Pierrepoint, the second Duke of Kingston-upon-Hull, who built her a home (Chudleigh House) and made her rich, partly by the gallant stratagem of paying his debts when they played cards but never claiming his winnings.[45]

But then she blundered. It looked as though her discarded husband, because his elder brother habitually fell ill, might become the
Earl of Bristol, as he eventually did. To prove her credentials as the
Countess of Bristol, she forged a parish register in Hampshire, thus
perfecting the otherwise imperfect record of her deliberately concealed marriage. Some years later, she moved in the opposite direction of seeking to deny her marriage because Hervey was threatening
to divorce her on the grounds of "the criminality of her conduct." She
took herself to the little-frequented ecclesiastical courts and sought a
"Jactitation of Marriage," a procedure "which put the onus on a person who claimed a wedding had taken place to prove it."[46] Since she
knew of the forged register and Harvey did not, the court ruled that
they had never been married at all. Now single, as far as the law had
bothered to determine, she proceeded in 1769 to marry her Duke of
Kingston and become a duchess. The duke died four years later and
she was bequeathed a very large income from his estate for life, but
on the condition she remain a widow.

The duke's family challenged the will on several fronts. In Chancery, they moved to disallow the will. In the criminal courts, they
sought to have her indicted for bigamy, in the hope that proving she
had never been legally married to the duke would assist their other
efforts. In 1776, she was indicted before the House of Lords in a show
trial in Westminster Hall. Aged retainers, once bribed by her to be
silent and now bribed by the duke's relatives to speak, managed to
tell the truth, and she was found guilty by 116 peers, without dissent.
Because she was a peeress—whether as Countess of Bristol or Duchess of Kingston did not matter—there was no punishment, though
branding and jail were usual for lesser folk found guilty of bigamy.
She did not even lose her munificent income, though sometimes legal
complexities and dilatory executors temporarily stemmed the flow of
money. However, she was faced with social ostracism, since the society that had not minded a closet bigamist was unwilling to receive
someone openly scandalous. So she left England, never to return, and
rattled around Europe for the rest of her life, with a strong prefer-

ence for countries whose courts were willing to receive her as the Duchess of Kingston. One such was Russia. In 1777, Elizabeth built for herself a frigate and set sail for Saint Petersburg, where Catherine the Great was hospitable. As a woman thought conservatively to have had twenty-one lovers in forty-four years, the tsarina was not one to reprobate sexual irregularity.[47]

In 1781, the duchess bought an estate beyond Narva. This consisted of the properties of Fockenhoff, Toila, and Orro, which she coalesced into a place she called Chudleigh after herself and her paternal family's Devonian origins. Missing home, she planned to turn it into a model English estate and for some years the docks at Narva received curious cargoes: English hunting dogs (spaniels, pointers), casks of seashells (for a grotto), trees and plants (lavender, polyanthus, periwinkle, daffodil, turnip), and a "hamper of pigeons." She built a house on the summit of a cliff, with a fine view of the Baltic. But she did not stay long or often and began to lean toward a residence in Paris, partly because the Empress Catherine had grown bored with her and the sensation created when Elizabeth had sailed into Kronstadt had long since faded. She acquired a mansion in Montmartre and, not long before her death, an estate at St. Assise outside Paris. She became friends with Maria Cosway, the painter with whom Thomas Jefferson was entranced. There in 1788 the duchess died, still a wealthy woman beset by lawsuits, but much forgotten, for old women who grow fat and drink too much are of less interest to wagging tongues. In Estland, the servants who remained to tend her estate and drink dry her excellent cellar were expelled, though, in 1813, it was still inhabited by an Englishman called Wilkinson, once her steward. By the mid 1820s, it was deserted and "occupied by a common farmer."[48]

Hence the village of Chudleigh, where Mrs. Adams stopped to change horses and postilions, on her less disreputable journey toward Paris. The conjunction of the scandalous duchess and the respectable diplomat's wife is not as incongruous as it might appear. The Duchess of Kingston had come from a world with which the traveler had been much acquainted, more so than Louisa was willing to acknowledge. It is difficult to understand Louisa Adams and what the world made of her, for good and ill, without realizing that the line that separated her from Elizabeth Chudleigh, though real enough, was thin. Mrs. Adams understood this truth about herself and knew that she had lived "a varied life in which temptation might have proved too strong to a heart in its nature warm and affectionate and to passions of a deep and powerful character which required the strongest curb to keep them within due subordination." But for lucky "preservatives from vice . . . I might and probably should have been a very vicious woman."[49]

Temptation to vice had been a problem in her English family. Louisa Johnson's grandmother and mother had been "not of maids the strictest," and her maternal grandfather Nuth had had a character that, as his granddaughter admitted, was "very indifferent." It is unlikely that he ever married Mary Young, by whom he had twenty-two children, of whom twenty seem to have been dispatched to an orphanage. Only two remained in his household. Both Mary and her daughter Catherine, one of the fortunate two, were probably illegitimate. In the case of Catherine Nuth (or Young), when about fifteen in 1772, she fell in the way of the very handsome Joshua Johnson, a Marylander come to make his fortune as a tobacco merchant in the great metropolis of the British Empire. On December 22, 1773, their child Nancy was born and baptized at St. Botolph Without Aldgate as the legitimate offspring of a married couple. But no record has ever been found of her marrying Joshua Johnson, though over the years several people have sought the evidence in many parish records. During 1773, Joshua Johnson often denied that he was married, and he may have been telling the truth.[50] Or he may not. It is possible he married Catherine later or, though this is less likely, that they had a common-law marriage. This last eventuality would not have been odd in William Hogarth's London. Many a young provincial came from Somerset or Maryland, tumbled into bed with a serving maid, was presented with a squalling baby, and did not bother with the niceties of Anglican rectitude.

A respectable woman or not, over the next twenty years Catherine Johnson bore seven daughters and a son, and the Johnsons became prosperous. They acquired a big house on Tower Hill, many servants, a carriage, silk dresses, and fashionable hairdressers. Thereby they came to mingle, not with the aristocrats of the West End, but with the merchant class of London, who needed to be close to the city's docks. Yet London was a swirling world, in which all classes were visible to all others. In the theaters, which the young Louisa came to love, she saw not only Mrs. Siddons perform but dukes in boxes, and she could glance nervously on rouged prostitutes fondling customers in the pit. It was a cold fact that her mother, the fashionable lady sitting next to her, had once been the fondling sort.

Coming of age in the 1790s in such a world, Louisa Johnson came to be a young lady who ventured to Ranelagh Gardens in Chelsea on warmer days and there might be mistaken for a fashionable beauty. As she remembered it: "In my own eyes I never possessed beauty; and yet strange to say, I was so familiarized to the idea of possessing it; that when I was often *mistaken* as I rode or walked for one of the most celebrated women in London, Lady Elizabeth Lambert; it never excited either surprize or vanity; as to my own eye there was no resemblance." The dandy George "Beau" Brummell thought Lady Elizabeth notable enough to include in his idiosyncratic system of ratings, in which London's female beauties were scored from 1 to 20 in nine categories, ranging from elegance to complexion. Of the sixteen beauties thus ranked, Lady Elizabeth gained, out of a possible 180, a score of 162, which placed her second in the table.[51]

But there is a different moral to this case of mistaken identity, for Lady Elizabeth Lambert was not only beautiful but scandalous, a teenager accused of "criminal intercourse with her own servant," a cause of a libel suit in which a barrister would speak of her "uncommon beauty, which was the theme of the public." In time she would marry a Mr. Ricketts, another sailor who went away to sea and returned to discover himself a cuckold. He successfully sued in the House of Lords for divorce by naming Captain Hargreaves of the Lancashire Fencibles as the corespondent, and producing evidence from a "chambermaid belonging to an inn, where they slept together." All this was widely reported, not least in the *Sporting Magazine*, whose business was to inform about "Transactions of the Turf, the Chace, and Every Other Diversion Interesting to the Man of Pleasure, Enterprize & Spirit." If Louisa Johnson was mistaken for such a woman in the street, the mistake was occasioned by no air of reticent demureness.[52]

In the spring of 1796, Louisa had stepped out to Ranelagh Gardens with her mother, her elder sister Nancy (dressed in an identical costume), and her young fiancé, John Quincy Adams. Six months earlier, he had visited London from his diplomatic post in the Netherlands to exchange the formal ratifying documents of the Jay Treaty, which had attempted to resolve the conflicts between Britain and the United States that had lingered since independence. While there, Adams had drifted into the orbit of the Johnsons, as most Americans did, because Joshua Johnson was the American consul and hospitable to his compatriots. (You were more welcome if from the Southern states, but even Yankees were not turned away.) What the young Adams saw in the Johnson household he liked, partly because he was unused to what he saw. There were six heedless girls, who sang, laughed, gossiped, competed, and liked games, in a manner guiltlessly remote from what Louisa would later designate as "cold harsh and gloomy calvinistic principles." But the chattering girls, who liked to compare notes on the young men who came their way, could not help but notice that Mr. Adams was a touch gauche. Trying to join in, he often blundered and was intriguingly opaque about his desires, a subject in which the young women were very interested, for every young American who entered the house was inspected as a prospect. Being ill-dressed was part of Mr. Adams's gaucherie. Even his mother, who cared more for morals than silk waistcoats, came to notice and worry about it.[53]

Planning the excursion to Ranelagh, Miss Johnson jokingly advised her fiancé that "if he went with us he must dress himself handsomely and look as dashing as possible." He said nothing, but was a little cold when they parted. The next day the Johnson party picked him up at his hotel at the Adelphi on the Strand, on their route from Tower Hill westward to Ranelagh, which sat next to Chelsea Hospital, where once Elizabeth Chudleigh had lived. Louisa was pleased to find him decked out in a blue coat and what later would be called a "large Napoleon hat," for this effort seemed to denote a willing heart and a pliant mind. So they reached the garden, paid their hefty entrance free, passed the Chinese pavilion, entered the great rococo rotunda, and strolled round and round, arm in arm, as lovers were supposed to do by way of display. Even Edward Gibbon, a pudgy and awkward lover, had noticed years before that Ranelagh was "the most convenient place for courtships of every kind . . . certainly the best market we have in England." The rotunda was a wonder of the age, immense like the Pantheon in Rome, but with the advantage of boxes where one might take tea, and of a great fireplace and chimney, in case the English weather should disappoint.[54]

Buoyed by all this—the flowers, the chinoiserie, the bustle of fashion, the sense of being fashionable—Miss Johnson complimented her beau on his appearance. As she was to remember it, "he immediately took fire," and told her in no uncertain terms that no wife of his should "take the liberty of interfering in those particulars." He "assumed a tone so high and lofty and made so serious a grievance of the affair" that she grew offended and told him that she "resigned all pretensions to his hand, and left him as free as the air to choose a Lady who would be more discreet." She then flounced off to her mother for the rest of the evening. (She had not frequented Drury Lane without learning a dramatic effect or two.) They made up, but the spat left "a sting behind," which she did not forget. A gulf had been indicated, small but symptomatic. She was to learn that "some enemy" of hers had told the young man that she "laugh'd at him."[55] As doubtless she had, as fashionable young women in London did at awkward young men from Massachusetts, young men who were unsure if blue was the right color for a coat or which way round hats were worn this year, young men who were very unsure whether a serious man ought to care about being dashing.

On balance, he decided he ought not to care. Back in the Netherlands, he worked on the "restoration of severe reason," and told his fiancée in letters that his recent residence in London, though "a time of delight," was also "a time of too much indulgence," of irresolution and idleness, even of an "abandonment to the fervour of [his] inclinations." After this realization, he had set to mastering himself by rigorous study and "uninterrupted exertions." Thereby he restored his true self, "the Man I was when you *first* knew me," and not "the Man I was for two or three months before I left you."[56] This was very satisfactory to him. But, for her, there began to be a problem. For it was the second man she had agreed to marry, not the first—the man willing to put on the blue coat and the Napoleon hat, not the man who lectured her under the dome of the Ranelagh Rotunda on the duty of wifely restraint.

Narva to Dorpat

(From Aaron Arrowsmith, *Map Exhibiting the Great
Post Roads, Physical and Political Divisions of Europe*
[London: A. Arrowsmith, 1810])

All that was now nearly twenty years ago. In 1815, onward from Chudleigh, Mrs. Adams's carriage and kibitka hastened on, their passengers' collars covered in the ice made by the freezing of breaths, their bells ringing, their postilions singing. For singing was customary among postilions, known locally in German as *Schwagers*, or brothers-in-law. It was still more usual for them blithely to ignore instructions from their indignant employers. Some years later, the German traveler Johann Georg Kohl was to claim, upon the authority of a Russian, that to get a response from a Livonian postilion it was necessary to "exclaim in a thundering voice, 'If you don't drive faster this moment, you rascal, I'll have you flogged like a dog at the next station, and tear your soul from your body.'"[57]

She was now heading south and, after eight miles, came to a fork in the road at Jewe. A right turn led to Reval, where her husband had gone a year before. But she turned left into regions less familiar and her carriage climbed gently uphill through fir forests, marsh, and cultivated hollows, in which sat small wooden houses. Out of these emerged yellow-haired women in what the undiscerning might think shapeless smocks. At the Kleinpungern posthouse hung the skins of bears, assiduously hunted in the nearby woods. Under her berline's runners the soil began to turn sandy, as she crossed the formal boundary between Estland and Livland and, in time, reached Lake Peipsi, whose northern shore she encountered before turning right, going on to Ranapungern and Nainal, and passing down the lake's western shore. Peipsi was the source of the river she had crossed at Narva and, being more than seventy miles long and nearly forty wide, the greatest body of freshwater in Europe west of Lake Ladoga near Saint Petersburg. But Peipsi was then frozen, "a wide desolate plain of snow" whose fishing smacks and rowboats were laid up for the winter, but over which passed "little dark spots . . . the numerous Russian and Esthonian sledges crossing the lake in different directions."[58]

Here she briefly reentered a Russian world, with long-bearded fishermen and craftsmen inhabiting neat villages of two-story houses, brightly painted and stark against the snow, with "walls, railings, gateways . . . all strongly built of strong logs of fir." These were Old Believers, who had fled persecution in Russia in the late seventeenth century, in order to live ancient lives of liturgical purity in isolation from the Swedish, German, and Estonian cultures around them, and to live beyond the reach of the reforming Patriarch Nikon of Moscow and, later, of Peter the Great. In time, the reach of Nikon's successors came to envelop them, but the Russian state had decided to leave these Raskolniki (or schismatics) alone, and to let them use two fingers instead of three when making the Sign of the Cross, to elect their own clergy, to have their services in Old Slavonic, and to decline to say "Hallelujah" three times but keep only to two.[59]

At Tschorna, she left the lake and turned southwest toward Torma. She would not have stopped in the town itself, but turned there to the left and proceeded southward past the manor house. A mile or so farther on, nestled inside a copse of trees ("clothed in their wintry finery of hoar-frost") was a modern Lutheran church with a high sharp spire, where once the pastor Johann von Schwarzenberg, a philosophical horticulturalist, had planted vegetables, established an orchard, and preached against serfdom. The Torma post station itself was about four miles south of the town on the brow of a hill. It was not the old-style barn, but a modern single-story building, Georgian in style, with a colonnaded entrance of five arches. (There was a similar station farther on at Englehardshof.) The Torma station was presided over by Herr Andersohn, a man said to be old and honest, who kept a good table. A decade or so later, Augustus Granville passed this same way, to find the station "comfortable, well arranged, and very well furnished," and his dinner accompanied by an "excellent Bordeaux" reasonably priced. His astonishment was great.[60]

Beyond Torma lay Iggafor, halfway to Dorpat. This part of the road was narrow, scarcely more than a single track on which only one vehicle could travel at a time. This occasioned problems at all times of the year, but especially in winter, because encountering an unyielding vehicle forced a carriage from the road and into the snow, which might be so deep as to come up to the horses' bellies. James Bayard and Albert Gallatin had this experience in January 1814, the worse because they "frequently met trains of loaded Kibitkas drawn by one horse of 25, 30 and 100 in succession." If the caravan was long, the Americans would give way, "but if the number was small the postilion with a thundering voice ordered them out of the road, which was always obeyed, tho the horse sometimes disappeared in the snow and the Kibitka and he were overturned together."[61]

Johann Christoph Brotze, *The Dorpat Stone Bridge* (1800)
(Latvian Academic Library, Riga)

She reached Dorpat by descending a long hill and turning right to cross a strikingly handsome triple-spanned stone bridge over the Embach River. She passed through its two triumphal Roman arches and directly into Town Hall Square. Such a modern bridge was notable, for over the miles Mrs. Adams encountered few. Rather, her carriage would often be compelled to ford many rivers, sometimes by wading through the water, sometimes by being hoisted on a barge, sometimes by hazarding temporary wooden constructions.

High on Toome Hill above her was a semiruined medieval cathedral and below a town of stone, not the wood common in Estland.

With one of those gestures of philanthropy and power she liked to make, Catherine the Great had forbidden wooden houses in Dorpat but permitted the townspeople to plunder the old stones of the cathedral and city walls. The bridge itself had been her gift. Dorpat in 1815 was doing well for itself. At a low point of war in 1710 there had been but four buildings and twenty-one people, but this had risen to about 3,500 in the late eighteenth century and would reach 8,500 by 1825. The reason for this growth was the town's university, the greatest center of learning between Saint Petersburg and Poland, an institution founded by the Swedes in 1632 as the Academia Gustaviana, at a time when in northeastern Europe only Uppsala had a university. But for much of the eighteenth century, the university had been defunct, because Dorpat was strategically significant and badly affected by the incessant warfare between Russians and Swedes. Oddly, it was Tsar Paul who in 1799 had ordered a resumption of the university. Unwittingly the tsar began a modest intellectual renaissance, whose consequences were more complicated than he imagined, for eventually some of the university's German professors ended up as sponsors of an Estonian cultural movement that would not serve the interests of Russian imperial power or even the interests of German professors.[62]

The official reopening of what was now called the Imperial University had been in 1802. So when Mrs. Adams arrived, she entered a place with many new buildings, a city that was a minor showplace of modern architecture. The town square had been rebuilt in the last three decades of the eighteenth century, in a style modestly reminiscent of Saint Petersburg. The bridge she crossed was a twin to one she had often crossed, the Chernyshev Bridge over the Fontanka River. The city hall, sitting at the top of the square, dated from 1786 and was a pastiche of the quasi-Palladian, quasi-baroque municipal buildings common in the Netherlands. The university's energetic architect, Johann Krause, had created an English-style park on Toome Hill, cleverly used part of the ruined Dome Cathedral for a university library, and constructed an elegant rotunda for the Anatomical Theater. Most strikingly, in 1809 Krause had completed at the foot of the hill a large neoclassical university building, with a portico in its facade, six Tuscan columns, rustication, and all the familiar hall-marks of the cosmopolitan, classicizing sensibility that Mrs. Adams knew well, but which she had little seen on her travels so far.[63] Dorpat was a standing reproach to the western travelers who saw in eastern Europe only melancholy and barbarism.

Being in a hurry, Mrs. Adams would not have stopped to look closely at the university, but it is doubtful she would have chosen to do so, even with world enough and time. As a woman, she had had little to do with universities, which were only places to which the men in her life went. What they learned, or failed to learn, there she often little respected. The propensity of college students to argue, for example, she found "most unpleasant and least amusing to me as they know little of sound reasoning and much of sophistry." She admired James Madison, despite his education at the College of New Jersey in Princeton. For her, Madison possessed a mind copious, yet "free from the pedantry and mere classical jargon of University Scholarship."[64] But then she came to know that education was one of the lesser purposes of colleges and later would write a play titled *The Wag or Just from College: A Farce*, in which the hero was most concerned with drinking, flirting, and practical jokes.

With learning that did not require universities, she would always have a conflicted relationship. For a woman of her class and time, she was well educated. This could not have been said of her mother or even her Maryland father, who, as a younger son among eleven children, was denied a classical education. But both her parents had been aspirant and took unusual care to school their children, even though almost all were girls. Louisa's first education was in a French convent school, for her father left England in 1777, when she was only two, and plied his merchant trade in Nantes.[65]

After the Treaty of Paris in 1783, the family returned to London and she was boarded out in Shacklewell, near Hackney Downs in east London, in a dame school run by a Mrs. Carter, a lady fat, eccentric, passionate, noisy, and unaccomplished. Her pupils were charged only with what eighteenth-century London deemed to be feminine skills (reading, dancing, singing, piano, drama); "modern studies" were eschewed, lest they lead girls toward mannishness. But Mrs. Carter was not the only teacher and masculinity was not so simply excluded. There was the "most extraordinary" Miss Young, the head teacher, whose uncle had had her educated with boys, who had worn boys' clothes, and who had acquired a minimalist classical education of "some little Greek and the rudiments of Latin." Unsurprisingly, her "person was masculine," her manners forbidding, and she was widely feared. But with her chosen ones, the crème de la crème, she shared a "mind full of the highest qualities," and she took to Louisa and to her best friend, the uncommonly talented and plain Miss Edwards from the East Indies, "very dark, with long black indian hair." Both girls were quick and apt, and to them Miss Young talked freely about books and taste, and intimated a less binary world than Mrs. Carter preferred, though even Miss Young formally reinforced the conventional premise that sensibility was feminine, learning masculine.[66]

In 1787, when Louisa was twelve, Miss Young went off to found her own school in Kensington, and soon after Mrs. Carter migrated to Baron House in Mitcham, then a Surrey village southwest of London. There, for another two years, Louisa boarded out. Then her father, concerned about the mounting expenses of educating so many children, brought the girls home and furnished a governess.[67]

The residue of these educational experiences was an ambivalence. On the one hand, Louisa had felt separate from the other schoolgirls, whom she regarded as trivial. She became the sort of girl who, when given a guinea on New Year's Eve, went out and bought "treasures to which I had long aspired," which were not ribbons and bonnets, but copies of John Milton's *Paradise Lost* and *Paradise Regained*, and John Mason's *Self-Knowledge: A Treatise, Shewing the Nature and Benefit of That Important Science, and the Way to Attain It: Intermixed with Various Reflections and Observations on Human Nature.* This did not stop her, however, when home during the vacations with her sisters, from dressing up in her mother's gowns, and thereby assuming "the titles of the great, [and] aping as far as we could their airs and manners."[68]

The result was someone who read widely and came (though late in life) to write freely, with no little conversational verve and command of grammar, though also with an inattention to punctuation and spelling not uncommon in her culture, which did not always think consistency of great moment. Louisa was to became skittish about bluestockings, far more so than her mother-in-law, Abigail Adams, whose education had been far more rudimentary and whose spelling often verged on the illiterate, but whose close friend was the historian Mercy Otis Warren, as bluestocking as a Bostonian woman could be. Louisa's ambivalence about what was masculine and feminine lay close to the heart of her resistance to female intellectuality. There was a tension between mind and body. Bodies had to be all feminine, but minds were not so single-sexed. Of a Miss Derville in Berlin, Louisa once wrote, "Her features were prominent and of the Roman cast; but somewhat too masculine." Dolley Madison was "tall large and rather masculine in personal discussions," though "her complexion was so fair and brilliant as to redeem this objection, in its perfectly feminine beauty." On the other hand, if a woman's mind and sensibility were inflected with the masculine, it need not incur criticism.[69]

It was less that Mrs. Adams mistrusted any woman with a quasi-masculine mind so much as she was uncertain whether she was capable of it. In Boston once, she met Martha Sullivan, wife of the Massachusetts attorney general, a woman whom Mrs. Adams thought had just such a "masculine mind," comparable to that of Madame de Genlis, the doyen of French bluestockings. In Mrs. Adams, the encounter occasioned an anxiety: "There is generally a want of feminine grace and sweetness, in these showy, strong minded Women; which produce fear in us lesser lights; and this has always been my first impression on becoming acquainted with them—yet they always appear to me to be *what God intended Woman to be*, before she was cowed by her Master *man*." For, in principle, she did not doubt that women had minds equal to men. In 1838, she was to write a letter of appreciation to Sarah Grimké, author of *Letters on the Equality of the Sexes and the Condition of Woman*, for a book that, as Mrs. Adams put it, demonstrated that men and women were "co-equal in mind" and showed that "we no where see an evidence of the inferiority in the female." But she feared too much mingling of sexual identities. In the 1840s, she urged that a granddaughter be prevented from appearing in amateur theatricals as a male, for "a Girl should never for a moment assume the masculine character." Girls should be pure, delicate, and modest. "To appear in the [male] garb is . . . unseemly; as the masculine stride; the bold look, the determined tone, and the haughty command necessarily assumed in the performance, have a tendency through the mere circumstance of momentary approbation; to destroy the timid and blushing graces of a Girl of sixteen on her entrance into her world, where feminine elegance has assumed a positive and fixed standard."[70]

From Dorpat, she proceeded southwest and passed through many small towns and two larger ones, Valk and Volmar. When about a hundred miles from Riga, in the vicinity of Valk, it started to rain. (She knew her location because by the side of the road the Russians put high and square markers, painted black and white, to denote a traveler's distance from Saint Petersburg.) The snow beneath her runners began to melt away and she had to stop, to have her servants remove the runners of the carriage and put on the wheels, which they had taken care to bring.[71] This transformation was impossible for the kibitka, designed only for snow, and it bumped along until they reached Riga, where it was sold. Thereafter the sledge's luggage and its two servant passengers were jammed on top of the carriage, whose interior was reserved for the genteel, which included only Mrs. Adams, her son, and Madame Babet.

This stretch of the road, especially the last thirty miles or so before Riga, was forested, hilly, and very sandy. From the road could be seen more wooden farmhouses, "small horses and diminutive horned cattle" quartered in barns for the winter. There were many public houses, "before the doors of which are usually seen a multitude of wretched carts and sledges, belonging to the peasants." At Hilkensfer,

Dorpat to Riga

(From Aaron Arrowsmith, *Map Exhibiting the Great Post Roads, Physical and
Political Divisions of Europe* [London: A. Arrowsmith, 1810])

she had to cross the river Aa on a ferryboat. Because of the rain and
thaw, she doubtless encountered the situation described a few years
earlier by George Green. If you "should [arrive] at the setting in or
going away of the ice," he observed, "you will find some difficulty in
getting your carriage over; however, for a silver rouble, the peasants
will exert their utmost endeavours." Thereafter her journey was short.
In the distance, she could see the gilt cupola of St. Peter's Church and
the tower of the Domkirche, sitting to the north of the river Dvina.
She arrived in Riga on Thursday, February 16, four days after leaving Saint Petersburg and "after as pleasant a journey as the Season
would admit," marred only by "the most trifling accident." This had

been a very good pace, about 350 miles at nearly ninety miles a day. A year earlier, Bayard and Gallatin had taken twice as long, because they had encountered driving snowstorms and trouble with broken vehicles. She had every reason to think that matters had started well.[72]

She found in Riga the greatest city she would encounter between Saint Petersburg and Königsberg, and the nearest thing to a capital that the western Russian Empire possessed. In it she found "tolerable lodgings," which almost certainly meant the Hotel Saint Petersburg, usually thought to offer the best accommodation. It is more probable that she stayed there because it was at the northern end of the Old Town in Castle Square and, as she remembered it, "we were barely settled in our Lodgings, when the Governor of Riga called to invite me to his house and to offer me the use of his carriage during my stay." She had sent over a letter of introduction from Levett Harris, to which the governor had promptly responded.[73]

This was Marquis Filippo Paulucci, who lived across the square in Riga Castle. He was already known to the Adamses, for he had met John Quincy Adams, at least, when visiting Saint Petersburg in 1812. He was an Italian from Modena, one of the cadre of foreigners who served the tsar, in Paulucci's case in various military capacities in the Asian territories. He had then helped to drive the French back from Riga in 1812 and been rewarded with the governorship of Livland and Kurland, a position he was to hold for several decades. Paulucci was a conservative, a friend to Joseph de Maistre and an enemy to liberalism and Jews, but also a man who gave to Riga esplanades and gardens by opening out the claustrophobic streets of the Old Town, a place that got mixed reviews from travelers. Francis Gray ungenerously called it "the mealiest city which I ever saw," and Nikolai Karamzin in 1803 had deemed it "not very elegant," because of its narrow passageways, though he acknowledged some handsome buildings, reminiscent of the high-gabled houses of Amsterdam.[74] Riga was, above all, a working town of merchants, its docks during the trading season filled with ships.

Paulucci was hospitable. He had invited both James Bayard and his fellow diplomat Albert Gallatin over from the Hotel Saint Petersburg to "the palace where [they] were led thro a long train of Apartments" to the marquis and his German Baltic wife, Wilhelmina, before escorting them to his box at the theater. It was a routine he followed with Mrs. Adams, who dined with him every day, who went to the theater with him, and who was introduced by him to the German elite of Riga, with whom she tried awkwardly to converse. The castle she visited had inherited the name but no longer embodied the form of a castle. Its fortifications had long since been dismantled, and it had come to look more like a grand city hall, though, as she crossed the square, she would have seen to her left a round tower that had once served a more belligerent purpose. To her right was the river, which in winter served as a "public walk, on which sledges, carriages, and skaters . . . rapidly [moved] to and fro."[75]

A day after arriving, a little before noon, she sat down to write two letters. One was to Levett Harris back in Russia, to inform him of her safe arrival (not to be taken for granted), to thank him for the letter of introduction to Paulucci, and to ask that Harris thank the minister of the interior, whose letter of safe conduct had made her travel so much easier. She spoke of money matters and a Mr. Mitchell who had called the previous evening when she was "just going to the Theatre with the Governor," but who was asked to return the next day. As she wrote, Mitchell and his wife appeared, so Mrs. Adams was able to conclude her letter by saying, "Mr Mitchel and his Lady have just left me I have given him notes to the amount of one thousand eight hundred R. he says that this Sum will be sufficient to take me to Memel I have therefore requested him to change it for the proper Money for the rout." In Riga and Kurland, roubles were not usable. Instead, travelers used Dutch ducats, silver crowns, florins, and marks. The Dutch ducat was the coin that was most acceptable in most countries, and John Carr, for example, stuck on the Finnish-Russian border in 1804 without roubles, was able to employ "the safety and convenience of this valuable coin."[76]

The second letter was to her husband, far off in Paris, to say that all was going well and to describe the Pauluccis, "a charming couple exactly suited to please me as they are entirely divested of the ostentatious manners which so generally pervade that class in the great City she is unaffected and pleasing and he . . . unites to frank and open manners the most hospitable and friendly attention and it is impossible not to feel gratified in his society."[77] With this sentiment, she stopped and would not resume the letter until she reached the Baltic coast.

It was her memory in both 1827 and 1836 that she stayed in Riga for four or five days, "to get my Carriage fixed and to dispose my kibitka." But her memory misled, for it is certain she reached Riga on Thursday, February 16, and she was in Memel on the Baltic coast by Monday, February 20, and it would not have been possible to have completed the next stage of her journey by leaving any later than early afternoon on that Saturday. Still, it is probable she reached Riga by about noon on Thursday, in time to dine and go to the theater with the Pauluccis, so she was there during Thursday, Friday, and part of Saturday. Memory might easily expand such a period, for it was the longest she stayed anywhere before reaching Berlin and she was enjoying herself.[78]

She was devoted to the theater and, for this, Riga was much above the provincial norm, for it was on the circuit for traveling companies who wended their way to Saint Petersburg. More unusually, the city had its own civic theater and a company of actors who performed through the winter season and toured local cities (Dorpat, Mitau) in the summer. The traveler Johann Seume observed in 1805, "The Riga theatre is well known, and may be compared to those of the higher order in Germany," which was high praise, given that this was a golden age for German theater. The Riga theater was at 4 Königsstrasse, had been built in 1782, and would remain the city's theater until 1863. It was unpretentiously small, with just five hundred seats, and a place where ladies in their boxes took out their knitting to make stockings. (Mrs. Adams was a knitter, too, though probably not there.) Bayard described it in 1814 as very crowded, "of common size, not very brilliant in its decorations," but with "an excellent orchestra." It did the usual German repertoire—Schiller, Schlegel's translations of Shakespeare, Klopstock—and understandably specialized in plays by August von Kotzebue, who had lived in and around Riga, there composing his elegant plagiarisms. But in its time, the theater had also sponsored masked balls, operas, singspiels, and concerts. Above the theater to which Mrs. Adams went in 1815 was an elite social club called Die Musse. It was in 1815 that the club itself came to own the theater, which had previously belonged to someone whose daughter Mrs. Adams knew well, whose son-in-law had once tried to seduce her, and whose grandson would in a very few years be the Russian minister to the United States, when John Quincy Adams was secretary of state. Riga was not so remote, after all, for someone whose adult life was spent at the intersections of cultures.[79]

The owner had been Baron Otto Herman von Vietinghoff, a high Russian government official and German landowner whose passion for the theater had led him to construct the auditorium, immediately next to his Riga town house at 2 Königsstrasse. There his daughter Julie was born in 1764, and eighteen years later she married a Livonian aristocrat and diplomat called Burchard Alexis Constantine, Baron von Krüdener. Like Mrs. Adams, Julie trailed around after her husband to various postings (Venice, Copenhagen) and, like Mrs. Adams, was uneasy in her marriage. Julie von Krüdener, however, took the drastic step of separation, which led her to wanderings in Italy, France, Switzerland, and Germany, sometimes led her back to her mother in Riga, and occasionally to reunions with her husband, reunions that seldom required fidelity on either side. It was on vacation in Bohemia that Mrs. Adams first met them, then again later in Berlin.[80]

At a Berlin supper party given by the Adamses' banker, Baron Krüdener once approached Louisa, expressed his great admiration, and, as she remembered it, "invited me to breakfast with *him*, tete à tete in a Pavillion in his Garden." She was amused, perhaps flattered, though she knew that his admirations were liberally distributed, for "he made the same proposals to all the ladies that he sat near; assuring them 'that his Lady was always engaged with her own affairs.'" That lady Mrs. Adams then lightly noticed as "a very handsome, but somewhat notorious person, of latitudinarian principles, with which for her own special comfort, she had innoculated her charming Caro Sposo." Later, lightness was not the appropriate tone, for Julie grew religious and mystic, even moral by her own lights. She went to Saint Petersburg and became very close to the tsar, successfully advised him to banish his mistress and contemplate his God, and was the single greatest influence that led him to transform the workmanlike and practical coalition that had overthrown Napoleon into a "Holy Alliance" with supernatural and Christian purposes.[81]

All this Mrs. Adams observed in both Prussia and Russia. "She was a woman of the most extraordinary character," she remembered, "noted for talents and accomplishments of a very high order, but her conduct very doubtful," indeed in Berlin "very guilty." Later "she became a fanatic, and roamed through Switzerland and Germany; where she became the leader or head of a considerable Sect of severe morality, and self denying doctrines; which she preached to very large audiences in the fields over whom she obtained prodigious Influence." Mrs. Adams never troubled to learn "the exact tenets of [this] religious faith," but she did know that Julie "exerted a powerful sway over the mind of the Emperor Alexander" and "changed his character."[82] Marquis Paulucci knew, too, and it would be surprising if the topic did not come up in his gubernatorial box at 4 Königsstrasse.

Mrs. Adams went to the theater everywhere she went, as did her husband, and this taste formed a bond in their marriage. As a teenager in Paris, he had fallen in love with a French child actress, had pined uselessly to meet her, and for several years had had his sleep disturbed by erotic dreams of her. When her husband was unavailable, Mrs. Adams dragooned whoever was at hand—a sister, an attaché, a son—to go, since ladies had to have chaperones and theater was a passion with her. But it is doubtful that Riga's theater would have entranced her, for she only went to the German theater when there was no alternative. She had tried the experiment in Saint Petersburg, only to note: "I do not understand the language and do not enjoy it—[the] Music is very sweet but the Germans scream to the very utmost extent of their voices and although great Musicians I dont like their screeching and I found it all very stupid." Her husband was, inexpli-

cably, "fond of it." The French theater, by contrast, was "an amusement in which I delight," though more for its comedy than tragedy,
since there was "something very stiff and cold in french tragedy."[83]

Her parents had taken the family to the London stage. From the
first, Louisa was drawn to the actresses; in fact she would hardly ever
notice actors. She took Elizabeth Farren and Sarah Siddons as models, despite the common opinion that the stage was little better than a
brothel. (It was a lifelong rule of John Quincy Adams "to make no
acquaintance with *Actresses*.") She came to know Mrs. Siddons off-
stage, too, and was struck by her regal dignity. Over the years, Louisa
came to see some great (Fanny Kemble, Ellen Tree) and many indifferent actresses, witness a few great (*Hamlet*, *Tartuffe*) and count-
less forgettable plays, hear much ravishing (*Figaro*, *Zauberflöte*) and
more jarring music. For the most part, she admired those performers
who achieved the illusion of naturalness. She disliked melodrama
and excess, ranting in tragedy or vulgarity in comedy. Her husband,
by contrast, preferred farce, and the broader the farce, the more he
enjoyed it. Her taste ran to the comedy of manners, to the likes of
Oliver Goldsmith, though also to Shakespeare, because he portrayed
the humanity of even the great, and showed Lear not just as a king,
but as a lost father.[84] Later in life she was to write lightly cynical plays
about secrets and lies, seduction and jealousy, set in the customary
theatrical scenes—English squirely households, inns, Turkish seraglios,
forest glades. Of all her compositions, these were the least successful.

What she learned from the theater went into her life, especially
her life as a politician's wife. While her husband drew little from his
theatergoing, because he regarded simulation as hypocrisy, she understood that public life had placed both of them on a stage, where
she was the better performer. John Quincy Adams often stared
blankly at the audience, ignored the prompter, and mostly sat in the
corner and read a book. At first, unwillingly, to fill the painful silence, she was forced into speaking the lines of the play, lest they be
pelted with orange peel and bad apples. Over time, she became good
at it, liked it when the audience laughed or shed a tear, and acquired
the showy habits of an actress. She took care with her costume, be-

came skilled at interacting, knew when to break a tension or force a crisis, and, in truth, sometimes flirted with being a ham, for the divide between naturalness and melodrama was too easily crossed. She once described a fictional counterpart of herself as "a singular compound of strong affections and cold dislikes; of discretion and caprice; of pride and gentleness; of playfulness and hauteur." And she quoted a gentleman saying of her, and to her, that "she was a being one could neither live with, or without."[85] This was high praise for an actress and made for an absorbing play, but could be hard work for those, like her husband, who had to live with her. But it was hard work for her, too, because she never shed a sense that she was in the wrong play, in the wrong theater, with the wrong audience.

The small boy, in Riga under the care of Madame Babet in the Hotel Saint Petersburg, would grow up adjacent to his mother's theatrical qualities, and came to observe them with mingled affection and exhaustion. In 1824, he wrote of her, "Although I am obliged to differ from her in opinion sometimes, and am forced to make a harsh judgment upon some of her actions or wishes, still there is something inexpressibly delightful in her manners and her affections are most powerful." In 1827, he would add, "Her feelings are constantly carrying her into extremes which she repents when it is too late." In 1828, after getting a harrowing letter from her, he glumly remarked, "It is difficult to deal with sensitive women."[86]

3

FROM RIGA TO BERLIN

A<small>FTER RIGA</small>, the journey became more difficult. Even before leaving, Mrs. Adams noticed a problem. In her last days in Saint Petersburg, Charles Francis had been presented with a silver cup as a keepsake by the Baron de Bussche Hunnefeldt, a Hanoverian who served as Westphalian minister, a man of worldly discretion and (he often claimed) a Francophobe, though there were those who suspected him of being a French spy. This cup had been in her carriage, but then it had disappeared, presumably into Riga's black market. She strongly suspected that the thief was Baptiste, the French prisoner of war, indeed felt there was "little doubt that he had made free with it." But she had no proof, so kept silent. With all the servants, she had to tread a delicate line between authority and complaisance, for she was a woman alone and vulnerable, not least because she was hiding bags of gold and silver. So she lied to them, declared she had little money, and said that in each town she exchanged letters of credit for only such cash as might take her to the next town.[1]

On Saturday, minus a silver cup and a kibitka, she crossed the Dvina. If the river was still hard frozen, she would have crossed on the ice, though it was common for passengers to walk or be conveyed in a light sledge so that a heavy carriage with passengers would not

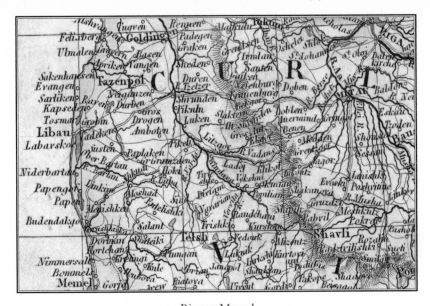

Riga to Memel

(From Aaron Arrowsmith, *Map Exhibiting the Great Post Roads, Physical and Political Divisions of Europe* [London: A. Arrowsmith, 1810])

break through. If the river had thawed, she would have traversed a long and wide plank bridge, which rested on poles, had a drawbridge for ships, and was inclined "under the wheels of heavy-laden carriages [to play] as if actuated by a spring."[2] She then headed southwest toward Mitau. The weather had worsened, as she had been told was likely, and the snow was deep. But now her carriage had wheels, not runners, and once or twice it stuck fast. When this happened, the postilions rang a bell and out of the flat countryside appeared muffled peasants armed with pickaxes and shovels to dig them out. The signal of the bell, she remembered, was "readily understood." If they were paid for this service, as doubtless they were, it was a regular winter emolument, for the road between Riga and Mitau was busy. The distance was short, only a little over twenty-five miles, and about halfway, at St. Olai, there were two obelisks that denoted the formal boundary between Livland and Kurland.[3] It was her plan only to stop in Mitau for food and rest, and then continue westward for another eighteen miles to the post station at Doblen for the night.

It was dark when she reached yet another wooden bridge and crossed the river Aa to a narrow island, before crossing a different branch of the same river to reach the market town of Mitau. On the island to her right, if she could see through the late afternoon gloom, was an oddly familiar sight. There stood a great baroque palace in the Saint Petersburg style, though not richly colored in salmon or green, but plastered and whitewashed. It had been designed in the mid-eighteenth century by Bartolemeo Rastrelli, the chief architect of the Winter Palace, for Ernst Biron, Duke of Kurland. In its flickering day, the palace had been richly splendid, a place where Giacomo Casanova had once danced minuets in a masked ball and, by his own account, been admired by "all the younger ladies." But there had been fires and neglect, and then Kurland had disappeared as an autonomous duchy. It used to be joked that "the palace was larger than the kingdom," but it was certainly larger than the revenues necessary for its upkeep. So there came to be disrepair, even during the period when the comte de Lille (later Louis XVIII of France), wandering safely far from his countrymen, had come to stay for more than six years in two spells, long enough for the French police to designate him "le roi de Mitau." Later, Napoleon's army, passing to and fro in its disastrous Russian campaign, had used the place as a hospital and amused itself by breaking things. But even before these depredations, it had grown uninviting, a "vast, inelegant, neglected palace . . . built of brick, stuccoed white, standing upon a bleak eminence, ungraced by a single shrub or tree," what Lady Sarah Lyttelton called in 1814 merely "a dismal barracks."[4]

At first sight, Mitau, too, was uninviting, a huddle of low wooden houses, "a long, straggling, ill-built town, and most wretchedly paved." Yet it was nonetheless "a cheerful sort of little capital," which drew people for many miles and was a center of music, theater, gambling, and amusement. This was especially so in the winter, when the painted houses were filled with German "noble families of small incomes, whose numerous equipages [gave] an aristocratic air to the place." It was often thought to be a more inviting place than even Riga, for Riga was large and tainted with trade, while Mitau was intimate and deemed civilized, a place concerned only with hospitality and manners, a city that in 1815 acquired a Kurland Society of Literature and Art, and would come to play a role in the creation of Latvian culture.[5]

Mrs. Adams stopped for some hours at an "excellent" house, "the best I had found," where "the People were very civil, and every thing very comfortable." This was yet another hotel called the Saint Petersburg, which was on the main square and "the best inn in the town, consisting of a great number of scattered apartments, a long billiard room, and two or three private sitting rooms near it, tolerably clean." Its landlord was a French émigré called Jean Louis Morel, who had come to Mitau as Louis XVIII's chef, but stayed on and married a local woman. By common consent, he was "a chatty old fellow," and he especially liked to reminisce about his days with the duc d'Enghien in Strasbourg, about fighting "many bloody actions" by the side of the Bourbons, actions in which he was "wounded, maimed, and rendered incapable of effective action." These experiences had bred in Morel a gossipy skepticism about his late royal employers, of whose private lives he had many stories. These yarns were the customary accompaniment

Johann Christoph Brotze, *Peasant Wagons in Estland* (undated)
(Latvian Academic Library, Riga)

to the excellent French food he served, which stood out in travelers' memories by its welcome contrast to the grim staples of German landlords, who tended to furnish black bread and beer soup ("beer, yolks of eggs, wheat and sugar, boiled together").[6]

Mitau was notable for more than the unexpected *fricassée*. It was the place where Mrs. Adams, moving westward from Saint Petersburg, first began to encounter numerous Jews, though in Mitau itself they were confined to residence in a single "Jews' Street." Kurland was a demographic and spiritual center for eastern Jewry, the northwestern home of the Yiddish-speakers known as Litvaks, who had migrated eastward from Germany and Poland in the late sixteenth and seventeenth centuries. Jews had by law once been confined to the countryside, though in practice they had worked as merchants, tradesmen, artisans, and tavern keepers, usually as agents for the German elite, who found "court Jews" to be useful, if distasteful for their long hair and longer black coats, and for their strange language with its many dialects. It was not until 1799 that Tsar Paul, of all people, decreed that they had a legal right to inhabit Kurland, though for reasons that flirted with anti-Semitism. We must, he said, "transform the Jews into a useful element and curb their avaricious pursuits." So, by his logic, they needed to be registered officially as burghers, merchants, and farmers, should be given family names, have their rabbis placed under the official scrutiny of Saint Petersburg, issue their religious works from a "government printing press," be banned from governmental positions, be forbidden to employ "Christian domestic servants," and be permitted Jewish schools for children under thirteen but not after. Above all, the tsar thought, "they should change their dress and speech." In its own cruel way, this was progress, for it advanced Jews from being illegal aliens to being not citizens but "non-Russians," or sanctioned foreigners. So although Alexander I was less amenable than his father and more bent on turning Jews into Christians, the Litvaks mostly supported the Russians when Napoleon came, because they feared that Napoleon would be more efficient in forcing assimilation, and they saw more hope in Russian inefficiency and inconsistency.[7]

The Litvak world had produced inventive theologians and believers, who quarreled fiercely. The basic division was between the Misnagdim and the Hasidim. The former were traditional and believed in Talmudic study, the life of the mind, rationality, elitism, and guilt. The latter were radical pietists who mistrusted the mind, put their faith in feelings and the common people, and mystically believed in joy, dance, and humor. An important leader of the Hasidim, a movement that originated in the Ukraine and reached the Baltic provinces in the 1760s, was Schneur-Zalmen of Lyozna, near Vibetsk, whose son became the first Lubavitcher rebbe. The leader of the Misnagdim was the rabbi Elijah ben Judah Solomon Zalman, known as the Gaon of Vilna, where he presided over an influential *beit midrash*, or study hall. In truth, near the Baltic the divisions were less abrupt than in the Ukraine, for the Misnagdim were a touch less rational, the Hasidim a little less ecstatic than their counterparts elsewhere, but this did not prevent the Gaon of Vilna from excommunicating his heretic enemies, nor the Hasidim from dancing in the streets when he died, nor the building of separate synagogues. Into this bitterness, or out of it, came the Maskilim, the small number of Jewish thinkers who looked toward the Enlightenment, the Königsberg of Immanuel Kant and the Berlin of Moses Mendelssohn. Prominent among these was David Friedlander of Mitau (though also of Berlin), but more famous was Solomon Maimon, who grew up near Mir on the estates of Prince Radziwill, whose family Mrs. Adams knew in Berlin. Maimon was admired by many (not usually Jewish) for his autobiography, his commentaries on Kant and Maimonides, and his hostility to ritualism. While he spoke the language with a "Yiddish accent that branded him as an *ostjude*," he wrote in German and was among the first eastern Jews to move westward to Berlin, in the belief that this was a movement toward the light.[8]

Travelers reaching Mitau and passing on habitually noticed this Yiddish world. Rarely was this done with a puzzled neutrality, as with the Scottish traveler William Rae Wilson in Königsberg, who observed that "the Hebrew race here is not a little numerous, and in walking along we observed several boards with inscriptions in their language." Further east, he "proceeded to an inn kept by a Jew, where we found ourselves surrounded by beings totally different in looks, dress and manners, from any we had hitherto met with." It was more usual to abandon neutrality and to declare that "Riga keeps itself clear of Jews; Mitau swarms with them." It was common to speak of "dirty villages swarming with Jews," of their "squalid appearance," of their "love of gain which acts as a ruling passion among those who, without country, rank, or character feel that money is the only thing that can secure to them even the outward tokens of respect." The novelist Leitch Ritchie observed that Mitau "absolutely swarms with these desperadoes; and, even in the courts of gentlemen's houses, if there is a nook at all capable of affording shelter, you see a Hebrew family nestling like a colony of mice."[9]

It is striking that Mrs. Adams, neither at the time nor later, said a word on the subject of the Jews. It is impossible for her not to have noticed them, because they dressed distinctively, were often postilions, and not infrequently owned inns, and Jewish peddlers were ubiquitous. In Mitau, one of the hotels was Jewish-owned, and Karamzin was to remember of the town: "No sooner had we set foot in the inn . . . than a number of Jews surrounded us with various trifles. One offered a pipe, another an old Lutheran Prayer-book and Gottscherd's Grammar, the third a telescope, and everyone assured us that he would sell his wares at the lowest prices 'to gentlemen such [as] you.'"[10]

Mrs. Adams's husband, by contrast, was not prone to silence on this subject. In 1781, he had passed through a Jewish village near Cologne and remarked that it was "a Nasty, dirty, Place . . . fit only for Jews to live in." When touring Silesia in 1800 with his wife, he went to Frankfurt on the Oder and noticed that a quarter of its inhabitants were Jewish. "It is, therefore," he noted, "distinguished by those peculiarities which mark all European towns where a large proportion of Israelites reside, and to express which, I suppose, resort must be had to the Hebrew language: the English, at least, is inadequate to it; for the word *filth* conveys an idea of spotless purity in comparison with Jewish nastiness."[11] Though he did not believe that a Jew, at least in the United States, should be disqualified from voting, he could refer to a Jewish congressman as the "alien Jew delegate," and he was not above the customary stereotypes when speaking of "stock jobbing and Jew-brokering tricks upon the Royal Exchange."[12]

It was not that Mrs. Adams was free of prejudices. She was, after all, a woman who in 1831 wrote a comic poem titled *The Black Ball*, which began: "Says Cuffee to Sambo, d'ya go to the Ball? / Yes! I was invited to day / And dey say we to dance in the great dining hall / Dey be taking the Carpet away." Her letters were freely scattered with references to "darkies," she did not mind employing a hired slave as a servant, and, though in fervent principle she disapproved of slavery, she was opposed to antislavery movements and sympathized with the cultural and economic dilemmas of slaveholders. It was just that anti-Semitism was not one of her prejudices. She had known many Jews, especially in her Berlin days. Then she had dined frequently with their "very polite" banker, Herr Schickler, who "lived in a very showy style, and entertained very handsomely." She had also frequented the salon of Ephraim and Pessel Cohen, "very rich Jews" who were "also very polite . . . and lived in a style of great elegance, entertaining the first and highest persons of rank in the City." Doubtless these homes did not administer a litmus test for an anti-Semite, for such people inhabited as high a society as was permitted to any European Jew. Schickler Brothers was Berlin's greatest banking firm, and whether she went to the home of David Schickler or his brother Johann Ernst makes little difference to the opulence she experienced.[13] Likewise Ephraim and Pessel Cohen ran one of the most favored salons in Berlin, a hospitality made possible by a cotton factory that employed hundreds of hands working English looms. Nowhere in such places did Mrs. Adams see men with long beards, long gowns, and broad slouch hats. In fact, while she was in Berlin, the Cohens converted to Christianity and became Ernst and Philippine.[14] Yet John Quincy Adams went to these homes and could still condemn Jewish filth elsewhere, while she was silent. Such silence was rare enough to be eloquent.

On the other hand, in Mitau she had other things to concern her.

After an hour at the inn, Mrs. Adams was visited by an acquaintance from her Saint Petersburg days. She remembered the visitor as Countess Mengs, a woman of "polished manners, fine sense and charming conversation," who lived a mile from the town. It seems likely, however, that she misremembered the name and this was Maria, Countess von Medem, who had extensive Russian family connections and who lived in Zala Castle, a late-eighteenth-century palace nearby, to the southwest of Mitau.[15] Her father was Count Peter von Pahlen, once the military governor of Saint Petersburg, the chief leader of the conspiracy that had murdered Tsar Paul, and an exile on his various Kurland estates, of which the most important was Kaucminde Castle, to the southeast of Mitau. But, whoever she was, the countess wished the distinguished visitor to see "all that was worth seeing" in the city and the area for two or three days, when introductions would be made to "some of her distinguished friends." For her usual reasons of haste, Mrs. Adams declined, and the countess left.[16]

Then dinner, taken in a private room, was finished and the dishes removed.[17] At this point the landlord Morel entered, unexpectedly looked around with suspicion, and shut the door carefully behind him. Seeing that there was something on his mind, Mrs. Adams invited him to sit down and asked why he had come and what he wanted to say. As she spoke, he glanced in a worried way at the doors, for the room had several entrances and he seemed concerned about intruders or eavesdroppers. This amused her by its theatricality. It also made her uncomfortable, for she did not know if this was only petty melodrama. But it had become a maxim with her that she should always appear unconcerned, so she "assumed an air of great calmness and patiently awaited."

Morel had two things on his mind. First, he told her that there had been a "dreadful" murder the night before, on the very road she was about to take. He advised that, in the circumstances, she should stay the night. Mrs. Adams replied "very coolly and decidedly" that she would not, for her plans were fixed. She was only going to the next post station and ought to reach it by nine or ten o'clock, and, besides, she had "two well armed servants," plus postilions who would be taking her on a well-frequented road. Perhaps, too, she quietly reflected that murders were part of the gossip of the road, that this slaughter might or might not have happened, and that landlords could be ingenious with tales that persuaded paying guests to linger, especially guests so evidently affluent. Morel later admitted as much, when he asked that she not consider his words to arise from "a mere innkeepers wish to keep his company."

During her cool reply, Morel looked grave and shook his head in polite dissent. But, after she had spoken, he admitted that this was, to be sure, an incidental matter, raised as a courtesy by an old man with "daughters of his own" to a friend of the countess and to a lady traveling with a young son. But there was another matter, the real occasion for shutting the door and his nervous glances.

When Mrs. Adams had arrived, as the carriage had unloaded its passengers and they had entered the inn, and as her servants had gone to the public areas to eat and drink, Morel had recognized Baptiste as a former soldier in Napoleon's army. Many in Mitau had experience of Baptiste, for he had stayed there for two years and, in that time, many had come to fear him, because he was "known to be a desperate Vilain, of the very worst character." His crimes extended beyond trifles like stealing silver cups. Morel did not think Mrs. Adams's life was safe with such a man. He advised dismissing him from her service, though not yet. Baptiste was doubtless acquainted with Morel, for an inn run by a gossipy Frenchman who liked to talk of French matters would have been a habitual resort for a French soldier, marooned in a small town among Germans, Jews, and Semigallians. If Mrs. Adams dismissed Baptiste instantly, there in the hotel Saint Petersburg on that early Saturday evening, and set out for Doblen without him, this would leave Baptiste alone at the inn, with a scrap of baggage, a grievance, and a suspicion, which could only fall on Morel, his wagging tongue, and his fondness for telling gaudy stories of past events. Might not Baptiste burn down his precious inn "over his head" as a revenge?

This was a more serious prospect or, at least, half serious. In truth, Mrs. Adams was not being offered much of a choice. Travel on and be murdered by footpads, which was possible but unlikely? Or travel on and be murdered by Baptiste, which was also possible but unlikely? For, as she told Morel, "the man had behaved very well so far," had been respectful, active, and attentive. To be sure, she did not like him and there had been the matter of the purloined silver cup, so she had her suspicions already, and this meant she was already on her guard. But suspicion was not proof, not even of larceny, let alone of prospective murder. And there was a matter of honor, hers as a lady. She had, after all, given her word "that he should be taken to his own Country; and that I was not to part with him unless he behaved improperly."

Morel acknowledged that "the case was difficult." Mrs. Adams, he advised, should perform an intelligent charade and play a longer game. She should "appear to place unlimited confidence" in Baptiste, she should "rely on him in any case of emergency," and she should "accept his advice if any difficulty occurred." But then, when she was safely among friends, she should rid herself of him. In the meantime she should keep silent, as candor would endanger both her and Morel. "I promised a perfect silence," she was to remember, "and said, that I would willingly postpone my departure; but as the hour had arrived for that departure, and the Carriage would be at the door directly, I was fearful that a sudden change of purpose, would excite suspicion, and do more harm than good; and I assured him I thought his advice excellent, and should adopt it thro the journey." He rose, full of apologies and confessions of honest purposes, and left.

Immediately the countess reappeared, "who had left a gay party at her house about a mile from the Town," renewed her invitation, and was again courteously refused. Mrs. Adams was determined to go on and, with the countess bidding a kind leave, the traveler and her son got into the berline and began the ride "under the most uneasy impressions." So far, traveling had been easy enough, mostly a

sleigh ride, a little theatergoing, and flattering courtesies from aristocrats and officials. Now, perhaps for the first time, she was sharply
conscious that this journey might be a test of character. She grew
more conscious of "the conviction that . . . the difficulties of my path
must be conquered, and it was as well to face them at once." She was
conscious, too, that this determination to press on might arise not
from a steely strength, but from a weakness, from "a proud and fool
hardy spirit." If so, she was being reckless, which a mother was not
supposed to be.

Things quickly went from bad to worse, because imagined dangers
gave way to real ones. They had gone four miles when the postilion
abruptly stopped the carriage, got off the lead horse, and came back
to tell her that "he had missed the road." By way of excuse, he said he
was a substitute for the usual postilion, who was experienced and
knew the way, but who was sick and absent that night. He, on the
other hand, "had never been [on] that road before, and . . . could not
tell where he was." The likelihood is that they were either northwest
or southwest of the post road that ran west from Mitau, for even an
ingénu postilion was unlikely to have taken the Riga road, and they
were on rough terrain, whereas the Riga road was flat. All they knew
for certain was that they were lost and it was very dark. The moon
was only in its first quarter and shed little light, and, as she remembered, there was "scarce a twinkling star to teach of living light."[18]
Unwisely, they went on, in the hope of hitting the right road. For
several hours they hit nothing but hills, swamps, holes, and valleys
"into which no Carriage had surely ever passed before." She became
very afraid, especially for the safety of her child, and in her fear she
prayed to her God, "the ever-protecting father of his Creatures."

One consolation proved to be that Baptiste and John Fulling were
watchful and took care to prevent the carriage's overturning, presumably by walking ahead and shouting back instructions. She followed Morel's counsel and "consulted Baptiste frequently and took
his advice as to the best mode of proceeding." This went on until

midnight. By then, the horses were exhausted and so were the people, though Charles Francis had remained asleep on the bed they had set up for him on the forward seat of the carriage. So they stopped, they consulted, and it was decided that Baptiste should unhitch a horse and search for help and the road. He mounted the horse and rode away, and they—Mrs. Adams, Charles Francis, Madame Babet, the servant, the postilion, and the remaining horses—were left alone in the deep dark, in a place where owls screeched, the wind moved through snow-laden larch and aspen trees, and wolves, bears, elk, and the "northern tiger" (lynx) walked at night.[19] Fifteen minutes passed, which must have seemed longer. Then she heard horses and not one voice, but several. She had been told a few hours earlier of footpads and murder, and there she was, in the middle of nowhere, her French soldier with his pistol gone away, she knew not where.

It turned out that Baptiste had come across a nearby house and woken up its sleeping family, and "a Russian officer came to him and, after inquiring what he wanted, offered his services to take us into the road, as it required great skill to keep the Carriage out of the gullies by which we were surrounded." In the middle of Baptiste's narrative, the officer appeared and, because Mrs. Adams spoke no Russian (though presumably Baptiste did) and the officer no French, she told her story in mangled German and gave him thanks for the offer of help. (*Danke*, fortunately, is uncomplicated.) "Lights were brought out" to pierce the dark, one of her servants mounted the officer's horse, and the Russian walked ahead over the terrain he knew, and they were guided in safety to an inn. There she "ordered refreshments for the gentleman, & coffee for ourselves," presented him with a handsome gift by way of thanks, for which he returned a courteous speech, as befitted an officer and a gentleman. He then instructed the innkeeper to take good care of her party and prepare horses for whatever departure Mrs. Adams might appoint, and went back into the night, with his horse, his present, and the comfort of a hard drink.

At this departure, she thanked her servants for their "prudence and discretion," advised that they would leave very early in the morning, retired to her room, prayed, and took stock. She decided she had been too easily alarmed, too mistrustful, and she "determined not to listen to any more bugbears to alarm my nerves and weaken my understanding." But this was not easy to do. She was prone to Gothic imaginings, had taken pleasure in them, and found it hard to make herself a cold rationalist. In Russia, she had been surrounded by people who believed in omens, people who thought it ill-luck if a hare crossed your path or the first person you met on the street was a priest, families who would not allow a saltcellar on their table lest the salt be spilled and occasion trouble, men who would never start a journey on a Monday. Mrs. Adams had a vivid memory of a New Year's Eve party in 1810, when they had all gone to the Colombis for the traditional celebration. They had gone at nine o'clock, played cards, danced, and took tea from great samovars until midnight, when they were invited into a different room. In its center was a table and, on it, they found cups and saucers, with the cups upside down. Everyone was asked to pick a cup, inside which was a strip of paper, which would tell a fortune. Louisa took hers and found "the simple word obstacles." Then they returned to the drawing room and everyone stood in the circle, men on one side, ladies on the other. "Small parcels of Oats were laid before every person, and then a Rooster and a Hen were turned out of a bag and suffered to run around." One stopped before Catherine Johnson and ate, then moved on to William Steuben Smith and did the same, at which the appointed speaker of oracles "declared that they would be man and Wife before the expiration of another year." (As they were.) Then there were two further forms of soothsaying, the first mysteriously consisting of "pouring boiling Wax in cold water, and making lead; from both of which long histories were told now forgotten; my fortune in all its forms were obstacles and disappointments." Second, cards were brought, everyone drew three, and a maidservant read them. Conde Colombi was told "that he would be buried in three Months." His wife was told that "she was to be immensely rich but shackled for life though a Widow."[20]

In the small hours, the Adamses went back to their apartment on the Moika Canal and laughed "at this ridiculous remnant of Superstition." But the Spanish count was not laughing, for "he took to his bed next day and in two Months the same party attended his funeral." His will decreed that his widow would inherit his great wealth and retain it only if she never remarried. She was then only twenty-eight and was to live for another sixty years. In the 1830s, Mrs. Adams had word of her "living in the utmost splendour; but her daughter the only object of her great ambition, rolling in riches, a perfect object of ugliness and deformity."[21]

Mrs. Adams was herself a lifelong reader of cards and a fortune-teller. In this, she was not singular. Many of the women in her life talked of dreams, ghosts, and nightmares, and peered anxiously into the future. In Berlin especially, she had known many such. There had been Mrs. Brown, the doctor's wife, who told "long stories of Welsh Superstitions," of strange events that she herself had experienced, tales deeply believed and "powerfully operating upon the imagination." There was the queen mother's maid of honor, Fräulein Bischoffwerder, who, after tea in the palace, once showed Louisa the great staircase down which came the "White Lady," who always appeared when a member of the royal family was about to die. If the wraith held a fan in her hand, it was a female who was doomed; if a glove, a male. Upon her own testimony, the *Fräulein* "was in familiar intercourse with Spirits," whom she "often saw," and who "conversed with her." There was Countess Pauline Néale, religious, mystical, rhapsodic, who related stories of Polish aristocratic families and their haunted fates. There was Lady Carysfort, in whose Irish mind "the spirit of superstition had taken the deepest and firmest hold," who told "many perfectly attested stories, of supernatural influences, which *she* or her *family* had actually witnessed; and of which she had not the smallest doubt."[22]

Mrs. Adams knew enough to know that such stories were the fashion, for she lived in the age of Horace Walpole's *The Castle of Otranto* and would live on into that of *Frankenstein*, and she lived in a Germany that was both a focus and a sponsor of such imaginings. She relished such tales as literature and, when her storytellers were literary and mannered, she was relaxed about the possibility of a dark realm where spirits walked. Fräulein Bischoffwerder, for example, when telling her supernatural stories gave the "appearance of worldly craft in her arrangement of the incidents, and in her manner of reciting; which blighted the interest by its artificial colouring." This was good, "but it [was] not life!!!" Louisa Adams, rather, was affected by stories told by those without literary skill, told with sincerity and faith, for these could produce "electric surprize, and suppressed fear," and produce "the wistful look and the half shuddering gaze; and the oft repeated glance at the door with sudden and abrupt pauses." Sometimes she would be skeptical and venture to lighten the mood. At this, Pauline Néale "would instantly turn pale; shudder, look round the room and say she had seen *too much* to doubt the reality of her assertions; and then drop the conversation." So, against her will, Mrs. Adams grew to believe in much of this. She would return home from hearing such stories "in a fever of excitement that . . . almost made my hair stand on end." She became conscious that, by these experiences, her mind had become permanently "tainted, and infected by a weakness, of which I have tried to be ashamed; but which still clings to me as if it was a part of my nature."[23]

The belief was nurtured by her religious instincts, for if she could believe in God, angels, and the devil, why should she not believe in wraiths, demons, and unseen forces? For her, religious faith and "these mysteries of Nature" were one and the same, both at odds with "the cold and artificial presumption of what we term reason, not always proved to be genuine wisdom." She came to think that "the subtleties of reason are often on a par with the refined subtleties of common superstition," that both involved a leap of faith. Still, there was faith, and there were the effects of faith. She might believe in moving spirits, but she was conscious that "the dread of things unknown . . . palsies the mind with fear," and leaves even "the wisest to a fearful imagination uncontrouled," for then "everything convinces us and [our] mind that there are things in this World, and the next, 'Men never yet hath dreamed of.'"[24]

So she traveled through an eastern European forest with a sense and a fear that she was moving through the landscape of a Grimm fairy tale. But at the same time, as she lay in her bed in the inn and tried to sort out her feelings and thoughts, she was conscious that this might be an unwise perspective, that she should try not to turn the ordinary into the extraordinary, that "the realities of life; of themselves dull straight forward and simple" could be "made of painful importance by extraneous circumstances," such as listening too much to "fanfaronade stories" of murder in the night. Against what she felt to be her nature, she resolved to be practical and commonsensical, as they moved the next day westward toward the Baltic.[25]

Twenty years later, when she tried to remember what came next, she got herself into a muddle about rivers, frontiers, and countries. In her memory, they left the inn at morning and traveled until four in the afternoon, when they reached the Vistula River, crossed it with great difficulty, cut across a small corner of Poland before reaching the Prussian frontier, suddenly encountered the sea, and pressed on to Königsberg. This was not possible. The Vistula lies to the west of Königsberg, not to the east, and in February 1815 the Duchy of Warsaw (what was then left of Poland) nowhere touched her route until she was beyond Königsberg.

What may have happened is elucidated by the letter to her husband she had started in Riga on Friday, February 17, and completed after reaching Memel on Monday, February 20. In that, she wrote of "passing through the greatest difficulties and even dangers." She said that ten versts beyond Mitau "the Snow was so deep as to render the roads almost impassible in addition to which the ground was not frozen and under Water almost all the way." She spoke of Charles Francis being overcome by "the sight of the sea," and said that "the rivers [were] almost all broken up," and these were "passed at the risk of our lives." From these hints, one can surmise the following.[26]

She left the inn, perhaps of Doblen, very early on the morning of Sunday, February 19, and encountered thawing snow. Slowly her carriage sloshed its way onward for about eight hours, deep in the forest, along a way that was scarcely populated and had little traffic, except for "waggoners and old fashioned berlins in which the Courland noblemen visit one another." At four o'clock in the afternoon, she reached Shrunden and the Windau (not the Vistula) River. When conditions were stable, this rapid current was crossed on "a flat bridge like a raft, formed of logs of wood." But she was caught between seasons; the ice was just beginning to break up, and the bridge had been removed. So she had to pause on the bank and look about for help. She was told that, unless she crossed at this spot, she would have to make "a very long and tedious detour," but that crossing here would be risky, even dangerous. The men who approached her said that they could "take long poles with hooks and attach the horses to the extreme end of the pole of the carriage and get over as well as they could." This was not an easy decision and took an hour to think through, before she decided on the risk and they pushed off from the eastern bank. She was getting into the habit of risk, although she must have wondered whether such men, with such poles, could hold the horses, the carriage, and its passengers if the fragile ice caused the horses to slip and the carriage to overturn. But the poles were attached to the horses, which pulled the carriage, and the men walked onto the ice, tapped to test its depth, and guided the horses and carriage along the firmest route. It nearly went wrong, because "the ice had given way on the border, and it required a violent effort in the horses to prevent the coach from upsetting on the bank."[27]

Thereafter she traveled on through the night toward the southwest, to Drogen and Tadliken. On this stretch of road from Mitau to the Baltic, the post stations offered no beds and grim food—black and sour bread (made from a mix of rye and barley), rancid butter, insipid soup, and what a Frenchman could only describe as bad meat and execrable beer *("mauvaise viande et bière détestable")*. At Tadliken, she turned to the left and headed south to Ober Bartau, where she encountered another river, one of many "pretty, clear streams, with high banks" in this area. Beyond Rutzau ("a bad little inn on the skirts of the great forest") and within the last few miles of Kurland, she stopped to rest and eat, though not to change horses. She spoke of doing this in a "small corner of Poland . . . where I saw the most

filthy and beggarly village that I ever had beheld in any country."
Legally, she was not in Poland. But informally she was right, for there
was "a mere slip of land, not broader than ten English miles," once
part of the old Polish-Lithuanian commonwealth that had reached to
the Baltic north of Memel and which, in the third Polish partition of
1795, had been annexed by Russia. It was common enough still to
speak of this small area as Polish. If she was within that slip of land
and somewhere without a post station, she was probably in Buden-
diekshof. By then, it was the morning of Monday, February 20.[28]

About nine miles further on, she reached the Russian-Prussian
border at Polangen, mostly a Jewish village with a discontented Roman Catholic minority, who signaled their feelings by erecting
"rows of crosses, about fifteen feet high" by the roadside, in protest
against those who had killed Christ. Sarah Spencer had rendered the
usual travelers' verdict when she described Polangen as "full of Jews
in long gowns and villainous faces; women with great turbans and
long veils." There Mrs. Adams stopped at the last Russian posthouse,
in front of which stood a "high and square pillar," on whose sides was
written in both German and Russian the information that she had
passed thirty-two post stations since Saint Petersburg and a distance
of 836 versts (552 miles) and, in the shorter run, had survived a journey since Saturday of 230 versts (152 miles) since Mitau.[29]

At this station she found the people to be "impudent," which may
have meant she was harassed by the Jewish peddlers who habitually
sold amber to travelers. This area was the historic source for amber,
which was picked up along the shoreline and found amid the sand
dunes, and hundreds of tons annually were converted into jewelry
and often exported to the Near East, where it was favored for the
heads of pipes and hookahs. Mrs. Adams bought no amber then, perhaps because the importuning was too urgent, but later, down the
coast at Königsberg, she would.[30]

At Polangen, she was forced to wait three hours for horses. Annoyed, she took this last opportunity to flourish her letter from Osip
Petrovich Kozodavlev, the Russian minister of the interior, and utter
threats of retribution from Saint Petersburg. This worked. The mas-

ter of the house grew alarmed, apologized, immediately found the horses he had been unable to find without menaces, and pressed upon her some extra horses, "as he thought the Carriage very heavy."[31] This last gesture, she well knew, was very little a courtesy. All along her way, she came to know that if you took more horses than you needed, you got them more quickly.

It was a short distance from the village to the border, which was passed in stages, framed by the Baltic shore to the west and a deep pine forest to the east. There was a Russian border post and, following, a sandy no-man's-land of about a mile, in the middle of which was placed "two old weather-beaten posts of demarkation, surmounted with the eagles of Prussia and Russia, badly painted." There was then the Prussian border post.[32]

The Russian side had a police office, a customhouse, and a guardhouse for the sentries. In the first of these, her passport authorizing her exit from the Russian Empire was shown and stamped. In the second, in whose yard were "several spacious magazines, serving as dépôts for merchandise introduced in Russia," her luggage was offloaded from the carriage and, in the house, carefully examined by officials, commissioned to be suspicious and prone to punishing presumption. It is possible that the pomp of her official letters made this process less thorough and intimidating than was usual, and she was spared the experience of a lady in the 1820s whose "cases of needles and thread were examined." But probably not, for it was normal procedure for the officials to unpack every bag and box, to remove everything from them, to single out items liable for duty, and then to present the bill. There was "an enormous pair of scales suspended from the ceiling," for things whose weight mattered to the calculation. In theory, one was not permitted to leave the country in possession of any Russian coins.[33]

With its luggage restored, the carriage then proceeded to the barrier, a red-and-white painted bar across the road held by a chain, attended by soldiers who emerged from a circular sentry box. It was usual for travelers to think these were Cossacks, though they may not have been, and Mrs. Adams would have known the difference, for she had spent years amid the complex epaulets of Russian soldiery. She made her way to the Prussian border post, where there was another bar to be raised, this one painted black and white, and where there were more officials, more stamps, and more scrutiny, for if there was a realm that equaled the Russian in authoritarian paranoia, it was Prussia. So she was subjected to "all the customary questions too tedious to enumerate." Who are you? Where do you come from? Where are you going? How long will you stay? Where will you stay?[34]

Safely inside Prussia, she went south along a road that passed very, very close to the sea, so much so that Charles Francis became suddenly alarmed that they were driving straight into the waves and nervously asked his mother if they were "going into that great water." This response was not idiosyncratic, for another traveler a few years later was to write of "a wilderness of sand and water, where it seemed, by the wheel tracts, that each carriage was in the habit of choosing its

Memel Lighthouse (1838)
(From Kęstutis Demereckas, ed., *Klaipėdos Uostas: Port of Klaipėda*
[Klaipėda: Libra Memelensis, 2007])

own way." So they proceeded to Memel, visible from a distance because of its double-spired church, citadel, windmills, and the lighthouse that, north of the city, guarded the entrance to the harbor and the inland waterway that swept away into the distance. The town was known for its "usually chill and stiff breezes," but also for its export of timber—the logs were floated downriver from the deeply forested interior on rafts. In Memel, the timber was fashioned in numerous sawmills into the great masts that powered the Royal Navy and much of the world's merchant marine, or, more humbly, into what were known as "Memel logs," made of a famously hard spruce.[35]

She entered via a modern bridge over the river Dange into a small city reminiscent of those in the Netherlands, a pretty merchants' town with a tidy grid of sandy streets and a central square surrounded by gabled brick houses and furnished with a theater built in 1775. On an island to the west was a low castle. There is no evidence of where she stopped for the night, but she did. There was a Memel stamp on her Prussian passport, the first of many, for any traveler was obliged to submit to official inspection upon entering any Prussian town of consequence. And she completed a letter to her husband on arrival, which expressed her determination to stay and proceed the next day. She was probably in the Hotel de Russie, which was the most highly regarded lodging, for it was her habit to go to the best places. More certain is that she acquired more cash for the next stage of her journey by drawing a bill upon her husband's Amsterdam bankers, Willink & Van Staphorst, for 1,218 florins and 19 cents, the equivalent of $487.57. When she left, she seems to have had in her possession 823 Prussian thalers and 22 groschen.[36] Beyond that, nothing is known of her time in Memel, because it is a curiosity of her memoirs that the town vanished from the narrative. This suggests that, when there, she forgot or was not reminded that Memel had a special resonance. For if she had walked to a small mansion on the north bank of the Dange River, halfway between the bridge and the harbor, she would have released a flood of memories, and this would have lodged Memel firmly in her mind.

The memories concerned Queen Luise of Prussia, who had come

twice as a refugee to that Memel mansion in 1807, and who was a woman Mrs. Adams had once come to admire and love. The war begun in 1806 had seen humiliating defeats for Prussia at Jena and Auerstedt, the French occupation of Berlin, and Napoleon's triumphal entry through the Brandenburg Gate. The Prussian royal family had been driven farther and farther into the eastern part of what was left of their realm, their dignity demeaned as they traveled. At Ortelsburg, they were forced into "one of the wretched barns they call houses," and could find no clean water or food.[37] In Königsberg, where in 1701 Frederick William III's ancestor had first declared that a Hohenzollern was a king, they set up court, until more military reverses forced them on toward Memel. Ill with typhus, the queen had been put into a traveling chaise, "placed on a bed . . . supported with pillows, covered with plumaux, and wrapped around with shawls," and compelled for three days, in a biting snowstorm, to inch her way along the great sandbank that brought her to the ferry over to Memel. Her first night on the road had been spent "in a miserable room with a broken window" and the melting snow had dripped onto her bed. At a post station, she had asked to share a warm room, but those already there refused to move, and elsewhere, it was reported, "a drunken peasant [had] bellowed out, 'O! you deserve this, and much more; for, if old Frederick had been alive, all this would not have happened.'" This was a truth she did not need to learn, for she was the one who had delivered the biting verdict after Jena: "We have fallen asleep upon the laurels of Frederick the Great."[38]

In Memel, Luise and her husband accepted the hospitality of a local merchant called Kauffman Consentius, in whose house they established a modest court, where they held receptions or levees three times a week, waited for the military tide fitfully to turn, and issued edicts that might never be obeyed. For some, exile turned into respite. The queen had time to read: Schiller on the history of the Netherlands, Gibbon on Rome's decline, and Shakespeare. For her close relative Princess Luise Radziwill, the world seemed to recede as spring came and "with fine weather Memel became a pleasant and peaceful refuge; the war and its discontents seemed thrown into a more distant background and the little town, with its pretty houses lining the seashore, reminded us of a season at the baths."[39]

Queen Luise had helped to form the young Louisa Adams's sense of what a consort might be. It had started when the latter had gone to the Prussian court in 1797 to be presented as the wife of the new American minister. She had been dressed in the fashionable clothes her father had given her: a white satin skirt trimmed with blonde lace, white satin shoes, kid gloves, a fan, and ostrich feathers in her hair, but otherwise no ornaments. She had thrown over this a pale blue satin robe, newly bought. During the formalities, the queen had soothed the debutante's wretched nerves, respected her limited means, and smiled. Long years later, Mrs. Adams was to—the word is not too strong—treasure, with grateful affection, the memory of this angel, this "Queen of Queens," who had grace, affability, sweetness, "and the most irresistable beauty." "Years have elapsed and I still see her in my minds eye moving in all the majesty of youthful royalty and followed by the admiring gaze of thousands who thought themselves blessed if they could catch a passing smile or have a glance of her beautiful form."[40]

As it happened, Mrs. Adams was among the first devotees of what would become a German cult. She had been in Berlin in late 1797 when Frederick William II died, his son became king, and the princess royal, Luise of Mecklenberg-Strelitz, ascended the queen's throne. So the American minister's wife came to have a third-row seat at the most dazzling debut for a queen in Prussian history, perhaps in any European history since Eleanor of Aquitaine. For Luise was not merely beautiful; she was erotic. This was a quality the artists had noticed, even before her accession. Johann Gottfried Schadow had sculpted a double portrait of Princess Luise and her sister Frederica, in which the former's body seemed to breathe through "a virtually transparent summer dress." Later this marble had to be shut away from public view, to avoid scandal. But the censorship was pointless, because there came to be so many other enticing images—paintings, engravings, porcelain, plaster busts sold along Unter den Linden. Luise was the more erotic for being unavailable, a family

Karl Wilhelm Wach, *Queen Luise as Hebe in Front of the Brandenburg Gate* (1812)
(Courtesy of the Stiftung Stadtmuseum, Berlin)

woman devoted to her awkwardly silent husband, yet a woman who loved to dress up, who defined fashion in her time and place, who liked an extravagant quadrille, and who loved being on display.[41]

Add to this that Luise was a powerful and often shrewd political adviser, and a precedent that Mrs. Adams was to follow through her life becomes discernible. If you rose too far above Queen Luise, as the Romanovs often did by being too splendid, too cold, and too remote, Mrs. Adams was dubious. If you fell too far below, by being vulgar, ugly, and graceless, Mrs. Adams was offended. But if you could hold together a family life, wear a tasteful dress that did not have to be prim, drop a useful hint into a politician's ear, and persuade a silent husband to fascinate a room, which your own charms had filled, Mrs. Adams thought the precedent set by Queen Luise was being honored. As it turned out, a family proved a hard thing to keep together, and learning the ropes in Berlin and pulling them later in Washington was liable to create cultural misunderstanding. Dolley Madison, the Quaker, would speak in 1820 of "Mrs. Adams . . . [keeping] up the fashion of dissipation." Even in 1807, the wife of the senator from Massachusetts knew of gossip about her "*supposed* aristocratic tastes," but she resolved never to change, because, if it was good enough for Luise of Prussia, it was good enough for her.[42] Whether it was good enough for Abigail Adams was another matter, for the other Mrs. Adams leaned toward plain living and high thinking, not elegant living and high feeling.

Moving on from Memel toward Königsberg, Mrs. Adams faced a choice. In summer, there were three ways to go. One could follow, in reverse, the route taken by Queen Luise in 1807. This involved loading one's carriage onto a ferry across the waterway known as the Kurisches Haff (or Curonian Lagoon), and then traveling for fifty miles down the Curonian Spit, a narrow sandbank swept by wind and inhabited by wolves and elk. There one's wheels often rested half in water and half on sand, dunes could move to block the road, postilions found the way by following the tracks of earlier carriages and

hoping the tide would not sweep the marks away, and the post stations were notorious for their high prices and bare facilities. Alterna-
tively, one could put one's carriage on a boat that sailed down the
lagoon. But in winter, the second option was impractical, and the first
was usually anticipated and remembered with a shudder. A few years
earlier, Kotzebue bleakly wrote that on the Curonian Spit, "nothing
meets the sickened eye but sea, sky, sand-heaps, stones, the remnants
of wrecks, and walls; with, every three or four miles, hovels erected
of boards, without door or window." The third choice was safer but
longer, a journey of about 120 miles, and required her to head southeast, on a road bordered by aged willows, through a flat and culti-

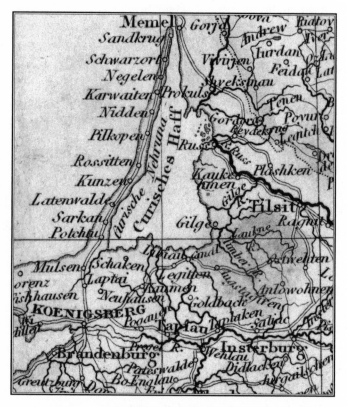

Memel to Brandenburg

(From Aaron Arrowsmith, *Map Exhibiting the Great Post Roads, Physical and
Political Divisions of Europe* [London: A. Arrowsmith, 1810])

vated countryside to Tilsit, where she would cross the river Niemen and then proceed westward, via Tapiau, to Königsberg. This third route was probably how she went, though it was hard traveling, all through the day and night of Tuesday, February 21, and into the next day. It was cold, it was "dreadfully gloomy," and her postilions were averse to her haste. They wanted to stop for the night and needed persuasion to go on. Everyone seemed affected by the blankness, the dreariness, and the cold. Her darkening thoughts turned superstitiously to what caused terror in "the ignorant, the learned, the romantic, the indifferent alike," and she reflected on "mystic shadows 'thwart our way."[43]

Tilsit was where, in June 1807, on a theatrical raft moored in the middle of the Niemen, Napoleon and Alexander I had met to negotiate a peace, and where Queen Luise had come futilely to plead with the French emperor for the cause of her humiliated husband. By 1815, the raft was gone, as were the "two superbly decorated pavilions of white canvas."[44] What Mrs. Adams began to see around her, instead, for the first time in her journey and her life, was what a generation of wars had wrought. All her life, she had been affected by war: the American Revolutionary War, which moved her as a child to France; the quasi-war between England and the United States, which killed her husband's career as a Massachusetts senator; and the Anglo-American war of 1812, which had taken him away from her to Ghent and, in time, forced her onto this cold and dreary road. But she had never seen the physical damage of war. Even when in Russia during the brutal events of Napoleon's invasion, she had been away from the killing. Napoleon had marched from Vilnius to Moscow and back again, but Saint Petersburg lay to the northwest of his march, and the city had never been attacked. Her discomforts had been minor: a less lively social life because many of the diplomats had left and the tsar was at the front, a few scarcities of food, and much trepidation, but little more. She had lived in a whirl of rumor, disappointment, worry, and triumph, for she was a partisan, if not of Russia, then at least of Alexander. But there were no corpses in her street, and she never had to bundle her child and possessions onto a cart to flee arson. And, on her journey so far, she had cut across the Baltic provinces through areas for the most part lightly touched by the campaigns.

At Tilsit and beyond, however, she entered the regions that, and began to encounter the people who, had been devastated by Napoleon's ambition, Alexander's vanity, and Frederick William's fumbling. It was an unsettling experience for her, but "deeply interesting." She saw "houses half burnt, a very thin population; women unprotected; and that dreary look of forlorn desertion, which sheds its gloom around all the objects, announcing devastation and despair." These were things that "forced themselves upon our attention." But at that moment, it did not occur to her that this was more than history and its remnants, a problem for the other people, the haggard faces on the road glimpsed through the carriage window. After all, Napoleon was safely on Elba, the diplomats and monarchs were then in Vienna nearly completing the postwar settlement, and "it was a time of peace," as she had firmly explained to a Russian countess a few days before leaving Saint Petersburg. Being now in Prussia, she felt increasingly safe, "as I was in a Country where I was very well known, as I had lived four years in Berlin, and was acquainted with the King, and all the Royal Family."[45]

In the "surprisingly mountainous" Königsberg, she stayed only a day, probably in Deutsches Haus, the best hotel in Prussia's second city, located in a "quiet and retired part of the town, and in a house which, from its appearance, must have been the residence of some grandee of old." She went to see her bankers to exchange a letter of credit for coins, she purchased some amber, and she thought about going to the city's small theater, before deciding she could not go without a gentleman to escort her. The city was, by far, the largest and most cosmopolitan of any on her route so far, with more than sixty thousand people, many from the usual groups (German Lutherans, Jews, Poles), many not (Dutch Mennonites, Huguenots). Its streets were old, narrow, ill paved, and winding; its bridges were many; and, from a distance, there were so many spires visible that an Englishwoman could be reminded of Oxford. Over the city brooded two great buildings: a castle, for Königsberg was a garrison town with many thousands of Prussian soldiers, and a clumsy redbrick cathedral, in which the body of Immanuel Kant had been deposited eleven years earlier. Louisa Adams would have found the former reassuring, the latter a matter of indifference, for she cared little for the "preposterously metaphysical." But Königsberg was not then very interested in celebrating the categorical imperative, for after Kant's death his old house was to be converted not into a shrine, but into a tavern where one could play billiards.[46]

She had hoped to set out early on the morning of Thursday, February 23, but it rained so hard that she had to wait until three o'clock in the afternoon. Again, she faced a choice of routes. She could go along the Baltic coast via Brandenburg, Braunsberg, Elbing, and Marienburg to Danzig, continue westward to Stolpe and Neugarten, and then turn south through Stargard and a different Königsberg to reach

Braunsberg to Graudenz

(From Aaron Arrowsmith, *Map Exhibiting the Great Post Roads, Physical and Political Divisions of Europe* [London: A. Arrowsmith, 1810])

Berlin. This had been John Quincy Adams's route when traveling eastward with Francis Dana in 1782. Or she could follow the same road as far as Marienburg, but turn left and go inland and southwest through Marienwerder, Graudenz, and Culm, eventually to turn west and cross the Vistula at Fordon, and then go through Schönlanke, Kustrin, and finally Berlin. She chose the latter.[47]

This part of the journey started with an awkward debate, for Baptiste was causing trouble. He had begun "to assume a tone not by any means agreeable" and she had grown uneasy, as had her other servant, John Fulling, who was frightened of the Frenchman. So Mrs. Adams tried to ease Baptiste out of the party. She explained that, being now in Prussia, she felt safer and needed him less for protection, and that he might leave her "as soon as he pleased." He drew back at this and reminded her that they had an agreement—he would serve her and she would take him home to France. Yes, she replied, but this agreement was contingent on good behavior. If he was "diligent and attentive," all would be well. They agreed to continue. Thereby she was taking a risk, but she knew that Baptiste understood the advantages of using a rich lady in a large carriage, someone who fed him and asked for services that came easily enough to a rough soldier. He was, after all, lucky not to have been one of those French prisoners whom Robert Johnston had once seen stumbling through Königsberg, wretched men wrapped in torn blankets who were missing hats and shoes, but also fingers and toes that frostbite had removed. So it was wise of Baptiste to improve his behavior, however erratically. He kept his "threatening look," which she endured but had to ignore, as they continued on.[48]

Seven miles west of Königsberg, in the vicinity of Ludwigsort but more than a mile from any habitation, the carriage suddenly lurched sideways and ground to a halt, because a front wheel had disintegrated. Since nightfall was coming on, the postilions suggested that one of them walk back to a house they had passed to fetch a means of transport, necessary because the mud was too thick for the ladies to walk. He was gone for some time, but eventually came back, driving "a miserable common Cart," into which unhappily went those (Mrs. Adams, Charles Francis, Madame Babet) who considered themselves above what was common and Baptiste, who had no such illusions. Fulling stayed behind to guard the marooned carriage. They made their way to "a hovel consisting of two rooms and a blacksmith's shop." Out of this came a woman, "dirty, ugly, and ill natured," and then some men, "very surly ill looking," with little interest in courtesy, but some in profit. Baptiste explained the problem and asked if the party could be conveyed back to Königsberg. No, came the reply.

They were asked again, and again the answer was no. But since this was a blacksmith's shop and they could make another wheel, they offered to let the party stay, so that the journey could restart in the morning. At this, there was a debate. Mrs. Adams feared staying in such a place, but Baptiste and the postilions were not keen on searching for another carriage and struggling back to the city, which might not be reached until past midnight. So it was decided to stay. From the Russian carriage, Charles Francis's bed was fetched and a postilion or Baptiste was left there as an extra guard, while another well-armed guard was put outside the bedroom in the hovel. Inside the room the child slept, while the two women stayed up a long, sleepless, hungry, and anxious night. In the morning, a clumsy and unpainted wheel was attached to the carriage, they ate some of their provisions, and they went on to the next post station at Brandenburg, where "on an eminence looking down on the river" they drank coffee.[49]

The incident is instructive. Mrs. Adams was used to encountering her social inferiors as servants and found it disconcerting to meet the undeferential. She never had learned the trick of familiarity, for she was (as she often admitted) proud, a quality that began early in life. Once, in London, the school dentist had tried to remove two of her teeth, she had refused, and the dentist had summoned a servant to hold her down. At this, Miss Johnson had submitted to the lesser violation of the dentist's yanking, for to be touched by a servant would be a pollution. "Do you think I will be held by a servant?" she had exclaimed, with a haughty vehemence that much struck her headmistress, who "always used to say she was sure I was intended to be a very great personage." Later, when traveling from Hamburg to Berlin, a liveried footman had been required to sit with her in the carriage, and she "felt as if the greatest insult had been offered to me," and understood this response as English rather than American, for "the American can never understand the sensation of mortified pride which I endured but an Englishman would blaze at the idea."[50]

By 1797, she had never lived in a republic, but only in the England of George III and the France of Louis XVI. She presumed that servants were deferential inferiors, who ought to feel gratitude and even love for the condescension of their betters. When leaving London in 1797, she had dismissed a female servant and been shocked at the woman's ingratitude, for she "showered down every horrible imprecation upon my devoted head until I was seated in the Post Chaise in which we drove away." When a servant acted in ways that violated class norms, Mrs. Adams could be angry, sorrowful, or amused, but seldom sympathetic. It was amusing when, in Berlin, her housemaid decked herself out in a pale blue satin cloak, trimmed with fur, and an elaborate bonnet in order to step out to church and the park on a Sunday. It was a matter for sorrow when, in Washington, one of her servants and her husband—"good but ignorant people"—were "seized with the mania of education" and tried to make a scholar of their daughter, but after five years of trying had made little progress with her literacy. This failure was a matter of little surprise for Mrs. Adams, who presumed that birth was fate, and felt only pity for the child's "ridiculous" command of geography.[51]

She was accustomed to a retinue. Her father in London had eleven servants and, as a young girl, she had been often asked to superintend household matters when her mother was unwell, as she often was. In Berlin, eventually, the Adamses had six domestics: a footman, a housemaid, a coachman, a cook, a valet, and a maid. The last two were Whitcomb and Epps, both of whom had come from the Johnson house in London and would stay with her until in Boston they married each other and set up as tradespeople. In Saint Petersburg, there were fifteen servants, and much later, in Washington, when she was the wife of an ex-president, she had even more: a steward, a butler, a porter, a housekeeper, upper and lower house maids, a laundry maid, a cook, a scullion, a coachman, an ostler, and boys to carry coal and serve at table. Only in the senatorial years, when money was thought to be scarce and she was forced to live simply in Quincy, did her household briefly disappear. Then she milked cows herself and cooked pies without help, before "a boy and two females" were procured. She did not appreciate the moral education implicit in this unassisted interlude and never developed a sense that work was enriching. In her lexicon *work* meant no more than her sewing. For the rest, it seemed to her an axiom that "toil and poverty must ever be intimately blended; for man by his nature is seldom inclined to work—it is thus wisely ordained that among that class destined thus to labor, the perceptions of the mind are generally less acute; the comprehension less vivid, the nervous system less subtle; and their bodies usually more sturdy and capable of supporting greater fatigue and exposure."[52]

On the road from Brandenburg, she traveled along the shore of the Frische Haff, the freshwater lagoon that stretched from Königsberg to Elbing. At Frauenberg, she passed through a village, dominated to her left by "an almost perpendicular hill," on the top of which lay a complex of medieval redbrick buildings, tightly encircled by great walls. Within these was the town's turreted fourteenth-century Gothic cathedral, in which lay the tomb of Nicolaus Copernicus, who had built there an observatory to study the stars and who had revolutionized cosmogony. From Frauenberg she proceeded past the hill and the "wretched village of Truntz" to Elbing, where she encountered a "pretty" and "very neat town, not unlike a swallow's nest, which is within very comfortable, and without nothing but sticks and mud." Past Elbing, the road passed to the south of the Nogat River, kept in place by large embankments, and she was now on a soft clay, which easily became rutted and tended to make a carriage sway. Next was Marienburg, a place that, more forcibly than anywhere else on her journey, conveyed a sense of the brooding militancy and power of the Teutonic Knights, the medieval conquerors of eastern Europe, though also of their disappearance. For the city was dwarfed by an immense fortress, where once had lived the grand master of the order, the grand commander, the grand marshal, the grand hospitaler, the grand keeper of the wardrobe, and the grand treasurer, all ensconced with their thousands of troops within a clanking and praying world of chapels, refectories, towers, and armories. By 1815, the order had long since gone from the castle. Over the centuries, much had been destroyed by siege, negligence, and plunder. Frederick the Great had carted away tons of building material for the innumerable barracks that underpinned his aggressively expanding domain. Only recently the French, who had used the fortress as a hospital, had pulled down the Holy Spirit Hospital, the Sand Gate, and many fifteenth-century walls on the southern and eastern side, a destruction readily visible to a traveler appearing from the northeast, advancing past the fortress toward the southwest, and keeping to the eastern bank of the Vistula River. But more than enough remained of the castle's "sombre towers" to bring "to mind tales of chivalry and blood," for those who cared to look past the town's "beauties, now obscured by dirt" to its past terrors.[53]

Keeping some miles from the Vistula to her west, Mrs. Adams now passed through a series of small towns, often with minor fortresses, palaces, and cathedrals in ill repair: Marienwerder, Graudenz, Ostrometz. More distinctive was Culm, though not for being founded by the Teutonic Knights in the thirteenth century, nor for being situated on a high hill surrounded by great redbrick walls, nor for having a rich collection of churches, nunneries, and guilds. What marked Culm out was that it had been planned from the first, even in the Middle Ages, as a city of geometrical regularity, with wide streets at right angles to one another and an immense city square, a medieval city into which it had seemed natural to introduce the Palladian regularities of seventeenth- and eighteenth-century architecture.[54]

Graudenz to Schönlanke

(From Aaron Arrowsmith, *Map Exhibiting the Great Post Roads, Physical and Political Divisions of Europe* [London: A. Arrowsmith, 1810])

After passing Graudenz, once notable for the "finest" of gallows set on a hill planted with "noble oaks," she left Prussia and entered the Duchy of Warsaw. She would remain within its domain until after she had crossed the Vistula River at Fordon, passed through Bromberg and Schönlanke, and skirted Filehne. It is doubtful that she much noticed the duchy, which was a scrap of territory organized by Napoleon in 1807 after the Treaty of Tilsit out of Polish lands formerly controlled by Prussia. Its duke had been Frederick Augustus, the king of Saxony, but its real rulers had been Napoleon and his ambassador in Warsaw, both of whom had treated the place as an economic resource, a recruiting post, and a springboard for war. By early 1815, however, the duchy was a puppet state without a puppet master, for the failure of Napoleon's invasion of Russia in 1812 had brought Russian troops onto the duchy's soil, and Prussia's role in the events that led to the defeat of Napoleon at Leipzig in 1813 had brought Prussian troops, too. Insofar as there was a government in early 1815, it was a provisional council, organized by the tsar for the administration of martial law. On her route, Mrs. Adams passed through not Russian- but Prussian-occupied territory, which would have felt little distinguishable from the East Prussia she had left and the Silesia she was to enter, for there were no frontier ceremonies to mark a traveler's passage.[55]

In all three regions were many medieval fortresses, many Jewish villages, and many sandy roads. Here it was common to find the post stations inefficient and to waste hours waiting for horses to be procured. "Bad post-houses, uncivil post-masters, sulky drivers, jaded horses and most abominable roads, are the agreeable attendants of Prussian posting" was doubtless too harsh a judgment, but hostility toward Prussian postilions in their dark blue livery with orange trimmings was general. "Travelers always inveigh against the rudeness of the Prussian postilions," it was familiarly observed. These were men not above making unscheduled stops at inns for a meal, a beer, or a schnapps, "while the passenger is left to look out at the carriage window" in enforced idleness. As Karamzin noticed, that the postilions often made these stops was evidenced by the fact that the king of

Prussia had forbidden the practice. Regulation, which in Prussia was meticulous, was often but a gesture against what was customary. Knowing this, some thought it wiser to furnish the schnapps in the first place, by way of bribing progress. Others thought the bribe futile. The traveler Robert Johnston, at least, believed such men were beyond intimidation or reform: "A Prussian is never grateful; the more he receives, the more avaricious he becomes. If he is offered a dram, he takes it most greedily, but never expresses the least sign of thanks . . . I would sooner deal with one hundred Russian postilions, than with one Prussian." Others agreed. "Protected by his royal livery, the Prussian postilion saunters on at the rate of one German mile an hour, and no bribes, intreaties, or threats, can induce him to exceed the regulation." He but smiled vaguely, smoked his meerschaum incessantly, and proceeded indifferently. In this, he differed from a French postilion, or so William Rae Wilson thought, for he was to remark upon "that silence and gravity so peculiar to German postilions, and forming so marked a contrast to those of France, who are all life and animation, and keep you constantly in good-humour by their loquacity and wit." With this, Wilhelm Render had agreed: "The French postilion is either singing, laughing, whistling, or swearing," while the German "drives his horses with a sort of clownish tranquillity."[56]

Past the blacksmith's hovel west of Königsberg, there had been little incident on Mrs. Adams's way toward Kustrin, except encountering a carriage "labouring through the mud" from the direction of Berlin. The carriages had come close to each other and, as they did so, "the servant stopped our drivers to ask concerning the desperate state of the road." By way of explanation, from within the carriage came the voice of a gentleman, a "Count somebody" who "enquired very politely of me, how many times I had been upset?" His own carriage had tumbled over on seven occasions so far. (Overturning was, in fact, not uncommon, and Mrs. Adams was unusual in never experiencing it.) Considering that he was journeying all the way to Saint Petersburg, he was anxious to know how many more times he might need to scramble out into the mud. He was very doleful, for he doubt-

Schönlanke to Berlin

(From Aaron Arrowsmith, *Map Exhibiting the Great Post Roads, Physical and
Political Divisions of Europe* [London: A. Arrowsmith, 1810])

less thought himself advancing from the better toward the worse,
and what he had left was bad enough. On the other hand, she was
experiencing the reverse and had not yet been overset. So she had
laughed, said she "hoped to escape the pleasure altogether," wished
him well, and gone on her way toward Berlin and the light.[57]

Kustrin, however, was seldom associated with light. As Thomas
Carlyle was later to observe, the city sat "among the Bogs of the
Oder" and looked over brown sedges and curlews. The city's long-
established purpose was to defend the eastern approaches to Berlin
by its impregnable fortress. In truth, the citadel was seldom impregnable, and in fact was known for surrendering without a fight, especially in 1807, when Napoleon's armies had come to call. The British,
at least, who preferred continental Europeans to struggle with subsi-
dized might against the French, noticed this trait and complained
that Kustrin (along with Madgeburg, Stettin, Spandau, and Hame-
lin), though "abundantly furnished with garrisons, artillery, ammunition and provisions, instead of making a valiant defence, instead of
gloriously perishing under their ruins, [capitulated] before a shot was
fired, or even the trenches were opened."[58]

The city and the fortress were still better known for being the
prison within which had been incarcerated in 1730 the young Frederick, not yet great. He had been placed there by his father, Frederick
William I, for the crime of trying to elope to England with Hans

Hermann von Katte. Then only eighteen, Frederick had been compelled to watch as his lover was taken to a gallows on the ramparts,
and been allowed to exchange melancholy farewells and apologies in
French, before fainting away. It was to be another two years before
the prince was released, after untold enforced tutorials in statecraft,
the means of war, and theology, required by a father who was anxious, among other things, that his successor learn to disbelieve the
doctrine of predestination.[59]

Mrs. Adams had a low opinion of militarism and her response to
the sight of the great fortress was to register her approval that "the
mutillating stamp of War" had damaged the bastion and stockade,
because the point of "military skill" was merely "to give dignity to
crime." The authorities did not permit travelers to enter the fortress,
so she saw it at a distance, from a "tolerable house." (In the 1820s, this
meant the Golden Hind.)[60] It is unclear whether she stayed overnight
or just paused, but in either case, she entered into conversation with
those she encountered and, with the fortress high above her, talked
about war, Napoleon, and recent history.

On Napoleon, she had long had mixed feelings and had not always embraced the view that the emperor was a rapacious despot, no
more, no less. Many Americans, including her husband, disliked tyr-
anny but admired ambition, and were not ill-disposed toward a man
who fought the British with implacable energy. In the beginning,
John Quincy Adams the Federalist tended gingerly to approve of a
man ("the comet of the day") who in the late 1790s, as first consul, had
ended Jacobinism and instilled order. From Berlin in 1800, it was his
opinion that "it is indeed impossible to consider him as a principled
man. His ambition, like that of other conquerors, scruples little what
means it uses; but it has certainly great and noble views, and the prospects of France in case of his failure are in every particular so much
worse, than what she may hope from seeing him established firmly,
but I believe this is really to be wished." Later, to be sure, back in
Quincy, he had thought the assumption of imperial glamour more
comic than impressive, as he told his wife in 1804: "As to titles, if
what we see in the papers be true the french are going to plunge into

them with all the fondness of children for new raffle—There is Imperial Majesty Josephine, Imperial Highnesses Joseph and Louis, Grand Elector, and High Constable, Serene Highness Arch Chancellor Cambaceres, and Arch Treasurer Lebrun; &c &c—was there ever so horrible a Tragedy, concluded with so ridiculous a farce?" Later yet, both Mr. and Mrs. Adams found themselves in a good location to study Napoleon, for Saint Petersburg was close enough to the tragedy of 1812 to require meditation on the invader's virtues and faults, but far enough away leisurely to allow it. Despite her sympathy with Alexander I, she was not uninterested in granting a parallel between Napoleon and Alexander the Great, and was willing, even when knowing the scale of his debacle, to entertain if not necessarily to believe tales of Bonaparte's personal courage. "It is said," she noted in her diary in December 1812, "that Napoleon has made his way into Russia at the head of [a] small band of chosen men that he stiles himself their Captain and marches on foot with all his Generals." This she regarded as a "trait which bespeaks the character of the man," though only "if true."[61]

For all that, having traversed an eastern European landscape where the human price of Napoleon's unintelligible ambition and cruel disregard was everywhere evident to her, she expected in Kustrin to find Germans who would loathe and berate the emperor, the enemy of their anointed king. She found the reverse. "To my utter astonishment I heard nothing but the praises of the gallantry of Napoleon, and his Officers, and great regret at the damage done to this beautiful fortress." She was told, too, that after Kustrin she would "travel over the most beautiful road in the world, which had been completed by his order," and, but for the victory of the Allies, "it would all have been finished in the same way." She found all this deeply incongruous, for Kustrin was so desolate, so "unutterably dismal." Like Sarah Spencer seven months earlier, she saw burned buildings on the outskirts, "old dark, weather-beaten fortifications and drawbridges, and moats, and great gates with black eagles upon them, [looking] half sublime, but most melancholy." Yet the tone of her interlocutors, despite their cheerful words in praise of Napoleon, was not untrue to this half-ruination. For everyone spoke with a "guarded tone," "suppressed sighs," and "the significant shrug."[62]

In particular, she noticed that "the Cossacks! the dire Cossacks! were the perpetual theme, and the cheeks of the Women blanched at the very name." This fear was not irrational, though it was influenced by legend. The Cossacks, who came from the vicinity of the Don and Volga Rivers, were Russian light cavalry and lancers, who served as scouts in front of a vanguard or as protectors of a rear guard, but seldom in pitched battles. They rode small and swift horses, guided only by the snaffle and the short whip, and they disdained the bridle and spurs. Their uniforms were irregular and their relationship to the chain of command still more so, since they received little pay, furnished their own horses, survived by plunder, and were often insusceptible to discipline that emanated from anyone but their own officers. Their atrocities were many, though whether they were crueler than other soldiers is unclear, because Cossacks stirred primeval fears. They were horsemen from central Asia and they summoned up dark imaginings of Attila the Hun, Tamerlane, and mountains of skulls. When they had been used in the Russian war with Frederick the Great in 1757, an English journal solemnly reported that, by the hands of Cossacks, innumerable "inhabitants of *Prussia* have been hanged, others have had their legs cut off, or been ript up alive and their hearts tore out." Towns were said to have been gleefully burned, children slaughtered, and at Memel a hundred women had leaped into the Baltic rather than "submit to the brutalities offered them by these monsters."[63]

Strengthened by such tales, Mrs. Adams deepened her mistrust of militarism. She was to write that Kustrin furnished "painful indications of the miseries of unholy Ambition, and the insatiate cravings of contaminating and soul corrupting War, with all its train of horrors." But it was not so with those around her. The men praised Napoleon's road, while the women damned Russian rape, and there was little balance in these judgments. It was a puzzle.[64]

But she did not spend much time puzzling. Once more the Prussians checked her passport, once more she climbed into her carriage,

and without incident—except for noticing a house where Queen Luise had stayed on the retreat from Berlin in 1806—Mrs. Adams passed
along Napoleon's excellent road to the Prussian capital, which
through avenues of poplars she reached on Saturday, March 4.[65] It
had been a week since she had left Königsberg, which was now nearly
four hundred miles behind her, beyond the mud, the Vistula, the fortresses, and the blacksmith's hovel. She was now nineteen days from
Saint Petersburg and she needed to rest.

4

FROM BERLIN TO EISENACH

Mrs. ADAMS had a strong sense of stepping back in time as she came through the Frankfurter Thor, crossed the river Spree, and at two o'clock arrived at the Hotel de Russie on the eastern end of Unter den Linden. This was the same hotel she had entered in 1797, when she had first come to Berlin, and outwardly the city had changed very little over the intervening years.[1] Her memory of that lost time came back with mingled pleasure and sadness. Much later, her sense of loss would grow, but in 1815 she remembered with gladness what it had been like once to be young, instead of forty, graying, and road-weary.

Yet her former days in Berlin had very often been marked by pain, even from the first. She had arrived pregnant, some four months after her marriage, and found herself in the Hotel de Russie ("a noisy and publick Hotel") among unintelligible strangers, whose manners seemed to her disgusting and indecent. She had had only the support of a seventeen-year-old serving girl, a husband she barely knew who was attentively affectionate but distracted by his duties, and a young brother-in-law as *ingénu* as herself. Within three days she had fallen dangerously ill, experienced "the most excruciating pain," miscarried her child, and nearly died. In fact, residents of the hotel had heard

Edward Savage, *Louisa Catherine Johnson* (ca. 1793)
(Courtesy of the National Park Service, Adams National Historical Park)

that she had died. They had told Thomas Boylston Adams of his bereavement and he had come into her chamber to ask the doctor if it
was so, as she lay in agony but conscious of the conversation around
her bed. It took her a month to be able to walk under the lime trees
and over two months to recover, though temporarily, because there
came to be a despairing cycle. Over the next three years, she became
pregnant three more times and, on each occasion, she miscarried.
Her husband's diary became peppered with entries that read, "Mrs.
A again very unwell," "Mrs. Adams very unwell so she could not go
out," "my wife yet very ill," "Mrs. Adams extremely ill all the morning . . . much alarmed for her." In time, he began to lose hope. "Mrs.
Adams ill again . . . I have no doubt of the issue. The cup of bitterness must be filled to the brim and drunk to the dregs." Finally, in
January 1800, he had to write, "Mrs. Adams taken ill this morning, in
the process of a fourth misfortune, like three others which she has
gone through since we arrived at Berlin . . . I can only pray to God
that there may never again be the possibility of another like event. A
better hope it were folly to indulge, for in cases like this hope itself is
but an aggravating misery."[2]

But she had been young and, in her own way, strong. She had felt
pain, she had fainted, she had bled, but then she had got up, left her
bedroom, tried a gingerly walk in the Tiergarten, and eventually
gone to the theater and the court. Curiously, Berlin was to give her
what may have been her happiest period, for then "life was *new*."
That memory of happiness was her strongest impression in 1815: "I
entered Berlin with the pleasant recollections of the past; and youth
seemed again to be decked with rosy smiles, and glad anticipations—
and I wandered in the bright images of vivid recollections which
every object called forth in fresher bloom, as if the scythe of time had
left them glowing as of yore."[3]

Though she would not have said so in late 1797, when she was ill,
frightened, and unsure, Berlin proved to be manageable. It was a
middling-sized city, with a population then of about 150,000, which
made it far smaller than London and Paris, if only somewhat smaller
than Saint Petersburg. Most of this growth was recent and, even in

1797, it was unclear whether Berlin had arrived as a center of culture and society, or whether it was, in the words of a condescending English traveler, only reminiscent of "a provincial town with a large garrison." This uncertainty was a spur to civic energy, which made the city a permanent building site, attractive to immigrants: Poles and Jews from eastern Europe, Huguenots from France, and any number of miscellaneous Germans who came for the multiplying offices of the Prussian army and bureaucracy and to work in the city's diversifying industries (pottery, armaments, textiles, furniture, silks). Though founded in the late twelfth century, Berlin had been but "a dirty provincial village" for centuries, until the growth of the parvenu and fragile Prussian state in the seventeenth century and the military successes of Frederick the Great in the mid-eighteenth century had made it a focus of Hohenzollern ambition and display. Most of the medieval city had been demolished, its old walls disappearing as early as 1669, and it was, though less systematically than Saint Petersburg, essentially a new town. So it had been made and remade at the whim of electors and kings, on a landscape that was flat, sandy, and undemanding, in a place that had little geographical reason for being. It was a city that felt spacious, for Frederick the Great had planned a larger city than the available people could fill. So the city's avenues were broad, most houses had only two stories, only a third of the land was covered with buildings, and there were still many "gardens, orchards, and fields."[4]

This modernity was offensive to some. Madame de Staël noted in her *De l'Allemagne* of 1810: "Berlin is a large city, with very broad streets, perfectly straight, the houses handsome, and the general appearance regular; but, as it has been but lately rebuilt, it displays no traces of ancient times. Not one Gothic monument remains amid its modern inhabitants; and nothing of the antique interrupts the uniformity of this newly created country." For her, this made the city featureless, a nowhere-in-particular, with "no marks of the history of the country, or of the character of its inhabitants." But others liked this freshness, out of distaste for the "wild chaos of randomly arranged alleyways and houses" that marked most German towns.

This regularity was not yet monumental and little neoclassical, for it would be the 1820s before architects like Karl Friedrich Schinkel would remake the cityscape into something that might plausibly engender a German Empire, which might imagine itself to be heir to the Caesars. By contrast, the late-eighteenth-century city was a place of stuccoed brick, not marble, and often baroque or rococo. It did not lack for very large buildings, notably the Royal Opera House and the Royal Palace—indeed, the latter was "the largest Baroque building north of the Alps"—but there were "hundreds of neat houses which [lined], with uninterrupted regularity, the streets of the Neustadt." And away from the fashionable area that centered on Unter den Linden and away from the parks (the Lustgarten, the Tiergarten), Berlin had more than its share of "dingy alleys such as one usually finds in country towns—so dark and narrow that when a coach drives through pedestrians have to stop and wait until it has passed," and of "poor, propped-up houses" in "desolate, unbuilt squares, with great piles of dung in front of the doors and the citizens showing in their features marks of extreme poverty." And everywhere were reminders that Prussia was a military state, in which a man was ten times more likely to be in the army than a man in Britain, and four times more likely than even in Russia. In Berlin, parade grounds, barracks, uniforms, pickets, and the sound of drum and fife were ubiquitous, since the Berlin garrison consisted of 25,000 men, a sixth of the city's population. Goethe was not alone in finding this presence disquieting. In 1778, he observed that the city's streets were full of "men, horses, wagons, guns, ammunition," and that such military regularity made the city but a "monstrous piece of clock-work."[5]

The young Louisa Adams, when she rose from her sickbed in the early days of 1798, quickly confronted the city's modernity, for her first permanent residence was in a building finished only five years earlier. She moved to apartments at the Brandenburg Gate, in the building to the left, if one stood under the lime trees and looked through the gate toward the Tiergarten. The gate then had a different name, the Gate of Peace. Above it was the Quadriga, the great statue of a chariot with four horses, which was driven not by Ares, the god of war, but by Irene, the goddess of peace. The sandstone relief below the Quadriga portrayed a "Procession of Peace." Only after 1815 would the formal meaning of the gate be transformed, when the goddess was redesigned to embody victory and martial glory. But even in 1798 it was hard to trust the formal symbolism. Mrs. Adams's apartments were above the guardhouse and, as she remembered, "few days nay even hours passed without my ears being assailed and my eyes shocked by the screams and blows which were bestowed on the soldiers," who were not only punished within the privacy of the guardhouse but in the publicity of the parade ground, upon which she looked down. In addition, the passage of the royal family through the central arch of the gate, which only they were permitted to use, had to be marked by the beating of drums. But drums were required for even ambassadors and "officers of distinction," so—considering how large was the royal family and how numerous the diplomatic corps and the high bureaucracy—these military noises were incessant, the more so because the Champs de Mars behind the gate was used for military exercises and parades.[6]

Within a few months, therefore, the Adamses moved to "a fashionable and central quarter of the Town," at 48 Behrenstrasse, where it intersected with the Friedrichstrasse. It was in the neighborhood where most of the diplomats lived; the Danish minister was at 18 Behrenstrasse, several others a street to the north on Unter den Linden. Though Berlin was relatively inexpensive by comparison with many other European capitals, nonetheless these quarters exceeded their means. The building itself was inhabited by the likes of Countess Golofkin, who kindly preferred a weekly standing invitation to call, but who set a standard not easy to reach. To maintain the illusion of adequacy, the Adamses had their drawing and dining rooms prettily furnished, but behind the scenes they stinted, though unequally. In Mr. Adams's study, there were pine bookshelves, a few chairs, and a secondhand sofa, but also a mahogany desk and a carpet. In Louisa's bedroom, there was a "very common" pine table covered in muslin, a plain mirror, six chairs, no fire, and *"no Carpet,"* as she was later to remember with some bitterness. In an attempt at comfort, she herself

made curtains for the windows and the four-poster bed, curtains
made of white cotton bordered with calico "cut from a striped print,"
though the cotton was "of the coarsest quality." In the drawing room,
however, she could assume the dignity of a foreign minister's wife,
even the exotic standing of an American president's daughter-in-law,
and think herself respectable.[7]

In Berlin, this economic constraint was less humiliating than elsewhere. As Karamzin observed: "The people of Berlin are praised for
their activity and frugal manner of living. Even the opulent, and
people of rank, do not spend their money in useless luxury; but observe the strictest economy in clothing, dress, the expences of the
table, and equipage." That is, the boundaries between the haute
bourgeoisie and the aristocracy were less sharply drawn than in Saint
Petersburg. Central to the bourgeois world was Dr. William Brown,
the English physician who tended to the aristocracy and the royal
family, especially to Queen Luise, and a man whose house was a focus
for most resident and traveling Britons. He had been sent for when
Mrs. Adams had fallen ill in the Hotel de Russie, and when recovered
she had quickly become an intimate of his family. She adopted the
Browns as a surrogate for the Johnson family from which she was
then exiled, and she reassumed her familiar role as an elder daughter.
The doctor himself was "a very handsome courtly gentlemanly man"
with a bearing somewhat above his station, for he was "showy in his
manners . . . and fond of distinction." (Others were less polite and
dubbed him "pompous.") But he was competent, fatherly, and hospitable, as were his wife and four children. Mrs. Brown—there is no
record of her first name—was motherly, unpretentious, and mirth-
ful; she was the ill-educated daughter of a Welsh curate, a sometimes
coarse woman who contented herself with domesticity. "She was the
beau ideal of a good, Honest, simple minded, kind hearted old Lady,
of the old School," Mrs. Adams was to remember. She always wore a
cap and apron, a dark silk gown, and a "neat muslin neck kerchief."
Of her three daughters, the eldest was Margaret, then about twenty,
a pretty brunette whose hard work and intellectual competence
alarmed girls and young men alike. By contrast, Louisa's acolyte Isa-

bella was feminine and gentle, a girl who, when on her premature deathbed, asked to be given a cap that Mrs. Adams had made for her and requested that it be buried with her. The youngest daughter was Fanny, the family's pet child of golden hair, roseate complexion, and soft blue eyes. Last was William, "very handsome and very wild." So, like the Bennet family in *Pride and Prejudice*, the Browns offered an eccentric and welcoming refuge, for theirs was a household that Mrs. Adams could enter at will and that would call on her at will, and where laughter, gossip, and confidences could be gladly exchanged without fear of betrayal or malice.[8]

The other pillar of Mrs. Adams's Berlin world was Pauline, Countess von Néale, who occupied a position of comfortably minor importance at the court as maid of honor to the king's cousin. Pauline Néale had been born in 1779, so was only eighteen when Mrs. Adams came to know her. That the American minister's wife was only four years older was part of the bond between them, as was the fact that the countess came from an Irish family and, though born in Berlin, was fluent in English and often visited Britain. Her father, Ferdinand, Count von Néale, had between 1776 and 1789 been chamberlain to the court of Prussia and in 1785 "grand cupbearer" to the monarch, so he had served both Frederick the Great and Frederick William II. His wife, Josephine, was mistress of the household to Prince Ferdinand, and hence courtly service ran in the family. The Néales were not a happy couple. He was a man of "violent temper" who treated his "kindly and sweet-natured" wife with great harshness. But little of this was evident to Mrs. Adams, who used to go often to the Néales "without form or ceremony at tea, taking a Supper of the most simple kind, of cold provision, often of bread and cheese (English) there deemed a great luxury."[9]

Pauline Néale was petite, "not handsome, but full of animation and ésprit," and unusually well-read and educated for a Prussian countess. She was more a woman for good times than bad, and later she would not take well to the rigors of exile and the flight to Memel. But times were more often good than bad and, of both sorts of experiences, she liked to tell stories. Over the years, she became someone to whom strangers would apply to learn ancient lore, for she became a spinster fixture at the Prussian court until her death in 1869. So when Queen Victoria's daughter, also named Victoria, married Frederick, the Prussian crown prince, in 1858, she came to Berlin and there met "some very old people," among whom was "a lady who was said to remember Frederick the Great" and who "could recollect with vivid intensity every detail and episode" of the Napoleonic years. Similarly, the German novelist Fanny Lewald talked to Countess Néale when writing *Prince Louis Ferdinand* (1848) and turned her into a character in the novel, as did the greater novelist Theodor Fontane in *Before the Storm* (1878). Over the years, Néale especially adopted the visiting English and was, for example, a close friend of Priscilla, Countess of Westmorland, whose husband was British ambassador to Prussia in the 1840s.[10]

All this was far in the future when Pauline Néale, full of advice, came to call on the recovering Mrs. Adams at the Brandenburg Gate apartment early in 1798. At that moment, there was a problem, of which the semi-American was oblivious. Mrs. Adams's recovery had been so protracted and her reclusiveness so marked that rumors had developed that perhaps she had not yet been presented at court because she was not respectable. Alarmingly, the queen herself "had said unless I was presented soon that she should suppose I was not married." So the countess set about propelling the Anglo-American ingenue into the Prussian world. Etiquette was explained, a dress was lent, the oddities of courtly persons were described, and a very young mentor established her sisterly role. "Whenever we met she gave me insight into the characters that passed before us; and this peep behind the scenes, was always amusing, beneficial, and instructive."[11]

Advice was imperative, because the royal family was complex. There was the very new court of Frederick William III and Queen Luise, which divided its time between the Stadtschloss, the Schloss Charlottenburg, and the various palaces of Potsdam. Around this were assorted lesser households, each with its presiding members of the royal family, to the female head of which a woman like Mrs. Adams needed to be introduced. Each had a guardian of etiquette, the mistress of the household—in French the *grande gouvernante*, in German the *Oberhofmeisterin*. This was invariably a lady of advanced years with a long memory for names, whose duty was to summon you, tell you where to stand, when to sit, what not to say, and how to go. In Queen Luise's court this was Sophie Marie, Countess von Voss. In 1797, she was sixty-eight years old, the daughter of a Prussian soldier who had fought with the Duke of Marlborough at Malplaquet and the widow of a diplomat called John Ernest von Voss. She had been a lady-in-waiting to a queen dowager as long ago as the 1740s. At first glance, even at second glance, she was dauntingly tall, thin, and straight. She wore a great hooped skirt of disused fashionability, a rich brocaded train and petticoat, short sleeves, double ruffles, gloves, jewels, and "what used to be called a fly Cap, placed on the back of her hair," which was frizzed in the manner of Martha Washington. She carried a fan, ready for tapping and pointing. It was to be said of her that "in her youthful days she had been trained to the Spanish style of Court manners, which was now going out of fashion," partly because Queen Luise had a fondness for spontaneity, even mischief, which was not the Spanish way.[12]

When Mrs. Adams was first presented to the queen, it was the sight of Countess von Voss that made her most tremblingly nervous. In fact, Voss was kindly and once wrote down firm but compassionate rules for an *Oberhofmeisterin* and seems to have abided by them. She believed such a person should "hold her head high and walk erect, should have a courteous but dignified carriage, and bow properly, not as is done now with the head only, but with the knees, curtseying respectfully and solemnly, and rising slowly and with dignity." She must be courteous to all, respectful to her seniors, but also kindly to her inferiors. With the young, she should not be too strict, because she ought not to forget "that she too was once young and has felt the power of love." She should earn confidences, but not be too familiar. She should see to the "acknowledged rules of etiquette," but "not fuss about trifles." She should be honest, devoted, cheerful, good-tempered and, remembering the pitfalls of age, "avoid long stories and repetitions, which fatigue every one."[13]

Mrs. Adams was to remember frequenting six lesser royal house-holds, presided over by the queen dowager, Princess Henry, Princess Ferdinand, the Princess of Orange, Princess Louis, and Princess Luise Radziwill. (It was the custom for wives to be designated by their husband's forename, if the husband was of superior rank.) This was a layering of three generations; that of Frederick the Great and his two brothers Henry and Ferdinand; that of Frederick William II, survived by his wife, Frederica Luise, and sister Wilhelmina; and that of Frederick William III.

In the middle generation was the queen dowager, Frederica Luise, whose husband had become king in 1786. She had been a second wife, and there was to be a third and a fourth in her own lifetime, for bigamy was permitted to kings if a marriage was morganatic. She was only forty-six when her unlamented husband had died, uncured by the "animal magnetizers" he had summoned, and was freshly in widow's weeds when Mrs. Adams called in respectful black and encountered an oddly dressed woman with "hair . . . scratched out on each side . . . a la crazy Jane." Also in the middle generation was the refugee Frederica Sophia Wilhelmina, wife of the Prince of Orange, who in 1795 had lost his position as hereditary stadtholder of the Netherlands to a revolution. Being indigent dependents, the pair entertained little, and Mrs. Adams's memory of the princess was therefore truncated, though there lingered that of a very tall woman, "so slender that she seem'd to stoop from weakness," whose situation elicited polite pity.[14]

In the oldest generation was Wilhelmina, the wife of Prince Henry. In his time, the prince had been an invaluable lieutenant to his jealous brother Frederick the Great, and a man who had won victories in the Seven Years' War. But now he was old, impatient of contradiction, and self-exiled in Rheinsberg, more than fifty miles northwest of Berlin. (Mrs. Adams was never to meet him.) This isolation arose partly from his open homosexuality, partly from his estrangement from Frederick William II (a nephew "weary of avuncular despotism"), and partly from an inveterate impatience with fools more powerful than himself. As the elegantly bitter epitaph he wrote for his own tomb was to explain, he had been "tormented by the passions of others and made restless by his own." So Princess Wilhelmina lived alone in a wing of her husband's huge palace on Unter den Linden, which would in time become the core of the University of Berlin. To Mrs. Adams, the princess seemed stately and rigid, the more so because, to support a weak spine, she wore an iron collar, little disguised by an abundance of lace. Once a week, she gave dull suppers with indigestible food, at which Louisa was expected to play cards for money with experienced "harpies" and rapacious officers, for whom whist was more than an amusement. (The Prussians were inveterate gamblers.) By mutual agreement, John Quincy Adams would fill his wife's purse with prudently little gold when she ventured out on a Monday night.[15]

For Mrs. Adams, most significant among the oldest generation was Luise, Princess Ferdinand, whose husband ("poor Ferdinand") was the quietest and most ineffectual of a turbulent set of brothers. In winter in the Saint John Palace on the Wilhelmsplatz and in summer at Bellevue at the western end of the Tiergarten, there existed the illusion of a harmonious family, a thing little known among the Hohenzollerns, who tended not to bother with affecting such illusions. These were places, therefore, which Louisa Adams—always in search of happy families and seldom finding them—was delighted to frequent on Friday nights, when Princess Ferdinand did her entertaining. The food was simpler and better, the card playing less tense, the atmosphere more relaxed, and it was common for ladies to sit together, to sew, and to chat. The princess herself was "a very fine looking woman tho' not handsome" and disconcertingly blunt, with a coarseness that Mrs. Adams came to associate with German ladies. ("I used to blush with astonishment at what I then thought her want of delicacy.") She was prone to abrupt and personal questions. How long have you been married? How old are you? Does your husband love you? A son-in-law was summoned and asked if he found Mrs. Adams to be pretty. At first, Mrs. Adams was confused and shocked by this intimate inquisition, until she got used to it and came to think, probably wrongly, that the princess meant no harm. It helped that the princess was but part of the scene. It was true that her husband, being "old and very sickly and not at all a prominent character in his family," was only intermittently present. (It is possible that the two sons were not his own, and there had nearly been a divorce.) But her sister Philippine, the Landgravine of Hesse-Cassel, at fifty still a great beauty, was habitually resident, had simpler tastes, was kindly, and especially welcomed Mrs. Adams into the sewing circle. Princess Ferdinand's only surviving daughter was often there, too, and worked hard to serve as a bridge between generations, since in 1798 she was twenty-eight. But it was uphill work, for she was "not a favourite with her mother," who was cold and censorious. This young woman was the princess to whom Pauline Néale was maid of honor, and in whose palace on the Wilhelmstrasse the countess had an apartment.[16]

Frederica Dorothea Luise Philippine, "a very large woman" sometimes known as Princess Luise but as often (to her mother's annoyance) as Princess Radziwill, had just been married in 1796 to Prince Anton Radziwill, though against the king's wishes. Younger than his consort, Radziwill was a Polish-Lithuanian aristocrat of much beauty, of great amiability, of inconstant fidelity, of musical talent, and of little money. ("It was by no means rare to encounter in his antechamber *landreuters* or bailiffs.") Mrs. Adams was to remember the princess as graceful, affable, and respectful of her guests' "social independence." Her posthumous memoirs display a woman of humanity and regretful realism, who sketched a more acute portrait of her world than any other courtly insider. This critical distance was achieved because she had stood a little aside, had been mistrusted by many for her liberalism, and had presided over the nearest thing to an intellectual salon that any member of the royal family managed. It was in the Radziwill Palace that Mrs. Adams was most likely to encounter a philosophe like Wilhelm von Humboldt.[17]

Last and eventually least was Princess Louis, who in 1793 had married the brother of Frederick William, the heir apparent, at the same time that her sister the future queen Luise had married the heir himself. But her marriage had been unsuccessful and her husband's death from typhus in late 1796, which left her a widow at eighteen, was a deliverance. Despite having charm and a coquettish sentimentality, Frederica had long stood in the shadow of her brilliant, beloved, and beautiful sister. Being second-best was not easy to live with and, eventually, Frederica's sense of duty slackened. She had an affair with the Prince of Solms-Braunfels, a penniless but handsome officer, and got herself pregnant. This became increasingly noticeable as her dresses grew unwontedly plain and full, and a woman who "had always vied with the Queen in her ornaments, and in the richness of her apparel" became "suddenly . . . very modest and precise." There had been a secret marriage and, when it was discovered, an angry king and a distraught queen ordered the hapless pair to a frontier garrison town. There, it was later reported by Mrs. Adams with gossipy satisfaction, "her brute of a husband [was] said to receive all his Officers while in *bed* with her, at five o'clock in the morning, smoking a Meerschaum: What a change produced by unbridled passion!!!" Later, after Solms died, she married the Duke of Cumberland, who became king of Hanover in 1837. In 1816, Mrs. Adams was to walk into a London drawing room, at a party given for the Duke of Cambridge, and there saw the Duchess of Cumberland sitting on a sofa with Lady Castlereagh. With the former, no introduction was necessary.[18]

Floating above the lesser households was the royal court itself, which often was little different in style, since there, too, on Sundays in alternate weeks during the winter season, courtiers played cards and women sewed. The queen preferred the game of casino, though the king did not play, and ladies like Mrs. Adams were required to sit at the queenly card table after supper. The royals formed an odd couple. ("Complementary" was the polite way of expressing this.) With flashes of humor, he was taciturn, grave, irresolute, and anxious. With flashes of seriousness, she was lighthearted, vivacious, shrewd, and decisive. Unusually for a Prussian king, he disliked the warlike "system of robbery and plunder" practiced by most great powers, while she came to favor it. For the most part, it was she who governed how the court behaved and she who stood conspiciously at its center, while her husband stood silently and benignly beside her. On the other Sundays, there were balls and masquerades, for the queen

loved dancing and theatricality, and she adored displaying her tanta-
lizing body in diamonds and pearls, which had been less available to
her in the provincial world of Mecklenberg-Strelitz. She had an especial weakness for elaborate quadrilles. Soon after her marriage in
1793, the court had staged a reenactment of Tasso's *Jerusalem Delivered*, and during Mrs. Adams's time, the Lutheran court strangely
chose to mimic the Roman Catholic marriage of Queen Mary (played
by Queen Luise) with Philip of Spain (played by the visiting Prince
Augustus of England). This latter enterprise took six weeks of re-
hearsal, close study of old paintings to get the costumes right, newly
commissioned music, and an abundance of crown jewels, page boys,
and courtiers with pretty ankles, who performed English, Spanish,
Italian, and Mexican dances.[19]

There is no reason to believe that Queen Luise treated Mrs. Adams with extraordinary kindness, for it was her habit to be courteous
and winning. Nonetheless there was kindness. When Mrs. Adams
was first introduced at court, she had been supposed to go forward to
greet the queen, but was so debilitated by her late illness and so nervous that she had frozen awkwardly and failed to move. The queen,
"perceiving my great embarrassment and pitying my situation,"
waived etiquette and came forward herself. She explained that, from
Dr. Brown, she knew of the illness and situation, and that she sympathized, for she was a young woman, too, often pregnant. And she
kept the interview short, so as not to be wearying. Later, during and
after supper, she "spoke to me sweetly." And this became a pattern,
this regal warmth and condescension, when Mrs. Adams sat and
played casino, when she danced with the king, when she sat at court
suppers, when she was "obliged to converse, or rather to answer to
the questions of their Majesties." Certainly the frequency of her miscarriages elicited the queen's sympathy, which explains why, when in
the spring of 1801 Mrs. Adams was close to bearing her first child
(and did), "the King had the ends of the Street barred up, [ordered]
that no carriages might disturb me; and the Queen sent every day to
enquire how I was." In fact, the queen could have felt herself responsible for the successful birth. More than a year earlier, she had asked

to see Mrs. Adams and told her "that she felt such a strong sympathy," because of the miscarriages. (The queen had once fallen down a flight of stairs and miscarried a daughter, and a second daughter had died after only five months in 1799.) So she had written to her aunt the Duchess of Darmstadt, "who was famed for her knowledge and still more for her cures of difficult cases." When in the autumn of 1800 Louisa once more became pregnant, she "received a large Packet from the Queen Sealed with the arms of Darmstadt and containing a *charm*." This packet was to be put under her pillow every night, but to remain unopened until after a successful delivery. In fact, Louisa did not even then open it, but put it away in a wardrobe. When packing to leave for America, she came across it and found "nothing but a yellow Powder" of an unknown substance.[20]

Nonetheless, Mrs. Adams's doting regard for Queen Luise came at a price, for John Quincy Adams, not a spontaneous or mischievous man, regarded the queen with misgiving. In 1807, when news of the reverses of the Prussian royal family reached the senator from Massachusetts, he wrote with satisfaction of "the vicissitudes of the world [that] have reached many of our old acquaintance there; and that beautiful and thoughtless queen whom we were accustomed to see so splendid has been brought to dance something less delicious and more vivid than a waltz."[21] He had not been pleased to see his wife drawn toward this erotic flame. There had been, notably, the bitter business about rouge.

At a ball in early 1799, soon after the disgrace of Princess Louis, Countess von Voss approached Mrs. Adams and said that the king proposed to partner her in the next dance. It was an English country dance, which meant that couples stood opposite each other in a line. So the dancers formed, the queen took her place with her own partner, and immediately next to his wife stood the king, who waited for Mrs. Adams. She tottered out with evident nervousness. Noticing this unease, the queen "took my hands in hers, and stood and talked for some minutes until I recovered." In the course of this conversation, "she told me I looked so pale that she must make me a present of a box of rouge." To this, Mrs. Adams replied that her husband would not let her wear rouge. The queen "smiled at my simplicity, and observed that if *she* presented me the box he must not refuse it, and told me to tell him so." At this, Luise "beckoned to the King, and told him to begin the dance." Mrs. Adams knew her husband's puritanism and republicanism better than the queen, for he did indeed say that she "must refuse the box, as he should never permit me to accept it." But matters did not rest there. The queen periodically "insisted upon the rouge, and threatened me with the box," though Mrs. Adams reluctantly stalled. For as her husband well knew, in American society no respectable woman then wore rouge. Beyond New Orleans, very few would until the mid-nineteenth century.[22]

It was common in Berlin to hold Venetian masked balls, or ridottos, events that the queen liked. On these occasions, it was the custom for ladies to wear a short-sleeved black dress cut very low, black shoes, a black Spanish hat, a Venetian cloak, and a black mask. This jet appearance was relieved by the flash of diamond earrings, diamond necklaces, and diamond or gold bracelets. This was well and good for ladies well supplied with diamonds, and better still for those whose complexions could bear the stark contrast of black. But Mrs. Adams was short of diamonds and very pale, so she was painfully conscious of looking "cadaverous," indeed "a *fright* in the midst of the splendor." Rouge would help. So on February 6, 1800, Mrs. Adams staged a stealthy rebellion. Going out to a ridotto, at the last moment she put on some rouge, rushed through the drawing room, and told her husband to put out the lights and follow her. He knew this was odd, examined her closely, spotted the scarlet impertinence, and led her to a table. He "then declared, that unless I allowed him to wash my face, he would not go." He seized a towel, put her on his knee, and wiped her face. So "all my beauty was clean washed away." For the moment, she took it well. They kissed and made up, and they "drove off to the party where I showed my pale face as usual."[23]

There the rouge controversy rested for nearly a year. But by February 1801, she was seven months pregnant and felt more than usually blanched and more than usually testy about "the everlasting tragedy" of her pale face. So she abandoned stealth, put on the rouge, and walked boldly forward to meet her obdurate husband. As usual, he insisted she wash it off. But she refused "with some temper." So he left her, went down to the carriage alone, and she remained by herself "crying with vexation." Her tears dried, she took off her evening clothes, put on something plainer, and went to visit the Browns, where she made no mention of the incident. There her husband came to fetch her and they "returned home as good friends as ever," for in 1801 anger "seldom lasted with me more than ten minutes." (It was to be different in later years, when her angers burned more steadily.) Nonetheless, for all this amiability, she "never went to any of the Courts after that" and she did not forget.[24] For at the root of this superficially insignificant spat lay a deeper social and marital tension, of which she was achingly aware and which Queen Luise helped to deepen.

So in Berlin for three and a half years, Mrs. Adams experienced a "giddy round of fashionable life," at first absorbing, later more a treadmill of ceremony. According to etiquette, invitations could not be refused except for reasons of illness. There was some compensation, therefore, for being often pregnant and ill. Save during these pained respites, the routine went around and around inexorably at the height of the season—Mondays at Princess Henry's; Tuesdays at a high official's, such as the foreign minister's; Wednesdays at the Queen Dowager's; Fridays at Princess Ferdinand's; Saturdays at another minister's; Sundays at the royal court. The opera, the theater, lesser balls, and still lesser engagements were squeezed in when and where there was a spare moment. Mrs. Adams complained and protested that she cared not a jot for the "gew gaws and vanities" of such a life, but really she loved this "constant round of company," as soon as she had gained some confidence. She liked it that she could say, "In the evening we were rarely alone." For this was the beginning of the years "when worldly taste occupied my attention; and social pleasures fascinated my spirits."[25]

In Saint Petersburg later, the life of the court was to occupy far less of her time and she lived more among the merchant and expatriate community. Berlin was more accessible and various. There were her Jewish acquaintances (the Cohens, the Schicklers), sundry aristocrats and officials (the Golofkins, the Bruhls, the Bischoffwerders), the diplomatic corps and their wives (the Parellas from Sardinia, the Panins from Russia, the O'Farels from Spain). Nonetheless, Mrs. Adams gravitated toward the English community, for "it was the only society natural to me" and "the only society I liked." For one thing, at first the British ambassador was single, and she came to be a surrogate hostess for the British embassy, a role deepened by a friendship with Hauptmann Garlike, the chargé d'affaires and "a sickly splenetic old Bachelor" fond of John Quincy Adams. For another, Berlin was now a destination on that lesser branch of the Grand Tour that led from Hamburg or Hanover to Berlin, Dresden, and Vienna. So English visitors appeared with exhausting, if engaging, frequency. Even as early as 1769, the English envoy in Dresden had complained of "an inundation of English, who have nearly eaten me out of house and home," and in 1774, now in Vienna, his heart sank at the sight of "half a score of Etonians," as well it might. In Berlin in the late 1790s, such people went with their letters of introduction to the embassy, they were led on to Dr. Brown's, and they came to know the Adamses.[26]

They came in all sorts and sizes—princes, aristocrats, diplomats, and gentleman and lady travelers. There were two younger sons of George III. Prince Frederick Adolphus appeared in 1801 on a minor diplomatic mission, though he was most interested in pursuing the delicate, alluring, and consumptive Mrs. Sanford, whose husband had brought her to Berlin precisely to evade the prince. By the undemanding standards of the Hanoverian dynasty, the prince was unusually courteous, a man who would ladle soup for the very pregnant Mrs. Adams, lest she be fatigued. His elder brother Prince Augustus Frederick had been around a few years earlier. He had been living out of England for more than a decade, latterly because in Italy he had secretly married Lady Augusta Murray, in contravention of the Royal Marriages Act. Keeping a safe distance from his father's displeasure, the amiable eccentric perambulated around the Continent with an African American valet and a small suite of odd friends, including William Brummell, brother of the peacock wit George "Beau" Brummell, whose beauteous cravats had so astonished London. One of Prince Augustus's eccentricities was that, because of his asthma, he slept only in armchairs, from which sometimes he roused himself to dance. He featured notably in Queen Luise's quadrille as King Philip of Spain, but also in others at Princess Radziwill's, where he appeared as Bacchus and, in drag, as Dulcinea. For the rest, he brought agreeable gossip about royal circles. Once, Mrs. Brown inquired of him about the famously dysfunctional marriage of Princess Caroline and the Prince of Wales. (They had slept together only three times, on the first two nights of their marriage, and thereafter both had thought it a bad idea.) At this question, Augustus "hesitated a moment; and then said 'my Dear Madam my brother is a Beast!!!'" As, in fact, he was.[27]

There were three British ambassadors to Prussia during Mrs. Adams's time, of which the first and third intruded on her world: the seventh Earl of Elgin, later the plunderer of the Parthenon and "a remarkably handsome roué" who flirted with and teased her; and from May 1800 the first Earl of Carysfort. The latter was of little interest to Mrs. Adams, who found him but "mild, silent, and good tempered" (this was not a rare opinion), but his wife, Elizabeth, mattered. Mrs. Adams came to love and cling to her "as if she had been my own mother." (She was to have several surrogate mothers through the years, which suggests her real mother did not suffice.) Her ladyship was a woman of high intellect, classical education, and stern manners, qualities that usually created timidity and fear in the young Louisa, though also a diffident envy. But Lady Carysfort was affectionate, wise, conversable, and surprisingly vulnerable for a Grenville, a lofty name of which she was pointedly proud. The two would meet in her ladyship's boudoir, "a sort of sanctum sanctorum . . . into which she never admitted any body, but her husband, and Children." There she would talk of her troubles, opinions, the death of her first son, religion, and fate. Thereby she exposed the conundrum of a mind "naturally strong, and so very highly cultivated," yet gripped by a "spirit of superstition . . . too deeply engrafted ever to be eradicated." In 1800 and 1801, this was a combination that fascinated Mrs. Adams, who even then had reasons to need the supernatural to compensate for a natural world that was often cruel. Later, when the world was yet more cruel, her fascination and need was to deepen.[28]

The other English and Irish who passed through offered only casual company and entertainment, though that was valuable enough to be memorable. There was the journalizing Melesina St. George, "a gay and dashing widow" from Ireland, and the newlywed Erringtons. There was the dotty Mrs. Elizabeth Orby Hunter, "one of the oddest, and most eccentric women to be *sane*" that Mrs. Adams ever met. Tall, badly dressed, smeared with rouge, she tormented gatherings by her propensity for flaming rows, violent language, hysteria, and weeping. She was, nonetheless, puzzled that all but Mrs. Adams received her visits with "chilling frigidity." When she left Berlin, she did so in a new carriage, expressly bought to convey her parrot, destined to become her heir. In 1813, she signed a will that granted to her "beloved parrot, the faithful companion of 25 years," a lifetime annuity of two hundred guineas, with elaborate provisions to prevent its murder, kidnapping, or expatriation. This was intended as a reproof to an unkindly world. "Many owe to me both gratitude and money," she observed, "but none have paid me either."[29]

These were the memories of Berlin that crowded Mrs. Adams's recuperating mind and body in the Hotel de Russie in 1815, memories of her ingenue time, recalled by a box of rouge, the squawk of a parrot, a jack of diamonds, the warmth of a velvet cloak, the chill of a ghost story, and the shape of a lime tree. But she and the world had changed over the last fourteen years.

Even her hotel, a place "particularly adapted for travelers of pleasure," had changed and, unusually, for the better. In 1797, she had found it rough and crude. Later, it was to earn a reputation for comfort and good living to match even "the first hotels in Paris," the sort of establishment that, at breakfast, furnished delicious coffee, butter, and rolls served on fine porcelain. In 1815, it was run by a widow called Obermann, who had played no small role in the Prussian resistance to French occupation, had often advanced money to those in need, kept the exiled Hohenzollerns informed of developments in their lost capital, and turned her hotel into something resembling "the headquarters of an army, or an established place of conference, rather than a tavern." For these services, Frederick William III would reward her with extensive lands in Silesia, so she was an unusually rich hotelier. Nonetheless, with perverse logic, she amiably over-charged her later English guests because "the French had plundered her of so many horses and valuables that she was determined the English should pay for it."[30]

From this place, Mrs. Adams quickly sent out letters, informing old friends that she was back. Pauline Néale "flew to meet" her and they agreed that, promptly on the next day, they would call on Princess Ferdinand and Princess Radziwill. So after a good night's rest, after arranging for the repair of her battered Russian carriage, and after hiring a new carriage for her stay, Mrs. Adams set forth into this changed world and stepped past the "female fruiterers, sitting before tubs filled with the finest grapes, and bergamot pears, [and] walnuts," who sat outside her hotel.[31]

The city's grander homes were semideserted, for the Congress of Vienna was still interminably meeting and many members of the court were in Austria: the king and Prince Radziwill and his sons, among others. Nonetheless, from those remaining (the Bruhls, the Golofkins, the Bischoffwerders), the old warmth still radiated, Mrs. Adams was made to feel at home, and "all the sweet sympathies of humanity [were] reawakened; and the sterile heartlessness of a Russian residence of icy coldness, was thawed into life and animation." Princess Ferdinand was kindly and her daughter Luise Radziwill was kindliest. Come every evening to dine at the Radziwill Palace, the latter said, and do not bother to dress elaborately, for now we live more plainly. As she explained, "The great people of Berlin had suffered so much from the War, that there was no pretention of style among them, and they were glad to see their friends sociably." The princess herself had aged, and the effect was not necessarily for the worse. There was "a softer shade of character on her face, than that which she possessed in the brilliancy of youth." The princess was conscious of the change. One evening as they sewed together, she asked Mrs. Adams whether the latter found the color of the princess's gown to be "very gay." Yes, was the polite reply. "She laughed, and observed, that she was rather *too old* to wear a bright couleur de rose; but she loved the dress, and must wear it, as it was a present from her Son, who had purchased it with the first money he had been allowed to spend; and had immediately on his arrival at Paris gone to a Magazine and selected it himself, as a first offering to a mother he adored."[32]

Princess Radziwill had been through much. In 1806, at Saalfeld, her impulsive brother Louis Ferdinand had been hacked down by a French hussar with six saber cuts, in 1810 her daughter Loulou had died, and in 1813 her father. She herself had been forced to flee Berlin without her parents (who were too old to move) in the knowledge that Napoleon was angry at her family and especially angry with Pauline Néale, who had once visited Paris, come to know Empress Joséphine, and written an unwisely candid and intercepted letter to her mother about Napoleon's megalomaniac plans. In Königsberg later, the princess was to read a newspaper account of Napoleon in Berlin. He was said to have asked Count von Néale where his daughter was. Eastward with Princess Radziwill, was the reply. "Well, if I had caught her here," said the emperor, "I should have had her hair cropped and sent her to Bicêtre for her interference in having political opinions and expressing them publicly." (Bicêtre was the lunatic asylum close to Paris, whose most famous inmate had been the Marquis de Sade.) So Princess Radziwill had a sharp, if exaggerated, sense that the French were coming personally for her, her family, and her dependents, as she passed along roads "blocked with fugitives" and crowded with the panicked carriages of her friends. In Königsberg, her son Wilhelm had nearly died from hospital fever, and she had been forced to stay and nurse him, even as everyone else had moved on to Memel and Napoleon advanced remorselessly toward her. Finally, she had been able to leave and then seen, on the horizon, the fires that signified that Eylau, where a battle was being fought, was burning. Later she was present at the mortifications of Tilsit. In time, by late 1810, she would be able to return to Berlin with a chastened king and a plainly dressed queen, where "it was painful to meet again persons who, in these times of trial, had shown equivocal behavior," the more painful because they were living there only because the French permitted it. In yet more time, after more "days of shame," there would be victory at Leipzig and Prussian troops in Paris, but the many days when the princess's "head swam to hear all the tidings that kept coming in, bit by bit, from hour to hour" had taken their toll.[33]

It was often the little things that told how hard war had been. The princess, though she hated the humiliations suffered by Prussia at the hands of the French, disliked to hear her enemy's humiliations celebrated by the vengeful. As she explained to Mrs. Adams, "She felt as a Christian, and she would permit no harsh and degrading language to be used in her presence; for the really great had fallen, and their punishment had overtaken them in all the horrors that unmitigated suffering could inflict; in addition to mortification and disgrace beyond the power of description." By way of illustration, the princess told the story of Louis Marie Jacques Amalric, comte de Narbonne-Lara, once deeply entrenched in the old order's *douceur de vie*, then in Napoleon's parvenu meritocracy. He was widely believed to have been the son of Louis XV by the comtesse de Narbonne-Lara, was baptized at Versailles with the future Louis XVI as his godfather, and for decades lived as an amiably dissolute, extravagantly indebted aristocrat, though one who troubled to read. The revolution and a liaison with Madame de Staël, who bore him a son, made him into a more serious man, propelled him very briefly into the position of secretary of war, and then forced him into exile in England. By 1801, he had returned to France, where Napoleon eventually began to use him as a soldier and diplomat, first as governor of Trieste and later as ambassador in Munich and Vienna, with spells as an emissary to Russia and Prussia. Though others mistrusted Narbonne as an émigré, Napoleon came to be an admirer, especially for what he saw on the Russian campaign. "Look at Narbonne!" he once said. "Never did leader inspire more zeal in his men; despite his age he undergoes fatigues and privations like a young man. Yet he is upheld solely by a sense of honour." With this, the duc de Vicenza agreed, for "M. de Narbonne was universally liked and appreciated." When in 1812 Narbonne was at Berlin, Princess Radziwill, too, was reluctantly charmed by a man who radiated "mildness and benevolence." "Though his position made his company embarrassing to me," she remembered, "he often succeeded in making me forget the master he served, and many were the curious and interesting anecdotes he told."[34]

The story that Princess Radziwill was to tell Mrs. Adams came without a date and is hard to verify, which is doubtless appropriate for an allegory about human fortunes. One day in Berlin, she said, she was brought "a Note on a Dirty bit of paper, earnestly entreating her to see a person who was in great distress." The request came with a condition, that the audience must be unobserved by anyone else and kept secret. The princess hesitated and asked about the source of the note. She was told it came from "a *Lady* who appeared in much trouble, [who] was waiting for admittance." So the odd request was granted and quickly there appeared someone "veiled and dressed in a blue Satin Pelisse." This person fell at her feet, implored assistance, confessed stark hunger, and claimed to have no clothes but those now on his back, which "had been charitably given to him by a Lady as a disguise." This was the comte de Narbonne-Lara, "flying from the Armies, in this utter and abject misery, who had thrown himself upon her mercy, to obtain the means of reaching Magdeburg." She pitied him and gave him money, clothes, and food. So he went on to the fortress of Torgau in Saxony, where soon after he "was killed by a fall from his horse . . . during the siege."[35]

This was a story about war. Mrs. Adams had formerly lived in a Berlin unusually at peace, during a moment of introspective domesticity. The intervening years had brutally smashed that moment and, looking around her in 1815, she saw the difference. People dressed and talked differently, and, it seemed to her, "all the Nationality of Costume &cc had disappeared, and french was almost universally spoken." She discerned "a foreign air . . . which damped the pleasure I had expected, in revisiting the scenes of my youth." This was a shrewd judgment, though at odds with the legend that was to develop in the nineteenth century. This legend described a Prussia that, humiliated at Jena in 1806, had pulled itself together, enacted sweeping reforms, placed itself at the head of German nationalism, and, by a succession of military victories (Leipzig, Waterloo, Sadowa, Sedan) and intellectual accomplishments, had turned Germany from an act of imagination into a political reality. Beyond the legend lay the awkward fact that the immediate purposes of reform after 1806 had been driven not by resistance to but acceptance of French hegemony. Frederick William III after 1809 had been opposed to "patriotic experiments of any kind." Mrs. Adams saw around her the cultural manifestation of this habit of compliance.[36]

The absence of many who were in Vienna contributed to the impression that all was "cold, and flat," that there was a "perfect stillness [which] seemed to cast a gloom over all the scenes, which had once been so gay, and brilliant." But then, she was acutely conscious that those former scenes had been "gladdened by the smiles and affability of the young Queen." And that queen was five years dead and now lay in a cold neoclassical mausoleum in Charlottenburg. So Mrs. Adams made her pilgrimage into the countryside three miles west of her old apartment at the Brandenburg Gate, out to the low baroque palace she used to visit. It was common to go by boat down the Spree, though she probably used her hired carriage. In either case, she would have crossed the broad *parterre de broderie* north of the palace and proceeded toward a narrow avenue of pine trees. Down that avenue, she found a small grove of sable pine, cypress, larch, and willow. Before her stood a rectangular building, narrower at the front, with eight steps framed by large stone urns. She walked up into a portico supported by four Doric columns, above which was a triangular pediment engraved with the ominous Greek letters alpha and omega. Through a tall double door lay the temple, which was divided into three levels. Intermediate was the entrance hall in which she first stood. Directly ahead were nine marble steps, leading down to an unornamented mahogany door, beyond which lay the queen's ashes. These were inside a leaden coffin with a simple inscription giving her names, her titles, and the place and time of her death in 1810. Into this Louisa Adams could not go, for the tomb was always locked, the

J. D. Laurens and F. C. Dietrich after F. A. Calau,
Mausoleum of Queen Luise (1818)
(Courtesy of the Stiftung Stadtmuseum, Berlin)

key kept in the possession of the occupant's widower, who had come alone after his 1813 victory at Leipzig and placed a laurel wreath on the tomb, and who came formally once a year on July 13 with his children to mark the anniversary. Looking up to the highest level, Mrs. Adams saw a white marble chamber, reached by a choice of two flights of eight steps on each side of the tomb's entrance. In daylight, this platform was lit with dramatic effect from above and sometimes by a window to the rear, usually concealed by curtains. Centrally, two sets of double Doric columns of porphyry framed an empty room into which, two months later in May, would be installed a white marble sarcophagus, high above which would hang an elaborate Grecian bronze lamp.[37]

The sarcophagus would become an icon. On a couch would lie a full-length figure of the queen asleep on her back, her upper body propped on a raised end, her arms crossed beneath her breasts, her legs crossed, her head turned slightly, wearing a diadem. As in Schadow's sculpture of the early 1790s, the queen's dress would cling to and expose her form, and hers was a sleep expressing sexual satiation as much as repose. It became the legend that the sculptor, Christian Daniel Rauch, who had once been a page to the queen, had been in love with her. However that may be, he understood the sexuality of her appeal. It is very doubtful that Mrs. Adams would have seen or been willing to acknowledge this eroticism, if she had visited a few months later. For her generation, Luise's temple expressed but "the undying love and respect" of the queen's subjects. As for the sarcophagus itself, it became usual to see a "smiling animation of innocence buried in a tranquil sleep," to discern "a scene of tender and melancholy recollections," to discern grace in the skillful folds of the dress, and to imagine that cool whiteness expressed that consoling peace that the just would encounter in a death stage managed by God.[38]

Back in Berlin, she settled accounts with her old banker Herr Schickler and enlisted the help of the Néales for a "Captain Norman, an American whom I had found dying of a fever in the upper story of the hotel for want of care and attention." On Friday, March 10, she had her Prussian passport stamped by the authorities and also called upon Victor Louis Charles de Riquet, duc de Caraman, recently appointed by the restored Bourbons as the French ambassador. She wanted a new French passport, as (for some reason) she was "not satisfied with the one given to me . . . [in] St. Petersburg." She had, in fact, delayed in Berlin longer than she had wished, because of what she called the "want of letters from Mr Adams."[39]

In the 1830s, she was to write, "My friends in Berlin had advised me to avoid Leipsic, as I should have to cross the battle-field so celebrated a year before." In fact, as a letter written from Leipzig to Levett Harris attests, she did go there and she did cross the battlefield, which lay to the north, east, and south of the city, and athwart the post road coming from the northeast. To reach Frankfurt am Main, her next major destination, it was very hard to avoid Leipzig and she seems to have followed the customary road. This involved going southwest from Berlin to Leipzig, then west through Weimar and Erfurt to Eisenach, then southwest again through Fulda and Hanau to Frankfurt.[40]

Until now, apart from her brief dip into the Duchy of Warsaw, she had only been in the Russian Empire and Prussia. Soon, until she crossed the Rhine and reached France, she was to pass through a more splintered political landscape, consisting of a series of states that, for the moment, nominally belonged to what Napoleon had invented as the Confederation of the Rhine (or Rheinbund). These were the kingdom of Saxony, two of the Saxon duchies (Saxe-Weimar-Eisenach and Saxe-Gotha-Altenburg), the principality of Erfurt (technically French, but occupied by the Prussians), what used to be the prince-bishopric of Fulda (occupied by the Austrians), the electorate of Hesse, the principality of Isenburg-Birstein, the free city of Frankfurt, the grand duchy of Hesse-Darmstadt, and the grand duchy of Baden. Early in 1815, most of these were poised in a political no-man's-land, for their future or lack of it was under fierce discussion in Vienna. The elegant and dark lord of European conservatism, the Austrian foreign minister Klemens von Metternich, wished to preserve the Rheinbund, though stripped of its status as a French protectorate, as a counterbalance to Prussia and any possible resurgence of Restoration France. For the opposite reason, the Prussians wished to dismember it and already had troops in Saxony, there since early November 1814, when the Russians had pulled out. The tsar had promised Frederick William III that the latter would receive almost all of Saxony, in compensation for the tsar's own annexation of the Duchy of Warsaw. This was a plan opposed by everyone else, including the British and, least effectually, the king of Saxony himself, Frederick Augustus. Only in late February had the Prussians been forced to abandon their most sweeping ambitions, and it became clear that Saxony would, for the most part, survive. But much else, especially for the lesser states, remained obscure. The Duke of Saxe-Weimar, because he was a relative of the tsar, bade fair to do well and had in theory already been transformed into a grand duke. The Duke of Saxe-Coburg, on the other hand, was heard to complain, "I am being pushed around, insulted. Metternich! That *scoundrel* Metternich! He treats me like a toy! . . . and, to add insult to injury, I am sent letters addressed with titles that I am claiming and being denied!"[41]

For Mrs. Adams, the immediate problem was that the practicalities of traveling became more vexatious, for these states had different currencies and post road regulations.

As to money, like later travelers she was to find "the difficulty of procuring, as well as comprehending, the endless variety of coin of each petty State through which the road runs." In Prussia, they had thalers, groschen, silver groschen, and pfennigs, but also the ducat and the frederic d'or. In Saxony, there were dollars, rix-dollars, and groschen, but also the augustus d'or and the ducat. In Baden, Hesse-Darmstadt, and Frankfurt am Main, there were florins and kreutzers, plus the ducat and the louis d'or. But a florin in one place might not be equivalent to a florin somewhere else, for local mints used different weights of silver. In general, ducats were safest to carry and Mrs. Adams, when in Leipzig, acquired a hundred of these to see her through at least as far as Frankfurt. But in Berlin she had been unable to get any "French money," and she was very conscious of not fathoming the complexities.[42]

As to post roads, the regulations were dizzyingly various. In Prussia, the *Wagenmeister*, or superintendant, got his own fee of four groschen per stage, but elsewhere this position often did not exist. In Prussia, regulations specified that "postillions [were] obliged to drive one German mile an hour on well-paved roads; one mile and a quarter on good roads not paved; and one mile within an hour and a half where the road is sandy." In Saxony, one paid 10 silver groschen per post-horse per German mile on rougher roads, but 12.5 on smoother. In Erfurt, it was 12.5 groschen for all roads, but 10 in most of the Saxon duchies. In Saxony, each postilion got a flat 3.75 groschen per mile, while in Prussia it was four. In Erfurt and many states on the Lower Rhine, the scale was graduated: 5 silver groschen for a single postilion up to three horses; 7.5 for a single postilion for four or five horses, but 5 groschen for each of two postilions for five or six horses; in the unlikely event of eight horses, it rose to 7.5 groschen per postilion.

In general, Hesse was more expensive than Frankfurt, for whereas in the latter each postilion per stage for up to two horses cost 40 kreutzers, in the former each postilion cost 45 kreutzers. When you had four horses, it was 1 florin per postilion in Frankfurt, but 1 florin and 5 kreutzers in Hesse. In many places, there was something called "greasing-money," which was compulsory even if the wheels of the carriage were not greased. The fee was higher if they were greased and was doubled if this greasing occurred in a larger place like Berlin, Potsdam, or Erfurt, rather than a village.[43]

These were constant confusions, which had long since vexed John Quincy Adams, a traveler who disliked local idiosyncrasies. In Saint Petersburg, such anomalies had led him obsessively to ponder the multifarious inconsistencies with which civilized countries measured things. Eventually, this would lead to his intellectually distinguished and politically quixotic *Report on Weights and Measures*, sent by him in 1821 as secretary of state to the U.S. Congress. Wishing this "Babel of confusion" to end, he was to recommend that the United States adopt the decimal system of the French and, he hoped, this would eventually become the standard for all nations. "*Uniformity* of weights and measures—permanent, universal uniformity—adapted to the nature of things, to the physical organization, and to the moral improvement of man," he observed in a philosophic rhapsody, "would be a blessing of such transcendent magnitude, that, if there existed upon earth a combination of will and power adequate to accomplish the result by the energy of a single act, the being who should exercise it would be among the greatest benefactors of the human race." It was not to be, and he pined for a "steam engine of moral power to stem the stubborn tide of prejudice, and the headlong current of inveterate usage."[44]

His wife was more resigned to this state of things, though not because, before their marriage, he had urged the stoic value of resignation. For he was always urging resignation and she never got the knack. "The hardships of traveling, by sea or by land are formidable to you," he had then noted, knowing that marriage to an Adams required her to become a traveling lady. "Yet you must be prepared to undergo them—The modes of life, the manners and customs of the people where you may have occasion to reside, will be entirely different from those which you have been used to; perhaps many of them would appear unpleasant to you. For your own happiness endeavour to acquire the faculty not merely of acquiescence, in unavoidable inconveniences, but even of a cheerful conformity to things which must be endured, and above all establish as an invariable rule for your conversation, to express no general or national reflections."[45]

She did not always do what he wished, especially when he lectured her. But her life and travels did obey this injunction, though not for his reasons. For they started from a different place. John Quincy Adams, however discontented he was with his own failings, knew with certainty who he was. He accepted cultural relativism because exotic customs touched him little. He traveled, he observed, he wrote in his diary, but he remained himself and he knew that, eventually, he would go home. And he knew where home was—those few square miles of Quincy, Massachusetts. He was, in truth, uncomfortable in that home and his life was, more than he ever admitted, an insistent flight from Quincy. But he never doubted that around this point his life and death were fixed, and that posterity would never fail to designate him an Adams from Quincy.

By contrast, Louisa Adams did not have a home. The warm protectiveness of her childhood had been irretrievably lost and, for this deprivation, she grieved for the rest of her life. Instead, she became a migrant and a visitor. She moved from country to country—England to France, to England, to Prussia, to the United States, to Russia, to England, to the United States. She was to have dozens of residences— on Tower Hill, on the Behrenstrasse, on Boylston Street in Boston, on Apothecary's Island, in Ealing, on F Street in Washington, in the old house at Quincy—and her life was measured out in packing cases. Like any woman in her society, she was expected to inhabit the family of her husband. In fact, she clung to her own family with greater tenacity than most wives of her era, and it was almost as often the case that her husband was the lodger in the Johnson family as she was the lodger in the Adams family. Still, the Adamses were as powerful a family as any, known for being fiercely clannish and introspective.

They treated in-laws as satellites, though in a kindly way, and there was no escaping their gravitational pull. This could be so even in death. When Louisa Adams died in 1852, she was not put among her own family in Rock Creek cemetery in Washington, but into a crypt in Quincy, where she still lies, at the end of a row of Adamses.

In 1826, when John Adams died, his son went to Quincy for the funeral and to execute his father's will. Briefly, there was doubt about the wisdom of retaining the ancestral estate and houses, for there were many debts. It was John Quincy Adams's newly strong sense that he had to keep this old home. "I cannot endure the thought of the sale of the Place," he wrote to his wife. "Should I live through my term of service, my purpose is to come and close my days here, to be deposited with my father and my Mother." For her, this instinct was intelligible but alien, and she cautioned against it. "That you should be desirous of owning the House that was your Fathers is natural, but that you should waste your property and burthen yourself with a large unprofitable landed estate, which has nearly ruined its last possessor, merely because it belonged to him, is scarcely prudent or justifiable . . . For myself I care not a pin where I die—I have never had a home since I left my fathers house, and it is a matter of perfect indifference if I never do."[46]

She had little sense of belonging, beyond the ties of family. Nations, places, and institutions were lesser things that came and went. But not belonging meant she was always being asked to meet standards she did not acknowledge, to follow rules she did not understand, and to pay penalties she did not merit. "I am always wrong" is how she put it later. "Why is it that every thing I do, I say, I think, even is misunderstood; misinterpreted; misconceived," she would ask herself. "I am as others, think, as others, act as others, speak as others! Yet can I never please or satisfy by any exertion whatever; and the more earnestly I labor to make people happy, the more impossible I find it to succeed." When calmer, she knew that she was not as others, not quite. She had been "engendered among a different people" and English values made her "odious" in America. "I am now nearly sixty five years old," she was to write in her commonplace book in

E. Malcom, *Water Color of the Old Adams House, Quincy* (1798)

(Courtesy of the National Park Service, Adams National Historical Park)

1839. Yet "no one understands me one bit better than they did the day I arrived; and I feel a desolate loneliness in the very midst of a family, that I have too much idolized." She had not entered American society until 1801, when she was already twenty-six and formed. To be sure, her father had been a colonial Marylander who, from London and Nantes, had avidly supported the American Revolution and taught his children to be patriots who revered George Washington. As she was later to point out when accused of being a European aristocratic cuckoo in the democratic nest of the White House, she had been an American since childhood. For "Mr. Johnson, fearful lest his long absence from his native country should deprive his children of the rights of citizenship, through the influence of his friends, had them naturalized in the Legislative Assembly of Maryland, where the names stand recorded." And the claim was true, as a look at those legislative records for 1784 attest. She had been, technically, an American since the age of nine.[47]

Yet she was stretching the point for political reasons and knew it. In private, she understood full well that her education had been English, her mother and siblings English, and her habits English. America had been an abstraction to her, a far-off republican dream that proved disorienting when it became real. It did not help that when she had first landed in Philadelphia in 1801, she had seen America through a haze of pain. She had a chest complaint; indeed Dr. Brown had diagnosed consumption and been unsure of her survival. She coughed, she was prone to colds and fevers, she had cramps and pain in her hands. In addition, she had been a semi-invalid, so damaged by a "drunken Accoucheur" during the delivery of her first son that she had temporarily lost the use of her left leg. She had been too weak to attend the christening, had had to be lifted into the carriage that left for Hamburg and the ship, and was unable to walk without help until some weeks after the crossing.[48]

Nothing much seemed to go right in those first days. In Maryland she had found her father ill and dying, and she had been forced to leave him, so that she could travel north to meet her in-laws in Quincy. She went, knowing that she might never see him again, all for the sake of meeting people she did not know and timidly feared, just so that John and Abigail Adams could look at a grandchild, who naturally mattered more to them than a daughter-in-law. On the way, she had been often drenched by torrential rain, her baby had cried incessantly, she had been jostled miserably on rough turnpikes, and she had been taken to doctors.[49]

"These were my first impressions of America!" she was to write later. "Suffering and sorrow, sickness and exhaustion, with anguish of mind, all combined to harass me." As was her way, she was conscious that somehow she was at fault, perhaps because in London and Berlin she had been "the spoilt Child of indulgence." Even before their marriage, her husband had stated this theme, by describing her as having lived in "the bosom of an excellent and happy family, where you have from your infancy scarcely formed a wish, but it was instantly supplied, and where the possession of fortune has accustomed you to the enjoyment of every indulgence." He had made it clear that, in marrying an Adams, she was marrying into people who mistrusted indulgence. In reply, she had done her best to embrace this ambivalent prospect: "I must not always expect cloudless skies I acknowledge my lot has been cast in a fair graine and on this ought to acquire a little of your philosophy." So when in late November 1801 she had taken the stage out to a very cold Quincy, she was depressed and resentful, the more so because she had been told to erase her past and not to speak of Berlin.[50]

In retrospect, she thought it was as well that she had been too ill and morose to say much, because she would have said the wrong thing. It was not that the elder Adamses were unkind. From the first, John Adams took to her warmly. Abigail Adams treated her with motherly care, and even gave her special food and delicate preserves. But there was an edge to this kindliness, for Louisa got the ineradicable impression that she was seen as a woman apart, a delicate European lady unable to cope, a piece of Meissen pottery, at best decorative and at worst pointlessly expensive. To be sure, in theory Abigail Adams mistrusted provincial prejudice. As long ago as 1778, she had written to her husband, then in Paris: "Let me Imitate and instill into my children the Liberal Spirit of that great Man who declared he had no Local attachments. It is indifferent to me say[s] he whether a man is rocked in his cradle on this Side of the Tweed, or on that, I seek for merrit wherever it is to be found. Detested be national reflexions they are unjust." But that is not how she usually thought or behaved. In the spring of 1796, when apprised that her son was planning a London marriage, she wrote to him: "I would hope for the love I bear my Country, that the Syren is at least *half Blood*."[51]

In Quincy, Louisa Adams realized she really was in a foreign place, and not just because she was being treated as a foreigner. Church services were different, they sang oddly, they took dinner at a funny time, they had strange manners, the old men were weird. "Quincy!" she was later to write. "What shall I say of my impressions of Quincy! Had I step[p]ed into Noah's Ark I do not think I could have been more utterly astonished." In Berlin, she had had a role. With no little difficulty, because it was what her husband needed, she had learned to be a courtier, to dance, to play cards, to converse with princes, to remember rank. In Boston, his need changed. She was to be the wife of a lawyer of little means, as he had long told her might happen. "I must . . . always be ready at an hour's warning to return to . . . private life and no fortune," he had said in 1796. So "you too must be prepared in connecting yourself with me and in order to be well prepared for it, consider rank itself as an object of no consequence since it must go."[52]

In Massachusetts, wives were housekeepers. This was the role Abigail Adams had played for decades. In her husband's long absences, she had run the farm, fed the chickens, instructed the servants, churned the milk, darned the socks, kept the accounts. Even the grander house the Adamses had purchased in the late 1780s sat in a rough farmyard, where fowl wandered and cider was pressed. Housekeeping was not a role Louisa Adams relished, but, even if she had, it was a role everyone in Quincy thought she could not discharge, because she was deemed but a fine and useless lady. Even her husband thought so and arranged their new household in Boston accordingly, with affairs managed by himself, his steward Whitcomb, and his housekeeper Eppes. Louisa Adams was reduced to being an observer, with little responsibility. This was a contemptible position and she was aware of being regarded with contempt. So she had withdrawn into herself: "I became cold and reserved, and seldom spoke at all—which was deemed pride." Nonetheless, she tried to learn Boston ways and her husband even tried to teach her, but "all went wrong, and the more I fretted the worse things grew." As a foreigner, she was a burden that could not be lifted, because cultural habits were ineradicable, something she "could not repair." From this, she drew a cold, devastating lesson that seemed as pertinent in the 1830s as in 1802. "I state this," she wrote in her memoirs, "merely to show how imprudent it is for a woman to form a connection in a foreign Country."[53]

But the late autumn of 1801 was a difficult moment for her in-laws. It was only months since John Adams had left the new presidential mansion, after three decades of traveling, politicking, and global significance. After the glory that had been 1776, when he had been the chief mover for American independence, and the fame that had been 1783, when he had helped to consummate peace in Paris, the 1790s had been anticlimactic. For eight years, he had served with irritated irrelevance as George Washington's vice president. For four years, he had endured a miserable presidency, in which he had contrived to avoid war with France if not with members of his own party, but had been increasingly fixed in the public imagination as a closet monarchist, a friend to British designs upon American freedom, and a destroyer of civil liberty. In 1800, he had been humiliated by Thomas Jefferson's easy victory. Adams's vision of American politics and society, even then, seemed to be destined for oblivion. Jefferson was proclaiming 1800 as a revolutionary moment, a resumption of the freedoms that the Federalists had taken away. A gloomy man like John Adams found it easy to believe, not that Jefferson was right, but that Jefferson would persuade posterity.

"The only question remaining with me," he had presciently observed after his defeat, "is what shall I do with myself? Something I must do, or ennui will rain upon me in buckets." In truth, John Adams did little. In late 1801, he was becoming but a diffident and morose farmer who restlessly sat, randomly read, bitterly remembered, and glumly contemplated "how much wall I lay up every day." Even his wife missed the wider world. Once she had been frightened to leave her known circle of Braintree, Boston, and Weymouth, but she had come to experience Paris, London, and Philadelphia, where she had been an eager politician and even, almost, a lady of fashion. But she missed it far less, because she was more rooted in Quincy and cared more for "the beauties which my garden unfolds to my view from the window at which I now write; [these] tempt me to forget the past, and rejoice in the full bloom of the pear the Apple, the plumb, and peach, and the rich luxuriance of the grass plats; interspersed with the cowslip the daffy & Collombine, all unite to awaken the most pleasing sensations, and to raise the mind from nature, up to natures God."[54]

John Quincy Adams, too, was at an awkward moment. He was a no longer young ex-diplomat of minor accomplishment who was undertaking to become a lawyer, but with little interest in practicing law. His mother knew that this was "a humiliating prospect."[55] And like his wife but less drastically, he, too, was caught between worlds. If, then, to his wife, he seemed remorselessly Bostonian, it was partly instinct, but partly an effort of will. After all, he had long been an American abroad, a traveler who had come home with a quasi-foreign wife and a taste for Tokay. This was awkward for a son whose father had helped to invent America and who had been taught that it was his duty to advance the American cause and become a great man. A Boston lawyer was, no doubt, respectable, but he was not a great man.

When a child and a youth, he had been given a wilderness of mandates that had pointed him toward the summit, which in 1801 seemed unreachably remote. Be virtuous, write with a clear hand, learn mathematics, keep a diary, skate with elegance, study but do not imitate the ancients, preserve your innocence, lose no time, this and much more he had been told. When ten, he had received a letter from John Adams that read: "There is an observation, which I wish you to make very early in Life because it may be usefull to you, when you grow up. It is this, that a Taste for Literature and a Turn for Business, united in the same Person, never fails to make a great Man . . . I hope you will keep these two Objects in view all your Lifetime." When thirteen, he had been advised by his mother: "These are times in which a Genious would wish to live. It is not in the still calm of life, or the repose of a pacific station, but great characters are formed . . . Great necessities call out great virtues. When a mind is raised, and animated by scenes that engage the Heart, then those qualities which would otherwise lay dormant, waken into Life, and form the character of the Hero and the Statesman." Lest he miss the point, she was specific. "Nor ought it to be one of the least of your excitements towards exerting every power and faculty of your mind, that you have a parent who has taken so large and active a share in this contest, and discharged the trust reposed in him with so much satisfaction." A few months later, she added: "Justice, humanity and Benevolence are the duties you owe to society in general. To your Country the same duties are incumbent upon you with the additional obligations of sacrificing ease, pleasure, wealth and life itself for its defence and security."[56]

These were not negotiable mandates, for John and Abigail Adams believed in parental authority, as much as in parental love. As she put it, "To your parents you owe Love, reverence and obedience to all just and Equitable commands," and she was not a woman who often thought her commands unjust. As she explained in 1783, "Ever keep in mind my son, that your parents are your disinterested Friends, and if at any time their advise militates with your own opinion, or the advise of others, you ought always to be, diffident of your own judgment, because you may rest assured that their opinion is founded in experience, and long observation, and that they would not direct you; but to promote your happiness." This was a doctrine the son tensely accepted, for when a parent himself and explaining to the American Congress how society worked, he was to write: "The relations . . . between parent and child import subordination and government; on the one side authority, on the other obedience." In his own childhood, this parental authority had been most absolute when it came to morality. "I had much rather you should have found your Grave in the ocean you had crossed, or any untimely death crop you in your Infant years, rather than see you an immoral profligate or a Graceless child," his mother had observed in 1778, when he was ten. "The least Stain upon your Character will do more harm to your Happiness than all Accomplishments will do it good," his father had added in 1782. So he was supposed to be great, virtuous, and American, all at once, with no allowance for shortcoming. "Let your ambition be engaged to become eminent," his mother told the fourteen-year-old boy, "but above all things support a virtuous character, and remember that 'an Honest Man is the Noblest work of God.'" In this endeavor, his steps should be "undeviating."[57]

This training had driven him back upon himself, so that he never showed much interest in belonging. In The Hague, Berlin, Saint Petersburg, even Washington, he was a man who resented the salon, took solitary walks, and preferred the seclusion of his study. The central irony of his marriage was that, in the United States at least, a man who did not care about belonging did belong, and a woman who cared for little else did not. When in 1815 she left her friends in Berlin and traveled toward Leipzig, she was traveling toward a life of cultural loneliness.

This movement into the twilight was one reason why she liked the traveling, why later she remembered it with such fondness, and why she attributed so much importance to what she had done. It was not that, in traveling, she found places to belong, except perhaps Berlin. As she admitted, she was "*alone, and without rank*; a mere voyageuse."[58] It was that, for those forty days, she was under no pressure to belong. She gazed out of the windows of her carriage, she saw the passing scenes, she stopped to eat and rest, she coped with problems, and no one gave her orders, no one scowled at a faux pas, no one excluded her. For once, she was in control. The carriage left in the morning when she said; it stopped when she commanded. To be sure, the journey mimicked her life in that, over the years, she seemed always in transition and seldom at rest. In a deeper sense, however, it defied the pattern of her life, which had been marked by transitions she had not sought and changes she could not control.

Berlin to Leipzig

(From Aaron Arrowsmith, *Map Exhibiting the Great Post Roads,*
Physical and Political Divisions of Europe

[London: A. Arrowsmith, 1810])

Early on the morning of Saturday, March 11, she climbed into her battered but refurbished Russian berline and for about eighteen miles went southwest toward Potsdam. She went past the post station at Zehlendorf and through an avenue of very tall poplars, with the river Havel to her right. There she could see Peacock Island, where Frederick William II had once kept a mistress, built a small palace in the form of "a dilapidated Roman country manor," and constructed a dairy oddly disguised as a Gothic ruin, and which she had once visited. During the day and a half of her traveling to Leipzig, Mrs. Adams was to pass along roads that, for the first and last time since leaving Strelna, were familiar to her. For she had gone along this road once before, though in the opposite direction. In 1800, the Adamses had visited Silesia by going eastward from Berlin to Frankfurt on the Oder, and then looping through Silesia back to Dresden and up to Leipzig. Her memory of the latter part of the journey was painful, for she had been overexerted and fallen very ill on the way back. They had been forced to stay for five weeks in Leipzig until she had recovered and was able to proceed back to Berlin, via Potsdam, a town she had little frequented, for Frederick William III and Luise had favored the exquisite rococo palace of "divine Sanssouci" as a retreat. In 1815, Mrs. Adams would not have stopped except to change horses, cross the wooden bridge into the "thinly inhabited" and nostalgically melancholy town, and move onward to the southwest. Things went quietly on these sandy roads, though she became conscious of a need for alertness. They encountered here and there "small straggling parties of disbanded soldiers loitering home" and so her two male servants "rode on the box armed." On that first Saturday evening when it grew dark, she "put on my son's military cap and tall feather, and lay his sword across the window of the carriage, as I had been told that anything that looked military escaped from insult." At post stations, she would quietly remove what might, for a more leisurely observer, seem an implausibly ferocious habit for a lady.[59]

The first station was at Beelitz, a small market town locally famous for its white asparagus and surrounded by meadows, with a rough redbrick church and old timber-framed houses curiously painted (wattle and daub of light pea green, wooden frames of dark green, and doors of yellow). The second station was at Treuenbrietzen, odiferous with a tannery, a brewery, a distillery, and manufacturers of woolens. The town's medieval walls had disappeared, but her carriage still had to enter through a gate, beside which stood a round medieval tower. Treuenbrietzen itself was little more than a very long street, along which were distributed more timber-framed houses and, halfway down, a town hall of unexpected height. The third station was at Kropstadt, set in a "forest of firs." By this time the livery of her postilions had changed from Prussian blue and orange to "the long yellow coat and large cocked hat" of the kingdom of Saxony. A few more miles and she could see the double octagonal spires of the Stadtkirche St. Marien, which sat on the ample market square of Wittenberg. This would have been a logical place to stop overnight, for she was then about halfway to Leipzig. However, Wittenberg was little enticing, for it had been besieged by the Allies in 1814 and much devastated, its Schlosskirche all but destroyed and its suburbs ravaged. "It is fast sinking into ruin, and nothing about it looked neat or in repair" is how one visitor described the town five years later. But to call it, as another traveler was to do, "insignificant as a town, unimportant as a fortress, and not very celebrated as a university" was harsh.[60]

Here Mrs. Adams began to enter the heartland of the German Reformation. In Wittenberg, in Leipzig, and in Thuringia beyond, she would be surrounded by stern Lutheran churches, gilded memorials to vanished martyrs, lofty pipe organs, and black leaden spires. The Schlosskirche, where in 1517 Martin Luther had nailed up his ninety-five theses, now contained his grave. Mrs. Adams liked to visit churches, although the Lutheran were low on her list, partly because she came to have a low opinion of martyrs, for tending "to inflame the arrogant passions of mankind, and to introduce schisms and heresies, calculated only to injure the religion, which they profess to amend." But she was very religious, becoming more so as she aged, until as an old woman she spent much time worrying about theology and writing religious poetry. Her own father had been a Unitarian, "but as those opinions were at that time much decried; he took particular pains to educate his Children in the Episcopal form as in regard to women he always said there was little danger in believing; there was *destruction* in doubt." In France as a girl, she had been educated by nuns and came back to England marked by "the strong impression made upon my imagination by the Roman Catholick Church," and remembering "the heartfelt humility with which I knelt before the Image of the tortured Jesus and the horror I felt at the thought of mixing with hereticks." This had been knocked out of her, but not entirely. Later she wavered about the merits of Catholic ritual, usually liking the music, sometimes liking the pomp, and often mistrusting the appeal to ignorant awe. But she never lost her need for a Christ who assumed the sufferings of the world, and who promised an afterlife free of pain.[61]

When she had married, custom expected her to attend whatever church was favored by her husband, which in Massachusetts meant the Congregationalists, but in Washington later usually meant the Unitarians or the nondenominational services held at the Capitol. When abroad, in Berlin and Saint Petersburg, the Adamses went together to the only English-speaking services available, which were

Anglican; this liturgy, for the most part, came closest to her taste and belief, though she mistrusted the sectarian and imagined that Christianity transcended denomination. But though they worshipped together in church and prayed together at home, the Adamses did not agree on religion, a difference of opinion of which she was more conscious than he was. She was less of a Puritan and "not fond of the old Puritan character" because "unnecessarily harsh, and unrelenting," although she respected the Puritans' sincerity and resistance to "mere worldly pursuits." She was much less a rationalist than her husband, but tried to believe in faith, simplicity, and practicality. She came very close to being anti-intellectual when it came to religion. Like most of her generation, she was an aficionado of sermons, and she disliked preachers who chopped logic, dissected texts, and demanded philosophical agility.[62]

At times, she attributed these differences to gender. In 1836, she was to take great exception to "a stiff Unitarian Minister who conversed very freely with Mr. Adams upon creeds of course condemning all but their own." Unusually, because irritated, she entered the argument. Afterward, she worried that her arguments had been unclear, but consoled herself that women tended to see to the heart of a matter, for "they come at correct conclusion with more ease, and frequently with more force, than the more highly and elaborately educated." Was it not true that "women dislike argument, and seldom know how to reason with perspicuity"? Rather, "they seize a question in its simplest form; and their opinion is rapid, and fixed." By contrast, "men reason pro and con until they bewilder themselves, and rather shake their own opinions than settle them." Indeed, "I have seldom met with a man at any period, who could *positively* and *honestly* answer what his religion was? They almost always evade the question or begin to talk of *religion*, without reverting to their own belief—With them it is rarely a feeling, therefore seldom a fix[ed] principle." And she was convinced that fixed feeling or faith was indispensable to the efficacy of religion, not only as a social force, but as a psychological necessity. Above all, for her religion was a balm for pain, both of body and mind. But especially of mind, for Christianity promised heart's ease. As she put it in 1813, "In religion alone have I found a gleam of comfort and in God who gives us strength to bear up against the afflictions which assail us in our passage through this vale of tears do I put my trust."[63]

From Wittenberg, Louisa had a choice of various routes, though it was usual to go through Kemberg, Duben, and Krensitz, mostly through forests, in one of which in 1804 one could puzzlingly have "read on a board an inscription, forbidding the emigrants from Wirtemberg to injure the trees."[64] She did not travel well, for Saxon roads were inferior to Prussian and she was to complain of a fatiguing journey. The road through the forest north of Duben ("a large, dirty, and scattered town") was little more than a track. "Did ever a traveler pass over this district without complaining of, and cursing the Saxon roads?" Kotzebue had asked, in the days before the elector of Saxony had become a king, and received an implausible explanation from his Wittenberg postilion: "'Why, says he,' putting some burning timber on his pipe, and enveloping my sullen complaints in a cloud of smoke, 'if the roads are so bad, it is because the Elector is a catholic; the Prince of Dessau would have changed that long ago.'"[65]

She reached the "level, well-cultivated, monotonous country" upon which Leipzig stood by the late evening of Sunday, March 12. She saw what her husband had once pleasantly described as "a small compact town, containing about thirty thousand inhabitants." It was surrounded by rivers and canals, and once by flourishing orchards and gardens, all placed where the old medieval walls had been. These "intricate mazes of . . . natural as well as artificial water-ways" were especially visible from the direction from which she came, for "on the north and west, [there was] a triple and natural barrier of water formed by the Parde, the Pleisse, and the Elster rivers."[66] But much had changed since 1800, when she and her husband had last been in Leipzig. Now she was traversing part of what had been one of the most calamitous battlefields of European history. For three days in mid-October 1813, some 200,000 French troops weary from a hard victory at Dresden had fought over 300,000 Allied soldiers. For two days, there had been a stalemate, with Napoleon having some 25,000 casualties, the Allies 30,000. On the third, with reinforcements arriving, the Allies had brutally prevailed, at the cost of still more carnage—40,000 killed and wounded for the French, some 54,000 for the Allies. In the final stages, with the French retreating across the Elster River to the northwest of the city, their engineers had placed explosives to destroy the bridge and hamper pursuit, but had detonated too early and killed many on the bridge itself. The explosion also trapped thousands of the Grande Armée on the wrong side. The Allies took about 30,000 prisoners.[67]

For ten miles around the city, there had been devastation. All the horses and cattle, all the pigs and sheep, had been killed or taken, the wheat fields stripped or burned. In some sixty villages, almost all the houses had been burned or demolished for firewood, their walls had become sites for attack and defense, their windows had been broken and converted into loopholes. The area acquired what one observer mournfully described as "a peculiar and repulsive physiognomy, resulting from such a variety of heterogeneous objects . . . The relics of torches, the littered and trampled straw, the bones and flesh of slaughtered animals, fragments of plates, a thousand articles of leather, tattered cartouche-boxes, old rags, clothes thrown away, all kinds of harness, broken muskets, shattered waggons and carts, weapons of all sorts, thousands of men dead and dying, horribly mangled bodies of men and horses,—and all these intermingled." The remnants of horses had soon disappeared, because horses were edible and famine had been the immediate aftermath of the battle. But after sixteen months human skeletons lingered, since burying the dead was then an episodic and voluntary activity of Christian peasants and not the business of governments, and peasants were often more interested in picking clean the bodies than in consecrating them to God. A battlefield was a site for entrepreneurs. Children collected lead bullets, cobblers "cut the covers off cartridge pouches to use for boots and soles," blacksmiths "pulled iron off empty powder-boxes and ammunition waggons, as well as horseshoes," and everyone looked for money. But even on an aging battlefield much remained, such as "discarded, rusty weapons and overturned wagons," and embedded cannonballs, too heavy to filch. And still missing were the fences that had been stripped and the trees that had been cut down for firewood. And beyond this recovering wasteland lay the scarred Halle Gate, still peppered with shot, by which she entered the city.[68]

From her experience in 1800, she would have remembered Leipzig at peace, as a place of books, students, and commerce, for it was the center of German publishing, had a famous university, and three times a year held a great fair, whose attendants could double the city's population. What she would have been unlikely to remember is that it had once been the home of Johann Sebastian Bach, for in 1815 few cared about Bach. The city's reputation was stubbornly commercial and not musical, which would not change until Felix Mendelssohn came to Leipzig in 1835 and revived the memory of the old Kapell-meister's cantatas. In 1815, the city's streets were scattered with "young coxcombs," who were enrolled as students, and full of bookshops, piled high with confusing stacks of new, old, and pirated books, even some in English, for the local publishers did not mind whether it was the copyright of Friedrich Schiller or Walter Scott they violated. Especially around the great marketplace, the city's houses were an arresting mix of old and new. The old houses were "highly decorated with fret-work, in the old German style," often six stories high. For Goethe, as a young student, they had seemed "immense . . . embracing a citizen-world within their large courtyards, built around with lofty walls . . . like large castles, nay, even half-cities." The new houses, in the unsympathetic opinion of an English traveler, bespoke "the progress of taste and luxury amongst the matter-of-fact, plodding and calculating people who inhabit them."[69]

The best inn in Leipzig was the Hotel de Saxe and, there or elsewhere, Mrs. Adams would have been presented with a dinner menu that would, almost certainly, have included "uncommonly delicious larks," the local delicacy. And she would have passed "a porter at the street-door, with a cocked hat and a halbert like an English sergeant-major." It was usual for hotels at dinner time to be frequented by professors and students, plus "mercantile travelers, or merchants of the town" who, struggling against the background of a musical band, talked about business and picked their teeth with table forks.[70]

On Monday, March 13, she took a letter of credit to Frege and Company, the city's most notable bankers. They had interests not only in Germany, but in Russia and the United States, and John Quincy Adams had used them from as long ago as the 1790s. The firm's patriarch, Christian Gottlob Frege, the second of that name, inhabited a great baroque mansion on the Katherinenstrasse and this doubled as the bank, so it was there that she went for ducats for her journey. It is likely that she departed promptly on the same day, for she was to reach Frankfurt late on the evening of Thursday, March 16, and had to traverse mountainous terrain. It is improbable that she could have traveled the 250 miles of that "great commercial road" in fewer than three days. In 1809, it took the exiled American Aaron Burr, ascending the mountain to Eisenach, eight and a half hours to cover twenty-three miles, in part because when a carriage had to climb a steep hill, commonly passengers got out and walked, so that the horses had less weight to pull.[71]

After leaving the plain on which Leipzig stood, this stretch furnished a landscape that was designated then as picturesque—fertile valleys, quaint villages, forests of oak and fir, rolling hills. But she was also covering the scorched earth over which Napoleon had swept

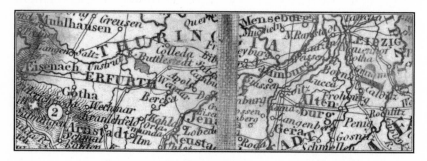

Leipzig to Eisenach

(From Aaron Arrowsmith, *Map Exhibiting the Great Post Roads, Physical and Political Divisions of Europe* [London: A. Arrowsmith, 1810]. The Arrowsmith map indicates no direct road from Erfurt to Eisenach, though such a road did exist in 1815)

in 1806, then been driven back in 1813. War had been a habitual pre-occupation of this region and its writers, notably Schiller, who had been drawn to the Thirty Years' War as an allegory of human folly. Mrs. Adams would pass many grim war memorials. Near the village of Lützen there was the Schwedenstein, or "Stone of the Swede," a collection of ancient rough stones shaped into a cross, out of which arose more stones, on which was carved "Gustavus Adolphus, king of Sweden, fell here, for liberty of conscience." It lay in a field, was surrounded by poplars, and was furnished with turf benches so that Protestant travelers might linger to muse on "the deeds and the fate of a heroic and chivalrous monarch," and Catholics contemplate a great and destructive heretic. After this, she entered the valley of the Saal River, and on each side were hills, gently rising and culti-vated with orchards and vineyards. Approaching Weissenfels, she crossed the river on a long and handsome bridge and then her car-riage slowly climbed a steep hill, went through the city gate, entered the modest square, and passed beneath an old castle, in the vaults of which moldered the coffins of many ancient, unremembered dukes. Beyond Weissenfels, she continued along the bank of the Saal and passed by more fruit trees and vines, until she reached Naum-burg, a larger and more commercial town, but with the usual supply of meticulous churches. After Naumburg, she recrossed the Saal at Kosen and ascended the high pass over the mountain before de-scending to Auerstedt, then passed on to Weimar, the epicenter of German civilization.[72]

It was customary for American and other visitors to call upon the last survivor of classical Weimar, for Goethe was politely hospitable and liked to talk, and this was one of the seasons (winter and spring) when he was in residence. In earlier years, the illuminati of Weimar had been so much vexed by travelers that the poet Christoph Wieland once received Nikolai Karamzin with great coldness and felt it neces-sary to explain himself. "It has become a fashion in Germany to travel with no other view than that of publishing ones travels," he said. "These travelers, whose number is not small, go from one town to another, and endeavour to introduce themselves to celebrated persons, only with the intention of afterwards printing what they hear from them." This was not a game played by Mrs. Adams and it was generally true that women played the game less often. Further, her acquaintanceship with German intellectual culture was intermittent. When in Prussia, her husband had acquired a reading knowledge of German, collected a good working library of German literature, and even translated Wieland's *Oberon*, Friedrich von Gentz's *Origins and Principles of the American Revolution*, and several of Christian Gellert's fables. Among the two hundred German titles John Quincy Adams owned, works by the luminaries of Weimar (Goethe, Schiller, Herder) were conspicuous. But for lack of funds, Mrs. Adams had taken no German lessons when earlier in Berlin, nor did she seem to read translations of German works, for there are very few references to German authors in her letters, diaries, and miscellaneous writings. (A Gothic poem of hers in the late 1830s mentions Goethe and Schiller, but glancingly.) To be sure, she did reluctantly attend the German theater, so she had some acquaintance with various plays by Klopstock, Kotzebue, and the rest. Nonetheless, for a woman who read widely in English and French literature, she was mostly indifferent to the German, beyond the indirect influence upon her of its partiality for ghosts, hobgoblins, and guilt.[73]

More relevant to how she might have behaved in Weimar is that, though she cared for books, she seems to have cared little for meeting authors. In 1804, for example, she read Madame de Staël's *Delphine* with fastidious disapproval—"the language is most beautiful but the morals appear to me detestable"—but when the Swiss lady passed through Saint Petersburg in 1812, her husband went to call but Mrs. Adams did not. Any number of authors crossed her path—Thomas Moore, Joseph de Maistre, Thomas Jefferson, John Marshall—but she seldom responded to them as authors. Later in life, she ran the nearest thing to a salon that Washington possessed, but it was a social and not an intellectual salon, however much she was willing to talk about her reading with whoever was interested. Insecurity had much to do with this diffidence about authors, for she feared that she might possess but "an erroneous education, a narrow mind, or an exaggerated sensibility." In 1842, when Charles Dickens came to lunch in Washington, she was mostly silent. "Dickens is an unpresuming lively and agreeable man," she wrote to her daughter-in-law, "and seemed perfectly delighted with the conversation of his Host . . . Of course in the presence of my superiors I could have but little conversation with them."[74]

So, though it is possible she stayed that Monday night in Weimar, for it was nearly a third of her way to Frankfurt from Leipzig, the likelihood is that she did little more than glance at the grand duke's palace and the theater, and otherwise have occasion to reflect that the town's literary reputation then exceeded its urban amenities. Its streets were thought by some to be "narrow, crooked, and ill-paved," and it was said that "the inhabitants . . . [took] a pride in having it considered merely as a large village."[75] What is known, with more certainty, is that she continued her journey deeper and higher into the Thuringian Forest past Erfurt and Gotha. Eventually she reached Eisenach, where she stayed the night.[76]

In Eisenach the world of her journey began to fall apart.

Eisenach and Wartburg (ca. 1700)

(Artist unknown. Courtesy of André Nestler)

5

FROM EISENACH TO FRANKFURT

W HAT MOST TRAVELERS KNEW about Eisenach was that its citadel had once kept Martin Luther hidden from a hostile world in what Samuel Taylor Coleridge called "a friendly imprisonment." In the high fastness of the Wartburg, the monk had translated the New Testament into German. But what struck most visitors about Eisenach was not its history, but its beauty. It lay in a valley surrounded by high ridges and forests, "many steep declivities, and lofty precipices," and nearby ran a tumbling river, sights that made travelers pause to contemplate "the primitive wildness of nature" in a place that seemed remote from the world's cares. The town itself had handsome houses, well-paved streets, and a large and inviting square, though the medieval walls were "in decay," which only added to its romantic appeal.[1]

However, 1815 was not a good time for Eisenach. The city had been on the road that Napoleon had taken eastward in 1806 to Jena and Berlin, in April 1813 to Dresden and Leipzig, and in October 1813 westward back toward Paris. The town had often seen the Grande Armée pass through, with its hundreds of thousands of troops, its cannon, its hospital wagons, its camp followers, and then seen Prussian and Russian troops pursuing them in the other direction. This had been more than an interesting spectacle, fit for curious children.

These armies, friend or foe, lived off the land. Wherever the column halted, magazines were established, and commissaries fanned out to strip bare the surrounding countryside and replenish "the bread and forage waggons." It was not just that chickens and potatoes were seized, cupboards and chests broken open, and every place "where troops spent a night lost doors, roof-thatch, straw from the barns, stocks of dry firewood, and furniture." It was that people fled, "so an army's route was marked by abandoned villages, half-demolished homesteads and mutilated trees." Arson was habitual.[2]

Eisenach, too, had been brutally raided for supplies, sex, and amusement. In 1810, a munitions wagon had passed along the Georgenstrasse in the center of the town and exploded; dozens of houses had been destroyed and sixty people killed. In late October 1813, Napoleon had returned there in haste and defeat, paused a night, and moved onward toward the Rhine. Along the road that led from Lützen to Eisenach and beyond, the disciplined corps that accompanied the swiftly moving emperor was followed by thousands of straggling and abandoned fugitives, sick and hungry, wounded and dying. Dazed with pain, many had wandered aimlessly into the Thuringian Forest, and there lay down to rot in the snow. In some places the roads had become impassable because of dead and dying men, dead and dying horses, and "blown up or destroyed ammunition and baggage waggons." The road that led from Eisenach to Fulda had been especially bad. "The dead and dying were frequently mixed together, lying in groups of six or eight, by half extinguished fires, by the road side," and, beside a corpse, there could sometimes be observed a rough walking stick, once used for hobbling.[3]

Amid this systematic carnage had been casual murder. Along Mrs. Adams's route from Eisenach, a French captain of the Fourth Regiment of the Line had noticed a wounded soldier briefly coming out of a house "to answer a call of nature," and, as he had reentered the house, "a pannier on a passing horse struck him right on the wound, which reopened." He had gone up to his room on the second floor, jumped from the window, and been killed by his fall, only a few feet from the captain. Above, in the window, a face had appeared and some soldiers had cried out that this peasant had thrown down the wounded man. They dragged him from the house, took him a hundred yards beyond the village, and shot him. The captain protested, but no one listened. "The staff officer who had taken the matter in hand insisted that he and no one else was right," and so the retreat went on, heedlessly.[4]

In 1819, at the first village beyond Eisenach, the postmaster was to remember the occasion when he had seen Napoleon on his return from the Russian campaign. The emperor had paused to change horses, but, like any common traveler, had been forced to delay. The horses were in a far pasture and had to be caught, brought to the post station, and fed. Napoleon stood sulkily, mostly silent except for the occasional expression of impatience. As he waited, he took great quantities of snuff, "till his clothes were completely besmeared with it." I saw Napoleon three times, the postmaster was to say, "the first in his glory on his way to Russia; the second time, in despair when he returned from thence alone; and the last time, in his fury after the battle of Leipsic, when my house, as well as every other in the town, was burnt by his orders, after all the provisions in them that were moveable had been taken away." Further down the road at Buttlar, the mistress of the post station had similar tales, of Napoleon passing through on five occasions, of houses being burned, and of the emperor's staying in her inn for two days in late 1813. That "he and his attendants ate and drank all she had, and paid nothing" was the least of her complaints.[5]

When Mrs. Adams reached Eisenach, she saw "a fortified town, once probably strong, but now in ruins, miserably conditioned, but guarded at its dilapidated gates by soldiers." She was tired, for it had been a long, uphill, and winding climb. So she decided to stay the night, possibly in La Klemme, which was part of an old château, but perhaps elsewhere. She climbed down from her carriage, entered the inn with Charles Francis and Madame Babet, and took a small chamber with two beds, one for herself, one to be shared by her son and the nurse.[6]

In conversation with the innkeeper, she was told of a rumor, though in a light tone, jokingly. Innkeepers were given stories by travelers, coming and going, and it was part of their trade to pass the stories on, suspecting they might be false, knowing they might be entertaining. Anyway, the innkeeper said, there was a story circulating that Napoleon had left the Mediterranean island of Elba, where he had been quarantined by the Allied Powers for nearly a year, and landed in France. Contrary to the innkeeper's tone, Mrs. Adams took the story seriously. This was not because she knew anything definite, but because she was superstitious. She remembered something from her last days in Saint Petersburg.[7]

On the Friday evening of February 10, two days before her departure, she had gone to take a farewell tea with Condesa Colombi. To her surprise, she found that the countess had a guest, who had come to stay, uninvited, for a few days. This was Countess Ekaterina Vladimirovna Apraxin, by marriage related to Peter the Great's famous admiral Fydor Apraxin and by birth Princess Galitzin, and hence doubly a great aristocrat. Since 1793, she had been married to Count Stepan Stepanovich Apraxin, who, for the most part, lived comfortably and hospitably in Moscow in a palace recently rebuilt, with an ample quantity of domes and porticoes. It had room for about five hundred residents or, as one visiting Frenchman amiably preferred to put it, a ridiculous number of parasites. The original had been burned down in 1812, when the city had been put to the torch. "That stately edifice," the count had told an English visitor, "was built in twenty-two successive years; it was destroyed in as many hours, and yet before twenty-two months are expired shall be renewed in the same state as before." The countess's son Vladimir had served in the Russian army in the campaigns of 1813, as aide-de-camp to the minister of war, and had been in the tsar's suite in Erfurt, a few miles from Eisenach. The countess was famous enough that, many years later, when writing *War and Peace*, Leo Tolstoy alluded to her, when Moscow society ladies were idly talking of "scandal, the weather and Countess Apraksin."[8]

Because the countess usually lived in Moscow, Mrs. Adams had never met her and was put out that this final parting from an old friend was thus disrupted. She was the more discomfited because the countess was "a fat coarse woman," who talked too much, mostly repeating scandal of who was sleeping with whom. After tea was done, since there was to be a journey, the countess insisted on telling the departing American's fortune. So the usual cards were laid out and Louisa was asked to choose a queen. At this, the countess launched into an inventive exposition, which caused great merriment. She observed that Mrs. Adams was very glad to be leaving Saint Petersburg, which was scarcely a secret, any more than that she was going to meet those from whom she had been separated. But then the prognostication took an unexpected turn. The countess said that, about halfway through the journey, Louisa would be "much alarmed by a great change in the political world, in consequence of some extraordinary movement of a great man which would produce utter consternation, and set all Europe into a fresh commotion." News of this would come to her "on the road," and she would be obliged to change her plans. The journey would become "very difficult," though she would make it through. At this, Mrs. Adams had laughed and expressed polite skepticism. For, as she explained, her journey was a simple one, Europe was at peace, and, anyway, she was not important enough to attract attention. So the ladies had laughed, but the countess had been serious and, when they had parted, had reiterated the point and requested that Mrs. Adams remember what the cards had said.[9]

In Eisenach, she did remember. Yet the innkeeper's tale was no more than a rumor, a fat countess's gossipy whim might mean nothing, and Napoleon was not Europe's only great man. But the memory of the cards was distracting, and when she went to her bedchamber and locked the door on the three of them, she did something she had not done before. She left her purse, with some gold in it, on the table next to a lamp. In the morning, the purse was there, but the gold was gone.[10]

So she left Eisenach with more urgency than usual. Down the forested mountainside she passed, hastily going through Berka, Vach, Hunefeld, the baroque munificence of episcopal Fulda, and Gelnhausen. She passed granite cliffs, red clay fields, "lofty and often

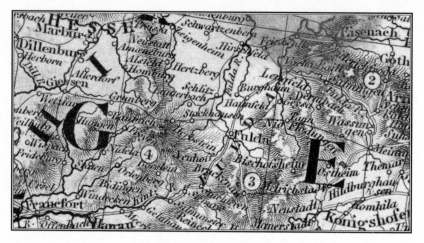

Eisenach to Frankfurt

(From Aaron Arrowsmith, *Map Exhibiting the Great Post Roads, Physical and
Political Divisions of Europe* [London: A. Arrowsmith, 1810])

abrupt hills," narrow valleys, forests of beech, and burned villages
that had only just been rebuilt. At each stop when changing horses,
the rumor about Napoleon was elaborated. Past Gelnhausen, she entered the dark of the Lamboi Forest and then suddenly emerged onto
a wide plain. A mile ahead of her was Hanau, encircled to its north,
east, and west by the river Kinzig, and which was entered along her
route by a narrow bridge.[11]

As she crossed the plain, next to the road she saw ditches and, in
them, innumerable graves marked with crosses. In the newly plowed
fields around, she looked across the rich black soil to see scattered
remnants of clothes, old boots in pieces, military caps, and "an immense quantity of bones." The postilion pointed to a board, which
explained that "this was the Field of battle, where the Bavarians had
intercepted the retreat of Napoleon, and that in this plain, ten thousand men had been slain." Perhaps because the plowing had starkly
thrown up this detritus of war, perhaps because the rumors were unsettling her, this sight affected her more than those she had seen before, at Leipzig and at Lützen. Now she felt nauseated and faint; her
pulse raced. It seemed suddenly real to her—the suffering, pain, and
death, all "the savage barbarity" of war.[12]

In 1813, Napoleon, too, had come down the post road from Eisenach and at Hanau encountered an Austro-Bavarian army of thirty
thousand men and fifty-eight cannon, a force commanded by Marshal Karl Wrede. Formerly, Bavaria had been Napoleon's ally: Wrede
had led its troops at the emperor's side at the battle of Wagram in
1809, and he had received the emperor's preferment. But only a few
weeks earlier, sides had been switched. Bavaria had attached itself to
the Allies, and its troops were part of the vanguard harassing the
French retreat. Arriving at Hanau from the east, Wrede did not expect to encounter Napoleon himself, who was supposed to be retreating into France along a northerly route. At best, Wrede anticipated a
smaller, flanking French army. Too casually, he deployed his men
east of Hanau, which he left unoccupied. Napoleon had about seven-
teen thousand men, scarcely more than half those available to Wrede.
But it proved more than enough. The emperor had the advantage of
surprise because his approach was masked by the forest, and he rapidly grasped that his enemy's position was very weak. Wrede's army
was concentrated too far to the south and was divided by a narrow
bridge that made rapid redeployment difficult, and its northern flank
was placed with its back to a river that cut off any retreat, save at the
Hanau bridge. (Napoleon is said to have remarked that he had been
able to make Wrede a count, but not a general.) The French victory
was decisive, so much so that Napoleon left the mopping up and occupation of the town to his subordinates. Wrede lost about ten thousand men, perhaps more, most dying on the field upon which Mrs.
Adams looked with such dismay, many drowning in the river when
trying to retreat. "This battle was one of the most murderous in this
campaign," a contemporary historian observed. "Eye-witnesses declare, that at no other place, not even at Leipsic, were so many dead
bodies found in an equal space." The town itself was taken and re-
taken several times and its suburbs were, past the moment when Mrs.
Adams was there, "still in ruins from conflagration."[13]

Reaching Hanau, she came to understand that the rumor of Napoleon's return was undoubted. For she was questioned closely by the
Hessian authorities, had to wait three or four hours for horses, and

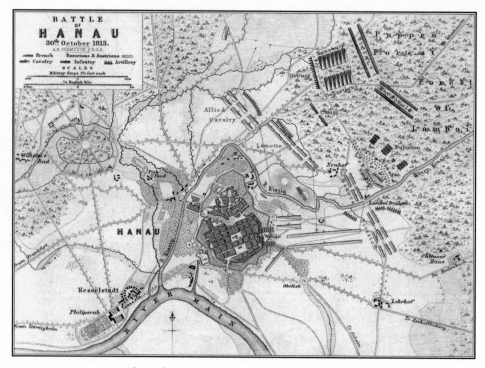

Alexander Keith Johnston, *The Battle of Hanau*
(From Archibald Alison and Alexander Keith Johnston, *Atlas to Alison's History of Europe*
[Edinburgh: William Blackwood, 1850], plate 90)

saw around her "measures . . . for calling the disbanded Troops together." It was now the afternoon of Thursday, March 16. As she was
beginning to learn, Napoleon had set sail from Elba on board the brig
L'Inconstant on February 26, more than two weeks earlier, when Mrs.
Adams had been somewhere in east Prussia. He had landed in the
south of France at Golfe Juan, near Cape Antibes and Cannes, on
March 1, when she was still three days short of reaching Berlin. He
had but 1,026 men with him and, at first, many were unclear about
his strength and purposes. It was widely thought he had only fifty
men, and some believed he would be heading for Naples and its king,
his old marshal and brother-in-law Joachim Murat.[14]

A courier had been dispatched from Genoa toward Austria with a report that Napoleon had gone missing from Elba, though with no information as to his destination. In Vienna, at six o'clock on the morning of March 7, Metternich was woken up by his valet and handed the urgent dispatch, which he ignored and laid on his bedside table. He slept on and off for an hour, then picked up the letter, opened it, and immediately rushed to see the emperor Francis. More exact news had reached Paris and Louis XVIII just after noon two days earlier. Late on that evening of March 5, when the literary forger Étienne Léon Lamothe-Langon was at the theater, he was summoned from his box by Comte Regnaud de Saint-Jean d'Angély. The two stood in the corridor and the comte whispered conspiratorially, "He has landed." Who "he" was required no elaboration. Many in Paris knew the bare news on the next morning, but not all. John Quincy Adams was only told of it on March 7, a few hours after Metternich, when Adams went to the Hôtel de l'Empire to visit a sick American diplomat, suffering with a cough and fever. "Mr. Bayard first mentioned to me that Bonaparte was in France," he noted laconically in his diary. "The proclamation of the King, declaring him a rebel and traitor, is in the Moniteur of this morning."[15]

On March 7, Mrs. Adams was still in Berlin, there reminiscing about old wars and oblivious of new ones. At nine on that same evening, Napoleon entered the gates of Grenoble, after the troops defending the city had switched allegiances. He now had an army grown to eight thousand men. By the time she reached Leipzig on March 12, he had reached Lyons, now with fourteen thousand troops, and left it the next day in a calèche drawn by six horses and flanked by "Polish lancers in red-and-gold uniforms." In the circumstances, it is surprising that it took until her arrival in Eisenach, which at the earliest was on the night of March 14, before any information reached her. By then, Bonaparte was on the road to Mâcon. In Paris the next day, March 15, John Quincy Adams was observing: "The public spirit in Paris now is confident and sanguine. It does not appear that Napoleon has advanced from Lyons. He is undoubtedly there, very weak; and formidable forces are marching from all quarters against him."

By March 16, when Mrs. Adams stood impatiently hoping for post-horses in Hanau, Napoleon was approaching Auxerre, more than three hundred miles to her southwest.[16]

As she waited, the people around her talked freely. That she understood little German and found it easier to converse in French doubtless skewed her listening, but she found that the talkative people were oddly proud of what Napoleon and his officers had accomplished during the battle of Hanau. She was given a narrative, especially of the struggle over the Hanau bridge, which it had taken three attempts by the French to seize. Outside the post station, they pointed out to her the scars of three cannonballs lodged in the fabric of the house. They remembered the French officers, whom they had been proud to quarter.[17]

Her servants listened and watched as she conversed. Baptiste, who had been to Russia and back, knew about war and had lost his taste for it. He and John Fulling "began to grow uneasy, and frequently talked about conscripts, and a renewal of the Wars." She noticed this, but was more preoccupied by her puzzlement, the same she had felt in Kustrin. "It was a very remarkable fact that in the course of my journey," she remembered later, "I heard but little praise of the Allied Armies, and unceasing admiration of the exploits of the French." It was puzzling because suffering and devastation had followed, wherever the French had appeared, and these crimes "seem to have [been] white washed . . . from their minds." What they did remember and did not forgive were "the renowned cruelties, and barbarities, of the Cossacks." What she neglected to understand, perhaps, was that the Allies were usually the last army to pass through, so memory of them was often freshest, and what they did could be the last, bitter blow. A schoolmaster in Buttlar certainly remembered that "the French in their retreat had eaten, carried away, or destroyed all the provisions that were above ground." But they left untouched the potatoes, buried in the soil and intended for winter provisions. The Russians had come and dug them up, and when winter came, a third of the local population of 1,500 had starved to death.[18]

Eventually, the six horses came and her carriage went quickly the last ten miles to Frankfurt am Main over a "luxuriant plain," past fields planted with wheat, rye, and potatoes. To her right, the Taunus Mountains rose gently. To her left, next to the river Main, were "handsome gentlemen's residences," for the city's businessmen had built themselves rich villas in the suburbs. But she looked very little at the landscape, because she was preoccupied with what she had heard and seen, especially the mustering of soldiers. She realized that there was a newly urgent atmosphere, part expectation, part fear: "There was a life and animation; altogether different from the dull monotony, which had pervaded all the former part of my travels."[19]

She entered through the elegant Obermain Gate and proceeded straight over the Langestrasse and down the Allerheiligen to the Zeil, the city's wide and central promenade, then perhaps beyond to the Parade Platz and the Rossmarkt. There were many hotels from which to choose, many of them on the Zeil. The city had well over forty thousand inhabitants and it attracted travelers going in Mrs. Adams's direction, but also those coming up and down the Rhine. "As the principal high roads of Germany lead through this city, all the persons of consequence . . . generally take Francfort in their way," Wilhelm Render had observed in 1801. The most common resorts for English-speaking visitors were the Maison Rouge and La Cour de l'Angleterre ("the most showy looking inn").[20] At the former, Thomas Jefferson had stayed in 1788, when it had been managed by John Adam Dick and was famous for "all Sorts of Genuine Hock or Rhenish Wine." It was very large, and it was not unusual when dinner was served at one o'clock each day for several hundred people to sit down together, both visitors and locals, noble and merchant. It was the custom that, during dinner, in the gallery a band should play, "occasionally accompanied with songs by ladies, who sometimes also play solos on the French horn."[21]

She arrived in the evening and the next morning wrote two letters. The first was to her Frankfurt banker to request an interview. The second was to her husband, in which she expressed her "severe disappointment in not receiving Letters more especially as the public

News renders my situation extremely unpleasant." Her irritation was understandable, though the logistics of correspondence were not easy. It was now March 17 and it was only five days earlier that, in Paris, John Quincy Adams had received her last letter from Saint Petersburg of February 12, and that from Riga and Memel of February 17/20, which had reached him on the same day. On March 15, he got her letter from Berlin of ten days earlier with its estimate that she would reach Paris "in ten or fifteen days."[22] So he expected her to reach Paris either immediately or by March 20.

She explained to him that it was her plan to leave for Mayence that evening, stay there overnight, leave at five in the morning, and then travel day and night to Paris. So "you must expect me very soon."

Between writing these words and seeing the banker, she had visitors. Baptiste and John Fulling asked to see her. They said that "circumstances having totally changed," they needed to resign her service. In Frankfurt, they might find work. In France, they might only find conscription into Napoleon's army. She tried to talk them out of it and offered them more money, but "no bribe could induce them to go on in their state of Panic." So, instead, she asked that they delay their going until she had taken the counsel of the banker.[23]

Almost immediately, he appeared. This was no ordinary functionary, but Simon Moritz von Bethmann, "le roi de Frankfort," among the richest of persons in a city that was the home of the Rothschilds, a city that, unusually, had prospered from the Napoleonic wars and was one of Europe's few viable banking centers.[24] For years, the great and the good had frequented Bethmann's home. It had been at a ball at Bethmann's in 1792 that the crown prince of Prussia had first set newly longing eyes on Luise of Mecklenberg-Strelitz. In 1813, on its way to conquer France for the first time, the Allied army had paused in Frankfurt and its leadership had availed itself of Bethmann's prudent generosity, so much so that the tsar had an affair with the banker's wife, Louise Henriette, whom Metternich unkindly called "a Dutch cow." Among other things, Bethmann was the Russian consul general to the Rheinbund, so being the tsar's cuckold was an inconvenience of his office.[25]

Johann Jakob de Lose, *Simon Moritz von Bethmann* (1812)

(Institut für Stadtgeschichte, Frankfurt am Main)

Needing an adviser at a moment of crisis, Mrs. Adams could not have fared much better than Bethmann. Not only was he famously polite, he was powerful and knowledgeable. "His connections in the mercantile world were so extensive," it was said of him, "that in no corner of the earth in which that valuable contrivance of commerce, a bill of exchange, is resorted to, was his name unknown." To this man, she explained her problem. In response, he suggested she remain in the city for a few days at least and see how the political and military situation developed. He would try to make arrangements for such a stay. He explained that "the consternation was universal," that her situation was "very unpleasant," that it would be very hard to find substitute servants, especially at short notice. It hardly needed saying that a lady, with a small boy and a French maid, could not go on alone, not into what might be a war zone. He urged great prudence. Normally, a man of such high authority might expect acquiescence. His guardianship and patronage at such a moment was not an offer to take lightly, nor would a detention have meant privation. Bethmann had a great mansion, a famous art collection, and many servants. At his dinners, behind the guests stood impressive men, looking like field marshals with rich uniforms and cocked hats with high green feathers, men whose sole duty was to assure that the right "luxuriant wines" went with the right dishes. Mrs. Adams could have stayed, visited his exquisite gardens, tasted his expensive Rhenish wines from the traditional green glasses, and abided until a better time. But she resisted.[26]

She said that it would be better to get to France "as soon as possible." She said that she would probably meet her husband on the frontier, for surely he knew about Napoleon's movements and knew that she was on her way, but in danger. She offered an analysis. Delay would only occasion more difficulty, not less. "At present," she contended, "the panic itself would prove advantageous; as it would require time to ascertain events, before the Governments could take decisive measures." Bethmann wavered. He reiterated that troops were gathering, that they would be sent to the frontier "by way of precaution," though he admitted that this would take time, for they had long been disbanded and were scattered. But she was insistent about going on and doing it now, so he changed tack. Go on, then, he said. But do not go by the most direct route, the one she had planned, the one intimated in the half-finished letter to her husband—Frankfurt to Mayence, Kaiserslautern, Metz, Verdun, Epernay, and onward. Take a more circuitous route, he suggested, for this would be safer. In the meantime, if she agreed, he would try to find someone to go with her.[27]

So they arrived at their illogical compromise. Perhaps Bethmann explained, perhaps he did not, why a circuitous journey would be safer and quieter. (In her memoirs, she did not.) Perhaps he presumed that German troops would move along the most direct route to the French frontier and French troops likewise, so an indirect route would be freer of their movements. Yet if she went more circuitously, she would take longer and risk losing her brief moment of opportunity. And doing what he now advised, she abandoned any hope that her husband would intercept her at the frontier, for he might go to Metz and she would not. In truth, her decision, made in haste and under pressure, was eloquent of her instinctive understanding that John Quincy Adams would probably not be hastening to the frontier. After all, she had just begun writing a letter in which she had complained of neglect. When Bethmann left on his errand, she turned back to the letter and finished it. She wrote, "Since writing the above I have seen Mr. Bethman who tells me that I must not think of going to Mayence but that I must go by Strasbourg and it will lengthen and add to the expence which has already frightened me." She subscribed it, as she often did, "God bless you my best friend and believe me ever most affectionately yours, Louisa C. Adams."[28]

But why worry about expense at such a moment? Why was she so determined to press on? And what sort of best friend was this husband?

In her memoirs, she explained this journey as a test of her individual competence, but also as proof that women, in general, could be competent. She wished to "show that many undertakings which appear very difficult and arduous to my Sex, are by no means so trying as imagination forever depicts them—And that energy and discretion, follow the necessity of their exertion, to protect the fancied weakness of feminine imbecility." But she had a larger, more anxious purpose. She wished to prove that she had existed at all, and that this journey substantiated a claim to being remembered. "It may perhaps at some future day serve to recal the memory of one, *who was*," she was to write in 1836.[29]

She was to leave little record of her tumbling thoughts while she waited in her Frankfurt lodging for Bethmann to return. She did recall her sense that this was a crisis, *"a situation."*[30] Ever since the moment when her carriage had been lost in the forests of Kurland, when she had resolved to control her fears, she had grown in the sense that this journey had a symbolic significance, that it had become a commentary on her life. Somehow the journey of her life and the act of traveling from Saint Petersburg to Paris had mingled together in her mind. To stop now would be an admission of failure, an acknowledgment that the men who thought women incompetent were

C.J.M. Whichelo, *South East View of All Hallows Barking (by the Tower)* (1803)
(Courtesy of Guildhall Art Gallery, City of London)

right. But it would also be an acknowledgment that she did not deserve to be remembered, and might as well not have existed. To understand why she felt this need to prove herself, why she had this bleak urgency, one must understand her marriage, the thing toward which she was traveling. For it was John Quincy Adams she needed to convince, though also herself. Of the two, it is difficult to know who was the more skeptical.

It had been a complicated, harrowing, and only sometimes satisfactory business—her marriage, her children, her place. There were signs of trouble even before she had gone to the altar at All Hallows Barking, signs that the two of them might not suit. His offer of marriage had been odd and unexpected—the family had thought he would ask Nancy, the elder sister—and Louisa's acceptance had been hasty, hard to explain even to herself, and reliant upon the conviction of others that John Quincy Adams loved her. But she was getting on, as marriageable young ladies in London went, and he was a very presentable young man with good prospects. She did not love him, but she resolved to make the attempt, as sentiment and custom required. When he got back to the Netherlands, they had started a correspondence. He was awkward at epistolary lovemaking and she did not like writing letters at all, but they did their best.

They used the language of friendship, which in their time could intimate more than friendship, as it had with John and Abigail Adams in their day. But with Louisa Johnson and John Quincy Adams, this was as yet a conjecture. (In time, it would become a habit, even a conviction about their relationship.) "I am your sincere and affectionate friend," she wrote. "Farewell my ever dear and amiable friend," he wrote back. In time he managed shyly to speak of himself as using "the language of a lover." Over the months, they settled into an awkward language of love, though it was a term most used when they had quarreled, as a sort of reproach, as when he complained, "It is *because* I respect as much as I love you, that this expedient did not please me."[31]

They had quarreled almost from the first. As she saw it, he had a bad habit of speaking *de haut en bas*, especially as a man to a woman. In his first letter after he had reached The Hague in June 1796, the tone was already there. There had been a storm in the Channel, a friend had told him that she had been anxious, and he wrote: "I hope and trust you exercised and discovered the species of Fortitude of which we have often conversed; not precisely what you mean by Philosophy, but a certain strength of mind, which improves and adorns even female sensibility without diminishing its force." "Do not think I am setting myself up for a Mentor," he later insisted, unconvincingly. His compliments had a way of being uncomplimentary: "Some People say the Ladies cannot keep secrets, but I am convinced the observation does not apply to you."[32]

She tried to please him. His father was elected president and she complimented him, but he said it was no matter for compliment. He was appointed minister to Portugal and she congratulated him, but he said it was no matter for congratulation. The position was but temporary and one ought not to care for "the parade of dignity annexed to rank . . . a thing for which I have no sort of respect." She was taken aback and then attempted conciliation, but eventually she decided that confrontation might be the better policy.[33] The immediate issue had been that John Quincy Adams grew very evasive about fixing the date of their wedding, partly for good reasons. He worried about money, about being able to care for a new wife, and had seen that in London she lived well, better than he could afford. He was appointed to Lisbon, but did not know when he would leave the Netherlands, how he would reach Portugal, or whether it was a place to take a wife. So he stalled and she grew anxious, as did her parents. Her problem was that her father's mercantile ventures were in flux and would require him to return to Maryland, she thought sooner rather than later, and she would have to go with him. Then an ocean would separate her from her fiancé, and the likelihood then would be a marriage postponed until John Quincy Adams returned permanently to the United States. No one knew when that would be. The minister made noises about disenchantment with a diplomatic life, though louder noises about how important it was to persist, to have fortitude, and to bear life's disappointments with philosophic resignation.

Since Adams made no moves to visit London, at the end of November 1796 she made a tentative suggestion: "I will endeavour to prevail on my Father to embark from Holland as I know he will shortly have a Vessel there." At this, Adams jumped to the conclusion that Joshua Johnson and his whole family would appear in The Hague, march him off to a marriage in an Anglican church, and then leave for their ship, minus their second daughter. In his reply of December 20, 1796, since she had not plainly avowed this purpose, he mingled bluntness with awkward compliment. Bluntly he expressed his opinion "that in the intention of urging your father to embark from Holland you have contemplated that of remaining with me." Awkwardly he attributed her failure to be explicit about this purpose to "delicacy, which is the glory of your Sex." If he was wrong in this, he asked her forgiveness, but the rest of his letter showed no glimmering of self-doubt. "I find myself compelled to assure you that the completion of our Union here would be impossible . . . While I remain here in my present unsettled condition, without orders, without authority, without power to remove, and exposed to dismission from the public service by a revolution far from improbable in the administration of the American government, to connect the fortunes of any amiable woman indissolubly with mine, would be an act of absurdity towards myself and of cruelty towards her . . . My sentiments on the occasion therefore cannot hesitate a moment. They are paramount to every other consideration, and fixed beyond the power of alteration."[34]

Her reactions were confused. She was conscious that, when Adams had left England, she had been too emotional, too sorry to see him go, and she suspected that the memory of this weak young woman had led to his mistrust of her fortitude, even her word. So she sometimes temporized, by expressing her frequent wish to recall her rash letters, and less often she became miffed: "I am almost angry when I read . . . your letter, as it implies a sort of doubt which I am sure I cannot have merited."[35]

Then Joshua Johnson wrote to express a willingness to detour to the Netherlands. Adams's reply was brisk and decisive. "If the object for which you propose to undertake this journey is to provide an opportunity to [accomplish] my matrimonial union, I regret sincerely the impossibility which would prevent me from concurring in a measure so conformable to my wishes." Worse, the next day to Louisa he added, "You will be sensible what an appearance in the eyes of the world your coming here would have; an appearance consistent neither with your dignity, nor my delicacy." To this, he added his customary homily about submitting cheerfully to adverse necessity. And he shuddered at the prospect of any abandonment to "childish weakness or idle lamentations." For "we should be indeed unfit for the course of life in prospect before us if we indulge ourselves in dreams of finding all our ways strewed with flowers or its borders lined with down."[36] For some time, she had been trying to go along with the homily, trying to play the role of the weak woman instructed by the wise man.

But then his letter of December 20 came to hand. Her response was volcanic, blisteringly ironic. She wrote of his "very decisive letter," his "authoritative stile," his "peremptory harshness." She insisted that, after the first suggestion, she had never pressed her parents to visit the Netherlands, and stiffly reasserted her acceptance of their marriage's indefinite postponement. She seems almost to have decided that this was not going to work, that they would end up going their separate ways, and hence that a valedictory subscription would be apt: "Adieu, that every happiness may await you, is the constant and heartfelt prayer of your truly and sincerely faithful Louisa C. Johnson."[37]

His reply was not conciliatory. Your letter, he said, "has given me as much pain as you expected, and more than I hope you intended." He denied being authoritative, commanding, unkind, harsh, and peremptory, though he admitted to intending decisiveness. He insisted that both she and her father, especially, had justified his inference of a plan to force a premature marriage in the Netherlands. Above all, he began to question her right to challenge his authority, though he did reluctantly admit that "spirit in a proper degree I do not disapprove, even when it bids defiance to myself." Still, it was clear he thought her expressions of spirit were in an improper degree.[38]

She began reluctantly to backtrack: "I regret most sincerely ever having expressed a wish to *meet* you in Holland, since it appears to have given you so much uneasiness." She added a thought that, over the years, would grow like a tumor: "Believe me I should be sorry to put it in your power or in that of the world, to say I wish to force myself upon any man or into any family." But even John Quincy Adams could notice this as a crisis, so he thought it wise to try a bribe or two, and sent over four etui cases for her sisters, a smelling bottle for her mother, earrings for Nancy, and a ring for Caroline. For Louisa, there was a pair of bracelets. Two days later, though he rehearsed his reasons for postponing their marriage, he also thought it best to talk of other things: the American election and her attempts to play the harp, though perhaps he did not get the tone of the latter right. "You imagine that I receive with anger the information that you pay little attention to the Harp, and cannot yet play a single song—By no means—I hear it with great indifference; it is indeed as you say a charming, but it is also a trivial accomplishment. It can amuse a moment of idleness, and discard some of the languor of tediousness, but it confers neither intelligence to the mind, nor virtue to the Heart. I trust therefore that your hours are employed in the acquisition of more valuable qualities."[39]

Gradually, they smoothed this crisis over. ("Now my most esteemed friend let us mutually forget the past, and by a constant, and tender correspondence, endeavor to alleviate the pang of inevitable separation.") He backtracked a little, apologized a little, though not for what he had said, only for having occasioned her interpretation of how he had said it. And she backtracked a lot. They had both looked into the abyss of a broken engagement and neither had liked what they saw. And she had learned something important about him. It concerned this matter of spirit. He had written, "You have again in this Letter repeatedly intimated that you think yourself obliged to assert spirit . . . Let us understand one another, Louisa . . . *Spirit* [should] never be needed or called in aid for the settlement of *our* differences . . . it is in its nature a *repellent* quality; that whenever it is used, and more especially when it is *professedly* used, it inevitably necessitates either a similar return of *Spirit*, or an acquiescence and obsequiousness painful to him who makes and unworthy of her who receives the sacrifice—I do most cordially wish my amiable friend that you may never have occasion to know whether I should possess a proper degree of Spirit or not, in opposition to you." For him, this was a ground rule for their relationship: he was who he was, and she should never try to change him. He seems to have thought that her role was to be a cheerleader for his character, especially his preference for bookish solitude.[40]

On the other hand, at her suspicion that he might think she was forcing herself upon him and his family, he expressed "the clear and unhesitating consciousness that the suspicion is without any foundation." And here arose a theme that he, perhaps, never grasped about her feelings, for it concerned the Adams family. "My *dignity*, my *Station* or *my family*, have no sort of concern with any subject of debate between you and me." This was disingenuous. Whatever he felt, whatever she felt, it was a cold fact that then, for most people, he was less John Quincy Adams and more John Adams's son, and his family was inescapable.[41]

That is where it rested. He was obdurate and a little sorry; she was angry and obliged to temporize. A gulf had been intimated, which turned on the matter of necessity. For the most part, he was a bleak pessimist who presumed that things would go wrong and, hence, that the essential art of life was learning to live with disappointment. As she put it, he was prone to a "continual contemplation of the dark side." In reply to this observation, he made clear that he did not understand the point: "To perceive all the dangers of futurity, to examine and scrutinize them, is the part of prudence—To shrink from them is the part of cowardice." Especially in their early days, she thought it possible that happiness might be made to exist, for she had seen it in her own family. He had seen it, too, in his own family, but his view had been so laced with the anxiety of influence, so laden with the sense that it would be impossible to match the standards of John and

Abigail Adams that it would be best to go on in life with pessimism. So he did not expect too much of his own marriage, in fact remarkably little. To his mother, he had suggested that marriage was little more than a good republican's duty: "I begin to think very seriously of the duty incumbent upon all good citizens to have a family," he had said in the spring of 1796. To his fiancée, he wrote with dispassionate equanimity: "I have always believed and still believe you to possess a virtuous Heart, an intelligent mind, an accomplished person and a gentle disposition, all of which qualities contributed to inspire the strong affection which I have for you; but I never seriously believed or pretended that I believed you exempt from the common and universal imperfections of humanity; or from occasional errors of the mind, and varieties of temper." For why would anyone yield to "the blindness of an irrational Love, or to the natural exaggeration of expression, which ardent sentiment often inspires"?[42] This was scarcely the philosophy of a lover at the beginning of a romance.

By mid-February 1797, she was writing that her family would go to America in three months and their separation would continue sine die. Their letters give the impression that both, with relief, were settling back into their own worlds—she into that of her family, he into his secluded study. However, quieter tensions persisted. He recommended reading to her, then criticized what she read. She worried that he was too bookish and unsociable, and he said that any time spent on books was healthy and sociability was a waste: "To my books I can return with pleasure, even from the most pleasing excursions of the fancy. They leave no languor, no saiety, no littleness of indolence upon the mind. They are therefore the only refuge of one to whom the common course of Society is now more than ever insipid." There was even a problem about names, for she began to speak of him habitually as "my Adams." He did not take to it, though he bore it in silence for several months, until patience ran out. "I do not like it—It is a stile of address that looks too much like that of novels. A proper name does not sound or look well for a Man in real life—I have endeavoured to habituate myself to it, because you appear fond of using it; but it looks to me more and more uncouth and awkward." Quietly, she dropped it. Nonetheless, there were also fond expressions, even moments when he tried to rally her propensity toward self-deprecation: "You speak of 'tiring me with your stupidity,' of 'sending me nonsense' in the latter of your 'ridiculous conduct' and your 'folly.' There is not one of these terms that can with any sort of propriety be applied to any thing that I ever observed of you." Nonetheless, even he began to notice "so essential a wideness of sentiment between us."[43]

That they got married when they did arose partly from circumstances, and it happened in a rush. Her father's business in the United States got pushed back, until it seemed likely that they would not go until July 1797. In the meantime, Adams received the official news that he was recalled from the Netherlands and commissioned as minister plenipotentiary to Portugal. Making his plans, he found difficulty during wartime in finding a passage from Amsterdam to Lisbon. In his capacity as a merchant, Joshua Johnson volunteered that one of his schooners sailing from London might be diverted to Portugal. Adams agreed to this possibility and, with some abruptness and much inconsistency with his earlier views, decided that he might as well get married in London and take his bride with him. By July 12, Adams was in London and married only two weeks later, though in the interim he had learned that his commission had been switched from Portugal to Prussia.[44]

So it had been a very bumpy courtship, in which incompatibilities had been intimated. But it was notable that courting loomed much larger in her mind than in his. The ebb and flow of their relationship, the good moments and the bad, were an absorbing topic for her. If his diary is a reliable guide, it was not so for him, because there Louisa Johnson appeared very infrequently, after those few months from November 1795, when he had first entered the Johnson household on Cooper's Row, to late April 1796, when he had proposed marriage under some pressure from Catherine Johnson, who had grown impatient with Adams's tendency to oscillate in his devotions between Nancy Johnson and Louisa. Between this agreement to marry and his departure for the Netherlands on May 28, there were many references to the Johnson family, but only two references to his fiancée by name, and between the last of these on April 26 and the day of their marriage over a year later, he never once mentioned her in his diary, even as part of the Johnson family. Over this period of fifteen months, they had what she remembered as a passionate correspondence, from which she learned much about what she might have to face as a woman married to this man. Whatever he may have thought, he never committed to paper. He never noted when he had received her letters, nor what was in them, though he chronicled when he wrote to his father, mother, and brothers, as well as to sundry political figures. Even when the final decision was made to marry, he was silent. A reader of his diary would have no notion that part of his intention in traveling to London in the summer of 1797 was to consummate his marriage. Yet John Quincy Adams was not a man uninterested in his own emotions. It was just that then she did not form part of his emotions, or too little to be worth recording. Over the long decades of his meticulous diary keeping, she was to appear very little as a character, except by way of his designating her presence or absence at an event, and at those moments when there was a crisis, usually her ill health. Though sometimes in letters to others, he would observe that she was "a tender, faithful, inestimable wife," the moments were fleeting. In his diary nowhere did he describe her, nowhere did he characterize her, nowhere did he pause and think it important to reflect on who she was and who they were together. So he was not understating the case when he described himself to her as "not a romantic lover."[45]

A look at his diary when he was a student casts some light on these matters, for there he contemplated love and marriage. On March 5, 1787, the Harvard branch of Phi Beta Kappa debated "whether Love, or fortune ought to be the chief inducement, to marriage?" The young Adams opted for fortune, despite knowing "the universal applause bestow'd on love matches, and the detestation of interested marriages." This was mostly because he had a very low opinion of love. "That pure, refined, and elevated passion, which we term *Love*," he explained, "is an heterogeneous compound of *Lust*, and *Vanity*, most frequently attended with *Jealousy*, a passion formed by the furies for the misery of mankind. It is captious, imprudent, whimsical, and utterly inconsistent with reason." In a marriage founded only on such a love, lust was satiated and this left vanity as the sole ingredient, necessarily breeding strife. But if a man sought not love but fortune in a marriage, the possession of wealth would occasion social importance and a benign temper. Husband and wife "would have reason to be pleased with themselves, and it would naturally follow, that they would please each other: no disappointed passion would divide them; no troublesome wants would make them burdens to each other." Serenely, they might discharge their obligations, including the education of their children. He admitted that some might designate these friendly sentiments as a form of love and he did not mind this. Yet there was a "difference between mutual esteem and love," and it resided in the former being "founded only upon reason, to which the other is diametrically opposite."[46]

A few months later, he wrote an essay on women, marriage, and courtship. In many ways, he took the hard patriarchal line that, throughout the civilized nations, women were reasonably "taught that it is their duty, to submit implicitly to the will of their lord," because men were stronger and women, being weaker, needed protection. Anything other than marriage was a disaster for a woman, for a spinster was "despised and neglected by all the world," was but a "dead weight upon the community." But he had a few unorthodox thoughts. He had some sympathy for what he understood to be the female predicament, their confinement to domesticity and their exclusion from "distinctions, military, civil, or even literary." From this insight, a more radical mind might have leaped to the notion that women ought to have a more expansive education and social role. Instead, he observed that these constrictions had a tendency to create overheated passions in women, that they did not have the emotional release associated with action, and, in particular, that it was unfair that a woman was expected to wait for a man to propose marriage. Rather, he thought it only fair that she should have the release of speaking first, if she wished. "Is it not therefore consistent with reason and justice, that the fair sex should have a right to express the tender passions, of which they are so susceptible?"[47]

John Singleton Copley, *John Quincy Adams* (1796)

(Photograph © 2010, Museum of Fine Arts, Boston)

Hence the man Louisa Johnson married in 1797 believed her to be inferior, emotional, and in need of protection. He further believed a marriage was best if it was not founded upon passion, but upon a rational equilibrium of esteem. And this was the message he kept reiterating to her during their courtship letters, that together they should be rational and philosophical, that she should not expect too much of life and people, that she should accept reverses with resignation. It was not a stance he ever revised. When in 1809 he set sail for Russia, he sat down in his cabin and wrote a letter to his sons. In it, he expounded his philosophy of marriage, which was curiously material: "The object of life, as it presents itself in the ordinary course of Providence to man, stands in this gradation—the means of subsistence for himself— of comfortable subsistence for himself and his wife—of subsistence, nurture, and education for a family of children. These are the first and the closest ties of human society. Without all these human society could not exist. They are founded on the universal law of self-preservation as applied to the individual and to the species."[48]

So for John Quincy Adams, marriage was a social duty and necessity, and its value lay more in what was done, less in what was felt. In this, he was not peculiar for his times; indeed, he was mildly progressive for admitting the principle of mutual esteem, which licensed the idea of a companionate marriage. For Louisa Adams, this was never enough.

As a result, even as they went to the altar, there were reasons to doubt that it would turn out well. However, what John Quincy Adams thought as a Harvard student need not have formed how he came to behave as a husband, and she was worldly enough as a Londoner, a reader, and a theatergoer to imagine love, for she knew the language. But something went immediately wrong, something she thought blighted the marriage irremediably.

Her father had been a merchant, dealing mostly in tobacco, as the London partner of an Annapolis firm. With many ups and downs, Joshua Johnson had prospered, for he was shrewd, jaunty, and bold, an essential quality in such a risky business. Most liked him, though some mistrusted him as a vain and weak social climber, overly concerned about appearances and driven on by "an ambitious and extravagant wife." In retrospect, Louisa herself conjectured that her parents' residence in Nantes had changed them, that her beautiful but ingenue mother had there "engendered *tastes*, and *ideas* perhaps calculated to lavish on her children a more expensive and higher order of education, [than] my Fathers station in life, or circumstances as a Commission Merchant prudently authorized."[49]

A merchant worked by securing credit, financing voyages, and using the profits to pay off the loans, so he was vulnerable if a voyage failed or the credit market changed. In 1796, Johnson entered into a scheme to import brandy from France. Because of the wars with France, British ships were forbidden to enter French ports, but an American neutral might, so Johnson and his partners floated loans and sent an emissary to Rochefort. Four hundred and twenty-nine pipes of cognac were purchased and loaded onto a ship, which sailed to the Channel Islands and at full tide anchored in Guernsey Roads. At night, with the captain ashore, the tide ebbed and the ship crashed over, "which stove every cask of brandy, and the ship herself." The underwriters refused to pay any insurance, since the ship had entered port without a pilot and the captain had declared his ship safely moored. Johnson had other problems, too: dropping prices for brandy in London, a ship that failed to arrive from the East Indies, and resentful creditors in Bremen.[50]

These multiplying troubles coincided with the presence of John Quincy Adams in London, but they did not gather an irreversible momentum until after his engagement to Louisa Johnson. By late 1796, Johnson knew it would be necessary to return to Maryland to sort out his business, and Adams seems to have been aware of some difficulties in the Johnson family's affairs. He certainly knew of the plan to return, though it is doubtful he knew exactly why the return was necessary. On July 17, the day before Adams learned he was being switched to Prussia, the bridal pair were inspecting their berths on the *Mary*, the ship Johnson had arranged for the voyage to Lisbon, and it is inconceivable that such an expedition would have been undertaken if Adams, at least, had anticipated a serious turn of events, beyond the readily anticipated pain of a daughter being separated from her family.[51]

But events did turn very serious. His diary between the marriage and the Johnsons' departure on September 9 gave bare hints. "Mr Johnson ill—The cause an unhappy one" is the entry for August 30. "The situation has become very painful," he wrote a day later. On September 8, on the eve of the Johnsons' departure, there was this: "After supper we had a distressing scene, while the whole family took their leave of Louisa; they go tomorrow morning at 4 o'clock, for Gravesend, there to embark immediately for America." A few weeks after, creditors came banging on Adams's London door and, in due course, Johnson was a bankrupt, his English property expropriated by the British government, his reputation destroyed, his family indigent.[52]

As Louisa was to tell the story, she had married under "the happiest auspices." In early July, her father had made an arrangement with his creditors, had a vessel in which to sail to America, and planned a return to England within two years to wind up his business. Thereafter "he expected to give each of his children a small fortune and to retire himself upon a handsome property without owing any one a shilling." (He had land in Georgia.) But two weeks after the marriage, his partner betrayed him, he was "obliged to stop payment for the sum of *five hundred pounds* in consequence of the failure of a remittance, and the non arrival of a large East India ship, and to quit the Country with his family in a very different manner and under very different circumstances than he had ever expected." For Louisa Adams, this bankruptcy and flight were a shock, developments that aged and disillusioned her. As a consequence, she was obliged to move to her husband's hotel and there she "too forcibly learnt that I had forfeited all that would give me consequence in my husbands esteem or in my own mind." In her later histories, these events were narrated bitterly and remorsefully. She claimed that her husband's response to this crisis was understandable, though permanently crip-

pling to her self-esteem. "Never have I, never can I blame Mr Adams
for his feelings on this trying occasion," she was to write, "for I felt
that thus situated my impressions would have been too strong to admit of either doubt or paliation, for he found himself exposed to a
situation full of difficulties and as he thought disgrace and after disappointment; from that hour all confidence was destroyed for ever in
me and mine." In her account, it is implicit that John Quincy Adams
somehow expressed the belief that he had been hoodwinked into
marriage, that the Johnsons had known matters were slipping toward
disaster and had cynically married off their daughter without saying
a word about the coming problem. He had expected a handsome
dowry and a respectable family connection, and got neither. It was
the loss of respectability that most rankled with her, "the harsh constructions generally adopted by an envious and ill judging world."
This is how she remembered the events of 1797, when in 1825 she
was newly settling into the White House: "Never never as long as
sense shall last shall I forget the worse than broken hearted look of
my adored family the last Even[ing] he passed with me in my own
house; my poor Mother too I was not aware that they were to leave
me so soon; but ere morning broke they had already left that Country
in which all his children were born, and in which he had so long lived
honoured and respected—When I arose and found them gone I was
the most forlorn miserable wretch that the Sun ever smiled upon—I
loved your father with the utmost sincerity but I learnt too quickly in
spite of his utmost exertions, how low I was sunk in his estimation
without hope of ever recovering the standing which was irreparably
lost. It was short and rigid justice and I had nothing to complain of—
Such was my honey moon."[53]

Over the years, she raked over these events continually, always
with a sense that her father needed defending, that he had been betrayed by others, that he had been innocent. Implicit was that she was
innocent, too, and had known nothing before the storm broke. A consequence was her powerful sense that she had entered her marriage
as an unequal partner, as more of a dependent than was usual even
for a woman and too illegitimate to have any authority. Moreover,

she felt the disgrace had distorted her feelings. This feeling was not something she kept to herself or to her husband, for she seems to have expressed it more widely, especially to her mother-in-law. In 1806, she wrote to Abigail Adams: "My education and the misfortunes which have pursued my family from the moment of what I may style my entrance into the world (I mean my marriage) may have given a harshness to my character which does not naturally belong to it and rendered me cold and fearful of forcing attentions w[h]ere they might not prove acceptable and the least appearance of unkindness or dislike acts so powerfully upon my feelings as to destroy every desire of pleasing or rendering myself agreeable where I have once perceived it." In 1810, she wrote: "It has however been an invariable rule with me as I had no fortune never to object or decline any thing which he thinks can tend to promote his ambition his fame or his ease."[54]

Abigail Adams was to insist that this "subject which preys upon your mind, and which you have repeatedly mentioned," was all nonsense, that no one in the Adams family blamed her, that her son was content not to marry money, and that financial independence would not have made her happier. The written record is all on Abigail's side. Nowhere in John Quincy Adams's diary or letters, nowhere in the correspondence of the Adams family, is there a hint of a reproach to his wife. On the part of his family and especially his mother, there was a careful solicitude and awareness of the pain attendant upon the losses of the Johnson family fortune, especially when in 1801 Joshua Johnson was declining in health and dying. Abigail Adams could be an exacting woman, but she was devotedly punctilious about family connections. She carefully wrote letters to Catherine Nuth Johnson for as long as the latter lived, especially to share news about their childrens' career in the world, but also to express condolences or pleasure at whatever befell the Johnsons and their various kin. She kept an eye on Louisa's brother Thomas Johnson when he was at Harvard and helped him get a position at the College of Charleston. Her presidential husband extended patronage in 1800, when Joshua Johnson was appointed superintendent of stamps, with an annual salary of two thousand dollars. As for John Quincy Adams, after his father-in-law died, he offered careful legal advice to the family about Johnson's lawsuit, *Joshua Johnson v. Charles Wallace and Eleanor Davidson, widow*, begun in 1799 in Chancery in England. In that correspondence, at least, Adams gave the impression that Johnson may have had a sound case and hence a valid grievance against his former partner.[55]

What cannot be known is what John Quincy Adams said to his new wife in the late summer of 1797, when the Johnson family was en route to the United States and the newly married couple were in Osborne's Hotel on the Strand. Something passed between them, though her memoirs are inexplicit. She was to speak of his "feelings." It seems very likely that her husband was upset and troubled, mostly on her account, partly on his own. For one thing, creditors and debt collectors kept appearing at their hotel door and he had the indignity of getting an outraged letter from a Bremen creditor of Johnson's, which he passed on to his father-in-law with words carefully poised between stricture, doubt, and compassion. "The turn of affairs here has not been such as your friends could have wished," he wrote, with some mildness. "Appearances and allegations are advanced which bring in question something more than merely your credit; and unfortunately your friends have not the means of refuting them in their power," he added, with more astringency. "Your affairs in America, as you represented them to me, are amply sufficient to satisfy every claim upon you in Europe, and to leave you still a decent property" was gently ambivalent. But "Let me urge you then Sir by every consideration of regard for yourself and your family to consider Justice to your creditors as the most imperious of your obligations" was a sterner reproach. "To render it speedily, and amply, however unkind you may think their treatment of you has been—I urge it, because I cannot suspect you of an unnecessary misrepresentation of your affairs to me, and because if your statement was correct it will be perfectly and largely within your power" was even more stern, because so laden with ifs.[56]

At the best of times, Adams could be grim, and this was not the best of times. Stern men have a way of being misread, since observers tend to assume that a critical temperament is indiscriminate, is always judging harshly, even when nothing is said or even thought. Louisa came to understand this of her husband. In retrospect, she felt she had misunderstood his letters from the Netherlands and, later, she had to repair some damage with her family, when his letters to the Johnsons were taken ill. In 1798, she wrote to her sister Nancy Hellen, "I am very sorry to understand by Mamas letter that some circumstance has happened to give her a very unfavorable opinion of Mr A. which gives me great uneasiness." But she was sure that "my husbands letters have been misunderstood," and recalled the winter of 1796/97. "You know Mr A's manner of writing and how often and severely I have suffered before I was married at the time of receiving letters from him which I am now fully convinced never were intended to give me a moments pain."[57]

So there may have been a misunderstanding, but it is likely that it came more from her than him. She overreacted very badly. It may be that she knew more than she claimed, probably not of the financial details, but of a longer history about her mother and father stretching back for years, and that this crisis set up a tension that she did not consciously know how to resolve. In later years, she was to construct a romantic myth about her childhood: how much her parents were in love, how beautiful her mother was, how handsome her father was, how much joy there was on Cooper's Row, how radiantly hospitable the Johnsons together had been. To be sure, her memoirs also remembered moments of pain, the difficulties of growing up, the complexities of siblings, but these remarks referred to herself, her sisters, and those she met. Her parents, and especially her father, move through her memoirs of the years before 1797 in a golden haze. This myth is at odds with the written record, such as it is.

In his early days and again in the late 1780s, Joshua Johnson had often found himself in "very ticklish" situations and this was not especially to his discredit, for his business was intrinsically unstable. At times, his partners thought that he fiddled the books, and certainly often numbers did not line up, though bookkeeping was then a rough-and-ready business.[58]

Louisa Adams after marriage seems to have written very few letters to her father, mother, or sisters, and the correspondence was often tense. In 1798, after hearing of Louisa's miscarriages, Catherine
Nuth Johnson wrote to her daughter: "Oh my Louisa what does your
Father & myself feel at not having a line from you to convince us of
your recovery, the anxiety we labour under for your preservation, the
solicitude we have ever shewn the principles we have endeavoured to
inculcate taught us to believe, that you would have embraced every
opportunity in your power to assure us of your undiminished affection." In 1800, writing during her visit to Silesia in the only letter to
her father that survives, Louisa expressed her extreme anxiety to hear
from her "beloved father," but also of trepidation: "As usual my beloved father I am fearful you will find [my letter] exceedingly tedious." In her memoirs, too, she was to speak of fear: "When roused
to anger, or to suspicion; [his eye] had a dazzling fixed severity that
was absolutely awful; and which seemed by its vivid scrutiny to dive
into the depths of the human heart."[59] So, although what survives
makes clear how much she loved her father, it does not show easy
relationships within the Johnson family.

The perception that she forced herself on John Quincy Adams
predated the crisis of July 1797. During the fierce debate over her
suggestion that she come to the Netherlands with her father, she
wrote: "Believe me I should be sorry to put it in your power or in that
of the world, to say I wish to force myself on any man or into any
family." The roots of her later bitterness lay here, in the fact that she
came from a family of dubious respectability. To be sure, her uncle
Thomas Johnson was a governor of Maryland, prominent in the
American Revolution, and was once nominated by President John
Adams to serve on the Supreme Court. But Louisa had little to do
with the Maryland Johnsons, even when she came to the United
States and lived close to them. In England, moreover, there were
many problems: Mr. Nuth and his twenty-two bastards, her grandmother and mother's illegitimacy, the obscurity of her parents' marriage. Truth about the Johnsons of London was elusive, which

suggests that untruth was necessary. Louisa herself became keen to stress her own sexual virtue, even to her children: "I can swear before the living God that I came pure and virtuous to [my husband's] arms, and that to this hour I have remained so; and that though the scorpion tongue of political slander assailed me ere I had been a wife a year; my Sons may look up with proud and unsullied honour to the mother who bore them who as far as chastity goes was pure as the azure of an unclouded sky."[60] Unlike some other people.

Louisa Johnson was marrying into a very different family. The Adamses of Braintree were farmers, deacons, lawyers—people of grave respectability. The Smiths of Weymouth, who furnished a wife for the young John Adams, were still more respectable and even more religious, and their only known weakness was a fondness for the bottle. While the Johnsons were metropolitan and worldly, wore silk, and saw church as an occasion for fashionable parade, the Adamses were rural, mistrusted the world, wore broadcloth, and thought church was for urgent prayer. Under normal circumstances, a Johnson might think herself sinking in the world to enter into an alliance with an Adams, or at least might be doubtful of rising. But John Adams had changed all that, not by earning much money, for the Adamses remained very pinched for money after decades of penurious public service, but by earning a fame even then thought likely to be lasting. By 1796, when Louisa Johnson became engaged, the awkward and garrulous Harvard lawyer of 1765 had broken free of his provincial world, helped to launch and win the American Revolution, become an able diplomat and turbulent author, been elected the first vice president of the new union, and looked likely to be the second president. Later, the world would come to know that his marriage was a republican parable. In 1796, the letters of John and Abigail were still private, and the world had little inkling of this, but the Johnsons had seen the Adamses in London in the mid-1780s, when John Adams had been the first American minister to the Court of Saint James. The Johnsons had known then that John and Abigail were a remarkable pair and hence, for Louisa Johnson as a fiancée, a daunting precedent. To be sure, John Quincy Adams did not like to speak of all this, for he dreaded being swallowed up by his father's name, and knew that the world presumed his preferment owed more to the father's position than the son's accomplishment. Nonetheless, he lived and breathed an Adams, not least for being passionately patriotic. ("My duty to my Country is in my mind the first and most imperious of all obligations; before which every interest and every feeling inconsistent with it must forever disappear.")[61] The Johnsons lived as most families did, looking about them for pleasure, employment, laughter, perhaps love, all ordinary things. The Adamses were aiming at the ages, at the prospect that posterity would come to chant the litany of the virtuously great and declaim: Solon, Cicero, Locke, Adams.

In 1796, when Louisa became engaged, the Johnsons had prosperity and standing, and most Americans who walked to Cooper's Row knew nothing of Mr. Nuth's twenty-two bastards. Then it was merely hard to marry an Adams. In late July 1797, when the roof caved in, it became almost impossible, but too late. So, miserably torn between shame, pride, and confusion, over time she adjusted the record in her mind. She eliminated the shadows from the Johnson history: the lust, the chicanery, and the guilt were talked away. And she cast a few shadows on the Adams record, shoveled a little clay on their feet, mostly by exploiting the darker side of republican virtue, its smug joylessness. In this way, she gave herself a fighting chance in her marriage.

It also needs to be observed that, though her memoirs were implicitly critical of her husband and mother-in-law, she never exploited the fact that there was another side to the Adams family. There was Abigail and John's second son, Charles Adams, who failed as a lawyer in New York, became an alcoholic, squandered four thousand dollars from his elder brother, died a pauper in 1800 when only thirty, and was denied burial in the family vault in Quincy by parents torn between grief and disapproval. There was the third son, Thomas Boylston Adams, who had many personal charms, but was another alcoholic, a gambler, a man plagued by debilitating self-doubt who ended up, along with his wife and many children, as a family incubus; he lived longer than Charles, though only to the age of fifty. There was the problem of William Stephens Smith, husband to John

Quincy's sister Abigail, who was a handsome and charismatic rogue, an adventurer who piled up debts in excess of $200,000, a man who had a spell in prison. It would have been easy for Louisa to note that this, too, was a family haunted by failure, quarrel, and regret.[62]

So the marriage of Louisa Johnson and John Quincy Adams had begun with concealments and anguish, with her most at a disadvantage, because she was penniless and shamed. But Berlin was a happy time for them, despite her miscarriages, for both had a respite from the pressures of their respective families far away and they contrived to live well together, or well enough. The next thirteen and a half years, from the moment of her arrival in Philadelphia in 1801 to her departure from Saint Petersburg in early 1815, went less well. It ought to have gone better. She came to the United States with a new-born son and in the next six years had two more, and so she had the basis for the family she so desired. But she never found and could never establish any stability. During those nearly fourteen years, she lived as a family with her husband and children for little more than a third of the time.[63] She lived with her husband, but not all her children, for nearly half the time. She had her children but not her husband with her for a tenth of the time, and for three months she lived alone, with neither husband nor children. This instability grew worse with the years. Until November 1805, they were all together for forty-four months out of fifty-two. Thereafter, until March 1815, they were all together for only eighteen months.

The patterns of this instability were various. From November 1801 until October 1803, she lived with her husband and son George in Boston, where John Adams II was born in July 1803. All four of them moved to Washington in November, after John Quincy's election to the Senate, and they stayed together there until the following April. Then John Quincy left by himself to spend the summer and fall in Quincy, and he returned to Washington in October 1804; there they stayed until March 1805, when all four went together to Quincy. But when the congressional session resumed in December 1805, the couple returned to Washington without the children, who were boarded out with Abigail Adams and Mary Smith Cranch, Abigail

Adams's sister, who also lived in Quincy. In May 1806, John Quincy left Louisa alone in Washington, because she was far along in a pregnancy, took bachelor quarters in Boston and Cambridge, but only visited his two sons. In July, she had a stillbirth, and when her health had recovered sufficiently, she joined him in Boston and the sons were returned to their household. In November 1806, he went alone to Washington and she remained in Boston with George, though for much of the winter John was with Abigail in Quincy; all four were reunited in April 1807 in Boston, where they stayed until October, though there were periods even then when John was with his grandmother in Quincy. Then, after the birth of Charles Francis Adams in August 1807, she went in October with her husband and the baby to Washington, while the two eldest boys were again in Quincy. After the conclusion of the congressional term and her husband's resignation from the Senate in April 1808, everyone was together in Boston, and this remained the situation until the summer of 1809, apart from a few months in early 1809 when John Quincy went to Washington to argue a case before the Supreme Court. When Louisa went to Russia in August 1809, she took Charles Francis with her. But George and John stayed with Mrs. Cranch in Quincy, until Abigail's sister died in October 1811, and then the boys were sent to the Atkinson Academy in New Hampshire and Abigail's other sister, Elizabeth Shaw Peabody. This remained the situation until John Quincy left Saint Petersburg in March 1814, when Louisa and Charles Francis lived alone in Russia. The whole family was not reunited until May 1815, in London.

How and why all this happened was complicated. Usually congressmen left their families at home. John Quincy Adams, at first, presumed that when Congress was not in session, they could live economically in the Adams house where he had been born and which his parents had occupied before their purchase of the larger Vassall house in 1788. But Louisa resisted, because she did not fancy six Quincy winters alone in a tiny house of very bare comforts, with only the company of her Adams relatives. Instead, she opted for the company of her own family, because she was able to live in Georgetown with her sister Nancy Hellen, now married to a Washington merchant. Reluctantly, John Quincy acquiesced, conscious that like his wife he was caught between conflicting loyalties: filial, conjugal, and parental. Unlike his wife, he worried about money, which would be a theme of his for as long as they were married, though his careful accounts give little evidence of probable ruin. The real problem lay with the children. If their parents were migrant or separated, where and with whom would they live? Abigail Adams, at least, was displeased at the thought that her grandchildren would stay in Washington and insisted on her rights and importance as a grandmother: "I have a great opinion of childrens being early attached to their grandparents, perhaps it may arise from the bias I formed for mine . . . more of their precepts and maxims remain with me, to this hour, than those of my excellent parents . . . I revered them as I do at this day their memories with respect and veneration, and I knew little difference of affection between them, and my parents." So Louisa had to give ground, not least because she had found separation difficult. The circumstantial evidence is that, given an impossible choice between husband and children, she mostly chose to live with her husband. So she was reduced to many valedictory letters. "Kiss my darling Children for me over and over again," she had to ask her mother-in-law in 1805, "and remind them constantly of their mother whose every wish on this earth centres in them should you have any apprehension of George having worms give him five drops of spirit of Turpentine upon a lump of Sugar every other morning." Abigail complacently suggested it would have been selfish of Louisa to have taken her children with her: "However reluctant you might feel, at being separated from them, I should suppose that your own judgment experience and good sense would have convinced you of the propriety of the measure without compulsion—I have experienced separations of all kinds from children equally dear to me; and know how great the sacrifice & how painfull the task—but I considered it the duty of a parent to consult the interest and benifit of their children."[64]

Thereafter, apart from a period in Boston after her husband had resigned from the Senate and before their departure for Russia, she had little or no control over her eldest sons or access to them, because of what she described as "the unsettled and divided life we at present lead." This worried her far more than it worried her husband, because what his sons were experiencing was close to what he had experienced as a child. Between his birth in 1767 and his departure for Harvard in 1785, John Quincy had lived with both his parents for about half the time, and seven of those nine years were the first years of his life, when his father was still a Massachusetts lawyer and not yet a revolutionary. Thereafter he was mostly reared by a single parent, either Abigail in Braintree or John in Europe. Nonetheless, he did usually have one of his parents around, unlike his two eldest sons, who usually had neither.[65]

In principle, John Quincy Adams favored a close family: "Thinking as I do that my home is the proper and only proper home of my wife and children, I should always feel the sweetest satisfaction in having them with me." But he, and to a lesser extent Louisa, acknowledged the claims of the extended family, which ran to grandparents, aunts, uncles, sisters, and in-laws, all of whom could be involved in the rearing of children. In this perspective, they were of their times, as this was how the eighteenth century, with its large families, saw matters. Joshua Johnson was one of eleven children, Catherine Nuth Johnson one of twenty-two, Louisa Johnson one of eight, and John Quincy Adams one of five. Even on the occasions when Louisa, John Quincy, and their children were in the same place, the children often moved between households. In Massachusetts, there were the various Adams and Cranch homes in Boston and Quincy. In the District of Columbia during the senatorial years, there was no such thing as an Adams household, because (along with Catherine Nuth Johnson and various unmarried sisters) they lived with Nancy and Walter Hellen. Further, whenever the Adamses did have their own household, there was almost invariably a relative visiting or resident for extended periods, since Louisa liked to have one of her sisters around. And, like all elite families, they had nursemaids and governesses, who had most contact with the children. It is a telling fact that, when Charles Francis Adams was growing up in Saint

Petersburg, he spoke English very poorly but German well, because while his parents spoke English, his nurse, Juliana Helm, was German, and he saw far more of the latter.[66]

Nonetheless, Louisa had a far stronger sense than her husband—and this marked hers as the more modern sensibility—that parents were peculiarly crucial to the emotional formation of their children. She was unsure there was much a parent could do to influence a child's character. As she put to her husband in 1814, "I believe contrary to the usual system of philosophers, that we come into the world with germs of character, which even the best education cannot eradicate, nor all the worldly experience that can be heaped upon us totally destroy." But for her, a mother's care was essential to a child's welfare; by affectionate care she inculcated principles, which acted as safeguards of future success. A parent, especially a mother, owed to her child "unsparing means," "anxious watching," "incessant love," as much as "the advantages of education, of accomplishment, of morals, and of virtue." It was Louisa's tragedy that she was unconvinced she could manage this: "I have had too many convincing proofs that I even with all the means in my power am not fitted to be or make others happy." But John Quincy Adams put less faith in the formative power of love, more in the power of education and example. "My design," he once said, "is to be the school master of my children."[67]

These were their differences and strains. Perhaps there were no more strains than in many marriages. Miscarriages, difficult in-laws, money worries, separations, and ill-fitting temperaments were and are ordinary enough experiences. The two of them had managed, she with the greater difficulty. But matters worsened drastically in the space of one month in 1809.

She knew in the spring of that year that James Madison, the new president, wished to send her husband to Saint Petersburg. But initially the Senate had been disinclined to send a minister at all, and the matter had been dropped. In March, John Quincy had informed his wife of this, with apparent satisfaction. But later in the summer, the issue had revived without her knowledge. According to her memoirs, she had been deceived by her husband's silence, had been shocked by the unexpected news, and had been stripped of any part in either the decision to go or the decision of who would go. "Every preparation was made without the slightest consultation with me and even the disposal of my Children and my Sister was fixed without my knowledge until it was too late to Change." She squarely blamed her husband's political ambition: "Oh this agony of agonies! can ambition repay such sacrifices? never!!—And from that hour to the end of time life to me will be [a] sucession of miseries only to cease with existence."[68]

Her memoirs telescoped events, perhaps for dramatic effect, perhaps by accident. It had been on July 4 that her husband had received the official letter about his successful nomination and he wrote back his acceptance the next day. She knew by July 6, because he was immediately besieged by young men seeking appointment as his secretary and she helped to fob them off. So she probably knew almost as quickly as he did, though whether he consulted her about his acceptance of the post or the disposition of their children, or indeed of her own disposition, is unclear from evidence independent of her memoirs. Most diplomatic wives stayed at home rather than go to Saint Petersburg, even those who came from elsewhere in Europe. The entry in his diary for July 23, which details the disposition of his two eldest sons, makes no mention of her. In that diary, as usual she appeared here and there, going to a dinner, visiting Quincy, performing a service for him, but no more. His entry for July 5, in which he laid out the considerations that had induced his acceptance, mentioned many things—a citizen's duty, his connection with Harvard, the confidence reposed in him by Madison, the welfare of the American union, the approbation of his countrymen, and "the continued consciousness of purity in my motives." He mentioned, too, as a motive for not going, the age of his parents and the infancy of his children. What he did not mention was his wife, what she felt, what she needed.[69]

She was to remember a sense of betrayal and powerlessness for the rest of her life. The blow had been so sudden, for she was on a ship for Russia within a month of the news. Obscurely she felt she ought to have had the power, ought to have been able to change the course of events. In time, she came to blame herself as much as, if not more than, her husband. In 1838, when Charles Francis Adams had a birthday, she wrote in her diary: "He is the only one of my Children whom I never deserted; therefore the only one to whom I have performed my duty—To my other two I failed; and God Almighty forgive me!"[70] Yet there had been almost no moment when she had chosen to be separate from her children. The impulse had habitually come from her husband, for his various reasons good, bad, and indifferent—political ambition, regard for his mother, expense, distraction. In their marriage, as in almost any marriage in her time, he had the final authority, but he had it the more because of her disabling sense that the dishonor of her family had evaporated her own authority.

Necessarily at the center of her world was her husband, the more so because her children were so often displaced and absent, and she was more consistently a wife than a mother. Later in life, she would offer a portrait of him, lightly disguised as "Lord Sharply," in her incomplete roman à clef, *The Metropolitan Kaleidoscope*, written in 1827. It is worth a full quotation:

> Lord Sharply was a man of outstanding talents; and great acquirements. He was the creature of Art rather than Nature. He had filled many high Stations most honorably and with great satisfaction to the Nation and Government he represented. His knowledge of mankind was vast formed however more from Books than from the actual and enlarged Study of man; which led him often to shock their prejudices and wound their feelings; dangerous things to trifle with, as prejudice is often the predominating impulse of their actions. His mind was stored with Classical and polite literature, and his every thought might be said to *teem* with learning. His taste had been cultivated in the best schools of modern refinement. Perseveringly laborious, there were few things too difficult for him to atchieve, and the natural coldness and reserve of his manners defied the penetration of the most indefatigably prying curiosity, to dis-

cover his thoughts, or to perceive his motives of action. The good of his Country was his constant aim; but he sometimes staggered the Nation, by the puppets he used to obtain his ends—Ardent and impetuous in his character and disposition, a constant and perpetual watchfulness enabled him to subdue the defects of his nature, and taught him to master them completely; only those who were the most constantly in his society, could sometimes observe the flashing of his eye, and the tremulous motion of his lip, conveying some faint idea of the volcano that burnt within but which seldom found vent and when it did the explosion was short and terrible—A fond father, a negligent and half indulgent husband, and utterly indifferent to almost all the other branches of his family, he often appeared to forget, or not to *conceive* that others had found obstacles in their path thro' life from which he had been entirely exempted and deemed things must be right because they actually existed. He was full of good qualities; but ambition absorbed every thought of his soul, and all minor objects had ceased to interest; and to the attainment of this object no sacrifice would have been deemed too great. Fortune had ever smiled on him, and the habit of wielding power had blunted in some measure his sympathy for others. He viewed mankind more as the medium through which the great plans he formed for the welfare of his Country were to be matured, than as rivals. He knew and hourly felt that many vied with him in talents and ability, many were more attractive in manners; but he also knew and *felt* that morality in conduct, sobriety, unceasing industry and endless application, even to the most trivial concerns of business, placed him in a scale far above the general run even of the gifted of mankind.[71]

This is as shrewd an assessment as any, early or late, though it described a man then in the White House, not a man in a Saint Petersburg apartment or a Paris hotel. Yet he did not change much over the years.

She captured his scholarly absorption, for he was a man who preferred to be alone in his study, where he read Tacitus and Cicero, Massillon and Madame de Staël, the Bible and Milton, and pondered how the Plantagenets organized their weights and measures. He was the most learned politician of his American generation, an eighteenth-century philosophe surviving into an antiphilosophical age. His own father's erudition was, by comparison, scattered and fragmentary. Louisa perhaps underestimated how much her husband studied men in life rather than in books, for his diaries are full of his conversations with diplomats, politicians, and gentlemen at dinner tables, and they often display an ability to grasp opinions not his own and some skill at portraiture. But she was not wrong to see that, for all that, he tended to form his opinions in the solitude of his study and mind, and often was jarring to those around him when he emerged into a drawing room, let alone a congressional chamber. This is something he knew about himself almost from the first. When in London in 1795, he wrote in his diary, "To myself at the close of the day I can only say, Oh! stupid Vanity! when wilt thou learn to be silent?" And "Dissatisfied again. I can never please myself but in solitude." James Bayard, who observed John Quincy Adams in Saint Petersburg, was not singular in offering this description: "He has little talent for society and does [not] appear to enjoy it. His address is singularly cold and repulsive. His manners are harsh and you seldom perceive the least effort to please any one." At best, Adams pleaded inadvertence. As he was to put it in 1821, "I am certainly not intentionally repulsive in my manners and Deportment." But inflexibility was almost a moral principle with him. He had the sense that he ought to stand for something and that pliability betrayed a weakness of character. He spoke of "the free and bold expression of my opinion, which I disdain to withhold."[72] He thought he should speak his mind, and it could puzzle him why anyone would be offended by a truth. It did not help that he had almost no sense of humor beyond heavy irony, although— like many humorless people—he liked to be made to laugh.

Many found him not rude, but inscrutable. As Louisa put it, "The natural coldness and reserve of his manners defied the penetration of the most indefatigably prying curiosity, to discover his thoughts, or to perceive his motives of action." His own children were often puzzled. In 1824, Charles Francis Adams was to write in his diary: "My father is, as usual, unpenetrating. He is the only man I ever saw, whose feelings I could not penetrate almost always, but I can study his countenance for ever and very seldom can find any sure guide by which to move." Shrewdly, he added, "He makes enemies by perpetually wearing the Iron mask." Worse than making enemies was that, after youth, he acquired only acquaintances. His wife made friends wherever she went and had the gift for it, but he did not. He came to notice the fact, mostly because it had political implications, in an American world where friendship and enmity almost defined politics. In 1820, he noted, "I [have] scarcely a single friend, personal or political, in the House, and, at the first session after I came here, not ten members with whom I had any acquaintance at all." But he would not have known where to start, because he would have had to trust someone other than himself, someone not an Adams, and he did not know how to do that. One of his mottoes was "Lean not on friendship or on time." Late in life, when things grew more bitter, he seemed even to want to exclude his wife, along with the rest: "If there is a lesson necessary for my peace of mind in this world, it is to form no strong attachment to any person or thing that it contains; and if I have a weakness growing upon me above all others, it is that of attaching myself inordinately both to persons and things—to persons from whom I must part; to things which bring me nothing but disappointment."[73]

Part of his character was a barely disguised indifference to what he found uninteresting. Not unjustly, this was read as coldness, though he was usually oblivious of this response. In 1819, when in the State Department, he was visited by a Mr. Jenkins, who brought with him a sheet full of Scripture, prayers, poetry, and "pious admonitions against duelling," which he intended to publish. Jenkins asked the secretary to sign a certificate recommending the venture. This was refused and a debate ensued. As Adams observed in his diary, "My wife, who was present, thought I had treated him harshly, and no doubt he thought so still more himself," though Adams felt he had borne the impertinence of the man "with composure." "[Louisa said] I looked all the ill temper that I suppressed in words." "The result is," he gloomily noted, "that I am a man of reserved, cold, austere, and forbidding manners; my political adversaries say, a gloomy misanthropist, and my personal enemies, an unsocial savage. With a knowledge of the actual defect in my character, I have not the pliability to reform it."[74]

More instructive, because less casual, is an incident in 1806. When the senator was boarding in Georgetown with Nancy and Walter Hellen, one of their young sons died. From Boston, Louisa wrote to her husband: "I know, and feel, how unnecessary it is, to urge you to offer all consolation, in your power, but there are a numberless little attentions, trifling in themselves, which it is in our power to offer on such occasions, and which afford the greatest consolation, to the unhappy. forgive, my friend this observation. I know how much your mind is occupied, and how *almost impossible*, it is for you, to attend to such circumstances, but I likewise know the goodness of your heart, and I am sure you will not feel offended at this suggestion. Nancy from a doubt of the strength of her *mind*, has repeatedly said, she was convinced you thought her too insignificant, to pay her any sort of attention." Louisa knew that his was but *"seeming unkindness,"* but also knew that this unintentionality was of little help to those ignored. So she urged him to "those little civilities, which by raising us in our own esteem, inspires us with gratitude, and thereby render us anxiously solicitous, to return by every means in our power, those sweet, and flattering attentions, which form the basis of mans happiness."[75]

By this he was taken aback. In his own eyes, as the man who rented the upstairs room, carried books in and out, went off to the Senate, and said very little, he was kindly enough and had noticed the Hellens. Yet his reply showed how awkwardly he understood such things. He said that he had been sincerely concerned, though he had been unsure whether expressing concern would have been of use. For he did "not know what are the *trifling attentions*, by which the heart of a mother can be comforted upon the death of a darling child." On the broader issue, he was regretful if Nancy had ever thought "my want of attention to her has proceeded from an unjust appreciation of her strength of mind," for he respected and admired her. Any inadequacy of gentlemanly manners on his part did not proceed from arrogance or self-importance. In fact, "for your sake and for that of your sisters I have often wished that I had been that man of elegant and accomplished manners, who can recommend himself to the regard of others, by *little attentions*—I have always known however that I was not, and have been sensible that I could never be made that man." He knew that the uncharitable would understand him to be unfeeling and could only hope, instead, that his conduct would "authorize persons disposed to kind construction, to describe my imperfections to [a] lighter shaded fault."[76]

This obliviousness in John Quincy Adams could shade into the comic. He was not a man who dressed very well, except when under compulsion, which his wife and mother often had to exert. As Louisa observed in 1845, from her long and exasperating experience: "He is a man with whom you cannot temporise . . . The little attentions which are mere common places in this world are utterly lost upon a man who thinks [it] a great offence to be asked to change his Coat or to put on a clean Shirt."[77] So the fierce rectitude of his opinions issued from a man whose cravat was awry or whose socks were oddly colored.

In *The Metropolitan Kaleidoscope*, Louisa was most shrewd to observe the fierce repression of his feelings, the emotions she could read but others could not. John Adams, too, had been prone to injudicious truth-telling, which his friends dubbed honesty and his enemies a loss of good sense. But no one ever doubted what John Adams thought or felt, because he was an open book. His son took a different path, in a hopeless attempt to evade the criticism, calumny, and failures that dogged his volatile father's career. This is what Louisa meant when she observed that her husband was "the creature of Art rather than Nature." For the son tried concealing his feelings, though seldom to himself. His diary fully justifies her sense of "the volcano that burnt within," for it is riddled with anxiety, self-doubt, and anguish of mind. This emotional turmoil was almost exclusively introspective; he looked constantly into his own mind and heart and constantly found shortcoming, though as constantly acquitted himself of impurity of principle and conduct. He had, moreover, no capacity for empathy. He observed what other people said and did, but had little capacity for understanding how they felt. The absence of a description of his wife's feelings is a striking feature of his diary, but it formed part of a wider neglect, for his relentless sense of morality and principle had a way of turning others into embodiments of what the eighteenth century termed "character," into types that personified morality or immorality.

His response to the death of his mother in 1818 was symptomatic. He was deeply upset, so upset he did what he never did, which was to vary his routine. He came home early from the State Department, shed tears—what he called "indulging the weakness of nature"—and the next day "omitted . . . my usual attendance at the office." He sat down to describe Abigail Adams in his diary. What he remembered of her was a catalog of virtues: she was a woman kindly, cheerful, guileless, calm, patriotic, with "a price . . . above rubies." This list denoted his powerful sense that, in what he saw as the essential business of life—which was that of virtue battling with fortitude against vice and adversity—his mother had fought the good fight. The best that he could say of her, and for him it was the best he could say of anyone, was that she had transcended humanity and achieved the repression to which he himself aspired and in which he took pride. "My mother was an angel upon earth. She was a minister of blessing to all human beings within her sphere of action. Her heart was the abode of heavenly purity. She had no feelings but of kindness and beneficence; yet her mind was as firm as her temper was mild and gentle. She had known sorrow, but her sorrow was silent. She was acquainted with grief, but it was deposited in her own bosom. She was the real personification of female virtue, of piety, of charity, of ever active and never intermitting benevolence." Of course, this was not Abigail Adams, but an abstraction. Grief can turn the dead into abstraction and grief is often allayed by this process. But when his grief ebbed, he did not revise this opinion, for in 1839 he concluded a biographical sketch of his mother by saying that she had left "to the women of her country an example which, could it be universally followed, would restore to mankind the state of paradise before the fall."[78]

However, that his diary after 1818 hardly ever mentioned his mother helps to justify another part of Louisa's portrait, her observation that he was, beyond his wife and children, "utterly indifferent to almost all the other branches of his family." This verdict is implausibly stringent, though it hovers around a truth. It might be better to say not that he cared nothing for his kin (for he obviously did), but that he seldom arranged his life to cement his relationship to them, beyond his summer visits to Quincy. This was partly because, as Louisa also argued too severely, "ambition absorbed every thought of his soul, and all minor objects had ceased interest; and to the attainment of this object no sacrifice would have been deemed too great." In such ambition, John Quincy Adams and his parents had long since entered into a pact. They had trained him to be ambitious, even though they knew that ambition attenuated family links. One reward of ambition, however, was that there was something to share. John Quincy Adams's long correspondence with his father and mother was almost exclusively political. It is a striking fact that, when the son sat down in the spring of 1801 to inform his mother about recent events in Berlin, he spent the first three and a half pages in a discussion of the political situation. In the last small paragraph, he wrote: "The day before yesterday, at half past three o'clock afternoon, my dear Louisa gave me a Son—She has had a very severe time through the winter, and is now so ill that I dare not write to her mother; to give her notice of this event—I will humbly hope that in a few days I may be relieved from my anxiety on her account and enabled to announce to her mother only news of joy—The child is well."[79] This, after four miscarriages.

He was not drawn to family history, except as a duty little discharged. Only occasionally, with a nervous side glance, did he formally contemplate what it might mean to be an Adams, though he knew it meant almost everything. In 1833, he wrote, "There is no passion more deeply seated in my bosom than the longing for posterity worthily to support my own and my father's name." But he would scarcely lift a finger to bring this about. In September 1824, he visited his father in Quincy. In his diary, he wrote: "I walked in the burying-yard, and viewed the granite tombstones erected over the graves of my ancestors by my father . . . Four generations, of whom very little more is known than is recorded upon these stones. There are three suceeding generations of us now living. Pass another century, and we shall all be mouldering in the same dust, or resolved into the same elements. Who then of our posterity shall visit this yard? And what shall he read engraved upon the stones?"[80] He lacked the desire, which his son Charles Francis was to have in abundance, to excavate his family's past to ensure that posterity would come to visit the moldering dust. Louisa was more assiduous in her familial historical awareness, especially of the Johnsons, but even of the Adamses.

In the days after his return to Quincy in 1829, after leaving the White House, John Quincy did try to arrange his father's papers, in order to prepare a biographical memoir, and he even read New England history in a desultory way. But little came of it, and his willingness to be elected to the House of Representatives in 1831 was, in part, driven by his desire to evade the obligations of *pietas*. In 1839, Louisa was to write to him with startling severity about this neglect. She reminded him that he owed everything to his parents: "You were their Son; not more highly gifted than their other children—But on you alone they lavished their substance; and brought you up in a Sphere of the highest order, and of great cost; procuring you every advantage, I may almost say at the expense of those, who with the same rights, could not attain the means to produce the same ends." She further reminded him that in 1836 she had showed him an old letter in which he had promised his mother to deal with his father's papers and spoken of this task as a "sacred duty." "Will you let this Letter go down to your posterity, to show the nothingness of such promises," she asked. "Can you trample over the manes of those who did so much for you, in the sacred Mausoleum where they are laid; and in the very presence of the Almighty treat their memories with neglect?"[81] In truth, the rough answer was yes.

Until he entered the State Department, Louisa Adams took little interest in the political and diplomatic issues that absorbed her husband's mind and time. She shared his Federalist conservatism, especially his mistrust of democracy as a system plagued by demagoguery, as well as his sense that intrigue too often trumped wise policy. She once wrote of "the buffoonery of the modern democracy" and habitually of loathing political intrigue and the persecution of public figures. She went beyond him in complaining about republics as a political form, not because she disapproved of republics or even the principle of equality—though her view on the latter is less clear—but because she became acutely conscious of the social hypocrisy inescapable in a society that preached equality but practiced social distinction. Her indifference to what he did in diplomacy and politics, however, put a barrier between them as husband and wife, for what he did was who he felt himself to be. So she did not know all of him or even most of him. For a long time, this was what he preferred. As she was to put it of her position in 1799, even in respect of news about the French Revolution, "I knew so little concerning politicks, I seldom heard, and never enquired what was going on—I only knew that it was a period of great events, which I did not understand; and in which I individually took no interest—Mr Adams had always accustomed me to believe, that Women had nothing to do with politics, and as he was the glass from which my opinions were reflected, I was convinced of its truth, and sought no farther."[82]

Nonetheless, while indifferent to the details, she respected what he did. Much of her regard for him rested on the fact that he had earned the respect of his world, that fellow diplomats trusted his judgment, that kings and emperors knew the American minister merited his place. As his wife, this respectability radiated to her and, after the humiliations of 1797, she stood in much need of this warm glow. Among the first words of her 1827 portrait are these: "Lord Sharply was a man of outstanding talents; and great acquirements . . . He had filled many high Stations most honorably and with great satisfaction to the Nation and Government he represented." But much earlier, too, she had written, "Talent acquirement, information and learning, is the only pass port which will ensure respect, and claim and maintain its station all over the world; and this was the sterling gold to which I bowed in the choice of my husband, and which in every position in which he has been placed in this world; has been *felt*, *understood*, and *granted* in the midst of trial, persecution, disappointment, and affliction—Such greatness bears its *own* stamp, and is the reward of *years*."[83]

His own estimate of their marriage was tempered and as much a judgment upon the institution as on the two of them, and so she tended to disappear into her social role as wife and mother. Yet he did notice idiosyncratic qualities, things that were Louisa or himself alone. In 1811, on his wedding anniversary, he wrote this: "I have this day been married fourteen years, during which I have to bless God for the enjoyment of a portion of felicity, resulting from this relation in society, greater than falls to the generality of mankind, and far beyond anything that I have been conscious of deserving. Its greatest alloy has arisen from the delicacy of my wife's constitution, the ill health which has afflicted her much of the time, and the misfortunes she has suffered from it. Our union has not been without its trials, nor invariably without dissensions between us. There are many differences of sentiment, of tastes, and of opinions in regard to domestic economy, and to the education of children, between us. There are natural frailties of temper in both of us; both being quick and irascible, and mine being sometimes harsh. But she has always been a faithful and affectionate wife, and a careful, tender, indulgent, and watchful mother to our children, all of whom she nursed herself. I have found in this connection from decisive experience the superior happiness of the marriage state over that of celibacy, and a full conviction that my lot in marriage has been highly favored."[84]

Her estimate was bleaker. There were moments, especially late in life when she was picking at her scabs, when she considered her marriage a mistake. But though there was bitterness, it was not always partisan. She understood that he was flawed, that she was flawed, that much had happened by accident, that pain could be unintentional. She spoke of him as "a negligent and half indulgent husband," and it is easy enough to document the negligence.[85] There were the long hours when he was in his study, at his office, walking alone on the Fontanka, and endlessly writing down words into his diary. There were the moments in social gatherings when he was rude or thoughtless or distracted, and this was a discourtesy to her, too. There were the quarrels about money, about whether they could buy a carriage or live with a son. There was her frequent fear that he was angry, that he was poised to criticize her. There were, most of all, the abrupt decisions he made about how her life would be shaped.

But he had another side, for which "half indulgent" is too belittling a phrase. For he was, in his own way, a very domestic creature. If he had been the sort of politician who went to the racetrack and hung around in taverns, she might have been less discontented, for then he would not have raised expectations that he could not satisfy. He inherited this sense of domesticity partly from his father, who had also disliked rowdy men, preferred his study, and liked the conversation of the family drawing room. For both father and son, however, the chief merit of domesticity was less what happened at home, more that home was a refuge. As the son put it in 1804, "It is in the bosom of domestic enjoyment alone that I can flatter myself with an alleviation from the thankless task which the public service will impose upon me; and if it pleases Heaven to restore me to you and our darlings with the blessing of health; all other cares will sit light comparatively speaking upon the mind of your ever affectionate friend." It would be well to remember that, for an upper-class man of that time, domesticity was mostly a matter of showing up. There were decisions to be made and accounts to be kept but, for almost everything else, there were servants and a wife, who might only be the first among his servants. Curiously, she felt that he would have been better served by a less domestic wife. As she put it, "Ambition was not one of my Sins and . . . I felt that my husband should have had a Wife fond of display, with a soaring mind and qualities of a much higher grade than those of a woman, who was content to live at home and nurse her tender babes." Yet this was wrong on almost all counts: she was ambitious, she liked display, and he disliked intellectual women.[86]

When at home and not secluded, there were things he liked to do, which she liked him doing. He would read to her in the evenings, sit and talk in her boudoir, lead prayers, play whist, and teach his children to speak French. He came especially to like gardening and "entered heart and soul in the pursuit of plants [and] wild flowers," while she loved flowers and wrote poetry crowded with roses, lilies, and heartsease. For all her worry about his anger, she was as conscious of his kindness, affection, and care. When she was ill, he would grow so anxious and restless and lose so much sleep that it almost worsened her predicament. "His kindness was unremited in promoting my comfort," she remembered, but "the perpetual anxiety which he displayed however had a tendency to defeat his wishes, and to keep me in a state of disquietude beyond my strength." So he was the sort of man who would lift his wife into a carriage when she could not walk, the sort of man on whose arm she could lean. He was very good in a crisis, so much so that over the years she had a tendency to melodrama as a way of getting his attention. When they were apart, she missed him. Her letters to him have an engaging, tumbling quality and betray someone who felt relaxed about her right to gossip, to relate her worries, to make her complaints, to gingerly offer her advice, and to talk about her reading. She was later to criticize George Bancroft's wife, Sarah, for being too deferential to her husband: "She is a very pleasing woman . . . [but] has a little too much of 'Mr Bancroft say's' introduced into her conversation—Now I like very well to adopt my husbands thoughts and words when I approve them; but I do not like to repeat them like a Parrot, and *prove myself* a non entity—When my husband married me he made a great mistake if he thought I only intended to play echo—I like the piquancy of contradiction which often calls forth new ideas, and it is fortunate for me that I have a goodly portion to gratify the taste—Socrates would have been but half a Philosopher had it not been for Xantippe."[87]

Taking both sides of the correspondence, one can see two people who were intimate. Probably their sexual relationship was important in this, though it is impossible to know, except that the frequency of her pregnancies suggest that intercourse was, at least, habitual or even too habitual. Now and again, he would end his letters with "I send you *les plus tendres baissers de l'amour*," which was as erotic a subscription as their culture permitted, and he would speak of flying "to the arms of my best beloved." In her turn, she would write, "God bless and speed you soon to the arms and heart of your faithful wife." On one occasion, he even ventured a sexual joke. "Did you see the account of the celebration of Independence somewhere in Vermont," he asked her in 1822. "The Oration of Miss Coke, and the 'four and twenty damsels all in a row' that represented the States—I liked it so much, that I wished a speedy downfall to the Independence of them all; for the benefit of the '*rising Generation*.'" To this, she drily replied, "I did not see the account you speak of in the Vermont paper, but your joke was not lost."[88]

So this was the marriage that, waiting in her Frankfurt hotel, she was anxious to resume. This history alone may be enough to explain why she wished to press on, to the point of folly. But there was one other thing in their life together that mattered deeply, which explains why Mrs. Adams wished to prove herself by going on. This was the matter of her daughter.

Late in 1810 in Saint Petersburg, she had become pregnant again and, in the spring and early summer of 1811, she endured her usual travails of morning sickness, headaches, and fever. There was the customary worry that she would miscarry, the usual ministrations of doctors who came to bleed her, apply leeches to her wrist, and give her laudanum. The Imperial family noticed her condition and were kindly. At a ball in mid-January, she was granted the condescension of entering the Winter Palace by the entrance reserved to the family itself and to the ambassadors, and she was given a special chair on which to sit.[89]

The pregnancy made her feel more than usually separated from her family in Washington and her sons in Massachusetts. "To give birth to another Child in a strange land after all I had suffered was a cause of incessant fear and anxiety," she noted. In the late spring, her sense of that remoteness was immeasurably deepened, because of unexpected bad news. On May 23, her husband received a bundle of American letters, sending word that Louisa's sister Nancy Hellen had died unexpectedly in childbirth, news that made Louisa restlessly ill.[90]

In the middle of July, the family was forced inconveniently to move. The tsar had decided to purchase the building in which they lived and, with a quick improvisation, they took a summer dacha on Apothecary's Island, some five miles to the northeast of the city and beyond the Peter and Paul Fortress. The cottage had a view of the Great Nevka River and its lazy boats, of the tsar's Stone Palace, and of the elegant rural retreat that belonged to their friends the Stroganoffs. Nearby, too, was the city's botanical garden. John Quincy was to remember this period with nostalgic fondness, for it was quiet and secluded, like a "hermitage a hundred miles from the city," and there were many sylvan walks by the river to ease his mind. For her it came at a bad time, for the move involved extra fatigue for a body already very tired and too often she had to travel back and forth to the city. But she liked the place, too. She would take a chair to the end of the garden, sit on the riverbank, and with Charles catch fish "not worth eating."[91]

On August 12, she was delivered of a daughter, who was christened as Louisa Catherine after her mother. In early October, the family moved back to the city for the winter, to a different and inferior apartment not far from where they had previously lived on the Moika Canal. In early November, the child was inoculated for smallpox and, as was usual, her arm became inflamed. In late November, she had the mumps, but recovered. Her mother had her usual winter illnesses (a fever, a cough), as did everyone else, but also had an inflammation of her breast occasioned by feeding the child. Still, she resumed a normal social life—going to the theater, the court's ceremonials. And the baby grew lovely. "Such a pair of Eyes!! I fear I love her too well."[92]

Then, at the end of January, there came more bad news from America, almost as bad as it could be. There had been four deaths. Louisa's mother had died on September 29 and her brother-in-law Andrew Buchanan, Caroline's husband, a few days later. On October 15, Richard Cranch had died and the next day his wife, Mary Smith Cranch; this was the couple, John Quincy's aunt and uncle, who had been looking after their sons George and John. In addition, there was word that Nabby Adams, John Quincy's sister, was ill of breast cancer. The Cranches were old, so this news was not too unexpected, but Catherine Nuth Johnson was only in her mid-fifties, Buchanan was still younger, and Nabby was forty-seven, only two years older than her brother. (She would die a year later.) Amid this "mortal affliction," Louisa grew even more conscious of the remoteness of her Russian existence, the more so because the human landscape of the America she had left was now irrevocably altered. She felt helpless. "My Poor Mother! After ten years of poverty dependence and severe suffering which at this great distance it was so utterly out of my power to mitigate or asuage—How different will home appear should we live to return." Having lost the woman above her in the chain of generations, Louisa clung the more to her "lovely beautiful Babe."[93]

In mid-July 1812, the baby sickened and their usual physician, Dr. Galloway, came and diagnosed dysentery. For some days, her health fluctuated, but into early August she improved. On her birthday, August 12, she was ritually measured and found to be two feet and three inches long. A day later, she was well enough to join the family on an expedition to see the tsar's palace at Oranienbaum, twenty-five miles from the city. A week later, however, the dysentery recurred, there was a high fever, and Galloway came again. It was suggested that it might help if Mrs. Adams resumed nursing the child, so she did. There was an improvement, then on August 23 a relapse. There were the old "violent symptoms" but also new ones "yet more alarming."

Galloway was sent for again, but word came that he was out of town for several days. So a Dr. Simpson was sent for instead, but he was out to dinner and not expected back until midnight. At eleven at night, they sent a carriage to wait upon him, with an urgent request that he come immediately. At midnight the carriage returned and a servant reported that Simpson had declined to come then, but promised attendance in the morning. John Quincy would not accept this, went himself to rouse Simpson from his bed, and brought the doctor back. Simpson examined the child, prescribed an emetic "and other things," and left. The father stayed up until two or three in the morning, his wife until four. The next day there was a small improvement, but the baby remained "yet dangerously ill" for several more days. On August 26, Galloway returned. Both he and Simpson recommended that the baby be taken into the countryside for a change of air. So they quickly scrambled to find a dacha. Annette Krehmer, who had a place in Octa, knew of a house a few doors away, and an arrangement was made. On August 30, before dinner Mrs. Adams went with the baby and a nurse to the dacha, and soon after they were joined by her sister and son, and their housemaid Maria Polana. John Quincy remained in the city, but commuted to the country as the situation warranted.[94]

It seemed to the family and doctors that part of the problem was the child's painful and debilitating teething. Every day she grew weaker. By September 4, the father was preparing himself for the worst. "After doing all that human power can do for its relief, I endeavour by reflection to brace my mind by reason and reflection to an event which I cannot disguise to myself to be probable. But reason has little if any more controul over the pains of the mind than over those of the body. I came home late this Evening with feelings which it is perhaps weakness to suffer, and which it were yet weakness to express." The next day Galloway came, but the baby was suffering "incessant torture" from her teeth. By September 7, there was a new symptom—convulsions. The next day, the doctors recommended that mother and child return to the city. By the tenth, they considered lancing the baby's gums, and a surgeon called Gibbes was sent for. He came almost at midnight, examined the child, noted that there were at least seven teeth coming at once, but "no one of them [was] sufficiently advanced to render lancing the gum advisable." He promised to come back the next day and reexamine by daylight. In the event, it was Galloway who came and, whether knowingly or not, contradicted the surgeon's advice and lanced one of the gums. Her illness grew more violent "and none of the physicians [had] any hopes of her recovery."[95]

The night of the eleventh was quieter, but in the morning she had more convulsions, which continued all day. Louisa herself became ill and had to leave the baby's side, after having been there incessantly for three days and nights. It was felt she should be "spared witnessing the last struggles" of her daughter. Catherine and the nurse remained, and John Quincy moved between child, mother, and the reading of sermons. Another night passed, and on the morning of September 14 Louisa returned to the side of the cradle. The doctors had been trying every remedy that their blunt science suggested—warm baths, injections of laudanum and digitalis, shaving the head. They applied to the back of her head a "blister," that is, a plaster (usually made of crushed Spanish flies) designed to raise a blister, which was then thought helpful for "spasmodic infections" and toothaches, but also risky. By eight in the evening, the final crisis began and everyone had abandoned hope. Catherine, who had been by the side of the cradle for the last two days, fainted with exhaustion and grief, then rallied and returned.[96]

At 1:25 on the morning of September 15, the baby died. John Quincy went to tell Louisa in the next chamber. She fainted and was unconscious for a few minutes. With satisfaction, for he was a man who believed in such qualities, he observed that she "received the shock with a resignation and fortitude, which manifested that her strength was proportioned to her trial." The doctors returned and bled Catherine, who had become ill. John Quincy began the business of arranging a funeral, while Annette Krehmer arrived to offer consolation and sympathy. For the rest of the day and the next, Louisa was very ill. On September 17, at eleven in the morning, the child's funeral service was conducted by the Reverend Pitt in the English Factory Church, the same church where she had been christened a year earlier. Mrs. Adams was too ill or too upset to attend and there were only a handful of people, just seven including the minister: John Quincy Adams, Charles Francis Adams, Levett Harris, Annette Krehmer, Chevalier Bezzara (the Brazilian minister), and William Steuben Smith. Afterward, the small group minus Bezzara accompanied the coffin across the Neva to Vasilevsky Island and the so-called Lutheran Cemetery, where all those who were not Russian Orthodox were buried, whether Lutheran, Anglican, or Jewish, whether German, English, or American. She was buried "on an elevated spot of ground, immediately behind the tomb of poor Blodget," another American.[97]

By all this, John Quincy Adams was greatly moved. In his diary, he kept meticulous track of the events, preached sermons of religious fortitude to himself, and gave way to raw emotion. He wrote of his "tenderly beloved child," of his "darling infant," and of having rejoiced in seeing her reach the age when "the first dawn of intelligence begins to reward the Parents pains and benefits." He wrote of her charms, the delight she gave, of "rapture and promise," of "her beaming intelligence and angelic temper." As always, he turned to religion as a consolation, to the expectation of his daughter's removal to a better place. But he admitted to a sense of desolation: "There is nothing upon Earth that can administer relief to my affliction. I cling more than ever to the bosom of my family; and I seek for the promises of hereafter, as the heart panteth for the cooling Brooks. I pray that the Calamity which has befallen me, may produce no unsuitable impressions upon my heart or mind!"[98]

It was a measure of his distress that it was six days before he wrote a letter to his mother to relay the news. It was even more the measure of his pain that he wrote only on this subject and, for once, ignored the political discussion that was their bond. "I can write you upon no other subject at present," he felt it necessary to explain. He was conscious of piling another bereavement upon all the other bereavements—those of Nancy Hellen, Andrew Buchanan, Catherine Nuth Johnson, Richard Cranch, and Mary Smith Cranch. "The turn has now come to me to ask your sympathy for our own peculiar Distress—we have lost our dear and only daughter—as lovely and promising a child, as ever was taken from the hopes of the fondest parent." He narrated the course of the crisis over its four weeks: the teething, the weaning and return to the breast, the dysentery and fever, the convulsions, the move to the country, the return to the city. He spoke of "inexpressible anguish," but was conscious that, as a man, he did not grasp how a woman and mother might feel. "The feelings of the Mother and the Nurse, can only be conceived by those who like you, have been called to pass through the same trial." He observed that the child's sufferings "were [so] severe the sight of them would have wrung with compassion a heart of marble." He praised his wife: "Her mother—at all times and to all her children one of the tenderest and most affectionate of mothers, attended her with the most unabating assiduity and vigilance night and day, until the close of the scene—Faithfully did she perform every duty, and exert every faculty that God and nature had given her, to preserve the darling of her heart." As in his diary, he praised "the calm Fortitude and pious Resignation of my dearest friend [which] has been as remarkable as her unbounded self devotion, and unremitting attentions had been while there was yet a spark of life which by any possibility could have been restored." He praised, too, Catherine, for her indefatigable kindness and vigilance. He praised even William Steuben Smith, who "gave us every assistance in his power, and we have not been without other kind and sympathizing friends." And, as he knew his mother would understand, he reiterated his religious and moral conclusions, indeed what had been his bleak anticipation. "There are passages in the Scriptures which seem to imply, if they do not directly assert, that the death of infant children is sometimes inflicted as chastisement for the transgressions of their parents." If this was so, he humbled himself "before the chastening hand, with a heart full of gratitude, for the blessings great and manifold, which are still left me." This bereavement was "an admonition to be prepared not only for my own departure a contemplation by no means painful, but for other privations no less terrible than that which I am now enduring."

"If there be a moral government of the Universe," he wrote—and the *if* was significant, especially at such a moment, the kind of moment that challenged even a believer's faith in God's order—"my child is in the enjoyment of blessedness or exists without suffering and [is] reserved for an alloyed bliss hereafter."[99]

He was sharply aware that his own suffering was not as great as his wife's and that this was a blow that might be permanently damaging. "Since the loss of my beloved child," he wrote in his diary by way of summary of the month of September, "our domestic condition is no longer the same as before. The privation and the vacuity are more keenly and constantly felt by her mother than by me. The maternal cares were the business as well as the enjoyment of life—The loss of them is a most severe if not an irremediable wound." As for himself, he resumed his "usual occupations," and there had been much going on in the world which offered distraction.[100] It was 1812, after all. In the midst of it all, the American minister had received word that on June 12 the United States had declared war on Britain. And on the day when the young Louisa Catherine Adams had died, Napoleon had entered Moscow. The next day, the city was in flames.

Mrs. Adams cared nothing then for Napoleon and Moscow, for the death of her daughter plunged her into the deepest depression and produced what she called "a great change in my character." She herself thought that she had drifted very close to madness: "I often involuntarily question myself as to the perfect sanity of my mind in this state of spirits." The tragedy brought all the torments, all the grievances, all the maladjustments of her life and marriage, into rancorous focus. However much the agony of the child's death had brought her and her husband together in grief, the aftermath drove them apart, far more than he realized, though he realized some of it.[101]

Her diary grew very fragmentary as it moved through the period when the child had sickened. It ends with four bleak lines:

3 August Went into the Country with my sick Child
9 Took my babe back to the City in Convulsions

Dr Simpson and Galloway both attend the Babe
15 My Child gone to heaven[102]

Then there was a silence.

It would take her seven months before she wrote to Abigail Adams and she only did so after her husband's letter announcing the death had reached Quincy and Abigail's letter of condolence had returned to Saint Petersburg. Her mother-in-law was practiced at these moments, was thoughtfully lyrical and kind, and as usual mixed the personal with high religious generality. "Distance secluded me from knowing your distress or sharing your sorrows, at the time when you most needed consolation but neither time, or distance has banished from my bosom, that sympathy which altho billows rise and oceans roll between us; like mercy is not confined to time or space, but crosses the atlantic and mingles tears with you over the grave of your dear departed babe." She herself had once lost a baby: "Early in life I was called to taste the bitter cup forty years has not obliterated from my mind the anguish of my soul upon the occasion." But she reminded Louisa that grief was inappropriate for the child, "whom with an eye of faith I behold with other innocents, surrounding the throne of their maker, and singing Halelujahs to the most high." Mourning was for the living, not the dead. "For ourselves only we can mourn, and how selfish is that sorrow?" And mourning would pass, for "we have yet so many blessings left us. Such I hope will prove to you, and to their father your surviving children, who most earnestly long for your return to your native Country."[103]

Writing to his son two months later, John Adams was less sensitive. "As I have experienced Griefs as exquisite as yours I have the better right to advise you. I have no doubt you have delighted in the hope and prospect of educating a Daughter under your own eye that should be a perfect Woman, a Daughter, a Sister, a Wife a Mother an Aunt a Grandmother, without Reproach or fault." He suggested that his son recollect the Roman rhetorician Quintilian (who had suffered the death of two young sons and a wife) and contemplate how easily worlds were destroyed, let alone babies. "Have you looked at this Universe, through the Telescopes of Herschell?" he asked. If John Quincy Adams had, he would know that self, posterity, the earth, the solar system were of little moment. "Should I and all my Posterity be split like Mackarel and broiled on a Grid Iron? . . . what is this to the Eight Millions of People who inhabit our own Country." In conclusion: "These ideas are none of my own; but they are Sublime. And what is more they are rational."[104]

As he usually did in moments of crisis, John Quincy Adams tried to move toward his parents' standpoint, to remember the sublime, the religious, the rational, the great lessons of resignation and fortitude. It was hard, no doubt, for "the wound of the heart still bleeds" and "can never be entirely healed." "Reason and Principle" were "at all times competent to expel" feelings of despondency and anxiety, even the "distrust of the goodness and protection of Providence." Yet these feelings, these "ideas I am constantly endeavoring to controul" had a way of returning, so the expulsion would need to be done again.[105]

His wife saw things very differently. She tried to control her emotions, but she knew they were beyond control. She sought distraction, she tried reading, she went to the theater, but when she came back to the same apartment where the child had died, she saw only coldness, blankness, dread. "My first object used to be my Child but alas now I see only the spot on which she died and every thing recalls her last agonies." As she confessed to Abigail, "Although the effort is almost too much for me I will endeavor to controul the pangs of my bursting heart and entreat you to compassionate and not condemn a grief which is beyond my reason to subdue." For Louisa, this was not a tragedy that had happened blindly, as a thing that God and Providence had visited upon them. For her, religion did not explain why this had happened, though it did offer a consolation, hard to retain. Like Abigail, she imagined the child to be among the seraphim. Like her husband, she thought she was being punished for sin. But his sense of sin was impersonal, an admission of the fallen nature of man.

Her sense was agonizingly personal and lay in "the evil propensities" of her own nature, of herself alone. She felt the responsibility for her daughter's death lay not with God, not with human nature, but with her. She had "secret and bitter reproaches." She had procrastinated and taken too long to send for the doctors. She had weaned too soon. To Abigail, she confessed a greater crime. "Had you witnessed the hard circumstances of my Angels death you would pity and forgive me my heart almost broken my health is gone and my peace of mind is I fear forever destroy'd dreadful as the loss of my dear Sisters Child was to her she has at least the happiness of knowing that it was not occasion'd by any accidental circumstance while I have the horrid idea that I lost my darling owing to a fall which I had with her in my arms in which I did not perceive that she had met with the slightest injury but which is said to have been the cause of her death."[106] So, in her own mind, she had killed her own baby. That it had been an accident did not make her any less a murderer.

Haunted by grief, guilt, and despair, she pined for death, as though the only expiation for her crime would be her own extinction. "I struggle in vain against the affliction that consumes me and I feel that all my wishes centre in the grave . . . surely it is no crime to pray for death . . . my heart is buried in my Louisa's grave and my greatest longing is to be laid beside her even the desire of seing my beloved Boys gives way to this cherished hope and I look forward with joy to that Bourne from which no traveler returns." This desire to be laid beside her child was specific. There was a space next to the grave in the Lutheran cemetery and there she wanted to be buried. She panicked when someone fell mortally ill. "They tell me that Mr Cabot is likely to die and I cannot describe the terror I feel lest they should usurp the little spot of earth which I have set my heart on that adjoins my Louisa's grave in vain I reason with myself the desire is uncontroulable and my mind is perpetually dwelling upon some means to procure this desired blessing."[107]

She began to have nightmares. In one, the guilts of her past and present jostled. She saw herself in the Octa dacha, to which she had futilely gone in the summer of 1812. There she was playing with her baby "who appear'd in pale health," but was summoned by her father and his gentlemen company in the next room, where she was directed to fetch wine from the cellar. She asked her sister Nancy Hellen to go with her. At the bottom of the stairs, in a deep vault, she "stumbled and fell over a body newly murdered from which the blood still appear'd to stream." She got up from the floor "and looked for my Sister who seem'd to stand as if immovable and as if just risen from the grave." Despite her sense of terror, she got three bottles and took them back to her father. But he was dissatisfied and said that what she had brought was not wine but porter "entirely spoiled." "With the usual inconsistency of dreams," the scene then switched. Louisa was playing with the child, who now was "all life and animation," when an electrical storm broke. There was thunder and lightning, and the sky "was entirely obscured." The child disappeared "and I was left alone." The thunder stopped and she looked up, to see "as it were a stream of Fire which extended completely across the Heavens in which was distinctly written, 'Be of good cheer thy petition is granted.'" At this, in the dream, she fainted.[108]

Amid all this, her relationship with her husband deteriorated. Fairly quickly, he settled back into his usual routines and manners, while she did not and could not. He was admirable in a crisis, but for him the crisis was past. For her, it was intensifying. Her diary, which she resumed five weeks after the baby's death, is crowded with a sense of grievance. On October 25, she wrote that Mr. Adams had read prayers to her, a bare fact that his own diary confirms. However, as she went on to say though he did not, there was a quarrel. For some time, she had been teaching Charles his prayers and the commandments. Now her husband "expressed himself dissatisfied" with how she had done this. She became angry ("I suffered myself to be hurried away by my temper in a very unbecoming manner") and then self-pitying. "I am peculiarly unfortunate for what I undertake with the best intentions almost always turns out exactly contrary I read I work I endeavour to occupy myself usefully but it is all in vain." She explained to herself the context, that her heart was "almost broken" and her "temper which was never good suffers in proportion to my grief." She did what her husband had always told her to do, to "strive against it and humbly implore heaven to fortify my soul and to teach me meekness and resignation." But he was displeased. "He complains of my being suspicious and jealous." Her own sense was that he was right, though "these were faults once foreign to my nature." She had changed because of him. These new traits had been "insensibly acquired by a perpetual coldness and restraint operating on a naturally warm and affectionate disposition." It all made her feel that she was "a burthen . . . to all around me." She pined for America, she pined even for Abigail—"in Mrs Adams I should have found a comforter a friend who would pity sufferings which *she* would have understood." But her husband was not a comforter, not a friend, or so she thought bitterly then, when she was pining for death.[109]

To distract herself, she started to read the memoirs of Frenchwomen, but even these drew her back to bleak conclusions, to a sense that everyone was helpless in the hands of fate, that there was "little we can do of ourselves," and that it was folly to run away from even a bad marriage. In the character of Louis XIV, she discerned her husband's self-absorption: "Self was the rule by which he measured every thing and every body." This she took to be a lesson. "My Children guard against the silly failing of Vanity," she advised. A superior man, led on by the world's adulation, would by imperceptible stages become "incapable of relishing the common occurrences and socialities of life," and come to presume that "every thing that surrounds him must live for him." With this egotism, "no sacrifices however great and painful in those who are so unfortunate as to belong to him can satisfy for he is to much absorb'd in himself to imagine that people so inferior can feel otherwise than flatter'd and honour'd" to be near him and to serve him. She was passionate in condemning this. "Remember my beloved Children that we are sent into this world to promote as much as possible the happiness of each other," and this was the duty of the lesser and the eminent alike, humbly to support those less gifted.[110]

Her mind had been long divided about ambition. When courting, she had insisted that worldly ambition did not concern her. "You *know* my friend I am not ambitious of any thing but your affection," she had said in 1796, when discussing her prospective father-in-law's election to the presidency. By 1804, she was ambivalent about his striving for high honors: "Form'd for domestic life my whole soul devoted to you and my children yet ambitious to excess my heart and head are constantly at war." In 1806, he contemplated leaving politics and resuming the practice of law, but she did not advise him toward the latter, despite the fact that such a way of life would have reunited her family. She knew he would not be happy and believed that he was "eminently calculated to shine and to be of real and essential service" to his country. Then she was willing to say that "self and family comfort must sometimes be sacrificed for the general good." "Think not that this desire proceeds from a foolish and weak ambition," she wrote. No, "if I know my own heart it springs from the purest motives which banish every interest but the public welfare." Then she believed in her husband's purity of virtue: "Nature produces very few really great men," and most of them were corrupted by power. He would be different.[111]

In 1813, after another miscarriage in January, she saw her husband very differently, though also herself. She was sick of the idea of ambition. "They say I am ambitious," she noted, but she acquitted herself of the charge. "The vain projects of the world" did not preoccupy her, by comparison with "those to whom I am the most nearly connected." For him, there was no thought for "peace happiness family." He neglected everything "for this one object" of ambition, which had made her life a wasteland. Rather, she desperately wanted "something to soften the casualties to which the best of us are liable." She needed "one being who will open his heart" to her. She was stifled by this mood of "dreadful restraint over the most trifling things," which destroyed her self-confidence and blighted even "that portion of happiness which we are allowed to enjoy."[112]

This was her mood at this worst of moments, which ran from the death of her daughter in September 1812 until the summer of 1813, when she was able to say that her "health and spirits are so much amended that I scarcely know myself." Even so, even then, though she thanked God "for his great mercy in having raised me up and comforted me in my severe afflictions," she was still looking "forward with the hope of soon being reunited to my Angelic babe." So though she was better, she knew she had been changed. Now she knew that there was no "hope of future happiness" and youth had died.[113] She realized her entrapment in the fallible world that she and her husband had made.

·*6*·

FROM FRANKFURT TO PARIS

THIS WAS THE WOMAN waiting in the Frankfurt hotel. Since the winter of 1812/13, when her self-confidence had been crushed, she had slowly healed. There was much scar tissue, but she had learned that even a damaged woman could function. The months spent alone, when her husband had left in the spring of 1814, had helped, for she had had to cope. Her son had sensed the pain and offered comfort. In 1846, she was to write to him: "When I lost my beautiful Babe in St Petersburg your little tender assiduities; attentions gentle and affectionate beyond your years, breathed new hope into my sinking spirits and an assurance of that affection which has never yet failed me in trouble or in joy—I look back with pleasure to those hours when you were my only companion in the foreign Country, when I found delight in your opening mind."[1] The preparations and traveling the long roads from Saint Petersburg had helped, too, as had the warm reception in Berlin, where she had been recognized for herself, not just for being a wife. In Frankfurt, however, the test was more serious. Fixing a broken wheel on the Baltic shore was one thing, braving Napoleon another. But she had learned that running away was no good, that John Quincy Adams and her sons were all that she had beyond herself, however imperfect they all were, however much unhappiness she knew was implicated in arriving in Paris. More, she was half in love with death. At least, that is what she had told herself. For all that, her pulse had raced when she had seen the white bones on the battlefield of Hanau.

So she waited in the hotel with her son, but no servants beyond Madame Babet—two women and a boy alone. After a short time, as he had promised, the banker Bethmann returned with help, though not much. With him was only a fourteen-year-old Prussian boy, "the only creature he could find willing to go." But the boy seemed "very smart and active," so Mrs. Adams took him into her service "to let me in and out of the Carriage." This agreed, the banker dealt with her need for money and gave her the equivalent of 962.13 florins, or $385.06. He then took them all down to the carriage, gave instructions to the postilions about the route he was recommending, and bade farewell "with the kindest wishes" and, doubtless, many misgivings about the imprudence of Anglo-American ladies in the midst of European wars.[2] So the carriage set out at four o'clock on the afternoon of Friday, March 17, not westward toward Mayence but southwest. For the banker had advised that she travel to the Rhine crossing at Kehl, then strike northwesterly toward Paris.[3]

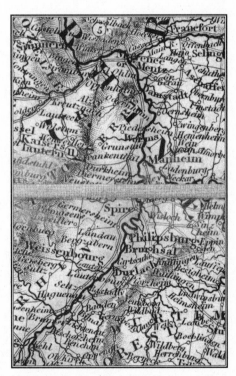

Frankfurt to Kehl

(From Aaron Arrowsmith, *Map Exhibiting the Great Post Roads, Physical and Political Divisions of Europe* [London: A. Arrowsmith, 1810])

As she traveled on, she began to talk to the Prussian boy. He proved of interest, because he shared some of her experiences of central and eastern Europe, but had a different perspective. In 1812, when only eleven, he had gone on the Russian campaign as a servant to a Prussian officer. (Napoleon had required his dependent ally Prussia to supply troops for the invasion.) This had been a great experience for one so young and naturally he liked to tell stories about it all. He had especially "a great many anecdotes concerning Napoleon during the retreat" from Moscow. About the emperor, he had very mixed feelings. He had witnessed the side of Napoleon that, over the years and the long campaigns, had led many soldiers to love and admire him, those moments when the great man would artfully mingle with his troops, sit down by their firesides, and share their soup "when they had any." On the other hand, the boy had seen how devastating were the consequences of the man's extraordinary ambition. No one who had seen and survived the retreat, a long march that Napoleon himself had rapidly abandoned when the hope of victory had disappeared in the freezing starvations of the winter, could have many illusions that the man was defined only by friendly gestures. So the boy, as she remembered, "expressed great hatred of the man, with all the petulance of boyish passion." These oscillating emotions Mrs. Adams observed, for "it was singular to watch the workings of this young mind, swayed equally by admiration and detestation, uttered in the strong language of natural feeling."[4]

All that is known from her memoir is that she went to Karlsruhe. She had no choice but to travel to Darmstadt and Heppenheim, but then she could have veered westward through Mannheim, or eastward through Heidelberg. Because shorter, the latter route was the more common.[5] If that is how she went, she started her journey by crossing the old stone bridge from Frankfurt to Saxenhausen, passed an old Roman tower, entered a wood of beeches, and passed over a sandy plain. Along her route were white distance markers, posthouses emblazoned with the Hessian lion, and "many fine, pleasant, and hospitable towns." She was now on much better roads. The Bergstrasse, the road between Darmstadt and Heidelberg that took its name from the mountainous ridge along which it passed, was celebrated for its smoothness. Decades earlier, Joseph II, the Holy Roman emperor, had persuaded the diet in Ratisbon to order that chaussées, or paved roads, be built throughout the empire. Most German states did nothing, but Hesse-Cassel and Darmstadt had acted, and their chaussées were "formed in a very expensive and beautiful style . . . generally very broad, and planted on both sides either with walnut or other fruit-trees and lofty elms, forming noble *allées*, which are kept in good repair."[6] From now on, Mrs. Adams would encounter better roads, for the French had in the eighteenth century far outstripped other European countries in the sophistication of their road construction. As early as 1716, they had established a department of Ponts et Chaussées, in 1747 founded a college of road engineering, and in 1775 appointed in Pierre Trésaguet an inspector general who reinvented the technology of road construction, by insisting that roads should be well drained, have surfaces impervious to water, be cambered, and have multiple layers of differently sized stones. In the 1780s, France had a "Corps of Roads, Bridges and Highways, with a staff of more than two hundred and fifty engineers and inspectors, and a budget of more than seven million *livres*."[7]

Entered through a two-mile avenue of poplars, Darmstadt was notable for the grand ducal palace of Hesse-Darmstadt, which was not too grand (indeed somewhat run-down). Several visitors thought the city reminiscent of an English spa like Tunbridge Wells, "with its regular buildings, its absence of the bustle of trade, and its quiet gentility," not to say its "well-bred listlessness and courtly demeanour." The posthouse where she stopped was the Hessian House. Next was Heppenheim, a small village on a tumbling stream where the inn was Le Soleil, from the windows of which one could see what remained of the ancient fort of Starkenburg, which Reichard designated the most beautiful of monuments to ancient chivalry, though in fact it had been built by a medieval abbot to defend himself against the military aggression of a bishop. Very quickly afterward, she passed into the grand duchy of Baden. The coats of the postilions became "buff turned up with red," and her road ran next to wheat fields and orchards to her right, with the Rhine in the far distance. In the fields worked peasant men who oddly wore "large cocked hats," and women whose own headgear was "of a monstrous size, flat, and [looking] like a sieve upon their heads." To her left were forested hills, often topped with stark and ruined castles, beyond which lay the Black Forest. Then she reached the old university town of Heidelberg, irregularly huddled beneath a great castellated crag. This was a famously romantic spot even then, especially for the high semidestroyed palace where once the Winter Queen, Elizabeth of Bohemia, had lived. Heidelberg was helping to define what Romanticism might mean, not least its sense that to visit exquisite dilapidation, a "green and beautiful decay," might offer a refuge from the bleak pressures of the new and lead one to "melancholy reflections upon the inconstancy of fortune, and the mutability of all human enterprizes."[8]

Finally, Mrs. Adams came to Karlsruhe. She reached it at about noon on Saturday, March 18, and stopped at an inn. If she stayed at the post station, it was La Croix, but there were other hotels, including La Cour de Darmstadt. Since she had come nearly a hundred miles, it is likely that she had traveled through the night. The city was another of those newly crafted communities (like Saint Petersburg and Washington) that she had so much inhabited, but it had not been laid out in 1715 with the usual parallelograms. At the city's northern edge sat the grand ducal palace of Baden, from which to its north radiated alleys of poplars projected into the Hardtwald forest. To the palace's south radiated more avenues, intersected by semicircular streets, so that the city seemed like a Spanish lady's fan. The result was "a masterpiece of the stately formality of the age," a place of elegant intimacy, which presented to the eye the appearance of "a large and very handsome country village," with buildings of "handsome gray stone," ruled over by what seemed "more like an English landlord amongst his peasantry, than an independent sovereign in his own capital."[9]

Here Mrs. Adams planned to pause and visit friends, who might give her useful information about the military and political situation. Karlsruhe was the family home of the Zähringen house of Baden, whose grand duke since 1811 had been Karl Ludwig Friedrich. Among his several siblings was his eldest sister, Princess Katharine Amalie

Christiane Luise (commonly known as Amalie), who was unmarried, and the former Princess Luise Marie Auguste, the woman who had become Tsarina Elizabeth Alexievna. Louisa Adams was under the impression that these two women, her old acquaintances from Saint Petersburg, were then in residence, along with Fréderica Bode, sister to Condesa Colombi and maid of honor to Princess Amalie. Fréderica was a woman whom a later traveler was to call "a singular instance of fascinating manners unconnected with beauty," in Karlsruhe the vivacious heart of every party and "the arranger of every pleasure."[10]

Mrs. Adams sent a message to the palace to ask for an audience, but word came back that, the day before, the empress and her sister had left for Munich. Prudently, they were moving away from Napoleon toward Vienna, where the tsar then was. The only person still in residence was the grand duchess, whom Mrs. Adams had never met, so she decided against going. Under the peculiar circumstances of March 1815, it would have been of interest to meet this "sparkling, smiling, actively graceful person," for, unlike her sisters-in-law, the grand duchess had little reason to fear the approach of Napoleon. She had been born in 1789 as Stéphanie de Beauharnais, the daughter of Claude de Beauharnais, comte de Roches-Baritaud, whose first cousin Alexandre, vicomte de Beauharnais, had in 1779 married a young woman from Martinique called Marie Josèphe Rose Tascher de la Pagerie, commonly called Joséphine. In 1796, two years after her husband's execution, this Joséphine had married a young officer called Napoleon Bonaparte. Since the pair had no children and it became useful for the emperor to have female relatives who might be married into other dynasties, he adopted Stéphanie, made her a *princesse de France*, and let her live in the Tuileries. In 1806, she was bargained away to the heir-apparent of the house of Zähringen, whose grandfather Karl Friedrich was helpfully made by Napoleon a grand duke.[11]

Instead of visiting the palace and seeing the gifts from Napoleon with which the grand duchess surrounded herself, instead of using the "tea-service of superb china, with [its] coffee-urn . . . of solid gold," Mrs. Adams stayed at her inn, resolved to push on in the afternoon, and had her plainer dinner. In Karlsruhe, it was customary for the table d'hôte to be available from twelve to one. While they were all eating, "the Master of the Inn came in, and informed me, that Napoleon had been taken, and that he had been tried immediately, and *Shot*." He was confident this report was true, "as it had just arrived at the Palace." With this, he left the room. Behind her, she heard a sharp noise, "an exclamation of horror," and looked around and saw the Prussian boy "pale as a ghost, and ready to faint." He looked distraught and piteous, and said, "O that great Man! I did not expect that!" In retrospect, she was to reflect that it was fortunate that the innkeeper had left the room and not seen this outburst of loyal grief: "He might have supposed me some violent Bonapartist, and the report would have been very unfavorable to my proceedings."[12]

At four o'clock, she procured her postilions, clad in the red-and-yellow livery of Baden, and departed without knowing how the political world stood or how her journey might now fare. The road that led to Kehl through Ettlingen, Rastadt, Stollhofen, and Bischoffsheim did little to diminish her incertitude, for it was full of wagons and soldiers "rushing towards the Frontier." They were singing or "roaring" their "national songs, and apparently in great glee at the idea of a renewal of hostilities." Since it was only about forty-five miles from Karlsruhe to Kehl and her passport shows that she was in the latter on the next day, she stayed the night somewhere along the way.[13]

Kehl was then a "low straggling town," which had been much damaged by the wars. It existed for two things: the great citadel that guarded one of the most significant entrances and exits into Baden (and Germany) and a bridge across the two channels of the Rhine to Strasbourg. It was hence a place crowded with soldiers and customs officials, the latter of whom were notoriously meticulous. Its wooden bridge "used to be reckoned the most stately structure of its kind in Europe," but the campaigns of 1814 had destroyed much of the German side and now, somewhat further downstream, there was an improvised crossing made of planks laid across boats. Her experience was the usual one: she was "questioned, and troubled" on the German side and "after some delay permitted to cross." On the French side, she was stopped again, her passports demanded, the luggage removed from the carriage and detained for close inspection. But the French officer showed some respect for her rank, suggested a good hotel for her, and "politely told me he would wait on me there." So, without her luggage, she went the few miles to Strasbourg through avenues of trees and past an obelisk that commemorated General Desaix, passed over the city's formidable entrenchments, and lodged herself in an "excellent" house. This may have been the Ville de Lyon, which Mariana Starke thought a "good inn." But there were also the Hotel de l'Esprit and the Maison Rouge.[14]

At her hotel, which she reached at about noon, she was immediately attended by its landlord, who was asked to dismiss the horses and postilions and in whom she quickly learned to repose confidence. He was a man of fifty or more, gentlemanly in his manners, and full of useful and canny, if somewhat mysterious, advice, especially about the customs official who would be coming to inquire further into her legal standing. "He told me the Officer would probably ask for Letters, and papers; and that as the moment was very *critical*, I had better cut the Seals before they took them, and in that state they would not read them, but suffer me to retain them." Much depended upon reputation, even when it came to passports. As it happened, she had two French ones. That from the French ambassador in Russia, Noailles, seems to have been of dubious service to her, but the second, which she had acquired in Berlin from Caraman, the French ambassador to Prussia, had been more useful, because "his name was popular and well known." After a while, the official came, informed her that her baggage was fine, and that her passports would be stamped. He would have collected from her, either before or then, a duty on her carriage, for any such vehicle was liable to an importation tax, technically a deposit equivalent to a third of the carriage's estimated value, three-quarters of which was refundable if it left France within two years. He advised her about the political situation, confirmed how unsettled matters were, and told her that, though Strasbourg was "very quiet," there was no doubt that Napoleon had returned and was on his way to Paris. Hence he cautioned that she faced a hazardous journey.[15]

On that afternoon of Sunday, March 19, the emperor was in Auxerre. There he was writing to his lost empress, Marie Louise, to explain that he would be in Paris before she got his letter and futilely asking that she, with their son the king of Rome, should come immediately to rejoin him in resumed imperial splendor. (A week earlier, she had renounced her claim to the French throne.) However wrong he was about his wife's intentions, however, Napoleon was not in error about the military situation. On the previous day, the situation of the royalists in Paris had begun to disintegrate. Troops were defecting and refusing to take orders. Aristocrats and the *haute bourgeoisie* were flocking to the Hôtel des Postes to get passports, flinging luggage onto carriages, and heading north and northwest out of the city. Twenty million francs had been withdrawn from banks or transferred abroad. Most ominously, the shopkeepers began to take down their signs, in order to erase the crested lily of the Bourbons and substitute the imperial eagle. The king had issued a forlorn proclamation to his errant officers and men, to ask them to throw themselves into the arms of himself, their father. But he knew they would not and began indecisively to make plans to flee, for he dreaded the fate of his executed brother. At noon on Sunday, as Mrs. Adams was approaching her Strasbourg hotel, Louis XVIII had scheduled a review of the Household Guard on the Champ de Mars, while having no intention of appearing. He dithered during the afternoon, as hostile crowds began to build up. He left the Tuileries at four p.m., went a few hundred yards, disliked what he saw, and scurried back. In the evening, he confided to his ministers that he was resolved to go, offered each a bribe of a hundred thousand francs in cash if they would follow him (they took the money), and finally departed for Lille at midnight, while Mrs. Adams was asleep.[16]

In Strasbourg earlier, Mrs. Adams was taking advice, within the constraints of her resolve to stay overnight and proceed toward Paris. To the landlord, who returned after the departure of the customs official, she argued that she would need more help than could be furnished by her Prussian boy and asked if "a respectable and confidential person to go with me as far as Paris" could be found. She promised to pay a handsome fee and the expenses of any return journey, and further pledged that he would be accorded all respect, for "I must rely entirely upon the discretion of this person, in the management and arrangement of my route; and should depend on him for advice, and assistance." The landlord thought such a person would be difficult to procure, "but that he had such a man in view, that he would see him directly, and prevail upon him to undertake the charge."[17]

She then had her dinner, perhaps boiled beef and sour cabbage, perhaps capon with truffles, because Strasbourg was poised culturally between France and Germany and offered both cuisines. Afterward, she took a walk about the town with Charles Francis. Later she was to remember the city as "very pretty," though oddly she found it reminiscent of Worcester, Massachusetts, not a place known for its Gothic cathedral, its medieval timbered buildings, and its encompassing intricate rivers and canals. Strasbourg's houses were high, so much so that they seemed likely to tumble down upon the walker in its many narrow streets. There were a few wide modern avenues, and its Place Broglie was a "handsome oblong square" surrounded by cafés and possessed of a new theater, its entrance supported in the modern style by Corinthian pillars. There were public walks along the banks of the Ill and the Breusch Rivers, notably the Jardin Christian close to the Porte des Pecheurs and the Jardin Baldener near the Porte des Boucheurs. There it was customary for the fashionable to promenade, as they probably were on that Sunday afternoon in early spring, amid the chestnut and acacia trees. It was usual for visitors to go to the cathedral, to try to fathom the humor of its satirical statues, to wonder at the delicate filigree carving that seemed to convert the heavy copper-colored building into a thing of "faëry-like lightness," to strain to see the stained glass now darkened with dirt and age, and to lament the neoclassical intrusion of Grecian pilasters in the nave. It was equally usual to visit the nearby church of Saint Thomas, celebrated for its monumental tomb to Maurice, comte de Saxe. On it were crowded many allegorical forms—a lion to stand for the Netherlands, a leopard for England, a weeping woman for the grief of France—all surrounding the armored soldier himself, in modern dress, crowned with laurels, holding his marshal's baton, and waiting before an open grave and the figure of Death.[18]

In the evening, back at the hotel, she was visited again by the landlord. With him was "a most respectable looking person" called Dupin, who seemed to her more than adequate as a servant for her travels, so she employed him and agreed on terms. She gave her orders, that the carriage be ready at the time she specified. Dupin asked if the Prussian boy would remain in their party. She did not know, so sent down for him and asked "if he would not prefer to be discharged there, and to return home." To this, he replied with some passion that "no! his object was to find his old Master in Paris, and that he would rather go on." Though he was now less necessary, she was conscious that he had served her well, so consented that he go along. But Dupin was worried that a Prussian might be a problem and insisted that the boy keep silent in any inn or post station where they might stop, and that Mrs. Adams must keep a close eye on him, at moments when Dupin was preoccupied. By contrast, Madame Babet was thought a risk by no one, for she was French, quiet, respectable, advanced in years, "very plain in her person, and manners, and very steady." These decisions were encouraging, but, as Mrs. Adams remembered her mood during that day, the strain was beginning to tell. "My health was dreadful, and the excessive desire I had to terminate this long journey, absolutely made me sick." Fatigue, excitement, fear, and expectation were wearing her down.[19]

It was her memory later that she told Dupin that they would leave the morning after next, which would have been Tuesday, March 21. But her memory of these last days was plagued by confusions about places and distances. Indeed, aware of this fact, in 1836 she cautioned her readers that they should not rely too much on her accuracy. She spoke of neglecting the embellishments customary to travel narratives and of confining herself only to "a brief sketch of the road," given "very often with a defective geography." As was her custom, she attributed this blundering to a mix of laziness, incapacity for research, and ignorance of the niceties of style and composition. The result, she felt, was confusion. So "those who may read this memento mori, must endeavour to extract light from the chaos which lies before them; and I wish them joy of the trouble."[20]

The trouble is as follows. In her account, she specified which towns she passed through on her way from Strasbourg to Paris in the following order: Nancy, Château Thierry, Epernay, Châtillon-sur-Marne, Sens, Meaux, and Bondy. As she had it, she left Strasbourg on March 21, traveled all day until one o'clock in the morning of the next day and stopped at an unspecified location for the night. She then resumed, changed horses at Nancy, and stopped the next night at Château Thierry. She then started again, passed through Epernay at midday, and stopped at a post station soon after for the third night. The next day was spent traveling onward to Châtillon-sur-Marne, which she reached in the evening, and there stayed for her fourth night. On the fifth day, she went on to Sens, then to Meaux, where she dined, and then she pushed on via Bondy to Paris. In her first account, she specified that she was in Meaux on March 20, but her revision of the narrative changed this to March 21. Hence, by her account, she was five days on the road and the fifth day was March 20 or 21.[21]

As she suggested, this is chaotic. Her travel from Strasbourg to Paris almost certainly occurred between the morning of Monday, March 20, and the late evening of Thursday, March 23, and hence involved four days of travel and three overnight stops. The later date is incontestable; because her husband's diary specifies the moment of her arrival.[22] The earlier date is less firm, but her French passport was stamped at Kehl and Strasbourg on Sunday, March 19. It is extremely unlikely that, as her memoirs suggested, she stayed for two nights (and hence left on Tuesday, March 21), because the three-hundred-mile journey from Strasbourg to Paris would have been very hard to achieve in three days, considering the delaying events she encountered. But it is equally unlikely that she did not stay overnight in Strasbourg. Hence the strong probability is a departure on Monday morning.

Her account of the sequence of towns is likewise implausible.

Château Thierry is west, not east, of Epernay; Châtillon-sur-Marne is not a day's journey from Epernay, but only thirteen miles; and Sens is miles to the south. What seems likely, instead, is that she never went to Sens and that, though she did eventually go to Château Thierry, she did not stop the night there, since it was only sixty miles from Paris on good roads. Overall she needed to travel 309 miles in four days and, if her pace had been even, she would have accomplished about seventy-seven miles a day. But her pace was not even: her first day was very long, her second normal, her third truncated, and her fourth again long. What is more plausible is an itinerary of Strasbourg to the vicinity of Velaine (ninety-seven miles) on Monday, Velaine to about Vitry-sur-Marne (seventy-eight miles) on Tuesday, Vitry-sur-Marne to Port-à-Binson (fifty-four miles) on Wednesday, and Port-à-Binson to Paris (eighty miles) on Thursday. However, the terrain was hillier in the earliest stages and it may be that she fell short of Nancy by late Monday.

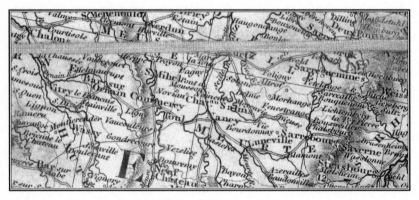

Strasbourg to Châlons-sur-Marne

(From Aaron Arrowsmith, *Map Exhibiting the Great Post Roads,*
Physical and Political Divisions of Europe [London: A. Arrowsmith, 1810])

On the first day of her journey on March 20, she went northwest.[23] She climbed the hills beyond Strasbourg, past Ittenheim and Wasselone to Saverne, whose main street climbed steeply up a hill. Parallel to the road lay the great château that had before the French Revolution housed the prince-archbishops of Rohan, but which for decades had lain indecisively empty, save for the disruptive billeting of troops. Here she was still in Alsace, where the postilions mostly spoke German with a French accent. But just beyond Saverne, she reached the province's boundary, marked to the right side of her road by an obelisk, on which was written in gilt letters ALSATIA. At the top of the pass that crossed the Vosges Mountains, she could pause to consider the panorama that stretched back to Strasbourg and the Rhine. Next she reached Phalsbourg, a town fortified by the seventeenth-century military engineer the Marquis de Vauban and surrounded by a deep fosse; it was entered by a drawbridge, raised by a great iron chain. Then there was Hommarting, where the post station looked like a farm house and food had to be foraged in a large kitchen with two long tables and a fire, in front of which might be found large mastiffs, which struck momentary fear into travelers. Sarrebourg, the next stop, was where one was likely to lose a German-speaking postilion and gain a French one, and beyond it at Héming one entered a valley, passed a "meandering rivulet," and changed horses next to a large fountain, where cattle drank. At Blamont, there was an old castle, fallen down, and an inn where even the *vin ordinaire* was said to be drinkable. Then there was a tiny place called Bénaménil, before one reached the large and busy town of Luneville, best known to travelers for the treaty signed there between France and Austria in 1801, but most striking for red tiles on roofs, for manufactories of cotton and porcelain, a city fountain that guidebooks fastidiously indicated had eight jets, and (opposite the posthouse) an ancient château. Finally, after Dombasle, a place of little note, there was Nancy, the most exquisite city she would pass on her present way to Paris.[24]

Nancy had its old town, its medieval and Renaissance quarters, and its old walls through which a traveler passed. But the city was most famous for its new town, its neoclassical gates of allegorical complexity, its eighteenth-century cathedral, its Place Carrière and Arc de Triomphe, which proclaimed in Latin the twin dedication of the French monarchy to peace and victory, both of which seemed ironic possibilities on the evening of March 20, 1815. In the city's central square, probably still known that morning as the Place Royale but very soon to be again the Place Napoleon, she changed horses.[25] She almost certainly did this in or near one of two low pavilions that sat at the same end of the square as the Arc de Triomphe, for the pavilions were reserved for shops, restaurants, and commerce. She was in one of the greatest urban spaces that the eighteenth century, so profligate of such spaces, had made. The square was more elegant than even the Nevsky Prospect, Regent Street, or Unter den Linden, the worlds Mrs. Adams had known. Ahead of her was the Hôtel de Ville, which had perhaps lowered the white flag of the Bourbons but may not yet have restored the *tricolore*. On each side, she was surrounded by four elegantly austere neoclassical palaces, at different times dedicated to high civic purposes (an academy, a library, a college of surgeons), the needs of the state (residences for the queen, the intendant, tax collectors), the needs of God (a bishop's palace), and private display (the *hôtel*, or mansion, of the Jacquet family). Geometrically distributed around the square were streets entered through gilded rococo gates, on which Bourbon lilies were ineradicable, and exuberant fountains in which sported Neptune and sundry damp sprites. Down upon Mrs. Adams and her Russian carriage frowned and laughed a multitude of stone faces, commenting with puzzlement and indifference on human folly.

This square was about sixty years old and, curiously, bridged the eastern European world Mrs. Adams had recently seen and the world she was now in. The rebuilding of Nancy had been sponsored mostly by Stanislaus Leszczynski, twice king of the Polish-Lithuanian commonwealth, but latterly exiled and made in recompense duc de Lorraine et de Bar. He had achieved this improbable transition by the grace of Louis XV, who was his son-in-law, and whose statue Stanislaus gratefully placed at the heart of the square, where it remained until 1793, when the "beloved king" had been removed by unloving republicans, and the square had been renamed the Place du Peuple. When Mrs. Adams arrived, the pedestal had been occupied for more than a decade by an allegorical winged spirit, which gestured in the direction of Paris, a symbol that was diplomatically vague about republics, consulates, monarchies, empires, and dynasties, and had no opinion about which flag ought to fly over post-horses and American ladies.

Around her in the square were troops mustering in support of Napoleon. These men, delighted at his progress, would not then have known how delighted they ought to be. If, as seems likely, she reached Nancy late on the evening of March 20, or even on the early morning of the next day, she was looking at troops who did not yet know that they had an emperor in residence in the Tuileries. Napoleon had reached Fontainebleau at 4:00 a.m. on that Monday morning, had slept for three hours, and then conferred with his staff, until word reached him at noon of Louis XVIII's flight twelve hours earlier. Promptly, he had set out for Paris, whose suburbs he reached after nightfall. His closed calèche arrived at the main entrance of the Tuileries at eight o'clock, where he was greeted by Mrs. Adams's old acquaintance the duc de Vicenza and jubilantly hoisted upon the shoulders of eager young officers, who had carried him up the Grand Escalier to his old, familiar apartments.[26]

Whether she was short of Nancy or beyond it, by one o'clock in the morning on Tuesday, March 21, Mrs. Adams had reached a point that exceeded the patience of her postilions. They insisted she stop at an isolated house and, with reluctance and upon Dupin's advice, she agreed. This was not a post station but a small and ill-furnished inn, with a long room, a pine table, bare benches, and "several very surly looking men." There she sat down and asked for food, but was offered nothing but a little milk. The men began to ask her son questions, at which he took fright. Mrs. Adams put them off in her good French, by claiming that her son was "too sleepy to talk." At this hint, Dupin asked if there was a chamber in which the lady could put her child to bed. A door was opened into a nearby chamber, "even more uncomfortable than the one we left." There anxiously she and Babet stayed awake all night, while the boy slept. Through the door came "the threatening conversation" of the residents, but also her own postilions. They boasted of what Napoleon would do, of how he would "drive out Louis dix huit and his beggarly Crew." Her postilions, in particular, "were vociferous in their exclamations; and there were many bitter anathemas against the Allied Powers and the horrible Cossacks." For a lady in a Russian carriage, this was not comfortable listening, all this talk of war and revenge by men drinking more than milk.[27]

The next day they went on, without incident. Beyond Nancy lay Velaine, approached through the cool and soothing forest of Hayes, crowded with elm, oak, lime, and beech. At Toul one crossed a moat through a tiny gate and found oneself on a round island city, freshened by kitchen gardens and dominated by a cathedral, which rose high above the flat countryside. Then there were Laye and Void, past meadows skirted by hills, and Saint Aubin, where the inn was "very little better than a common ale house in England." Afterward the road broadened out and, on the outskirts of Ligny, descending a hill she could see to her right an old castle, before she entered the town through a gate of "chaste Tuscan architecture" and went along the Rue de Strasbourg. Soon after she reached Bar-le-Duc, sharply divided into a high and low town, with the post station at the Hotel du Cygne in the lower half, at the bottom of a very steep hill. Its landlord, Monsieur Fatalot, was famous for his jams in a town celebrated for its fruits. Fatalot's daughter was accustomed to serving the local wines and to reminiscing to travelers about her mother, who carefully hid her daughters away when armies went through, especially the Cossacks, whom Mademoiselle Fatalot called *Turques*. So it was probably the case that then, when Mrs. Adams was passing, the young woman was nowhere to be seen.[28]

Beyond the sugared gooseberries of Bar-le-Duc and past the local vineyards, Mrs. Adams proceeded through Saudrupt ("little better than a miserable village"), Saint Dizier, Longchamp, and La Chaussée. It is possible that she reached Vitry-sur-Marne or perhaps as far as Châlons-sur-Marne. At the former, the best inns were La Cloche d'Or and La Pomme d'Or; at the latter, La Croix d'Or. And there was an inn in Châlons probably then in grave doubt about its sign, because it oscillated between announcing itself as the Palais Impériale and the Palais-Royale. Wherever she was, she found a place of "good beds, and comfortable refreshment," though she was to be troubled by an inquisitive and sententious gendarme who, as the travelers ate, instructed an annoyed Charles Francis that he must be a good boy "and not speak a word on the road, for that little children of his age often did a great deal of mischief." As for Mrs. Adams, he "expressed great astonishment at my travelling towards Paris in such a state of things, and seemed by no means contented with my answers, which were very simple."[29]

Châlons-sur-Marne to Paris
(From Aaron Arrowsmith, *Map Exhibiting the Great Post Roads,
Physical and Political Divisions of Europe* [London: A. Arrowsmith, 1810])

On the next morning, they resumed. The weather and the roads were good, their spirits were high, and "every thing seemed propitious" as they passed between the wheat fields. At one o'clock they stopped to dine at Epernay, almost certainly at the Poste-aux-Chevaux. This was a town nestled among steep hills and close to the river Marne to its north, a river that Mrs. Adams would shadow, cross, and recross for many miles to come. On it floated "a multitude of barges . . . with their cargoes of fire-wood and coals" bound for Paris. Epernay had sundry industries—quarries, potteries, a factory for hosiery, a woolen mill, paper mills—but was most abundantly famous for its wine. Mrs. Adams was now in Champagne and everywhere between the Marne and the slopes of the valley were vineyards, where then the vines were being pruned, because this was done in late March and early April. Epernay was the chief place where local vintners sent their bottles to be stored. The town had immense caves, carved with precise regularity into the chalk, into which in the 1820s as many as six or seven million bottles of *vin blanc mousseux* alone would come to be annually placed. In 1815, the caves were emptier than usual, because the Russian troops who had occupied the town in 1814 had helped themselves to approximately 600,000 bottles by way of pleasant recompense for the burning of Moscow.[30]

Mrs. Adams was familiar enough with champagne, because in Russia "champagne corks flew about abundantly."[31] In the United States, a taste for the wine had helped to drive Thomas Jefferson into debt, for he liberally dispensed it at the White House dinners that Louisa Adams had once had to endure. Still, in Saint Petersburg her husband had kept relatively few bottles in his cellar and seems to have preferred claret and sauternes as his staples, with Margaux as a more expensive option. This may explain why she had not ordered any champagne with her "capital dinner" in Epernay. But the waiter was insistent that she ought to try some, because he claimed she would find nothing better in Paris. The meal being good, the weather and the road that morning having been as good, she acquiesced and ordered a bottle. Later in the century, there would have been little doubt about what she would have been given. But in 1815 there were different discriminations about the champagnes (red, white, rosé, sparkling, still) produced in villages like Sillery by owners like Jean Remy Moët. Then the sparkling was mostly reserved for export to those with inferior palates and was sweeter than later taste preferred. For locals as for Thomas Jefferson, who came to Epernay in 1788, it was the *vin blanc non-mousseux* that occasioned grave connoisseurship. It was thought proper then to serve it over ice, for "the wine was so delicate, that the difference of five minutes more or less remaining in the ice would make a sensible difference to the palate." So it was probably a *vin blanc non-mousseux* on ice that Mrs. Adams had. To her pleasure, it turned out to be "superior to any that I have ever tasted before, or since."[32]

After less than an hour, they set out again in a confident mood, because the townspeople had said that troops were not expected in the vicinity for another day and there was no need for hurry. So they climbed the steep hill that led westward out of Epernay and, after a mile or so, began to descend a gentle incline to a flat stretch of road. To her right, past the sloping wheat fields, lay the Marne and its bus-

George Lewis, *Beggars Surrounding a Carriage, Epernay* (1823)
(From George Lewis, *A Series of Groups, Illustrating the Physiognomy, Manners, and Character of the People of France and Germany* [London: John and Arthur Arch, 1823], plate 26)

tling barges, which carried Epernay's wines down the river to Paris, and beyond the river were forested chalk hills. Above her, to the left of the road, lay the forest of Epernay.

Then, from within the carriage, she heard the sound of women shouting obscenities. She looked out and saw that they had caught up with a group of camp followers. They were quickly in the midst of a troop of the Imperial Guard, part of the elite corps that had come to function as the spearhead of the Grande Armée. Their blue uniforms and bearskin caps with a high feather, the golden eagles they carried before them, and their swagger and fierce loyalty to Napoleon had long made them an object of fascination, resentment, and fear. Now, after a year of defeat and humiliation, they were moving joyously toward Paris and their restored emperor.[33]

Mrs. Adams began to make out what the women were shouting— "Tear them out of the carriage"—"They are Russians"—"Kill them." Madame Babet heard this, too, went pale, and began to shake.

Abruptly the carriage stopped. Soldiers surrounded it, grabbed the horses, and turned their muskets on the postilions. Mrs. Adams sat frozen with fear. She had taken the risk of traveling on, even knowing it could go wrong. She had been told often enough of the risks. She had been traveling for weeks through scenes of war, heard stories of mindless violence, seen burned houses, observed faces sick with exhausted anger, and witnessed battlefields strewn with bones. But it had been going well. A moment ago, the weather, the roads, and the champagne had been reassuring, and Paris beckoned. Now suddenly she was reduced to fumbling for her passports, in the hope that affidavits and rank might help.[34]

As she did so, men on horses rode up and stopped by her carriage window. She gave the leading officer her passports, he examined them, and he called out to his men that she was an American lady "going to meet her husband in Paris." At this news, that the travelers were not Russians deserving death, the soldiers shouted, *"Vive les Américains!"* But they also demanded that the American lady shout back, *"Vive Napoleon!"* So she did and, for extra measure, leaned from the window of the carriage and waved her handkerchief. Reassured, the soldiers shouted back, *"Vive les Américains!"* again and, for extra measure, declared, *"Ils sont nos amis!"* With this the crisis lessened, though only a little. The officer gave orders that the carriage proceed at a walking pace, that the soldiers go in front of the horses, and that any attempt by the carriage to accelerate should be met by firing. The staff of officers formed an escort by the side of the carriage and, as they went on, the chief of staff explained to her that she was in much danger, for his men were undisciplined and unpredictable, but that she should appear "easy and unconcerned," and always echo their patriotic cries. He advised that, when they reached the post station, he would try to persuade the landlady to let Mrs. Adams's party stay the night. Further, he suggested that the next morning, she should delay her departure "until the troops had all passed, and then take a circuitous route to Paris; as the whole Army would be in motion, to Greet the Emperor."[35]

MICHEL.

Lieutenant Général.

B. de Belport, *Claude Étienne Michel* (1826)

(Courtesy of Christel Poirrier)

As it chanced, Mrs. Adams had fallen into the hands of a considerable soldier. This was Claude Étienne Michel, and, as best he could, he was commanding what a few days earlier had been the Corps Royal de Chasseurs, a regiment of light infantry assembled in 1814 out of men once in the Garde Impériale, a status they had now resumed. He was then forty-two years old, a veteran of many wars and a carrier of many wounds. He was the son of a surgeon in Pointre and had entered the revolutionary armies in 1791. He had twice been a prisoner of war, detained by the Prussians from 1793 to 1795 and again by the British in 1799, when he had tried ferrying war supplies to Irish rebels and been intercepted. He had served in Saint-Domingue, when French troops had been sent futilely by Napoleon to crush the great slave rebellion of Toussaint L'Ouverture. He had been in many of the later Napoleonic campaigns and served his emperor in Prussia in 1806, Spain in 1808, Russia in 1812, Saxony in 1813, and lastly in defense of the walls of Paris in 1814. Gradually he had risen through the ranks, from sous-lieutenant in 1792 to divisional general in 1813. With Napoleon's banishment to Elba, Michel had accepted a commission from Louis XVIII and had even been awarded la Croix de Saint-Louis, which he was able to add to his temporarily disused standing as a baron d'empire and commandant de la Legion d'Honneur. But, like most of the army, he was a Bonapartist by conviction and a Bourbon royalist only by necessity, so when Napoleon had returned, he and his men had gladly resumed their old, glorious allegiance. As he and Mrs. Adams moved slowly along the *route impériale*, he was moving toward disaster. In Paris the next day he would be made a comte d'empire, be sent by Napoleon to aid the Armée du Nord, and at Waterloo would help to lead the assault upon the ground held by the Duke of Wellington, an assault in which Michel was to die. So the considerate man on the horse had only three months left to live. He was to leave as part of his legacy a remark that some were to treasure as the quintessence of gallantry, others to think the height of folly, and many to attribute to someone else: *La garde meurt mais ne se rend pas*—the guard dies but does not surrender.[36]

Michel was happy to do his best for Mrs. Adams, but a dead American here or there was of little consequence at such a moment. For Charles Francis Adams, however, the shouts, the bayonets, the obscenities, and the slow creak of the trapped carriage were petrifying, and he sat close to his mother "like a marble statue." For Mrs. Adams, her cheeks flushed, her pulse racing, it was a severe test of composure. Luckily, she spoke an idiomatic French, a fact upon which she was complimented by Michel, who hazarded that this would help in survival by diminishing her status as an ominous foreigner. As they talked, they went up and down gentle slopes through copses, while the soldiers periodically bellowed "brutal threats" at her drivers. On each side of the road were drunken men, shouting *"À bas Louis dix huit! Vive Napoleon!"* Later, remembering the incident, her mind was to run to poetic and Gothic images of noisy confusion, of skies rent with screeching midnight owls, of dire alarums, and of startled ears.[37]

What happened next, when it happened, and where it happened are unclear. Mrs. Adams was to remember traveling until midnight and reaching a post station. There Michel spoke to the landlady, who at first refused to admit the travelers. With more persuasion, she consented to let them in for the night, upon the understanding that they hide in a back room, that the servants be concealed, and that the carriage be hidden away inconspicuously. Then Michel left in the direction of Toul, occupied by Claude Victor-Perrin, duc de Bellune, a former Napoleonic marshal now loyal to the Bourbons. But this account makes little sense, for Toul is almost a hundred miles to the east, Michel is known to have reached Paris the next day, and Bellune was then not in Toul but in Lille with his king.[38] Moreover, it is deeply unlikely that Michel, a general of the Garde Impériale, would at such a critical moment have spent eight hours trotting next to a foreign lady's carriage in a direction opposite to that which she claimed was necessary to his military purposes.

Much more likely is that they went to the next post station and Michel did as Mrs. Adams described, but then, his chivalric responsibility

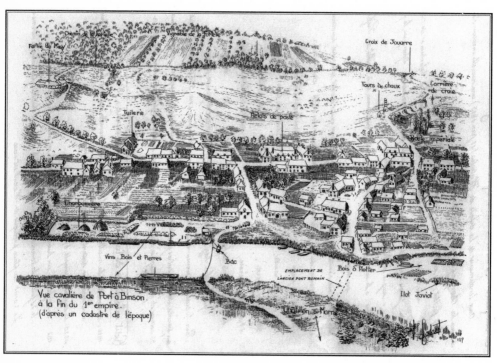

Port-à-Binson in 1815

(From an unpublished manuscript history of Port-à-Binson by
Jean Godart, Mairie de Mareuil-le-Port, France)

rapidly discharged, he went on immediately with his men toward Paris. If so, she spent the night in Port-à-Binson. Her memoirs suggest that, the next day, she was advised to go not directly toward Paris, but to make a detour to Châtillon-sur-Marne.[39] From Port-à-Binson, such a detour is logistically intelligible. But if she had proceeded to further post stations (Dormans, Paroy, Château-Thierry), she would in going to Châtillon-sur-Marne have been going backward.

It is the more likely that she was in Port-à-Binson, where wood and charcoal were traded, because Mrs. Adams was to write of the post station being run by a woman, and the *relais de poste* in Port-à-Binson was under the charge of Gabrielle Victoire Larangot, née Leclerc.[40] She had been born in the local municipality (Mareuil-le-Port) and in 1783 had married an older local man, though a little to the north in Soissons, a husband by whom she was to have eleven children. His name was Jean Larangot and his family had held the royal commission as *maître de poste* in Port-à-Binson since 1706; first, there had been Jacques Larangot, then his son Antoine, then Jean himself, and eventually his wife. Mrs. Adams was to remember "a showy pleasant faced woman, of about forty," though Gabrielle Larangot was then about fifty-five and, in fact, would be dead before the year was out. Like most *maîtres de poste*, the Larangots were important local figures and Jean had, in his time, been mayor of Mareuil-le-Port. This prominence was common, because a post station was usually attached to a considerable estate.[41] The Larangots owned a large farmhouse at Cerseuil nearby, 120 hectares of land, 3 vineyards, 25 meadows, and some 300 head of sheep. This affluence had been helped in the past because, under the ancien régime, a *maître de poste* had been exempt from the *taille*, or land tax. Further, a post station returned a very good living, for it was a complex industry in its own right. Apart from the revenues attendant upon the fees paid by travelers and royal couriers, the station was at once a hotel, a restaurant, a stable, a forge, a saddlery, a storeroom, and a hayloft, while in the surrounding fields were kept more than fifty horses, for the use of the public diligences, private carriages, individual horsemen, and locals in need of a mount.

So Gabrielle Larangot had a position in her world not much inferior to the lady who stepped from her carriage in a state of nervous exhaustion. And Madame Larangot had an air of authority, though also of conversational playfulness, which long experience of crisis had bred. Turbulent soldiers and frightened travelers were not novelties to her, for her post station had been an unwilling spectator to passing revolutions and wars, amply supplied over the thirty years she had been married to Jean Larangot. Hence she briskly disposed matters: the carriage was concealed, while Mrs. Adams, her son, and the nurse were placed in a shuttered and close-barred room, with the comfort of a fire. There they waited and listened, shut away but also trapped. Outside, Michel's guards marched away, but assorted other soldiers kept appearing, crowding into the inn, drinking, shouting. A "very kind old gentleman" appeared in the chamber and tried to be encouraging by expressing the hope that they "should get through the night without farther molestation." He left and they were alone again. Then Madame Larangot appeared, followed by a female servant bearing coffee. The former apologized for her inattentiveness, but explained that she was concerned the soldiers would plunder the house, so she had opened casks of wine and was trying to keep them in a good humor.[42]

Their danger was real. Murder was unlikely, but rape was a strong possibility, as Mrs. Adams well knew, though later she was to remark implausibly that she had been "fortunately neither young nor beautiful; a fact in itself calculated to prove my safeguard." Little wonder that she had a headache, was nauseated, and fainted a few times, so great was her justified fear. Madame Babet was still worse and "really appeared to have lost her senses." She continually clasped and unclasped her hands, wept, and cried out that she was lost, "for the Revolution was begun again, and this was only the beginning of its horrors." Later in Paris, she would be so affected by the experience that she had a nervous collapse, which continued for at least two months. Of the three, only Charles Francis managed some equanimity, enough to fall asleep, while the two women listened for hours on end, until eventually Madame Larangot felt it safe to lock her doors

Post station, Port-à-Binson
(From an unpublished manuscript history of Port-à-Binson by Jean Godart,
Mairie de Mareuil-le-Port, France)

against the stragglers, who banged to demand entry and then moved on. Only then was it possible to get a few hours' sleep.[43]

At nine Mrs. Adams was awake and emerged to find that the only sufferer in the night had been the Prussian boy, whom the soldiers had prodded playfully but harmlessly with a bayonet and whose cap had been burned by way of entertainment. Relieved of immediate anxiety, Mrs. Adams's party breakfasted well, while the carriage was retrieved, the horses attached, and the postilions employed. Pleasantries were exchanged with her hosts, thanks were given, and Jean Larangot advised that, to keep away from the army, it would be best to divert to Châtillon-sur-Marne. This would mean they would avoid the *route impériale* and the post stations at Dormans and Paroy, but instead travel along the northern shore of the Marne, to rejoin the route at Château-Thierry. It also meant the postilions would need to travel much farther than was usual.[44]

So, on a very rainy day, Mrs. Adams left the *relais de poste*, went down a short slope to the Marne, put her carriage on a barge, and on the other side quickly climbed a steep hill covered in vines to reach Châtillon, long ago the birthplace of Pope Urban II. Then, down the other side of the hill, she passed through villages (Verneuil, Vincelles, Barzy-sur-Marne, Chartèves) close to the river before returning to the main road at Château-Thierry. There she encountered the public diligence coming from the direction of Paris. Its passengers told her not to go on, "as there were forty thousand men before the Gates; and a battle was expected to take place." At this information, she was startled, but as usual decided to press on. Dupin advised that they could proceed to the outskirts of Paris and there reconnoiter the situation. If necessary, from so close a vantage point, they could get a message to John Quincy Adams, who would find the means to help.[45]

Dupin thought they might proceed because he had been encouraging a useful rumor. He had heard it said that, because Mrs. Adams was so oddly and singularly proceeding toward Paris when the roads were empty of the usual traffic, and as she was traveling in a large carriage pulled by six horses, she must be someone of great importance. Dupin had heard it whispered that she was one of Napoleon's sisters, moving in haste to greet her brother. When asked the truth of this conjecture, Dupin had adopted the policy of shrugging and smiling, so that the rumor might spread and those along the route might be pleased to leave them unmolested. It was not an absurd rumor, at least as it concerned one of Napoleon's sisters.[46] Caroline Bonaparte Murat was alone and serving as regent in Naples, while Elisa Bonaparte Bacciochi, grand duchess of Tuscany, was in Bologna. But the scandalous Pauline Bonaparte was another matter. She had stood by her brother in 1814, had joined him on Elba, and had bid him farewell as he had set sail for Cap d'Antibes, and it was not irrational to imagine that, a few days behind him, she would be hastening to the Tuileries. In fact, she was in Viarreggio and would never see France again.[47]

So on Mrs. Adams went. Close by the cathedral in Meaux, she stopped for dinner, probably at La Sirène. Here she encountered more evidence of "the murderous horrors of savage war, with all its detestable concomitants." The inn had furniture "almost in ruins," the landlady talked of Cossack atrocities, and Mrs. Adams was taken to view the graves of six local girls who had been raped and killed. By now, it was approaching nightfall and she was almost to Paris. There were only two more post stations.[48]

After passing the first station at Claye, they entered the long and deep forest of Bondy, a place dark with myth. There were many stories of malevolent men who lurked behind trees and pounced on the unwary and wary alike, but the most famous legend concerned murder and a dog.[49] In the fourteenth century, during the reign of Charles V, a man called Aubri de Montdidier was traveling through the forest of Bondy with his favorite dog, Dragon. There Montdidier was set upon, murdered, and buried. Dragon stayed close to the grave for days until, starving, he returned to Paris and barked to gain admission to the house of his late master's friend. Then, by crying out and by dramatic motions, he persuaded members of the family to follow him to the forest, where he led them to the grave. Back in Paris, some days later, the dog encountered in the street Chevalier Macaire, whom without provocation he attacked. This assault became so spoken of that word reached the king, who sent for the dog. To his surprise, he found an amiable beast, not the savage of report. But by chance, Macaire entered the king's presence and again the dog attacked. It was known that Macaire had been an enemy to Montdidier, so the king, suspecting foul play, ordered that there be a trial by combat between Macaire and the dog, to be held on the Île de la Cité. The chevalier was given a bludgeon, but the dog had right on his side, and the chevalier duly had his throat ripped out, to the satisfaction of all.

This was a story often told, and in 1814 it was turned by René Charles Guilbert de Pixérécourt into one of the definitive melodramas of the nineteenth century, *Le chien de Montargis, ou, la forêt de Bondy*. Quickly there was an English translation, which ran for thirty-nine performances at Covent Garden in late 1814. In this version, much was elaborated from the original legend. There was a love interest (the mute boy Florio in love with the beauteous Lucille), a case of mistaken identity and accusation (Florio condemned and acquitted), and an altered conclusion, for Macaire is not killed by the dog, but guiltily flings himself over a waterfall. English audiences liked all this, for they had a weakness for dogs and a fondness for dead French-men. Theatrical critics were more skeptical, but even they were re-luctantly won over. As one put it stiffly, "Quadruped performers are a disgrace to the stage, but the dog of this piece must be exempted from the general censure."[50]

It is unclear whether the play reached Saint Petersburg in her time, but Mrs. Adams knew that the forest was "celebrated for Ban-ditti," and her recent experiences had filled her mind with forebod-ing about "the cruel evils to which the fiend like passions of men expose the world." By the time she had occasion for such dark pon-derings, it was around nightfall and the forest was darkening, rainy, and ominous. Behind her, she heard the sound of a horse's hooves. She looked back and saw a lone horseman at a distance, but riding hard toward her carriage. With a mind prepared for catastrophe, she feared the worst. After so many days of strain, she was incapable of imagining other than the worst. It was familiarly said of French highwaymen, at least by the English, "that to escape detection, their *robberies* are always accompanied by *murder*." Inexplicably to her, the postilions suddenly slackened the carriage's pace and what she fully expected to be a highwayman caught them up. But he turned out to be no more than a polite gentleman who, for some time, had been apprehensive that one of her carriage wheels was about to fall off and the berline overset. So they thanked him for the courtesy, he rode on, and Dupin examined the wheel. He recommended that, for the mo-ment, they could do no more than roughly fasten the wheel, return to the post station at Claye, and there get an adequate repair. So they did this and, though it was now past nine at night, they set off again through the forest.[51]

Emerging safely from the trees, just before the village of Bondy, they reached the post station. For those who knew recent history,

Bondy and its post station were known for two things. In March 1814, it had been Field Marshal Blücher's headquarters for the final assault of the Allies on Paris, over the heights of Montmartre. (Mrs. Adams's late companion, General Michel, had tried to stand in the Prussian's way.) More poignant, however, for a woman like Louisa Adams who had a soft spot for royalty, was an incident at the Bondy post station at around midnight on June 20, 1791. Two hackney carriages had stopped, and from them had stepped six travelers whose names were Durand (a *valet de chambre*), a Madame Rocher and her companion, Rosalie, and a Baroness de Korff with her two daughters, Amelia and Aglaë. In fact, this party was the disguised French royal family, attempting their escape from imprisonment in the Tuileries— Louis XVI, Marie Antoinette, the king's sister Élisabeth, the royal governess the marquise de Tourzel, and the dauphine and dauphin of France (Marie Thérèse Charlotte and Louis Charles), the latter disguised as a girl. In Bondy, they rendezvoused with servants and bodyguards, and transferred to a berline, the same kind of carriage that was bringing Mrs. Adams from Russia. From Bondy, they set out on a southerly route that had deliberately been chosen as little frequented, before passing northward through Châlons-sur-Marne and reaching Varennes. There they were recognized, captured, and returned to Paris, where later the king and queen were executed. This experience explains why, as Mrs. Adams paused in Bondy, eight miles to her west Napoleon was in the Tuileries and Louis XVI, anxious not to repeat the experience of his brother, had, about four hours earlier, left Lille in the direction of Mannheim and a place safely remote from a guillotine.[52]

All this while, Mrs. Adams and Dupin had seen no evidence of military movements, no sign of troops massed for battle, so they felt safe to proceed quietly, anticlimactically. She could have had little sense then of what was to come, after she reached Paris and began the rest of her life. She was pessimistic enough to fear the worst. She would not have been surprised to learn that there would be more of the same—a miscarriage, quarrels, difficult relatives, betraying politicians, an opaque husband, what the slip of paper in Saint Petersburg

William James Hubbard, *Louisa Catherine Adams* (1828)

(Courtesy of the Adams family)

had called "obstacles." But there was to be more death, more grief, and more bodily pain than even she might have expected. And there was to be more success, though she seldom acknowledged success when it came, because she feared it was ephemeral and undeserved, especially by her. The husband waiting for her in Paris had little reason then to expect succeeding his father in the White House. He had for years been exiled at the ends of the earth and being a signatory of the Treaty of Ghent was a modest claim upon preferment. So she had no special reason to expect dinner parties in Washington, political celebrity, years of gossip, and a death that would lead the United States Congress to adjourn in her honor. She had even less reason to expect that she would take to writing, that she would become the author of her own story, and that her desire to be remembered as someone *"who was"* would be gratified.

On the heights of Paris, Louisa Catherine Adams, Charles Francis Adams, Madame Babet, Monsieur Dupin, the Prussian boy, and two postilions went past the Canal de l'Ourcq to their right, paused at the customhouse and barrier at Pantin, and descended through the Rue du Faubourg Saint-Martin.[53] At the bottom of the hill, they passed the Porte de Saint-Martin, the last of the innumerable triumphal arches she encountered on her journey. Her carriage turned right into the Boulevard Saint-Martin, moved along the Boulevard Poissonière, and eventually turned left into the Rue de Richelieu. Near its northern end, she entered a courtyard, stopped, and got out with her son. She did not know if her husband was still in residence at the Hotel du Nord, but she entered, found that he was, and climbed the several stories to the rooms he had rented. It was eleven o'clock at night on Thursday, March 23, 1815, and her fortieth day since Saint Petersburg.

It was his memory that, after an evening at the Théatre des Variétés on the Boulevard Montmartre a few streets away, he had returned to the hotel. Very soon thereafter his wife and son arrived.[54]

In her memory, he was not yet there.[55]

APPENDIX: PLACES

The following is a list of the places through which Mrs. Adams passed on her journey from Saint Petersburg to Paris. In the text above, I have noted where her route is more difficult to reconstruct and may have varied, but this appendix gives my best estimate. Many of the places on her route have changed their names, sometimes several times, as political states have come and gone. Changes have been more common east of Berlin and less common in western Europe, but have occurred everywhere. So this appendix is arranged in two columns. The left-hand column gives the name of the place and the political jurisdiction under which it fell in 1815. The right-hand column gives the name and political jurisdiction in 2009. It is worth stressing, however, that maps and travel guides early in the nineteenth century varied in their spellings, especially of places in eastern Europe. I would be misleading the reader if I asserted that any decision about which spelling to use can be rigorous. It is also worth noting that, in the early months of 1815, the volatile political situation meant that political jurisdictions were often insecure, states were frequently occupied by foreign troops, and the existence of a legitimate authority was sometimes uncertain; this was especially true of southwestern Germany.

RUSSIAN EMPIRE	RUSSIA
Saint Petersburg	Saint Petersburg
Strelna	Strelna
Kiepena	Kipen'
Koskova	Kas'kovo

Cherkovitza	Chirkovitsy
Opolie	Opol'e
Yamburg	Kingisepp

ESTLAND
(PROVINCE OF RUSSIAN EMPIRE)

	ESTONIA
Narva	Narva
Vaivara	Vaivara
Chudleigh	Voka
Jewe	Jõhvi
Kleinpungern	Väike-Pungerja
Ranapungern	Rannapungerja

LIVLAND
(PROVINCE OF RUSSIAN EMPIRE)

Nainal	Ninasi
Torma	Torma
Iggafor	Igavere
Dorpat	Tartu
Uddern	Uderna
Ringen	Rõngu
Teilitz	Tõlliste
Valk	Valga

	LATVIA
Valk	Valka
Gulben	Gulbene
Stakeln	Strenči
Volmar	Valmiera
Lentzenhof	Lenči
Roop	Straupe
Engelhardshof	Inciems
Hilkensfer	Murjani
Neuermühlen	Ādaži
Riga	Riga
Saint Olai	Olaine

KURLAND
(PROVINCE OF RUSSIAN EMPIRE)

Mitau	Jelgava
Doblen	Dobele
Berghof	Brocēni
Frauenberg	Saldus
Schrunden	Skrunda
Drogen	(defunct)
Tadliken	Tadaiki
Ober Bartau	Bārta
Rutzau	Rucava

LITHUANIA

Polangen	Palanga

KINGDOM OF PRUSSIA

Nimmersat	Nemirseta
Memel	Klaipėda
Prokuls	Priekulė
Heideckrug	Šilutė
Szamitkehmen	Žemaitkiemis

KALININGRAD OBLAST, RUSSIA

Tilsit	Sovetsk
Ostwethen	Zilino
Insterborg	Chernyakhovsk
Taplaken	Talpaki
Tapiau	Gvardeysk
Pogauen	Vysokoe
Königsberg	Kaliningrad
Brandenburg	Ushakovo
Hoppenbruch	(defunct)

POLAND

Braunsberg	Braniewo
Truntz	Milejewo
Elbing	Elblag
Marienburg	Malbork

Marienwerder	Kwidzyn
Graudenz	Grudziadz

DUCHY OF WARSAW

Culm	Chelmno
Ostrometz	Ostromecko
Fordon	Fordon
Bromberg	Bydgoszcz
Nakel	Nakło
Wirsitz	Wyrzysk
Grabionne	Grabówno
Schneidemühl	Pila
Schönlanke	Trzcianka
Filehne	Wieleń

KINGDOM OF PRUSSIA

Driesen	Drezdenko
Friedberg	Strzelce Krajeńskie
Landsberg	Gorzów Wielkopolski
Balz	Białcz
Kustrin	Kostrzyn

GERMANY

Dolgelin	Dolgelin
Müncheberg	Müncheberg
Vogelsdorf	Fredersdorf-Vogelsdorf
Berlin	Berlin
Zehlendorf	Zehlendorf
Potsdam	Potsdam
Beelitz	Beelitz
Treuenbrietzen	Treuenbrietzen

KINGDOM OF SAXONY

Kropstadt	Kröpstadt
Wittenberg	Lutherstadt-Wittenberg
Kemberg	Kemberg
Duben	Bad Düben

Krensitz	Krensitz
Leipzig	Leipzig
Lützen	Lützen
Weissenfels	Weißenfels
Naumburg	Naumburg

GRAND DUCHY OF
SAXE-WEIMAR-EISENACH

Auerstadt	Auerstedt
Weimar	Weimar

PRINCIPALITY OF ERFURT
(PART OF FRANCE,
BUT OCCUPIED BY PRUSSIA)

Erfurt	Erfurt

DUCHY OF SAXE-GOTHA-ALTENBURG

Gotha	Gotha

GRAND DUCHY OF SAXE-WEIMAR-
EISENACH

Eisenach	Eisenach
Berka	Berka/Werra
Vach	Vacha

FORMER PRINCE-BISHOPRIC OF
FULDA (UNDER AUSTRIAN CONTROL)

Hunefeld	Hünfeld
Fulda	Fulda
Neuhof	Neuhof

ELECTORATE OF HESSE

Schlüchtern	Schlüchtern
Saalmunster	Bad Soden-Salmünster

PRINCIPALITY OF ISENBURG-BIRSTEIN

Gelnhausen	Gelnhausen

ELECTORATE OF HESSE

Hanau	Hanau

FREE CITY OF FRANKFURT

Frankfurt am Main	Frankfurt am Main

GRAND DUCHY OF HESSE-DARMSTADT

Darmstadt	Darmstadt
Heppenheim	Heppenheim

GRAND DUCHY OF BADEN

Weinheim	Weinheim
Heidelberg	Heidelberg
Wiesloch	Wiesloch
Bruchsal	Bruchsal
Karlsruhe	Karlsruhe
Ettlingen	Ettlingen
Rastadt	Rastatt
Stollhofen	Stollhofen
Bischoffsheim	Rheinbischofsheim
Kehl	Kehl

FRANCE

FRANCE	FRANCE
Strasbourg	Strasbourg
Ittenheim	Ittenheim
Wasselonne	Wasselonne
Saverne	Saverne
Phalsbourg	Phalsbourg
Hommarting	Hommarting
Sarrebourg	Sarrebourg
Héming	Héming
Blamont	Blâmont
Bénaménil	Bénaménil
Luneville	Luneville
Dombasle	Dombasle-sur-Meurthe
Nancy	Nancy
Velaine	Velaine-en-Haye
Toul	Toul

Laye	Lay–Saint Rémy
Void	Void-Vacon
Saint Aubin	Saint-Aubin-sur-Aire
Ligny	Ligny-en-Barrois
Bar-le-Duc	Bar-le-Duc
Saudrupt	Saudrupt
Saint Dizier	Saint-Dizier
Longchamp	Perthes
Vitry-sur-Marne	Vitry-le-François
La Chaussée	La Chaussée-sur-Marne
Châlons-sur-Marne	Châlons-en-Champagne
Jâlons	Jâlons
Epernay	Epernay
Port-à-Binson	Port-à-Binson
Châtillon-sur-Marne	Châtillon-sur-Marne
Château Thierry	Château-Thierry
La Ferme-de-Paris	La Ferme–Paris (close to Coupru)
La Ferté-sous-Jouarre	La Ferté-sous-Jouarre
St. Jean	Saint Jean-les-deux-Jumeaux
Meaux	Meaux
Claye	Claye-Souilly
Bondy	Bondy
Paris	Paris

NOTES

ABBREVIATIONS

The following abbreviations are used in the notes; unless otherwise specified, all manuscript sources can be assumed to be in the Adams Papers, Massachusetts Historical Society, Boston.

AA	Abigail Adams
ABA	Abigail Brooks Adams
AFC	L. H. Butterfield et al., eds., *Adams Family Correspondence*, 8 vols. to date (Cambridge, Mass.: Belknap Press of Harvard University Press, 1963–2007)
CFA	Charles Francis Adams
JA	John Adams
JQA	John Quincy Adams
JQA Diary	John Quincy Adams diary: online at http://www.masshist.org/jqadiaries/
LCA	Louisa Catherine Adams
LCJ	Louisa Catherine Johnson
Memoirs	Charles Francis Adams, ed., *Memoirs of John Quincy Adams, Comprising Portions of His Diary from 1795 to 1848*, 12 vols. (Philadelphia: J. B. Lippincott, 1874–77)
Narrative (1)	Louisa Catherine Adams, "Narrative of a Journey from Russia to France 1815," manuscript dated June 27, 1836; unpaginated

by LCA, so I have ascribed page numbers, of which there are forty-eight

Narrative (2) Louisa Catherine Adams, "Narrative of a Journey from St Petersburg to Paris in Feby 1815," undated manuscript, only partly in LCA's handwriting; a slightly revised version of *Narrative (1)*; this is also unpaginated, but runs to fifty pages

Nobody Louisa Catherine Adams, "The Adventures of a Nobody," manuscript dated July 1, 1840; inconsistently paginated and often unpaginated, so I have ascribed page numbers; when the manuscript reproduces a diary entry, I have indicated the date of the entry

Record Louisa Catherine Adams, "Record of a Life or My Story," manuscript dated July 23, 1825; since this text was only paginated by LCA for the first nine pages, the numbering is mine

I. SAINT PETERSBURG

1. *Narrative (1)*, 2; LCA to JQA, October 16, 1814.
2. These names are conjectural, because the evidence about the identity of LCA's servants is contradictory. 1) LCA's Russian passport specifies a chambermaid (Maria Blot) and two servants (Englebert and John Fulling). 2) LCA, "Mrs J. Q. Adams," *Mrs A. S. Colvin's Weekly Messenger* (June 12, 1827): 304–305, says she departed with "two men servants, a French waiting maid, and her son Charles; only one of these persons being known to her." 3) *Narrative (1)* names a nurse (Madame Babet) and a servant (Baptiste), but also indicates a third, unnamed servant. LCA to JQA, January 31, 1815, makes clear that she had employed a Madame Babet, so either the Russian authorities mistook her name on the passport or Maria Blot was dropped at the last minute. One may be reasonably confident that Fulling was the first male servant, but it is possible that LCA misremembered Englebert's name as Baptiste: *Narrative (1)*, 15, has "Baptiste I believe that was his name (but no matter)."
3. Elizabeth Donnan, ed., *Papers of James A. Bayard, 1796–1815*, in *Annual Report of the American Historical Association for the Year 1913: Vol. II* (Washington, D.C.: American Historical Association, 1915), 472; LCA to JQA, February 20, 1815; on Kozodavlev, see Alexander M. Martin, *Romantics, Reformers, Reactionaries: Russian Conservative Thought and Politics in the Reign of Alexander I* (DeKalb: Northern Illinois University Press, 1997), 114, 159–63, 188, 205.
4. *Narrative (2)*, 27.
5. LCA to JQA, November 25, 1814; December 14, 1809, *Nobody*, 240; LCA to CFA, April 21, 1846.
6. LCA to JQA, December 30, 1814; in 1822, she weighed 102 pounds: see LCA to JQA, September 19–20, 1822.

7. AA to JQA, May 20, 1796; *Record*, 10, 27.

8. *Record*, 79.

9. LCA to AA, July 10, 1814; LCA to JQA, June 24, August 22, June 7, August 15, 1814.

10. JQA to LCA, December 27, 1814.

11. LCA to JQA, January 31, March 5, January 20, 1815.

12. On this requirement, see John Carr, *A Northern Summer; or, Travels Round the Baltic, Through Denmark, Sweden, Russia, Prussia, and Part of Germany, in the Year 1804* (London: Richard Phillips, 1805), 381–82; J. T. James, *Journal of a Tour in Germany, Sweden, Russia, Poland, During the Years 1813 and 1814*, 2nd ed., 2 vols. (London: John Murray, 1817), 2:121; Robert Johnston, *Travels Through Part of the Russian Empire and the Country of Poland: Along the Southern Shores of the Baltic* (New York: Davis Longworth, 1816), 146; and Marquis of Londonderry and H. M. Hyde, eds., *The Russian Journals of Martha and Catherine Wilmot* (London: Macmillan, 1934), 252.

13. Meyer and Bruxner to Schwink and Koch, January 29, 1815; LCA to JQA, January 31, 1815.

14. *Nobody*, 229; CFA to Abigail Brooks, September 15, 1828; August 5, 1809, *Memoirs*, 2:3; LCA to "My Children," May 1, 1828; July 1, 1809, JQA Diary; "List of the Officers and Crew of the Ship Horace," in JQA, memorandum book entitled "The Chaos."

15. *Nobody*, 229–33.

16. Alfred W. Crosby, *America, Russia, Hemp, and Napoleon: American Trade with Russia and the Baltic, 1783–1812* (Columbus: Ohio State University Press, 1965), 152; September 27, October 5, 1809, *Memoirs*, 2:30, 38; October 2, 1809, *Nobody*, 232; LCA to AA, October 21, 1809.

17. *Nobody*, 235.

18. Mrs. Hugh Wyndham, ed., *Correspondence of Sarah Spencer, Lady Lyttelton, 1787–1870* (London: John Murray, 1912), 169; George Soloveytchik, *Potemkin: A Picture of Catherine's Russia* (London: Percival Marshall, 1949), 112–15 (quotations on 114); Simon Sebag Montefiore, *Prince of Princes: The Life of Potemkin* (London: Weidenfeld and Nicolson, 2000), 190, 237, 590–91; Marina Ritzarev, *Eighteenth-Century Russian Music* (Aldershot, U.K.: Ashgate, 2006), 136, 333; Alan Palmer, *Alexander I: Tsar of War and Peace* (London: Weidenfeld and Nicolson, 1974), 37–38; Sophie de Tisenhaus, comtesse de Choiseul-Gouffier, *Historical Memoirs of the Emperor Alexander I and the Court of Russia* (London: Kegan Paul, Trench, Trübner, 1904), 239; http://www.batguano.com/catno30.html (accessed March 1, 2008); Desmond Gregory, *Malta, Britain, and the European Powers, 1793–1815* (Madison, N.J.: Fairleigh Dickinson University Press, 1996), 105; Jean-Henri Castéra, *The Life of Catherine II, Empress of Russia*,

4th ed. (London: T. M. Longman and O. Rees, 1800), 255; Jean-François Georgel, *Mémoires pour servir à l'histoire des évémens de la fin du dix-huitième siècle, depuis 1760 jusqu'en 1806–1810*, 6 vols. (Paris: Alexis Eymery, 1818), 6:188–91.

19. The following description of her presentation, with quotations, is drawn from *Nobody*, 236–37, and November 12, 1809, *Memoirs*, 2:60–61.

20. On the entrance, see George Matthews Jones, *Travels in Norway, Sweden, Finland, Russia and Turkey, Also on the Coasts of the Sea of Azof and of the Black Sea*, 2 vols. (London: John Murray, 1827), 1:427.

21. Tatyana Pashkova, Tatyana Semionova, and Liudmila Toshina, *The Hermitage: The History of the Buildings and Halls*, trans. Paul Williams and Valery Fateyev (Saint Petersburg: Alfa-Colour Art Publishers, 2007), 29–41.

22. Sarah Spencer observed in 1813 of this ritual, "She [the Empress] is only rather too modest, shrinking from everything like ostentation; she won't suffer any woman to kiss her hand, but always embraces quite cordially": Wyndham, *Correspondence of Sarah Spencer*, 173.

23. Londonderry and Hyde, *Wilmot Journals*, 214; on friendship, see Richard S. Wortman, *Scenarios of Power: Myth and Ceremony in Russian Monarchy: Volume One: From Peter the Great to the Death of Nicholas I* (Princeton, N.J.: Princeton University Press, 1995), 195, 204, 206, 208; Adam Czartoryski, quoted in E. A. Brayley Hodgetts, *The House of Hohenzollern: Two Centuries of Berlin Court Life* (London: Methuen, 1911), 247–48; Choiseul-Gouffier, *Memoirs of Alexander I*, 23, 82; Janet M. Hartley, *Alexander I* (London: Longman, 1994), 1–18; Adam Zamoyski, *Rites of Peace: The Fall of Napoleon & the Congress of Vienna* (New York: HarperCollins, 2007), 353.

24. Wyndham, *Correspondence of Sarah Spencer*, 173; Madame de Staël, *Ten Years of Exile*, trans. Doris Beik (New York: Saturday Review Press, 1972), 201; Princess Louise of Prussia, *Forty-Five Years of My Life* (London: Eveleigh Nash, 1912), 385; "Her voice is very sweet & low, & she speaks as quick as lightening": Londonderry and Hyde, *Wilmot Journals*, 171.

25. Pashkova, Semionova, and Toshina, *Hermitage Buildings*, 101; for a view of the apartments, see the painting by Sergei Zaryanko of the Palace Enfilade, reproduced in Yevgenia Petrova, ed., *St Petersburg: A Portrait of the City and Its Citizens* (Saint Petersburg: State Russian Museum, 2003), 144–45.

26. Henri Troyat, *Alexander of Russia: Napoleon's Conqueror*, trans. Joan Pinkham (London: New English Library, 1982), 4, 112; Wortman, *Scenarios of Power*, 250–54; Elizabeth Alexievna to Amalie of Hesse-Darmstadt, September 10, 1807, quoted in Palmer, *Alexander I*, 148; Carr, *Northern Summer*, 258.

27. Carr, *Northern Summer*, 257.

28. These seem to have been her standard questions, since they were also asked of Catherine Wilmot in 1805: Londonderry and Hyde, *Wilmot Journals*, 177–78.

29. Priscilla Stucley Zamoyska, *Arch Intriguer: A Biography of Dorothea de Lieven* (London: Heinemann, 1957), 23; Johann Gottfried Seume, *A Tour Through Part of Germany, Poland, Russia, Sweden, Denmark, &c. During the Summer of 1805* (London: Richard Phillips, 1807), 43; Palmer, *Alexander I*, 45, 185–88.

30. Wortman, *Scenarios of Power*, 8; LCA to JQA, August 7, December 27, 1814; February 9, 1811, JQA Diary; Thomas Raikes, *A Visit to St. Petersburg, in the Winter of 1829–30* (London: Richard Bentley, 1838), 80, 289; January 13, 1810, November 14, 1809, July 25, 1811, *Nobody*, 242, 238, 266; James Holman, *Travels Through Russia, Siberia, Poland, Austria, Saxony, Prussia, Hanover, & c. & c., Undertaken During the Years 1822, 1823 and 1824, While Suffering from Total Blindness*, 2 vols. (London: George B. Whittaker, 1825), 1:129.

31. LCA to AA, June 2, 1810; October 26, 1835, LCA Diary.

32. December 23, 1809, January 1, 1810, *Nobody*, 240–41; LCA, "Mrs J. Q. Adams"; however, both the tsar and tsarina were absent from Saint Petersburg in February 1815.

33. LCA to JQA, November 8, 1814; January 13, 1811, *Nobody*, 259.

34. April 29, 1810, *Nobody*, 248.

35. December 22, 1810, January 13, 1811, *Nobody*, 258–60 (quotation on 258–59).

36. May 23, 1811, *Nobody*, 250; Paul C. Nagel, *The Adams Women: Abigail and Louisa Adams, Their Sisters and Daughters* (New York: Oxford University Press, 1987), 186, 233–34.

37. Palmer, *Alexander I*, 151, 149; February 3, 1810, *Nobody*, 245; LCA to "My Children," May 1, 1828. There is a halfhearted defense of Constantine in Seume, *Tour*, 50–51, though he does observe, "It must not be denied that an unexampled violence of disposition, sometimes, it is said, exercised beyond all controul, gives him a temporary appearance of greater depravity."

38. Holman, *Travels*, 1:180, 184–85; November 30, 1810, *Memoirs*, 2:192–93; John Proud Greene to Eliza Greene, October 5/17, 1812, and Journal of Peter Allaire, 1774, in Nina N. Bashkina et al., eds., *The United States and Russia: The Beginning of Relations, 1765–1815* (Washington, D.C.: U.S. Government Printing Office, 1980), 883, 25; Charles B. Elliott, *Letters from the North of Europe* (Philadelphia: Key and Biddle, 1832), 200–201. Jones, *Travels*, 1:289, says that Saint Petersburg annually had 114 days of rain, 72 of snow, 92 unsettled, and 97 "bright."

39. Joseph Allen Smith to Rufus King, September 16/28, 1802, in Bashkina, *United States and Russia*, 358; LCA to AA, May 13, 1810.

40. Geraldine Norman, *The Hermitage: The Biography of a Great Museum* (1997; London: Pimlico, 1999), 23.

41. Wortman, *Scenarios of Power*, 4; James Hassell, "Implementation of the Russian Table of Ranks in the Eighteenth Century," *Slavic Review* 29 (June 1970): 283–95; Arthur L. George and Elena George, *St Petersburg: The First Three Centuries* (Stroud: Sutton Publishing, 2004), 181–82; Orlando Figes, *Natasha's Dance: A Cultural History of Russia* (London: Allen Lane, 2002), 6.

42. "Peter the Great and his successors seem to have taken their capital for a theatre": Astolphe, marquis de Custine, *The Empire of the Czar; or, Observations on the Social, Political, and Religious State and Prospects of Russia, Made During a Tour Through That State*, 3 vols. (London: Longman, Brown, Green, and Longmans, 1843), 1:153.

43. Penelope Hunter-Stiebel, ed., *Stroganoff: The Palace and Collections of a Russian Noble Family* (Portland, Ore.: Portland Art Museum in collaboration with Harry N. Abrams, 2000); January 3, 1811, *Nobody*, 258; on Le Brun in Russia and the Stroganoffs, see Gita May, *Elisabeth Vigée Le Brun: The Odyssey of an Artist in an Age of Revolution* (New Haven, Conn.: Yale University Press, 2005), 127–51.

44. November 12, 1809, *Memoirs*, 2:59; October 23, 1810, *Nobody*, 279; Troyat, *Alexander of Russia*, 113.

45. JQA to AA, January 27/February 8, 1810; October 22, 1809, *Nobody*, 233.

46. Georgel, *Mémoires*, 6:178; Augustus Bozzi Granville, *St. Petersburgh: A Journal of Travels to and from That Capital; Through Flanders, the Rhenich Provinces, Prussia, Russia, Poland, Silesia, Saxony, the Federated States of Germany, and France*, 2nd ed., 2 vols. (London: Henry Colburn, 1829), 1:466; Raikes, *Visit to St. Petersburg*, 38; October 23, 1809, *Memoirs*, 2:48; *Nobody*, 234–35 (quotation on 234); Johnston, *Travels*, 130.

47. Holman, *Travels*, 1:108; May 31, 1810, October 8, 1811, August 27, 1812, JQA Diary; LCA to JQA, June 7, October 16, 1814. Little Officer's Street is now Dekabristov Street; the Hotel de la Ville de Bordeaux may have been Demuth's other hotel.

48. JQA to AA, January 27/February 8, 1810, has "fifteen hundred or two thousand dollars, that is, six or seven thousand rubles" for the rent, while LCA to AA, July 9, 1810, says $1,500.

49. JQA, Personal Financial Record, 1802–22, indicates this was the exchange rate in late 1809, though by 1815 he was calculating that a dollar was equivalent to about 5.5 roubles, rather than the 3.15 of 1809. Such fluctuations were mostly driven by the Napoleonic wars. A rouble was worth thirty-one English pence in 1805, twenty-one in 1809, fourteen in 1810, and twelve in 1814: see Crosby, *American Trade with Russia*, 189, and Johnston, *Travels*, 154.

50. Quinzard Accounts, 1810–13; September 24, December 17, 1810, in *Memoirs*, 2:171, 193–94; Joel R. Poinsett to Joseph Johnson, January 1807, in Bashkina, *United States and Russia*, 465; Alexander Pushkin, "The Queen of Spades," in *The Collected Stories* (New York: Everyman's Library, 1999), 268.

51. Figes, *Natasha's Dance*, 21.

52. Leitch Ritchie, *Russia and the Russians: A Journey to St. Petersburg and Moscow Through Courland and Livonia* (Philadelphia: E. L. Carey & A. Hart, 1836), 102; Figes, *Natasha's Dance*, 18; LCA to CFA, February 4–14, 1838 (entry for February 5).

53. George and George, *St Petersburg*, 182–84; Crosby, *American Trade with Russia*, 36; Carr, *Northern Summer*, 236.

54. February 7, 1810, *Nobody*, 244; Donnan, *Bayard Papers*, 451, 458–59, 461–62, 467, 486, 492; JQA to Alexander H. Everett, June 10, 1813, reprinted in Bashkina, *United States and Russia*, 969–71. Sebastian's brother was called Benedict and the family sometimes spelled their name as Cramer: see Peter Littke, "Benedikt Cramer, Director of the Russian and American Company," online at http://www.irah.org/frameset/articles/Cramer.pdf (accessed May 14, 2008).

55. James Dowling and Archer Ryland, *Reports of Cases Argued and Determined in the Court of King's Bench, During Hilary, Easter, and Trinity Terms, in the Second and Third Geo. IV. [1822-Trinity Term, 1827]*, 9 vols. (London: S. Sweet, 1822–31), 2:697; November 4, 10, 1812, *Memoirs*, 2:420–22; on Thomas Gisborne, see Robert Hole, "Gisborne, Thomas (1758–1846)," in *Oxford Dictionary of National Biography*, ed. H.C.G. Matthew and Brian Harrison (Oxford: Oxford University Press, 2004; online ed., ed. Lawrence Goldman, October 2005), http://www.oxforddnb.com/view/article/10782 (accessed November 19, 2007).

56. October 26, 27, 1809, January 7, 1810, August 5, 1812, *Nobody*, 234, 241, 277; LCA to JQA, October 16, 1814.

57. March 28, 1811, *Nobody*, 263; on the Colombi and Bode genealogy, see http://www.feunedecolombi.com/familytree.htm (accessed November 20, 2007); William Shakespear Childe-Pemberton, *The Baroness de Bode, 1775–1803* (London: Longmans, Green, 1900), 62–72 (quotations on 67–68).

58. Childe-Pemberton, *Baroness de Bode*, 171, 226–48 (quotations on 171, 225–27, 231, 236, 241, 244, 248).

59. Donnan, *Bayard Papers*, 423–24; March 29, 1811, *Nobody*, 263; Nicolas d'Ydewalle, *Monseigneur de Soultz: de l'Alsace à Saint-Pétersbourg, 1775–1812: Correspondance et mémoires de la Baronne Mary de Bode* (Gerpinnes: Quorum, 1999), 156–57; LCA to ABA, December 24–27, 1833.

60. August 3, 1811, May 20, 1812, *Memoirs*, 2:287, 372; Alexander von Solodkoff, "St Petersburg," in *Dictionary of Art*, ed. Jane Turner, 34 vols. (London: Macmillan, 1996), 27:576; Werner Keller, *Are the Russians Ten Feet Tall?* trans.

Constantine Fitzgibbon (London: Thames and Hudson, 1961), 168, 170, 180; June 24, 1814, June 24, 1810, *Nobody*, 276–77, 251; Juan van Halen, *Narrative of Don Juan Van Halen's Imprisonment in the Dungeons of the Inquisition at Madrid* (New York: J. & J. Harper, 1828), 195, 210–11. Jones, *Travels*, 1:361, speaks of Bétancourt as heading the "Corps des Ponts et Chaussées" and as a builder of bridges, beautifully designed but defectively constructed.

61. February 7, June 25, 1810, October 25, November 27, 1809, February 8, 1810, *Nobody*, 245, 251, 234, 239, 246; Gustav Heinrich Wetter von Rosenthal to General William Irvine, June 24/July 6, 1804, in Bashkina, *United States and Russia*, 416.

62. February 8, 1810, *Nobody*, 246.

63. Nikolai P. Rumiantsev to Maksim M. Alopeus, October 6/18, 1807, and Andrea Ia. Dashkov to James Madison, July 2/14, 1809, which speaks of "Mr. Levett Harris . . . whose wise, intelligent, and upright conduct has merited the high approbation of His Imperial Majesty": Bashkina, *United States and Russia*, 495, 571.

64. LCA to JQA, August 6, 1822, December 2, 1814; Donnan, *Bayard Papers*, 416; deposition of Christian Rodde, December 4/16, 1814, in Bashkina, *United States and Russia*, 1098; Crosby, *American Trade with Russia*, 276–79.

65. Choiseul-Gouffier, *Memoirs of Alexander I*, 61; Troyat, *Alexander of Russia*, 50, 71; Palmer, *Alexander I*, 60, 74–75, 353–54; *Nobody*, 117; Zamoyski, *Rites of Peace*, 351–53. For a different perspective on Maria Federovna's view of "the importance of marriage and marital love," see Wortman, *Scenarios of Power*, 251.

66. January 3, 1810, November 20, 1809, *Nobody*, 241, 239; February 8, 1811, JQA Diary.

67. Joseph de Maistre, *St. Petersburg Dialogues, or, Conversations on the Temporal Government of Providence*, ed. and trans. Richard A. Lebrun (Montreal and Kingston; Ontario: McGill-Queen's University Press, 1993), xvii–xviii.

68. November 8, 1809, January 3, 1810, *Nobody*, 235, 241; November 10, 1809, September 27, 1811, January 12, 1812, *Memoirs*, 2:57, 311, 333–34; Maistre, *St. Petersburg Dialogues*, xvii–xviii.

69. François Gabriel, comte de Bray, *Essai critique sur l'histoire de la Livonie, suive d'un tableau de l'état actuel de cette province* (Dorpat: J. C. Schünmann, 1817); idem, *Mémoires du comte de Bray, ministre et ambassadeur de S. M. Maximilien, premier roi de Baviére, au près des cours de Saint-Pétersbourg, Londres, Berlin, Paris et Vienne* (Paris: Plon-Nourrit, 1911); idem, *Voyage pittoresque dans le Tyrol aux salines de Salzbourg et de Reichenhall: et dans une partie de la Bavière* (Paris: Gide fils, 1825); Kasper Maria, Graf von Sternberg, et al., *Essai d'un exposé géognostico-botanique de la flore du monde primitif* (Ratisbonne: Christophe Ernest Brenck, 1820–26).

70. Andrei Ia. Dashkov to Nikolai P. Rumiantsev, December 3/15, 1811, in Bashkina, *United States and Russia*, 804, 807.

71. Aleksandr A. Bezborodko to Iva A. Osterman, June 21/July 2, 1782, and Alexander I to Levett Harris, July 16/28, 1806, in Bashkina, *United States and Russia*, 158, 454; Crosby, *American Trade with Russia*, 156. On the Russian representation, see Bashkina, *United States and Russia*, 553.

72. June 4, 1811, *Memoirs*, 2:271; Alexander I to Fedor P. Pahlen, December 27, 1809/January 8, 1810, in Bashkina, *United States and Russia*, 633; Crosby, *American Trade with Russia*, 96.

73. LCA to JQA, November 22, 1814.

74. D. Chrétien Muller, *Tableau de Pétersbourg, ou lettres sur la Russie, écrites en 1810, 1811, et 1812*, trans. C. Léger (Paris: Treuttel et Wurtz, 1814), 3.

2. FROM SAINT PETERSBURG TO RIGA

1. On such perceptions, see Larry Wolff, *Inventing Eastern Europe: The Map of Civilization on the Mind of the Enlightenment* (Stanford, Calif.: Stanford University Press, 1994); Charles Lloyd, *Travels at Home, and Voyages by the Fireside: For the Instruction and Entertainment of Young Persons*, 2nd ed. (London: Longman, Hurst, Rees, Orm & Brown, 1815), 114–15; "I have really acquired the reputation of a heroine at a very cheap rate": LCA to AA, June 12, 1815; Augustus von Kotzebue, *To Serve as Italy, in the Years 1804 and 1805*, 4 vols. (London: Richard Phillips, 1806), 1:3–4.

2. See, for example, JQA to AA, May 2, 1811, which compares Carr and Porter.

3. John Carr, *A Northern Summer; or, Travels Round the Baltic, Through Denmark, Sweden, Russia, Prussia, and Part of Germany, in the Year 1804* (London: Richard Phillips, 1805), 2; on Carr, see T. F. Henderson, "Carr, Sir John (1772–1832)," rev. Elizabeth Baigent, *Oxford Dictionary of National Biography* (Oxford: Oxford University Press, 2004), http://www.oxforddnb.com/view/article/4749 (accessed October 15, 2008). Green (sometimes Greene) was an Englishman of little fortune, who worked as a land steward in France in the 1790s and subsequently lived in Russia: see Gordon Goodwin, "Greene, George (b. 1747/8, d. in or after 1816)," rev. Elizabeth Baigent, in *Oxford Dictionary of National Biography*, ed. H.C.G. Matthew and Brian Harrison (Oxford: Oxford University Press, 2004), http://www.oxforddnb.com/view/article/11415 (accessed October 15, 2008).

4. Useful guides to women travelers include Jane Robinson, *Wayward Women: A Guide to Women Travellers* (Oxford: Oxford University Press, 1990) and Shirley Foster and Sara Mills, eds., *An Anthology of Women's Travel Writing* (Manchester: Manchester University Press, 2002). On the general topic of traveling, see Peter

Hulme and Tim Youngs, eds., *Cambridge Companion to Travel Writing* (Cambridge: Cambridge University Press, 2002) and Jás Elsner and Joan-Pau Rubiés, eds., *Voyages and Visions: Towards a Cultural History of Travel* (London: Reaktion Books, 1999).

5. Katie Hickman, *Daughters of Britannia: The Lives and Times of Diplomatic Wives* (London: HarperCollins, 1999); *AFC*, 5:358–86; Anne Disbrowe, *Original Letters from Russia, 1825–1828* (London: Ladies' Printing Press, 1878).

6. On American epistolary diaries, see Steven E. Kagle, *American Diary Literature, 1620–1799* (Boston: Twayne, 1979), 88; for LCA's autobiography, see LCA, "Mrs J. Q. Adams," *Mrs A. S. Colvin's Weekly Messenger* (June 12, 1827): 304–305.

7. *Narrative (1)*, 34.

8. See Heinrich August Ottokar Reichard, *An Itinerary of France and Belgium; or, an Account of the Post and Cross Roads, Rivers, Canals, Principal Inns, Coins, Modes of Travelling; a List of the Diligences, Voiture, Etc. with Their Various Destinations* (London: Samuel Leigh, 1816).

9. Edme Theodore Bourg Saint-Edme, *Itinéraire complet de l'empire Française, de l'Italie, et des provinces Illyriennes*, 3rd ed., 3 vols. (Paris: H. Langlois, 1812), 1:1–11; see also Leopold, Graf von Berchtold, "Observations générales et pratiques sur les voyages," in Heinrich August Ottokar Reichard, *Guide des voyageurs en Europe*, 3 vols. (Weimar: Bureau d'Industrie, 1805), 1:iii–lxii.

10. Mariana Starke, *Information and Directions for Travellers on the Continent*, 5th ed. (Paris: A. and W. Galignani, 1826), 352.

11. March 13, 1815, JQA Diary; April 19, 1814, *Memoirs*, 2:605; *État général des postes du royaume de France, avec les routes qui conduisent aux principales villes de l'Europe, dressé par ordre du Conseil d'Administration* (Paris: De L'Imprimerie Royale, 1814), 134–35, 138–41.

12. Robert Johnston, *Travels Through Part of the Russian Empire and the Country of Poland: Along the Southern Shores of the Baltic* (New York: Davis Longworth, 1816), 59; Richard Smith, *Notes Made During a Tour* (London: C. & J. Rivington, 1827), 77; Elizabeth Donnan, ed., *Papers of James A. Bayard, 1796–1815*, in *Annual Report of the American Historical Association for the Year 1913: Vol. II* (Washington, D.C.: American Historical Association, 1915), 413.

13. "The length of each [Russian] stage is graduated according to the nature of the ground and is from eleven to twenty-six versts": Juan Van Halen, *Narrative of Don Juan Van Halen's Imprisonment in the Dungeons of the Inquisition at Madrid* (New York: J. & J. Harper, 1828), 185.

14. Saint-Edme, *Itinéraire complet*, 1:44; William Rae Wilson, *Travels in Russia, &c. &c.* (London: Longman, Rees, Orme, Brown, and Green, 1828), 170; Kotzebue, *To Serve as Italy*, 1:30–31; Smith, *Notes During a Tour*, 76.

15. William Jacob, *A View of the Agriculture, Manufactures, Statistics, and State of Society, of Germany, and Parts of Holland and France: Taken During a Journey Through Those Countries, in 1819* (London: John Murray, 1820), 80.

16. Carr, *Northern Summer*, 427–28; April 28, 29, 1814, *Memoirs*, 2:603–6; Alexander H. Everett to JQA, August 13/25, 1810, in Nina N. Bashkina et al., eds., *The United States and Russia: The Beginning of Relations, 1765–1815* (Washington, D.C.: U.S. Government Printing Office, 1980), 690; Kotzebue, *To Serve as Italy*, 1:31: "We do not pay so much for ten horses in Russia, as five in other countries."

17. *État general (1814)*, 20–41; Mariana Starke, *Travels on the Continent, Written for the Use and Particular Information of Travellers* (London: John Murray, 1820), 15–18.

18. On berlines, see László Tarr, *The History of the Carriage* (London: Vision, 1969), 226–27; http://www.carriagesofeurope.com/index.cfm?pid=14&letter=B#Berlin (accessed November 21, 2007); and E. Poppele, *Manuel des postes pour l'Allemagne et les routes principales de l'Europe*, 4th ed. (Frankfurt: Frédéric Wilmans, 1831), 132.

19. "Des choses necessaires pour les voyages," in Reichard, *Guide des voyageurs en Europe*, 1:lxxiv; Carr, *Northern Summer*, 268, 190; Eduard Kolbe, *Recollections of Russia During Thirty-Three Years' Residence by a German Nobleman*, trans. Lawrence Wraxall, 2nd ed. (Edinburgh: Thomas Constable, 1855), 141; *Narrative (1)*, 13, 43; LCA to Levett Harris, February 5/17, 1815, Dr. Mavis Kelsey Collection of Adams-Harris Papers, Special Collections Department, Bryn Mawr College Library (hereinafter Adams-Harris Papers); LCA to JQA, March 17, 1815.

20. JQA, Account Book, 1809–1819; JQA, Financial Ledger, 1802–1813; for dollar equivalences in 2007, the latest available data, see http://www.measuringworth .com/calculators/uscompare/ (accessed June 24, 2008).

21. There are suggestions for what to take in "Choses necessaires."

22. Starke, *Travels on the Continent*, 5–7; on drag chains, see Jeremy Black, *The British Abroad: The Grand Tour in the Eighteenth Century* (New York: St. Martin's Press, 1992), 173.

23. Bayard Taylor, *Travels in Greece and Russia, with an Excursion to Crete* (New York: G. P. Putnam, 1859), 420; Johann Gottfried Seume, *A Tour Through Part of Germany, Poland, Russia, Sweden, Denmark, &c. During the Summer of 1805* (London: Richard Phillips, 1807), 26; Wilson, *Travels in Russia*, 217; Augustus Bozzi Granville, *St. Petersburgh: A Journal of Travels to and from That Capital; Through Flanders, the Rhenich Provinces, Prussia, Russia, Poland, Silesia, Saxony, the Federated States of Germany, and France*, 2nd ed., 2 vols. (London: Henry Colburn, 1829), 1:395–96; George Matthews Jones, *Travels in Norway, Sweden,*

Finland, Russia and Turkey, Also on the Coasts of the Sea of Azof and of the Black Sea, 2 vols. (London: John Murray, 1827), 1:333.

24. Carr, *Northern Summer*, 216–17; Julie A. Buckler, *Mapping St. Petersburg: Imperial Text and Cityshape* (Princeton, N.J.: Princeton University Press, 2005), 164–65; April 28, 1814, *Memoirs*, 2:603; LCA to JQA, May 20, 1814.

25. *Narrative (1)*, 2; JQA to LCA, May 1, 1814; David Kirby, *The Baltic World, 1772–1993: Europe's Northern Periphery in an Age of Change* (London: Longman, 1995), 48, observes that, in winter, one could get from Saint Petersburg to Reval in two days by sledge.

26. Wilson, *Travels in Russia*, 215; Seume, *Tour*, 25; Mrs. Hugh Wyndham, ed., *Correspondence of Sarah Spencer, Lady Lyttelton, 1787–1870* (London: John Murray, 1912), 187; Seume, *Tour*, 26; J. G. (Johann Georg) Kohl, *Russia* (1844; New York: Arno Press, 1970), 353, 349; Kirby, *Baltic World, 1772–1993*, 48; Granville, *St. Petersburgh*, 2:514; on the "See saw movement on the Ice," see Marquis of Londonderry and H. M. Hyde, eds., *The Russian Journals of Martha and Catherine Wilmot* (London: Macmillan, 1934), 63.

27. Johnston, *Travels*, 359–60; Wyndham, *Correspondence of Sarah Spencer*, 187; Leitch Ritchie, *Russia and the Russians: A Journey to St. Petersburg and Moscow Through Courland and Livonia* (Philadelphia: E. L. Carey & A. Hart, 1836), 10–11; Jean-François de La Harpe, *Lycée, ou cours de littérature ancienne et moderne*, 3 vols. (Paris: Agasse, 1805), 3:217, quoted in Kirby, *Baltic World, 1772–1993*, 46.

28. Donnan, *Bayard Papers*, 498; Wilson, *Travels in Russia*, 213; George Green, *An Original Journal from London to St. Petersburg, by Way of Sweden; and, Proceeding from Thence, to Moscow, Riga, Mittau, and Berlin* (London: T. Boosey and J. Hatchard, 1813), 132.

29. Carr, *Northern Summer*, 419; Taylor, *Greece and Russia*, 421; Green, *Original Journal*, 133; Alexander Pushkin, "A Novel in Letters," in *The Collected Stories* (New York: Everyman's Library, 1999), 65; Jones, *Travels*, 1:283, 488–89; Mary Holderness, *Journey from Riga to the Crimea, with Some Account of the Manners and Customs of the Colonists of New Russia*, 2nd ed. (London: Sherwood, Gilbert, and Piper, 1827), 12–13; J. T. James, *Journal of a Tour in Germany, Sweden, Russia, Poland, During the Years 1813 and 1814*, 2nd ed., 2 vols. (London: John Murray, 1817), 2:307–308; Seume, *Tour*, 42; Jean-François Georgel, *Mémoires pour servir à l'histoire des événems de la fin du dix-huitième siècle, depuis 1760 jusqu'en 1806–1810*, 6 vols. (Paris: Alexis Eymery, 1818), 6:6; Pushkin, "The Stationmaster," in *Collected Stories*, 107; for other instances of swindling, see Londonderry and Hyde, *Wilmot Journals*, 335.

30. Peter Kolchin, *Unfree Labor: American Slavery and Russian Serfdom* (Cambridge, Mass.: Belknap Press of Harvard University Press, 1987), 42; Johnston, *Travels*, 170–71; Carr, *Northern Summer*, 421; Londonderry and Hyde, *Wilmot Journals*, 32.

31. For descriptions of such bridges, see Daniel Wilson, *Letters from an Absent Brother, Containing Some Account of a Tour Through Parts of the Netherlands, Switzerland, Northern Italy, and France, in the Summer of 1823*, 4th ed., 2 vols. (London: George Wilson, 1824), 1:77; Nathaniel Hazeltine Carter, *Letters from Europe, Comprising the Journal of a Tour Through Ireland, England, Scotland, France, Italy, and Switzerland in the Years 1825, '26, and '27*, 2nd ed., 2 vols. (New York: G. & C. & H. Carvill, 1829), 2:396; *Diary of Occurrences on a Journey Through a Part of Belgium, Holland, and up the Rhine to Mayence, and Thence to Paris, in the Months of August and September 1828* (London: J. Ridgway, 1829), 48–49. For a technical discussion, see "Of Flying Bridges," in *The London Journal of Arts and Sciences: Vol. VIII*, ed. W. Newton (London: Sherwood, Gilbert and Piper, 1832), 289–94.

32. Ritchie, *Russia and the Russians*, 31; Wilson, *Travels in Russia*, 213; Halen, *Halen's Imprisonment*, 186; Georgel, *Mémoires*, 6:18.

33. April 29, 1814, *Memoirs*, 2:605; Wilson, *Travels in Russia*, 209; Ritchie, *Russia and the Russians*, 30; Indrek Rohtmets, *A Cultural Guide to Estonia*, trans. Liivamägi and Tiina Randviir (Tallinn: Varrak, 2006), 166.

34. Donnan, *Bayard Papers*, 498; June 4, 1812, *Nobody*, 276; Mati Laur et al., *History of Estonia* (Tallinn: Avita, 2002), 132; William Coxe, *Travels in Poland, Russia, Sweden, and Denmark*, 5th ed., 5 vols. (London: T. Cadell and W. Davies, 1802), 2:238, hazards 9,000 Swedes in the battle against 32,000 Russians, with Russian casualties of 6,000.

35. Detlev von Uexküll, ed., *Arms and the Woman: The Diaries of the Baron Boris Uxkull, 1812–1819*, trans. Joel Carmichael (London: Secker & Warburg, 1966), 17–18; Carr, *Northern Summer*, 420; Ritchie, *Russia and the Russians*, 30.

36. *Narrative (2)*, 2; Donnan, *Bayard Papers*, 498–99; April 29, 1814, *Memoirs*, 2:605; Green, *Original Journal*, 134; LCA, "Mrs J. Q. Adams"; LCA to Levett Harris, February 5/17, 1815, Adams-Harris Papers; *Record*, 5; LCA to ABA, March 2, 1834; Nicolai Karamsin, *Travels from Moscow, Through Prussia, Germany, Switzerland, France, and England*, 3 vols. (London: J. Badcock, 1803), 1:10.

37. *Record*, 75; Laur, *History of Estonia*, 120–21, 129.

38. *Hand-Book for Northern Europe: Including Denmark, Norway, Sweden, Finland and Russia* (London: John Murray, 1849), 578, 393; Francis C. Gray to JQA, October 4, 1811; Carr, *Northern Summer*, 419, 421.

39. Laur, *History of Estonia*, 31; Ants Viires, *Old Estonian Folk Life* (Tallinn: Ilo Publishing House, 2004), 13–14.

40. Léon Renouard de Bussière, *Voyage en Russie: lettres écrites en 1829* (Paris: F. G. Levrault, 1831), 267; Laur, *History of Estonia*, 55–154.

41. Granville, *St. Petersburgh*, 1:392; Elizabeth Rigby, *Letters from the Shores of the Baltic*, 2nd ed. (London: John Murray, 1842), 117; Jones, *Travels*, 1:476, speaks of

"Chudleigh, so celebrated as the residence of the Duchess of Kingston." "Tschudelei" is the spelling in *Hand-Book for Northern Europe*, 579.

42. April 29, 1814, *Memoirs*, 2:605; when traveling in Devon, John Adams noted in his diary: "Strachleigh did belong to the Chudleighs the Dutchess of Kingstons Family": August 7, 1787, L. H. Butterfield, ed., *Diary and Autobiography of John Adams*, 4 vols. (Cambridge, Mass.: Harvard University Press, 1961), 3:210.

43. T. A. B. Corley, "Chudleigh, Elizabeth [married names Elizabeth Hervey, countess of Bristol; Elizabeth Pierrepont, duchess of Kingston upon Hull] (c.1720–1788)," *Oxford Dictionary of National Biography* (Oxford: Oxford University Press, 2004), http://www.oxforddnb.com/view/article/5380 (accessed December 3, 2007). The following account is drawn from Claire Gervat, *Elizabeth: The Scandalous Life of the Duchess of Kingston* (2003; London: Arrow Books, 2004).

44. Vic Gatrell, *City of Laughter: Sex and Satire in Eighteenth-Century London* (London: Atlantic, 2006), 207; Gervat, *Scandalous Life*, 43–45.

45. Gervat, *Scandalous Life*, 59.

46. Ibid., 85.

47. On Catherine's lovers, see George Soloveytchik, *Potemkin: A Picture of Catherine's Russia* (London: Percival Marshall, 1949), 22.

48. Gervat, *Scandalous Life*, 208–11, 218, 222–23; Jones, *Travels*, 1:476; Green, *Original Journal*, 134; Maria Cosway to Thomas Jefferson, September 20, 1786, speaks of an abortive dinner with the duchess in St. Cloud; see John P. Kaminski, ed., *Jefferson in Love: Love Letters Between Thomas Jefferson & Maria Cosway* (Madison, Wisc.: Madison House, 1999), 59.

49. LCA to CFA, July 10, 1828.

50. *Record*, 4; undated memorandum on LCA's genealogy, quoted in Joan Ridder Challinor, "Louisa Catherine Johnson Adams: The Price of Ambition" (Ph.D. diss., American University, 1982), 28; Michael O'Brien, *Henry Adams and the Southern Question* (Athens: University of Georgia Press, 2005), 31–32; Challinor, "Price of Ambition," 27–38.

51. *Nobody*, 22–23; William Jesse, *The Life of George Brummell, Esq., Commonly Called Beau Brummell*, 2 vols. (London: Saunders and Otley, 1844), 1:163–65.

52. *New Annual Register, or General Repository of History, Politics, and Literature for the Year 1792* (London: G.G.J. and J. Robinson), 25–26; *The Times* (London) (July 10, 1792); *The Sporting Magazine or Monthly Calendar of the Transactions of the Turf, the Chace, and Every Other Diversion Interesting to the Man of Pleasure, Enterprize & Spirit: Volume the Thirteenth* (London: Rogerson & Tuxford, 1799), 330.

53. May 11, 1796, JQA Diary; LCA to CFA, April 21, 1846; AA to LCA, December 8, 1804.

54. *Record*, 63–64; Edward Gibbon to Dorothea Gibbon, April [18?], 1768, in J. E. Norton, ed., *The Letters of Edward Gibbon*, 3 vols. (London: Cassell, 1956), 1:226; Gervat, *Scandalous Life*, 22.

55. *Record*, 64–65.

56. JQA to LCJ, February 28, 1797.

57. Jones, *Travels*, 1:489; Carr, *Northern Summer*, 428; Londonderry and Hyde, *Wilmot Journals*, 63; Thomas Holcroft, *Travels from Hamburg, Through Westphalia, Holland, and the Netherlands to Paris*, 2 vols. (London: Richard Phillips, 1804), 1:28; Kotzebue, *To Serve as Italy*, 1:31; Kohl, *Russia*, 349.

58. Taylor, *Greece and Russia*, 422; Ritchie, *Russia and the Russians*, 29; Carr, *Northern Summer*, 421; Kohl, *Russia*, 349.

59. John Dundas Cochrane, *A Pedestrian Journey Through Russia and Siberian Tartary, to the Frontiers of China, the Frozen Sea, and Kamtchatka* (Edinburgh: Constable, 1829), 38; Laur, *History of Estonia*, 115; Kohl, *Russia*, 349. For nineteenth-century accounts of the Old Believers, see Charles François Philibert Masson, *Secret Memoirs of the Court of Petersburg: Particularly Towards the End of the Reign of Catharine II and the Commencement of That of Paul I* (Philadelphia: John Conrad, 1802), 247–48; and Frédéric Lacroix, *The Mysteries of Russia* (Boston: Coolidge and Wiley, 1848), 95–96.

60. Ritchie, *Russia and the Russians*, 11; historical marker at Torma Church; Ivar Sakk, *Estonian Manors: A Travelogue*, trans. Ants Pihlak (Tallinn: Sakk, 2004), 206; Ulrich von Schlippenbach, *Erinnerungen von einer Reise nach St. Petersburg im Jahre 1814*: Th. 1 (Mitau: J. F. Steffenhagen, 1816), 59; Granville, *St. Petersburgh*, 1:389.

61. Donnan, *Bayard Papers*, 499.

62. Malle Salupere, *Millenary Tartu: City of Youth and Good Ideas*, trans. Alexander Harding (Tartu: Tartu University Press, 2006), 23–29, 46–49; this book is better than its title.

63. Ibid., 73–111.

64. August 15, 1821, LCA Diary; *Nobody*, 170.

65. Jacob M. Price, ed., *Joshua Johnson's Letterbook, 1771–1774: Letters from a Merchant in London to His Partners in Maryland* (London: London Record Society, 1979), ix–x; *Record*, 4–7; LCA to ABA, March 2, 1834.

66. *Record*, 8–9, 17–18.

67. Ibid., 18–24.

68. Ibid., 26–27, 18.

69. *Nobody*, 16, 170, 101.

70. Ibid., 145; LCA to Sarah Grimké, January 11, 1838; LCA to ABA, [pre–August 7, 1846].

71. LCA to Harris, February 5/17, 1815, Adams-Harris Papers; Thomas Raikes, *A Visit to St. Petersburg, in the Winter of 1829–30* (London: Richard Bentley, 1838), 28, 327; Halen, *Halen's Imprisonment*, 185; Carr, *Northern Summer*, 200–201; Wilson, *Travels in Russia*, 167.

72. Carr, *Northern Summer*, 427; Charles B. Elliott, *Letters from the North of Europe* (Philadelphia: Key and Biddle, 1832), 274; Granville, *St. Petersburgh*, 1:381; Halen, *Halen's Imprisonment*, 189; Starke, *Travels on the Continent*, Appendix, 265; Georgel, *Mémoires*, 6:164–65; Kohl, *Russia*, 340; LCA to Harris, February 5/17, 1815, Adams-Harris Papers; Donnan, *Bayard Papers*, 497–500.

73. *Narrative (1)*, 3; Maurizio Lo Re, *Filippo Paulucci: L'Italiano Che Governò a Riga* (Livorno: Book and Company, 2006), 9; LCA to Levett Harris, February 5/17, 1815, Adams-Harris Papers. For accounts of the hotel, see Starke, *Travels on the Continent*, Appendix, 265; Granville, *St. Petersburgh*, 1:379.

74. October 24, December 25, 1812, *Memoirs*, 2:416, 435–36; Arnolds Spekke, *History of Latvia: An Outline* (1948; Riga: Jumava, 2006), 261; Francis C. Gray to JQA, October 4, 1811; Karamsin, *Travels from Moscow*, 1:14. On Paulucci, see also H. G. Schenk, *The Mind of the European Romantics: An Essay in Cultural History* (New York: Doubleday, 1969), 107; Josifs Šteimanis, *History of Latvian Jews* (Boulder, Colo.: Eastern European Monographs; New York: Columbia University Press, 2002), 23; Albert Blanc, ed., *Correspondance diplomatique de Joseph de Maistre, 1811–1817; Tome Premier* (Paris: Michel Lévy frères, 1860), 30; Kohl, *Russia*, 330.

75. Donnan, *Bayard Papers*, 501; Re, *Filippo Paulucci*, 14; LCA, "Mrs J. Q. Adams"; Halen, *Halen's Imprisonment*, 187–88. For the appearance of the castle, see the illustrations following 128 in Māra Caune, *Rīgas Pils—Senā un Mainīgā* (Riga: Jumava, 2004).

76. LCA to Levett Harris, February 5/17, 1815, Adams-Harris Papers; Carr, *Northern Summer*, 199; on ducats, see also James, *Journal of a Tour*, 2:220. Her money-changing visitor was probably John Mitchell, a Riga merchant, whose father, James Mitchell, had retired in December 1814; see Mungo Ponton Brown, *A Treatise on the Law of Sale* (Edinburgh: W. & C. Tait, 1821), 158; and J. Potter, "The British Timber Duties, 1815–1860," *Economica* n.s. 22 (May 1955): 126.

77. LCA to JQA, February 17–20, 1815.

78. *Narrative (1)*, 3. Her narrative speaks of reaching the post station beyond Mitau by eight or nine o'clock at night, of spending several hours in Mitau, and of a journey from Riga to Mitau delayed by the snow, so it is very unlikely that she left Riga much after noon, if not before. In the late 1790s, Kotzebue took three days to get from Polangen to Mitau: Augustus von Kotzebue, *The Most Remarkable Year in the Life of Augustus von Kotzebue; Containing an Account of His Exile*

Into Siberia, and of the Other Extraordinary Events Which Happened to Him in Russia: Written by Himself, trans. Benjamin Beresford (London: Richard Phillips, 1802), 34–35.

79. Laurence A. P. Kitching, "A Baltic-German Lessing? Johann Friedrich Recke's Mitau Dramaturgy," *Journal of Baltic Studies* 31 (Spring 2000): 44–47; Seume, *Tour*, 15; Halen, *Halen's Imprisonment*, 188; on knitting, see LCA to CFA, February 4–14, 1838 (entry for February 12); Donnan, *Bayard Papers*, 501; Heinrich Bosse, "The Establishment of the German Theatre in Eighteenth Century Riga," *Journal of Baltic Studies* 20 (Fall 1989): 207–22.

80. Ernest John Knapton, *The Lady of the Holy Alliance: The Life of Julie de Krüdener* (New York: Columbia University Press, 1939); *Nobody*, 83.

81. *Nobody*, 106; Richard S. Wortman, *Scenarios of Power: Myth and Ceremony in Russian Monarchy: Volume One: From Peter the Great to the Death of Nicholas I* (Princeton, N.J.: Princeton University Press, 1995), 229; Knapton, *Lady of the Holy Alliance*, 143–66.

82. *Nobody*, 116–17.

83. JQA to LCA, August 28, 1828; October 8, 10, November 10, 1810, November 19, 1811, *Nobody*, 253–57, 268.

84. JQA to LCA, August 28, 1828; *Record*, 19, 59, 23; LCA, "A Rejected Address on the Opening of the National Theatre at Washington"; June 16, 1838, September 15, 1839, LCA Diary; July 6, 1810, November 19, 1811, *Nobody*, 252, 268; *Nobody*, 95, 83.

85. LCA, *The Metropolitan Kaleidoscope*, 21–22.

86. September 23, 1824, October 12, 1827, July 10, 1828, in David Herbert Donald et al., eds., *Diary of Charles Francis Adams*, 8 vols. (Cambridge, Mass.: Belknap Press of Harvard University Press, 1964–86), 1:332, 2:171, 255.

3. FROM RIGA TO BERLIN

1. November 16, 1809, March 18, 1811, April 4, April 8, 1816, *Memoirs*, 2:69, 247, 3:322–26; *Narrative (1)*, 3–4, 11.

2. Augustus Bozzi Granville, *St. Petersburgh: A Journal of Travels to and from That Capital; Through Flanders, the Rhenich Provinces, Prussia, Russia, Poland, Silesia, Saxony, the Federated States of Germany, and France*, 2nd ed., 2 vols. (London: Henry Colburn, 1829), 2:515; Charles B. Elliott, *Letters from the North of Europe* (Philadelphia: Key and Biddle, 1832), 273; George Green, *An Original Journal from London to St. Petersburg, by Way of Sweden; and, Proceeding from Thence, to Moscow, Riga, Mittau, and Berlin* (London: T. Boosey and J. Hatchard, 1813), 136; William Coxe, *Travels in Poland, Russia, Sweden, and Denmark*, 5th ed., 5 vols. (London: T. Cadell and W. Davies, 1802), 2:245; Mary Holderness, *Journey from Riga to the Crimea, with Some Account of the Manners and Customs of the*

Colonists of New Russia, 2nd ed. (London: Sherwood, Gilbert, and Piper, 1827), 8; Mrs. Hugh Wyndham, ed., *Correspondence of Sarah Spencer, Lady Lyttelton, 1787–1870* (London: John Murray, 1912), 189.

3. *Narrative (1)*, 4; Elliott, *North of Europe*, 372; William Rae Wilson, *Travels in Russia, &c. &c.* (London: Longman, Rees, Orme, Brown, and Green, 1828), 180; J. G. (Johann Georg) Kohl, *Russia* (1844; New York: Arno Press, 1970), 323; for a photograph of the obelisks, see Karl-Otto Schlau, *Mitau im 19. Jahrhundert: Leben und Wirken des Bürgermeisters Franz von Zuccalmaglio (1800–1873)* (Wedemark-Elze: Harro v. Hirschheydt, 1995).

4. Modris Eksteins, *Walking Since Daybreak: A Story of Eastern Europe, World War II, and the Heart of Our Century* (Boston: Houghton Mifflin, 1999), 37, 39; Wilson, *Travels in Russia*, 178; Arnolds Spekke, *History of Latvia: An Outline* (1948; Riga: Jumava, 2006), 27, 234–35, 260; Giacomo Casanova, *The Memoirs of Jacques Casanova de Seingault*, trans. Arthur Machen, 6 vols. (New York: G. P. Putnam's Sons, 1959–61), 5:487; Coxe, *Travels*, 2:249; Jean-François Georgel, *Mémoires pour servir à l'histoire des évémens de la fin du dix-huitième siècle, depuis 1760 jusqu'en 1806–1810*, 6 vols. (Paris: Alexis Eymery, 1818), 6:148–55; John Carr, *A Northern Summer; or, Travels Round the Baltic, Through Denmark, Sweden, Russia, Prussia, and Part of Germany, in the Year 1804* (London: Richard Phillips, 1805), 430; Wyndham, *Correspondence of Sarah Spencer*, 189.

5. Carr, *Northern Summer*, 430; Wyndham, *Correspondence of Sarah Spencer*, 189; Leitch Ritchie, *Russia and the Russians: A Journey to St. Petersburg and Moscow Through Courland and Livonia* (Philadelphia: E. L. Carey and A. Hart, 1836), 15; Wilson, *Travels in Russia*, 177; Kohl, *Russia*, 321; Eksteins, *Walking Since Daybreak*, 40.

6. *Narrative (2)*, 5; *Narrative (1)*, 4; Thomas Raikes, *A Visit to St. Petersburg, in the Winter of 1829–30* (London: Richard Bentley, 1838), 29–30; Granville, *St. Petersburgh*, 1:366–67; Ritchie, *Russia and the Russians*, 11; Carr, *Northern Summer*, 431; Schlau, *Mitau im 19. Jahrhundert*, 28; Georgel, *Mémoires*, 6:148.

7. Josifs Šteimanis, *History of Latvian Jews* (Boulder, Colo.: Eastern European Monographs; New York: Columbia University Press, 2002), 10, 12, 14–16, 21; Masha Greenbaum, *The Jews of Lithuania: A History of a Remarkable Community, 1316–1945* (Jerusalem: Gefen, 1995), 163–64, 167–69.

8. Dovid Katz, *Lithuanian Jewish Culture* (Vilnius: Baltos Lankos, 2004), 120–37, 202–10; Greenbaum, *Jews of Lithuania*, 82–85, 115–18; Šteimanis, *Latvian Jews*, 160, 24; Solomon Maimon, *An Autobiography*, trans. J. Clark Murray (Urbana: University of Illinois Press, 2001), ix–xxx (quotation on xx).

9. Wilson, *Travels in Russia*, 148, 164; Kohl, *Russia*, 319; Bayard Taylor, *Travels in Greece and Russia, with an Excursion to Crete* (New York: G. P. Putnam, 1859),

425; Elliott, *North of Europe*, 283; Ritchie, *Russia and the Russians*, 15; see also Robert Harrison, *Notes of a Nine Years' Residence in Russia, from 1844 to 1853* (London: T. Cautley Newby, 1855), 11, on "the dirty crowded villages of Jews."

10. Šteimanis, *Latvian Jews*, 20; Nicolai Karamsin, *Travels from Moscow, Through Prussia, Germany, Switzerland, France, and England*, 3 vols. (London: J. Badcock, 1803), 1:17–18; Wyndham, *Correspondence of Sarah Spencer*, 190, speaks of Jewish postilions.

11. John Quincy Adams, *Letters on Silesia, Written During a Tour Through That Country in the Years 1800, 1801* (London: J. Rudd, 1804), 5–6.

12. July 12, 1781, Robert J. Taylor et al., eds., *Diary of John Quincy Adams*, 2 vols. (Cambridge, Mass.: Belknap Press of Harvard University Press, 1981), 1:94; Adams, *Letters on Silesia*, 5–6; May 16, 1842, *Memoirs*, 11:162; JQA to George Joy, September 13, 1814, Worthington Chauncey Ford, ed., *Writings of John Quincy Adams*, 7 vols. (New York: Macmillan, 1913), 5:138. The brief discussion of JQA's anti-Semitism in George A. Lipsky, *John Quincy Adams, His Theory and Ideas* (New York: Crowell, 1950), 122–23, is exculpatory.

13. LCA to ABA, January 30, 1835; LCA to JQA, May 18, 1837; LCA to CFA, May 14, 1847; LCA to ABA, January 27–February 4, 1848 (entry for January 29); LCA to CFA, February 4–14, 1838 (entry for February 7); LCA to ABA, February 28, 1831; *Nobody*, 68; *Memoirs*, 1:203, 208, 222; see also Victor Hugo Paltsits, ed., *Berlin and the Prussian Court in 1798: Journal of Thomas Boylston Adams, Secretary of the United States Legation at Berlin* (New York: New York Public Library, 1916), 8.

14. The Schicklers' father, Johann Jacob Schickler, served as banker to Frederick the Great, but also to James Boswell in 1764; see James Boswell, *Boswell on the Grand Tour: Germany and Switzerland, 1764*, ed. Frederick A. Pottle (New York: McGraw-Hill, 1953), 20, 22, 76, 100. On the Schickler brothers, see W. O. Henderson, "The Rise of the Metal and Armament Industries in Berlin and Brandenburg, 1712–1795," *Business History* 3 (June 1961): 73; on the Cohens' conversion, see Steven M. Lowenstein, *The Berlin Jewish Community: Enlightenment, Family, and Crisis, 1770–1830* (New York: Oxford University Press, 1994), 124, and Deborah Hertz, *Jewish High Society in Old Regime Berlin* (New Haven, Conn.: Yale University Press, 1988), 103–104.

15. *Narrative (2)*, 6. I surmise the misidentification because I can find no evidence of a Mengs family in Mitau; on Zala, see Alberts Zarāns, *Latvijas Pilis un Muižas* (Castles and Manors of Latvia) (Riga: A. Zarāns, 2006), 156–57; on the Medems, see Rosalynd Pflaum, *By Influence & Desire: The True Story of Three Extraordinary Women—the Grand Duchess of Courland and Her Daughters* (New York: M. Evans, 1975).

16. Alan Palmer, *Alexander I: Tsar of War and Peace* (London: Weidenfeld and Nicolson, 1974), 40, 42–45, 55; Zarāns, *Latvijas Pilis un Muižas*, 116–17; Eksteins, *Walking Since Daybreak*, 18–24; *Narrative (1)*, 5.

17. The following account of LCA's experience at the Mitau inn is taken from *Narrative (1)*, 5–8, and *Narrative (2)*, 6–9.

18. On getting lost, see *Narrative (1)*, 8–10, and *Narrative (2)*, 9–11; on the phase of the moon, see http://sunearth.gsfc.nasa.gov/eclipse/phase/phases1801.html (accessed December 14, 2007).

19. Carr, *Northern Summer*, 431; Granville, *St. Petersburgh*, 1:362; Kohl, *Russia*, 311–12; Conrad Malte-Brun, *Universal Geography, of a Description of All the Parts of the World, on a New Plan, According to the Great Natural Divisions of the Globe*, 5 vols. (Philadelphia: John Laval and S. F. Bradford, 1829), 4:280.

20. James Holman, *Travels Through Russia, Siberia, Poland, Austria, Saxony, Prussia, Hanover, & c. & c., Undertaken During the Years 1822, 1823 and 1824, While Suffering from Total Blindness*, 2 vols. (London: George B. Whittaker, 1825), 1:260; LCA to ABA, December 24-27, 1833. LCA remembered this as a Christmas Eve party and suppressed the names, but January 12, 1811, *Memoirs*, 2:211–12, and January 12, 1811, *Nobody*, 258, confirms the Colombis; the count died in March 1811.

21. LCA to ABA, December 24–27, 1833.

22. LCA to JQA, December 30, 1814, September 19–20, 1822; *Nobody*, 73, 74, 115. LCA says the ghost was described to her as being Frederick the Great's wife, but this is an error: see Princess Louise of Prussia, *Forty-Five Years of My Life* (London: Eveleigh Nash, 1912), 50, which speaks of "*The White Lady* [who] has been familiar for centuries," and Constance Wright, *Louise, Queen of Prussia* (London: Frederick Muller, 1970), 37.

23. *Nobody*, 74, 73, 75.

24. Ibid., 115–16.

25. *Narrative (1)*, 11.

26. LCA to JQA, February 17–20, 1815.

27. Karamsin, *Travels from Moscow*, 1:21; Wilson, *Travels in Russia*, 172–73; *Narrative (1)*, 12. The Windau is now called the Venta River.

28. Georgel, *Mémoires*, 6:19, 379; Wyndham, *Correspondence of Sarah Spencer*, 190; *Narrative (1)*, 12; Carr, *Northern Summer*, 431.

29. Elliott, *North of Europe*, 277; Carr, *Northern Summer*, 431. Granville, *St. Petersburgh*, 1:359, says Jews were 600 out of the 1,400 inhabitants, but Elliott claims it was "inhabited principally by Jews" (277), an opinion shared by Juan Van Halen, *Narrative of Don Juan Van Halen's Imprisonment in the Dungeons of the Inquisition at Madrid* (New York: J. & J. Harper, 1828), 185.

30. *Narrative (1)*, 13; Granville, *St. Petersburgh*, 1:355–56, 359–60.

31. *Narrative (1)*, 13; Granville, *St. Petersburgh*, 1:355. In the 1820s, the postmaster was Jewish, though also young, so he may not have been there in 1815.

32. Granville, *St. Petersburgh*, 1:354; Carr, *Northern Summer*, 432; Raikes, *Visit to St. Petersburg*, 27.

33. John Dundas Cochrane, *A Pedestrian Journey Through Russia and Siberian Tartary, to the Frontiers of China, the Frozen Sea, and Kamtchatka* (Edinburgh: Constable, 1829), 35; Granville, *St. Petersburgh*, 1:355–56; Wilson, *Travels in Russia*, 163; Carr, *Northern Summer*, 432; Elliott, *North of Europe*, 277–78.

34. Georgel, *Mémoires*, 6:379; Ritchie, *Russia and the Russians*, 6; *Narrative (1)*, 13; Karamsin, *Travels from Moscow*, 1:67, 72; on misidentifying Cossacks, see John Scott, *A Visit to Paris in 1814; Being a Review of the Moral, Political, Intellectual, and Social Condition of the French Capital*, 4th ed. (London: Longman, Hurst, Rees, Orme, and Brown, 1816), 213.

35. Ritchie, *Russia and the Russians*, 2–3; C. W. Rordansz, *European Commerce; or, Complete Mercantile Guide to the Continent of Europe* (London: Baldwin, Cradock, and Joy, 1818), 118; Robert Johnston, *Travels Through Part of the Russian Empire and the Country of Poland: Along the Southern Shores of the Baltic* (New York: Davis Longworth, 1816), 68; Elizabeth Harriot Hudson, *The Life and Times of Louisa, Queen of Prussia: With an Introductory Sketch of Prussian History*, 2 vols. (London: W. Isbister, 1874), 2:269; Walter Nicol, *The Practical Planter; or, a Treatise on Forest Planting* (London: J. Scatcherd, 1803), 54; Halen, *Halen's Imprisonment*, 184; for early-nineteenth-century views of Memel, see Kęstutis Demereckas, ed., *Klaipėdos Uostas: Port of Klaipėda* (Klaipėda: Libra Memelensis, 2007), 12–13, 28, 36–37, 44. In Walter Scott's *Guy Mannering*, a character exclaims, "How could there be a foot mark on the ground, when it was a frost as hard as the heart of a Memel log?"

36. Nijolė Strakauskaitė, *Klaipėda, Curonian Spit, Königsberg*, trans. Aušra Simanavičiūtė (Klaipėda: R. Paknio leidykla, 2005), 36; Wilson, *Travels in Russia*, 159; Wyndham, *Correspondence of Sarah Spencer*, 191; Johnston, *Travels*, 56, 66; Granville, *St. Petersburgh*, 1:353; *A Hand-Book for Travellers on the Continent: Being a Guide Through Holland, Belgium, Prussia, and Northern Germany* (London: John Murray, 1836), 333; Karamsin, *Travels from Moscow*, 1:24–25; JQA, Personal Financial Record, 1802–22 ["Waste Book and Journal"]; JQA, Financial Ledger, 1802–1813; JQA, Account Book, 1809–1819.

37. Christopher Clark, *Iron Kingdom: The Rise and Downfall of Prussia, 1600–1947* (London: Allen Lane, 2006), 312; Ortelsberg is today called Szczytno. On Napoleon's entry into Berlin, see Catherine Hyde, marquise de Govion Broglio Solari, and Louis François Joseph, baron de Bausset-Rocquefort, *Private Anecdotes of Foreign Courts*, 2 vols. (London: H. Colburn, 1827), 1:326.

38. Sophie Marie Voss, *Sixty-Nine Years at the Court of Prussia: From the Recollections of the Mistress of the Household*, trans. Emily Stephenson and Agnes Stephenson, 2 vols. (London: Richard Bentley & Son, 1876), 2:61; Hudson, *Louisa, Queen of Prussia*, 2:217–18, 223–25; Sylvanus Urban, *The Gentleman's Magazine: And Historical Chronicle: For the Year 1809* (London: John Nichols and Son, 1809), 435; J.A.R. Marriott and C. Grant Robertson, *The Evolution of Prussia: The Making of an Empire*, rev. ed. (Oxford: Clarendon Press, 1946), 193. Wright, *Louise*, 173, claims Luise's remark about Frederick's laurels was made to Napoleon during dinner at Tilsit.

39. Richard Smith, *Notes Made During a Tour* (London: C. & J. Rivington, 1827), 100; Strakauskaitė, *Klaipėda*, 21; Louise of Prussia, *Forty-Five Years*, 261.

40. *Nobody*, 18–19; *Record*, 79.

41. Clark, *Iron Kingdom*, 314–19 (quotation on 316); on family, see John Russell, *A Tour in Germany, and Some of the Southern Provinces of the Austrian Empire, in the Years 1820, 1821, 1822*, 3rd ed., 2 vols. (Edinburgh: Archibald Constable, 1825), 2:52.

42. Dolley Payne Madison to Sarah Coles Stevenson, ca. February 1820, in David B. Mattern and Holly C. Shulman, eds., *The Selected Letters of Dolley Payne Madison* (Charlottesville: University of Virginia Press, 2003), 239; January 1, 1808, *Nobody*, 217.

43. Wright, *Louise*, 146; Wilson, *Travels in Russia*, 152; Strakauskaitė, *Klaipėda*, 73; Raikes, *Visit to St. Petersburg*, 24; Augustus von Kotzebue, *To Serve as Italy, in the Years 1804 and 1805*, 4 vols. (London: Richard Phillips, 1806), 1:33; Johnston, *Travels*, 62; Karamsin, *Travels from Moscow*, 1:24; *Narrative (2)*, 14. That LCA went via Tilsit cannot be certain but seems very probable, partly because the route along the Curonian Spit was so memorable that it is unlikely she would have left it unmentioned, partly because the scenes she describes better fit the Tilsit road, partly because her husband had gone along the Haff in 1781 and found it a disagreeable experience; see Taylor, *Diary of John Quincy Adams*, 1:99.

44. Henri Troyat, *Alexander of Russia: Napoleon's Conqueror*, trans. Joan Pinkham (London: New English Library, 1982), 102.

45. *Narrative (2)*, 15, 21, 16.

46. Wyndham, *Correspondence of Sarah Spencer*, 192; Georgel, *Mémoires*, 6:21; *Narrative (2)*, 15; Manfred Kuehn, *Kant: A Biography* (Cambridge: Cambridge University Press, 2001), 166, 59; December 16, 1822, LCA Diary; Carr, *Northern Summer*, 438; Cochrane, *Pedestrian Journey*, 32; Granville, *St. Petersburgh*, 1:349; Green, *Original Journal*, 150; *Leigh's New Descriptive Road Book of Germany, Containing a Detailed Post Itinerary* (London: Leigh and Son, 1837), 188; Jedidiah Morse and Sidney Edwards Morse, *A New System of Geography, Ancient and*

Modern, for the Use of Schools (Boston: Richardson and Lord, 1822), 196; Smith, *Notes During a Tour*, 87.

47. *Narrative (2)*, 15; Edward Augustus Domeier, *A Descriptive Road-Book of Germany* (London: Samuel Leigh, 1830), 135–36; Taylor, *Diary of John Quincy Adams*, 1:99; François Gandini, *Itinéraire de l'Europe*, 2nd ed. (Milan: Sirtori, 1819), 229. It is clear that LCA did not go to Danzig, since the road to Berlin via Kustrin did not go through Danzig. However, after Braunsberg, travelers sometimes cut further south through Preussisch Holland, Preussisch Mark, and Rissenbourg before reuniting with the other road at Marienwerder; for this route, see Heinrich August Ottokar Reichard, *Guide des voyageurs en Europe*, 3 vols. (Weimar: Bureau d'Industrie, 1805), 3:372.

48. Johnston, *Travels*, 58; *Narrative (1)*, 15–16.

49. *Narrative (1)*, 16–17; Wilson, *Travels in Russia*, 147.

50. *Record*, 17, 76.

51. Ibid., 74; *Nobody*, 91–92; August 29, 1832, LCA Diary.

52. *Record*, 24; *Nobody*, 36, 189, 68; LCA, "Instructions for Servants"; August 29, 1832, LCA Diary.

53. Carr, *Northern Summer*, 440–42; Granville, *St. Petersburgh*, 1:346; Johnston, *Travels*, 53, 49–50; Cochrane, *Pedestrian Journey*, 31; Mieczyslaw Haftka, *Malbork and Surroundings* (Warsaw: Festina, 2004), 7–27; Smith, *Notes During a Tour*, 78–79; Elliott, *North of Europe*, 282. For a modern work on what used to be Frauenberg, see Tadeusz Piaskowski and Henryk Szkop, *Zabytki Fromborka* (Frombork: Muzeum Mikołaja Kopernika we Fromborku, 2003).

54. See Anna Grzeszna-Kozikowski, *A Guide to Chełmno*, trans. Dorota Sobierajska (Toruń: PWR Publishing House, 2004) and, especially, the handsomely illustrated Marek Chelminiak, *Chełmno: Zabytkami Malowane* (Bydgoszcz: Margrafsen, 2006).

55. Kotzebue, *To Serve as Italy*, 1:56; Johnston, *Travels*, 395.

56. Karamsin, *Travels from Moscow*, 1:59; Thomas Holcroft, *Travels from Hamburg, Through Westphalia, Holland, and the Netherlands to Paris*, 2 vols. (London: Richard Phillips, 1804), 1:28; Johnston, *Travels*, 277; Augustus von Kotzebue, *The Most Remarkable Year in the Life of Augustus von Kotzebue; Containing an Account of His Exile Into Siberia, and of the Other Extraordinary Events Which Happened to Him in Russia: Written by Himself*, trans. Benjamin Beresford (London: Richard Phillips, 1802), 18; Wilson, *Travels in Russia*, 43; Wilhelm Render, *A Tour Through Germany; Particularly Along the Banks of the Rhine, Mayne, &c. and That Part of the Palatinate, Rhingaw, &c. Usually Termed the Garden of Germany*, 2 vols. (London: A. Strahan, 1801), 1:24–25.

57. Jeremy Black, *The British Abroad: The Grand Tour in the Eighteenth Century* (New York: St. Martin's Press, 1992), 173; *Narrative (2)*, 18.

58. Thomas Carlyle, *History of Friedrich II of Prussia, Called Frederick the Great*, 3rd ed., 4 vols. (London: Chapman and Hall, 1859), 2:274; William Hunter, *Reasons for Not Making Peace with Buonaparte*, 2nd ed. (London: John Stockdale, 1807), 87.

59. Carlyle, *Frederick the Great*, 2:290–91, 278.

60. *Narrative (2)*, 17–18; Mariana Starke, *Information and Directions for Travellers on the Continent*, 6th ed. (London: John Murray, 1828), 544.

61. JQA to JA, May 20, 1797, JQA to AA, June 12, 1800, Ford, *Writings of JQA*, 2:169, 462; JQA to LCA, July 19, 1804; December 5, 1812, LCA Diary; for JQA's retrospective judgment, see June 22, 1828, *Memoirs*, 8:40. There is a brief discussion of JQA on Napoleon in Samuel Flagg Bemis, *John Quincy Adams and the Foundations of American Foreign Policy* (New York: Alfred A. Knopf, 1949), 222–23.

62. Wyndham, *Correspondence of Sarah Spencer*, 194; *Narrative (1)*, 18–19.

63. *Narrative (1)*, 18–19; Alexis Eustaphieve, *The Resources of Russia, in the Event of a War with France: With a Short Description of the Cozaks* (Boston: Munroe and Frances, 1813), 85–96; Sir Robert Wilson, *Brief Remarks on the Character and Composition of the Russian Army, and a Sketch of the Campaigns in Poland in the Years 1806 and 1807* (London: T. Egerton, 1810), 25–49; Scott, *Visit to Paris*, 210–14; Philip Longworth, *The Cossacks* (London: Constable, 1969), 226.

64. *Narrative (1)*, 18–19.

65. Johnston, *Travels*, 397; *Narrative (1)*, 19; on the retreat, via Kustrin and Graudenz, see Wright, *Louise*, 130–38.

4. FROM BERLIN TO EISENACH

1. Mrs. Hugh Wyndham, ed., *Correspondence of Sarah Spencer, Lady Lyttelton, 1787–1870* (London: John Murray, 1912), 193; LCA to JQA, March 5, 1815; *Nobody*, 5; November 6, 1797, *Memoirs*, 1:203; William Jacob, *A View of the Agriculture, Manufactures, Statistics, and State of Society, of Germany, and Parts of Holland and France: Taken During a Journey Through Those Countries, in 1819* (London: John Murray, 1820), 191.

2. *Record*, 77; JQA to Catherine Nuth Johnson, February 7, 1798, copy in JQA diary; November 12, December 1, 1797, February 12, 17, March 21, June 18, 1798, January 8, 9, 1800, JQA Diary.

3. *Nobody*, 15; *Narrative (2)*, 20.

4. Jacob, *View of the Agriculture*, 192, indicates 124,730 civilian inhabitants in 1797; Richard Chevenix Trench, ed., *The Remains of the Late Mrs. Richard Trench, Being Selections from Her Journals, Letters, & Other Papers* (London: Parker and Bourn, 1862), 120; Matt Erlin, *Berlin's Forgotten Future: City, History, and Enlightenment in Eighteenth-Century Germany* (Chapel Hill: University of North Carolina Press, 2004), 25; Alexandra Richie, *Faust's Metropolis: A History of Ber-

lin (London: HarperCollins, 1998), 70, 52, 1–2, 54; Elizabeth Harriot Hudson, *The Life and Times of Louisa, Queen of Prussia: With an Introductory Sketch of Prussian History*, 2 vols. (London: W. Isbister, 1874), 1:305. Cf. Thomas Raikes, *A Visit to St. Petersburg, in the Winter of 1829–30* (London: Richard Bentley, 1838), 14: "The quiet streets, the scanty equipages, and the little movement which is seen . . . give to Berlin rather the air of a great provincial town with a numerous garrison, than the animated aspect of a great and busy capital."

5. Madame de Staël, *Germany*, ed. O. W. Wright, 2 vols. (Boston: Houghton, Mifflin, 1859), 1:111–12; Frederick Wilhelm Taube, "Thoughts on the Beautification of Cities" (1776), quoted in Erlin, *Berlin's Forgotten Future*, 3; on stucco, John Carr, *A Northern Summer; or, Travels Round the Baltic, Through Denmark, Sweden, Russia, Prussia, and Part of Germany, in the Year 1804* (London: Richard Phillips, 1805), 460; Ronald Taylor, *Berlin and Its Culture: A Historical Portrait* (New Haven, Conn.: Yale University Press, 1997), 40; Augustus Bozzi Granville, *St. Petersburgh: A Journal of Travels to and from That Capital; Through Flanders, the Rhenich Provinces, Prussia, Russia, Poland, Silesia, Saxony, the Federated States of Germany, and France*, 2nd ed., 2 vols. (London: Henry Colburn, 1829), 1:259, 332; August Friedrich Julius Knüppeln (1798), quoted in Taylor, *Berlin and Its Culture*, 60; "Introduction: The Rise of Prussia," in *The Rise of Prussia, 1700–1830*, ed. Philip G. Dwyer (Harlow, U.K.: Longman, 2000), 14; Richie, *Faust's Metropolis*, 66, 72; Johann Wolfgang von Goethe, "Briefe an Charlotte von Stein—Reise nach Berlin, 17 Mai 1778," in Friedhelm Kemp, *Goethe: Leben und Welt in Briefen* (Munich, 1978), 171, quoted in Richie, *Faust's Metropolis*, 76.

6. Peter Feist, *The Brandenburg Gate*, trans. Ilka Laxczkowiak (Berlin: Kai Homilius, 1998), 6–17; *Record*, 78; Granville, *St. Petersburgh*, 1:266.

7. *Address-Kalender der Königliche Preussischen Haupt-und-Residenz Städte* (1799), reproduced in Anneliese Harding, ed., *John Quincy Adams: Pioneer of German-American Literary Studies* (Boston: Boston Public Library, 1979), 29; Granville, *St. Petersburgh*, 1:272; Carr, *Northern Summer*, 464; *Nobody*, 29–32.

8. Nicolai Karamsin, *Travels from Moscow, Through Prussia, Germany, Switzerland, France, and England*, 3 vols. (London: J. Badcock, 1803), 1:113; Constance Wright, *Louise, Queen of Prussia* (London: Frederick Muller, 1970), 65; Hugh Elliott, the British minister to Saxony, quoted in Trench, *Remains of Mrs. Trench*, 112; *Nobody*, 6, 8, 11–14, 120.

9. Francis Gray to JQA, October [26?], 1811; Rose Weigall, ed., *The Correspondence of Priscilla, Countess of Westmorland* (London: John Murray, 1909), 104; Princess Louise of Prussia, *Forty-Five Years of My Life* (London: Eveleigh Nash, 1912), 32–33, 430–31, 36. The countess's sister, Fräulein von Keller, was governess to the young Princess Luise, hence the bonds between the Néales and the family of Prince Ferdinand were extensive.

10. *Nobody*, 15; "Pauline Néale found the hardships of our flight hard to bear, and, for all her goodness of heart, afforded me no comfort": Louise of Prussia, *Forty-Five Years*, 242; *The Empress Frederick: A Memoir* (London: J. Nisbet, 1913), 79; K. D. Reynolds, "Fane, Priscilla Anne, countess of Westmorland (1793–1879)," in *Oxford Dictionary of National Biography*, ed. H.C.G. Matthew and Brian Harrison (Oxford: Oxford University Press, 2004), http://www.oxforddnb.com/view/article/9140 (accessed January 22, 2008); Weigall, *Westmorland Correspondence*, 104, 402–403, 447, 468–69; Linda Rogols-Siegel, "Fanny Lewald's 'Prinz Louis Ferdinand' and Theodor Fontane's 'Vor dem Sturm' and 'Schach von Wuthenow,'" *Modern Language Review* 88 (April 1993): 367. However, though Pauline's father appears in Lewald's novel with verisimilitude, the character called "Pauline" bears little relationship to the real person, not least for being married.

11. *Record*, 78; *Nobody*, 15.

12. Sophie Marie Voss, *Sixty-Nine Years at the Court of Prussia: From the Recollections of the Mistress of the Household*, trans. Emily Stephenson and Agnes Stephenson, 2 vols. (London: Richard Bentley and Son, 1876), 1:3; *Nobody*, 52; Hudson, *Louisa, Queen of Prussia*, 1:330.

13. Voss, *Sixty-Nine Years*, 1:182–83.

14. Louise of Prussia, *Forty-Five Years*, 158; Hudson, *Louisa, Queen of Prussia*, 1:341; *Nobody*, 20; *Record*, 82. Frederick William II married Julie Amalie Elisabeth von Voss in 1787, and, after her death, Sophie Juliane, Countess von Dönhoff, in 1790.

15. Hans-Joachim Giersberg, *The Splendor of Prussia: The Royal Palaces of Berlin and Brandenburg* (Munich: Prestel, 2007), 50; Chester V. Easum, *Prince Henry of Prussia, Brother of Frederick the Great* (1942; Westport, Conn.: Greenwood Press, 1971), 377, 245, 248; Richie, *Faust's Metropolis*, 74; Christopher Clark, *Iron Kingdom: The Rise and Downfall of Prussia, 1600–1947* (London: Allen Lane, 2006), 332–33; *Record*, 82–83; *Nobody*, 48, 27; Honoré-Gabriel de Riquetti, comte de Mirabeau, *Secret Memoirs of the Court of Berlin*, 2 vols. (London: Grolier Society, n.d.), 1:86. On Prince Henry's homosexuality, see Eva Ziebura, *Prinz Heinrich von Preußen* (Berlin: Stapp, 1999): I am grateful to Christopher Clark for bringing this work to my attention.

16. Easum, *Prince Henry*, 5, 343; Louise of Prussia, *Forty-Five Years*, 328, 8, 59–60, 95, 418; Mirabeau, *Secret Memoirs*, 1:47; *Record*, 84–85. Prince Ferdinand occupied the Saint John Palace in his capacity as Grand Master of the Order of Saint John, and later the Radziwill Palace would become Bismarck's Reich Chancellery and the site for the 1878 Congress of Berlin.

17. *Nobody*, 34, 48; Wright, *Louise*, 45; Louise of Prussia, *Forty-Five Years*, 140, 9, 400; David L. Montgomery, "From Biedermeier Berlin: The Parthey Diaries:

Excerpts in Translation, with Commentary and Annotation," *Musical Quarterly* 74, no. 2 (1990): 208–209; Hermann Ludwig Heinrich, Fürst von Pückler-Muskau, *Tour in England, Ireland, and France, in the Years 1826, 1827, 1828, and 1829* (Philadelphia: Carey, Lea and Blanchard, 1833), 7; Catherine Hyde, marquise de Govion Broglio Solari, and Louis François Joseph, baron de Bausset-Rocquefort, *Private Anecdotes of Foreign Courts*, 2 vols. (London: H. Colburn, 1827), 1:323; E. A. Brayley Hodgetts, *The House of Hohenzollern: Two Centuries of Berlin Court Life* (London: Methuen, 1911), 294.

18. Hudson, *Louisa, Queen of Prussia*, 1:339; *Nobody*, 60, 111, 53, 59; Jane-Eliza Hasted, *Unsuccessful Ladies: An Intimate Account of the Aunts (Official and Unofficial) of the Late Queen Victoria* (London: Robert Hale, 1950), 163–90; July 21, 1816, *Memoirs*, 3:406.

19. *Nobody*, 66–67, 19, 121; Hudson, *Louisa, Queen of Prussia*, 2:20, 23, 1:319–20; *Record*, 80–81; "Prussia During the French Revolutionary and Napoleonic Wars, 1786–1815," in *The Rise of Prussia, 1700–1830*, ed. Philip G. Dwyer (Harlow, U.K.: Longman, 2000), 247; Brendan Simms, *The Impact of Napoleon: Prussian High Politics, Foreign Policy and the Crisis of the Executive, 1797–1806* (Cambridge: Cambridge University Press, 1997), 288.

20. *Record*, 80–81; LCA to ABA, December 18, 1833; Wright, *Louise*, 33, 53.

21. JQA to LCA, February 16, 1807.

22. *Nobody*, 61–62, 93; Daniel Walker Howe, *What Hath God Wrought: The Transformation of America, 1815–1848* (New York: Oxford University Press, 2007), 10.

23. *Nobody*, 63, 95.

24. Ibid., 107–108.

25. *Record*, 82; *Nobody*, 47, 59, 62, 58; LCA to CFA, January 27, 1842.

26. *Record*, 84; *Nobody*, 40, 111; Jeremy Black, *The British Abroad: The Grand Tour in the Eighteenth Century* (New York: St. Martin's Press, 1992), 10. For Garlike's forename, see Harding, *JQA: Pioneer*, 29.

27. Hasted, *Unsuccessful Ladies*, 172; Hubert Cole, *Beau Brummell* (New York: Mason/Charter, 1977), 49; *Nobody*, 69–70, 119, 118, 50, 51, 57, 56.

28. G.F.R. Barker, "Proby, John Joshua, first earl of Carysfort (1751–1828)," rev. E. A. Smith, *Oxford Dictionary of National Biography* (Oxford: Oxford University Press, 2004; online ed., January 2008), http://www.oxforddnb.com/view/article/22832 (accessed January 28, 2008); *Nobody*, 101, 108–109, 115.

29. *Nobody*, 101, 66, 109–10, 112; Trench, *Remains of Mrs. Trench*; Hunter's will can be read at http://www.thebookofdays.com/months/oct/16.htm (accessed January 29, 2008).

30. John Bramsen, *Letters of a Prussian Traveller*, 2 vols. (London: H. Colburn, 1818), 1:27–28; *Nobody*, 5; Carr, *Northern Summer*, 463; Granville, *St. Petersburgh*, 1:273; Mariana Starke, *Travels on the Continent, Written for the Use and Particular*

Information of Travellers (London: John Murray, 1820), 179; Jean-François Georgel, *Mémoires pour servir à l'histoire des évémens de la fin du dix-huitième siècle, depuis 1760 jusqu'en 1806–1810*, 6 vols. (Paris: Alexis Eymery, 1818), 6:26; Hyde and Joseph, *Private Anecdotes*, 1:265, 347–49 (quotation on 349).

31. *Nobody*, 22; Carr, *Northern Summer*, 463.

32. *Narrative (1)*, 23–26.

33. Louise of Prussia, *Forty-Five Years*, 225, 247–48, 306–307, 229, 255, 238, 243, 250, 258, 321, 336, 341; Clark, *Iron Kingdom*, 352.

34. *Narrative (1)*, 24; Adam Zamoyski, *1812: Napoleon's Fatal March on Moscow* (London: HarperCollins, 2004), 111; J. Christopher Herold, *Mistress to an Age: A Life of Madame de Staël* (Indianapolis: Bobbs-Merrill, 1958), 94; Madelyn Gutwirth, *Madame de Staël, Novelist: The Emergence of the Artist as Woman* (Urbana: University of Illinois Press, 1978), 80–84; Jean Hanoteau, ed., *Memoirs of General de Caulaincourt, Duke of Vicenza*, 3 vols. (London: Cassell, 1935–38), 1:107, 542–43; Adam Zamoyski, *Rites of Peace: The Fall of Napoleon and the Congress of Vienna* (New York: HarperCollins, 2007), 13; Ernst Otto Innocenz, Baron von Odeleben, *A Circumstantial Narrative of the Campaign in Saxony in the Year 1813*, trans. Alfred John Kempe, 2 vols. (London: John Murray, 1820), 1:255; Louise of Prussia, *Forty-Five Years*, 338.

35. *Narrative (1)*, 24–25; on his death in 1813 when governor of Torgau, see the obituary in Sylvanus Urban, *The Gentleman's Magazine: And Historical Chronicle, from July to December 1814: Vol LXXXIV* (London: Nichols, Son and Bentley, 1814), 197.

36. *Narrative (1)*, 22–23; Clark, *Iron Kingdom*, 338, 352; Dwyer, "Prussia, 1786–1815," 253, adopting the arguments of Brendan Simms, *The Struggle for Mastery in Germany, 1779–1850* (Basingstoke, U.K.: Macmillan, 1998), 75–90.

37. *Narrative (1)*, 23; Giersberg, *Splendor of Prussia*, 30–31; Granville, *St. Petersburgh*, 1:326–27; William Rae Wilson, *Travels in Russia, &c. &c.* (London: Longman, Rees, Orme, Brown, and Green, 1828), 106–7; Hudson, *Louisa, Queen of Prussia*, 2:336–40; Ednah Dow Littlehale Cheney, Friedrich Eggers, and Karl Eggers, *Life of Christian Daniel Rauch of Berlin, Germany* (Boston: Lee and Shepard, 1893), 69. In the 1820s, at least, the mausoleum was only "open in summer on the 19th of each month": see Richard Smith, *Notes Made During a Tour* (London: C. & J. Rivington, 1827), 189, and Jacob, *View of the Agriculture*, 205, which has: "I did not see, it being open only on the day of her death, the nineteenth of each month." If these were the rules in 1815, Mrs. Adams would have needed a special dispensation to visit, since she was not in Berlin on the nineteenth.

38. Fritz Novotny, *Painting and Sculpture in Europe, 1780 to 1880* (Harmondsworth, U.K.: Penguin, 1960), 219–20; *Narrative (1)*, 24; Granville, *St. Petersburgh*, 1:327; John Russell, *A Tour in Germany, and Some of the Southern Provinces of the*

Austrian Empire, in the Years 1820, 1821, 1822, 3rd ed., 2 vols. (Edinburgh: Archibald Constable, 1825), 2:49. On Rauch and the sarcophagus, see Philipp Demandt, *Luisenkult: Die Unsterblichkeit der Königin von Preussen* (Köln: Böhlau, 2003).

39. LCA to JQA, March 5, 1815; LCA, French passport, March 10, 1815; *Narrative (2)*, 27; LCA to Levett Harris, March 13, 1815, Adams-Harris Papers.

40. *Narrative (2)*, 28; LCA to Levett Harris, March 13, 1815, Adams-Harris Papers; map of the battlefield in Charles William Vane, Marquis of Londonderry, *Narrative of the War in Germany and France, in 1813 and 1814* (London: Henry Colburn and Richard Bentley, 1830), following 168; Mariana Starke, *Information and Directions for Travellers on the Continent*, 5th ed. (Paris: A. and W. Galignani, 1826), 422–23; Edward Augustus Domeier, *A Descriptive Road-Book of Germany* (London: Samuel Leigh, 1830), 124; E. Poppele, *Manuel des postes pour l'Allemagne et les routes principales de l'Europe*, 4th ed. (Frankfurt: Frédéric Wilmans, 1831), 17, 41.

41. Zamoyski, *Rites of Peace*, 108–109, 340, 195, 240, 348, 410–11, 427–28, 299.

42. Granville, *St. Petersburgh*, 1:187; Domeier, *Road-Book of Germany*, 13–16; JQA, Personal Financial Record, 1802–22; LCA to Levett Harris, March 13, 1815, Adams-Harris Papers.

43. Starke, *Travels on the Continent*, 172–77; Starke, *Information and Directions for Travellers on the Continent*, 417–19; Domeier, *Road-Book of Germany*, 4–13.

44. "Weights and Measures: Communicated to the Senate, February 22, 1821," *American State Papers, 16th Congress*, 2nd Session, Miscellaneous: Volume 2, 675, 704, 687.

45. JQA to LCJ, August 13, 1796.

46. JQA to LCA, July 14, 1826; LCA to JQA, July 18, 1826.

47. October 16, 1839, October 27, 1835, LCA Diary; Louisa Catherine Adams, "Mrs J. Q. Adams," *Mrs A. S. Colvin's Weekly Messenger* (June 12, 1827): 304–305; *Laws of Maryland, Made Since M, DCC, LXIII, Consisting of Acts of Assembly Under the Proprietary Government, Resolves of Convention, the Declaration of Rights, the Constitution and Form of Government, the Articles of Confederation, and, Acts of Assembly Since the Revolution* (Annapolis: Frederick Green, 1787), 383.

48. LCA to JQA, September 22, 1801; *Nobody*, 120–21.

49. *Nobody*, 124–30.

50. November 23, 1801, January 1, 1802, *Nobody*, 130, 132; JQA to LCJ, December 20, 1796; LCJ to JQA, August 25, 1796.

51. *Nobody*, 132–37; AA to JA, November 12–23, 1778, *AFC*, 3:120; AA to JQA, May 20, 1796.

52. January 1, 1802, *Nobody*, 131; JQA to LCJ, September 12, 1796.

53. *Nobody*, 133–34.

54. JA to Cotton Tufts, December 26, 1800, JA to Thomas Adams, June 29, 1801, quoted in David McCullough, *John Adams* (New York: Simon & Schuster, 2001), 568, 571; AA to Catherine Nuth Johnson, May 8, 1801.

55. AA to Thomas Adams, July 5, 1801, quoted in McCullough, *John Adams*, 572.

56. JA to JQA, March 16, 1777, AA to JQA, March 20, 1780, *AFC*, 2:177, 3:311.

57. AA to JQA, March 20, 1780, June [10?], 1778, November 20, December 26, 1783, January 21, 1781, JA to JQA, April 28, 1782, *AFC*, 3:311, 37, 5:273, 284, 4:317, 68; *Weights and Measures*, 658.

58. *Nobody*, 32.

59. Robert Semple, *Observations Made on a Tour from Hamburg Through Berlin, Gorlitz, and Breslau, to Silberberg* (London: Robert Baldwin, 1814), 212; J. T. James, *Journal of a Tour in Germany, Sweden, Russia, Poland, During the Years 1813 and 1814*, 2nd ed., 2 vols. (London: John Murray, 1817), 65; Bramsen, *Prussian Traveller*, 1:43; Giersberg, *Splendor of Prussia*, 114–23, 70; *Nobody*, 89, 42; John Dundas Cochrane, *A Pedestrian Journey Through Russia and Siberian Tartary, to the Frontiers of China, the Frozen Sea, and Kamtchatka* (Edinburgh: Constable, 1829), 1:21; *Narrative (2)*, 27–28.

60. Jacob, *View of the Agriculture*, 257, 259; Helmut Vorkastner, *Treuenbrietzen: Ein Märkisches Landstädchen mit Geschichte* (Horb am Neckar: Geiger, 2004), 7; Smith, *Notes During a Tour*, 203; *A Hand-Book for Travellers on the Continent: Being a Guide Through Holland, Belgium, Prussia, and Northern Germany* (London: John Murray, 1836), 296; Thomas Hodgskin, *Travels in the North of Germany* (Edinburgh: Archibald Constable, 1820), 1:65; Granville, *St. Petersburgh*, 1:246.

61. July 26, 1825, LCA Diary; *Record*, 11, 4.

62. JQA to LCA, December 17, 1806: "I do not precisely understand what you mean by saying we shall never agree upon this subject"; September 15, 1839, LCA Diary.

63. July 9, 1835, LCA Diary; LCA to AA, April 4, 1813.

64. Augustus von Kotzebue, *Travels from Berlin, Through Switzerland, to Paris, in the Year 1804*, 3 vols. (London: Richard Phillips, 1804), 1:8; the other route was via Gräfenhainichen, Bitterfeld, and Delitsch; on this, see *Hand-Book for Travellers: Holland Etc.*, 296; puzzlingly, Domeier, *Road-Book of Germany*, 142, suggests a route from Wittenberg to Schmiedeberg, then to Duben and Krensitz.

65. Hodgskin, *Travels*, 57; Cochrane, *Pedestrian Journey*, 19; Kotzebue, *Travels from Berlin*, 1:6–7.

66. Russell, *Tour in Germany*, 1:226; John Quincy Adams, *Letters on Silesia, Written During a Tour Through That Country in the Years 1800, 1801* (London: J. Rudd, 1804), 260–61; Hodgskin, *Travels*, 47; Karamsin, *Travels from Moscow*, 1:145; Granville, *St. Petersburgh*, 1:242–43.

67. Alistair Horne, *How Far from Austerlitz? Napoleon, 1805–1815* (London: Macmillan, 1996), 341–42, has a brisk narrative of the battle; James Lawford, *Napoleon: The Last Campaigns, 1813–15* (Maidenhead, U.K.: Sampson Low, 1977), 62, says 50,000 French prisoners, while F. Loraine Petre, *Napoleon's Last Campaign in Germany, 1813* (London: John Lane, 1912), 383, only 15,000.

68. Frederic Shoberl, *Narrative of the Most Remarkable Events Which Occurred in and near Leipzig, Immediately Before, During, and Subsequent to, the Sanguinary Series of Engagements Between the Allied Armies and the French, from the 14th to the 19th October, 1813*, 7th ed. (London: R. Ackermann, 1814), x–xi, 51, 16; Antony Brett-James, *Europe Against Napoleon: The Leipzig Campaign, 1813, from Eyewitness Accounts* (London: Macmillan, 1970), 240; Karl Gustav Carus, quoted in Brett-James, *Leipzig Campaign*, 239; on the storming of the Halle gate, see James McQueen, *A Narrative of the Principal Military Events During the Memorable Campaigns, of 1812, 1813, 1814, in Russia, Germany, Spain, France & America* (Glasgow: Edward Khull, 1814), 445.

69. Smith, *Notes During a Tour*, 260–61; Toma Babovic and Edgar S. Hasse, *Leipzig* (Leipzig: Ellert & Richter, 2005), 35; Karamsin, *Travels from Moscow*, 1:154; Russell, *Tour in Germany*, 1:230–39; Granville, *St. Petersburgh*, 1:233; Johann Wolfgang von Goethe, *The Autobiography of Johann Wolfgang von Goethe*, trans. John Oxenford, 2 vols. (Chicago: University of Chicago Press, 1974), 1:262.

70. Georgel, *Mémoires*, 6:27, 437; Granville, *St. Petersburgh*, 1:238–39; Smith, *Notes During a Tour*, 1:270; Karamsin, *Travels from Moscow*, 1:154; Pückler-Muskau, *Tour*, 3; Hodgskin, *Travels*, 53–54; James Holman, *Travels Through Russia, Siberia, Poland, Austria, Saxony, Prussia, Hanover, & c. & c., Undertaken During the Years 1822, 1823 and 1824, While Suffering from Total Blindness*, 2 vols. (London: George B. Whittaker, 1825), 2:301.

71. JQA, "Monies Received," 1796–1801; LCA to Levett Harris, March 13, 1815, Adams-Harris Papers; Robert Beachy, *The Soul of Commerce: Credit, Property, and Politics in Leipzig, 1750–1840* (Leiden: Brill, 2005), 48–49, 106, 146; Russell, *Tour in Germany*, 1:217; Matthew Davis, ed., *The Private Journal of Aaron Burr, During His Residence of Four Years in Europe; with Selections from His Correspondence*, 2 vols. (New York: Harper and Brothers, 1838), 1:379; Holman, *Travels*, 2:251–52.

72. Cochrane, *Pedestrian Journey*, 18; Russell, *Tour in Germany*, 1:223–24, 219; Hugh Murray, *The Encyclopedia of Geography*, 3 vols. (Philadelphia: Lea and Blanchard, 1839), 2:114; *Hand-Book for Travellers: Holland Etc.*, 352; Jacob, *View of the Agriculture*, 324–26; Domeier, *Road-Book of Germany*, 55–56.

73. Russell, *Tour in Germany*, 1:83; Karamsin, *Travels from Moscow*, 1:179; Walter J. Morris, "John Quincy Adams's German Library, with a Catalog of His German

Books," *Proceedings of the American Philosophical Society* 118 (13 September 1974): 321–33; LCA, "The Queen's Ghost: A Tale of the Olden Time."

74. LCA to JQA, May 13, 1804; September 6–7, 1812, *Memoirs*, 2:399–401; LCA, *The Metropolitan Kaleidoscope*, 24; LCA to ABA, March 17, 1842. However, it is relevant that LCA was much preoccupied in September 1812.

75. Jacob, *View of the Agriculture*, 337; Russell, *Tour in Germany*, 1:59, whose view is challenged in Granville, *St. Petersburgh*, 1:205–206.

76. *Narrative (1)* reads: "We went on a different route, to a fortified Town in Prussia, the name of which I cannot recollect." *Narrative (2)* has: "We took the route I think to Eisenach a fortified Town." The deletion of "in Prussia" is significant, since Eisenach was not in Prussia.

5. FROM EISENACH TO FRANKFURT

1. Samuel Taylor Coleridge, *The Friend*, in *The Collected Works of Samuel Taylor Coleridge*, ed. Barbara E. Rooke, 2 vols. (Princeton, N.J.: Princeton University Press, 1969), 1:136; Jean-Pierre-Guillaume Catteau-Calville, *Voyage en Allemagne et en Suède, contenant des observations sur les phénomènes, les institutions, les arts et les moeurs*, 3 vols. (Paris: J. G. Dentu, 1810), 1:268; William Jacob, *A View of the Agriculture, Manufactures, Statistics, and State of Society, of Germany, and Parts of Holland and France: Taken During a Journey Through Those Countries, in 1819* (London: John Murray, 1820), 365–66; Nicolai Karamsin, *Travels from Moscow, Through Prussia, Germany, Switzerland, France, and England*, 3 vols. (London: J. Badcock, 1803), 1:196; Matthew Davis, ed., *The Private Journal of Aaron Burr, During His Residence of Four Years in Europe; with Selections from His Correspondence*, 2 vols. (New York: Harper and Brothers, 1838), 1:380.

2. Frederic Shoberl, *Narrative of the Most Remarkable Events Which Occurred in and near Leipzig, Immediately Before, During, and Subsequent to, the Sanguinary Series of Engagements Between the Allied Armies and the French, from the 14th to the 19th October, 1813*, 7th ed. (London: R. Ackermann, 1814), 6; Antony Brett-James, *Europe Against Napoleon: The Leipzig Campaign, 1813, from Eyewitness Accounts* (London: Macmillan, 1970), 12–13.

3. Reinhold Brunner, *Geschichte der Stadt Eisenach* (Gudensberg-Gleichen: Wartberg, 2004), 62–63; Charles William Vane, Marquis of Londonderry, *Narrative of the War in Germany and France, in 1813 and 1814* (London: Henry Colburn and Richard Bentley, 1830), 189–90; James McQueen, *A Narrative of the Principal Military Events During the Memorable Campaigns, of 1812, 1813, 1814, in Russia, Germany, Spain, France & America* (Glasgow: Edward Khull, 1814), 459; see also John Philippart, *Campaign in Germany and France, from the Expiration of the Armistice, Signed and Ratified June 4, 1813, to the Period of the Abdication of the*

Throne of France by Napoleon Buonaparte, 2 vols. (London: C. J. Barrington, 1814), 1:237.

4. Captain Jean-Baptiste Auguste Barrès, quoted in Brett-James, *Leipzig Campaign*, 274–75.

5. Jacob, *View of the Agriculture*, 370–71.

6. Mariana Starke, *Travels on the Continent, Written for the Use and Particular Information of Travellers* (London: John Murray, 1820), 182; Edward Augustus Domeier, *A Descriptive Road-Book of Germany* (London: Samuel Leigh, 1830), 53; *Narrative (2)*, 28.

7. *Narrative (1)*, 27.

8. Ibid., 20–21; Arthur L. George and Elena George, *St Petersburg: The First Three Centuries* (Stroud, U.K.: Sutton Publishing, 2004), 58, 104; Emile Dupré de Sainte-Maure, *Pétersbourg, Moscou et les provinces*, 3 vols. (Paris: Pillet Ainé, 1830), 3:267; J. T. James, *Journal of a Tour in Germany, Sweden, Russia, Poland, During the Years 1813 and 1814*, 2nd ed., 2 vols. (London: John Murray, 1817), 2:212–13; Louis François Joseph, baron de Bausset-Rocquefort, *Mémoires anecdotiques sur l'intérieur du palais et sur quelques événemens de l'Empire, depuis 1805 jusqu'en 1816, par servir à l'histoire de Napoléon*, 4 vols. (Paris: Levavasseur, 1828–29), 1:316; Leo Tolstoy, *War and Peace*, trans. Anthony Briggs (1868–69; London: Penguin, 2005), 39, 42, 105 (quotation on 42).

9. *Narrative (1)*, 21–22; see Simon Sebag Montefiore, *Prince of Princes: The Life of Potemkin* (London: Weidenfeld and Nicolson, 2000), 193, on Apraxin and incest.

10. *Narrative (1)*, 27–28.

11. Jacob, *View of the Agriculture*, 371; John Russell, *A Tour in Germany, and Some of the Southern Provinces of the Austrian Empire, in the Years 1820, 1821, 1822*, 3rd ed., 2 vols. (Edinburgh: Archibald Constable, 1825), 1:326; Augustus Bozzi Granville, *St. Petersburgh: A Journal of Travels to and from That Capital; Through Flanders, the Rhenich Provinces, Prussia, Russia, Poland, Silesia, Saxony, the Federated States of Germany, and France*, 2nd ed., 2 vols. (London: Henry Colburn, 1829), 1:188, refers to this forest as "the magnificent wood of Kinzigheimerhof."

12. Jacob, *View of the Agriculture*, 383; *Narrative (1)*, 28–29.

13. George Cathcart, *Commentaries on the War in Russia and Germany in 1812 and 1813* (London: John Murray, 1850), 369–74; Marquis of Londonderry, *War in Germany and France*, 198–99; McQueen, *Memorable Campaigns*, 460–61; F. Loraine Petre, *Napoleon's Last Campaign in Germany, 1813* (London: John Lane, 1912), 388–93; McQueen, *Memorable Campaigns*, 461; Charles Edward Dodd, *An Autumn on the Rhine; or, Sketches of Courts, Society, Scenery, &c. in Some of the*

German States Bordering on the Rhine (London: Longman, Hurst, Rees, Orme, and Brown, 1818), 96.

14. *Narrative (1)*, 28; on Murat, see Helen Maria Williams, *A Narrative of the Events Which Have Taken Place in France* (London: John Murray, 1815), 13. The following account of Napoleon's movements draws upon Alan Schom, *One Hundred Days: Napoleon's Road to Waterloo* (1993; London: Penguin, 1994), 2–33.

15. Adam Zamoyski, *Rites of Peace: The Fall of Napoleon and the Congress of Vienna* (New York: HarperCollins, 2007), 442; Schom, *Hundred Days*, 34; Étienne-Léon, baron de Lamothe-Langon, *Evenings with Prince Cambacérès, Second Consul, Arch-Chancellor of the Empire, Duke of Parma, &c. &c. &c.* (London: Henry Colburn, 1837), 286–87; March 7, 1815, *Memoirs*, 3:165.

16. Schom, *Hundred Days*, 29; March 15, 1815, *Memoirs*, 3:171.

17. *Narrative (1)*, 29.

18. Ibid.; Jacob, *View of the Agriculture*, 372.

19. Dodd, *Autumn on the Rhine*, 79; Jacob, *View of the Agriculture*, 395; *Narrative (1)*, 30.

20. Russell, *Tour in Germany*, 1:39; Wilhelm Render, *A Tour Through Germany; Particularly Along the Banks of the Rhine, Mayne, &c. and That Part of the Palatinate, Rhingaw, &c. Usually Termed the Garden of Germany*, 2 vols. (London: A. Strahan, 1801), 1:41; on the Maison Rouge, see Starke, *Travels on the Continent*, 184, and [Jonathan Gray], *Letters Written from the Continent During a Six Weeks' Tour in 1818; and Afterwards Published in the York Chronicle* (York: W. Blanchard, 1819), 71; on La Cour d'Angleterre, see John Chetwode Eustace, *A Classical Tour Through Italy, an. MDCCCII* (Philadelphia: M. Carey, 1816), 47, where it is described as a byword for a good, clean hotel.

21. John R. Hailman, *Thomas Jefferson on Wine* (Jackson: University Press of Mississippi, 2006), 166, 173–74, illustration following 304; Render, *Tour Through Germany*, 1:38, 47–48; there is a similar description of the table d'hote in Russell, *Tour in Germany*, 1:37–38, and *Letters Written from the Continent*, 72, confirms that the timing of dinner had not changed between 1801 and 1818.

22. LCA to JQA, March 17, 1815; March 12, 15, 1815, JQA Diary.

23. *Narrative (1)*, 30.

24. Unusually for a Christian banker, Bethmann only mildly resented the Rothschilds: see Niall Ferguson, *The House of Rothschild: Money's Prophets, 1798–1848* (London: Penguin, 1999), 138, 140–41.

25. Charles Tennant, *A Tour Through Parts of the Netherlands, Holland, Germany, Switzerland, Savoy, and France, in the Year 1821–2* (London: Longman, Hurst, Rees, Orme, Brown, and Green, 1824), 331; John Carr, *A Northern Summer; or, Travels Round the Baltic, Through Denmark, Sweden, Russia, Prussia, and Part of Germany, in the Year 1804* (London: Richard Phillips, 1805), 474; Elizabeth Har-

riot Hudson, *The Life and Times of Louisa, Queen of Prussia: With an Introductory Sketch of Prussian History*, 2 vols. (London: W. Isbister, 1874), 1:274; Richard Smith, *Notes Made During a Tour* (London: C. and J. Rivington, 1827), 432; Granville, *St. Petersburgh*, 1:159; Zamoyski, *Rites of Peace*, 122; Wilfried Forstmann, *Simon Moritz von Bethmann, 1768–1826: Bankier, Diplomat und Politischer Beobachter* (Frankfurt am Main: Waldermar Kramer, 1973), 270; Davis, *Journal of Aaron Burr*, 1:402; Carl-Ludwig Holtfrerich, *Frankfurt as a Financial Centre: From Medieval Trade Fair to European Banking Centre* (Munich: C. H. Beck, 1999), illustration following 112. However, Constance Wright, *Louise, Queen of Prussia* (London: Frederick Muller, 1970), 15, says that Frederick William first saw Luise at the French Theater in Frankfurt.

26. Granville, *St. Petersburgh*, 1:156; *Narrative (1)*, 30–31; Tennant, *Tour Through Parts*, 331; *Letters Written from the Continent*, 73. The most famous piece in Bethmann's art collection was Heinrich Dannekar's *Ariadne on the Panther*: for contemporary responses, see Dodd, *Autumn on the Rhine*, 70–71; John Bramsen, *Letters of a Prussian Traveller*, 2 vols. (London: H. Colburn, 1818), 2:343; *Letters After a Tour Through Some Parts of France, Italy, Switzerland, and Germany in 1816; with Incidental Reflections on Some Topics Connected with Religion* (Edinburgh: Oliphant, Waugh, and Innes, 1817), 326–27; and Russell, *Tour in Germany*, 1:41–42.

27. *Narrative (1)*, 31; for the route via Metz, see E. Poppele, *Manuel des postes pour l'Allemagne et les routes principales de l'Europe*, 4th ed. (Frankfurt: Frédéric Wilmans, 1831), 45–46.

28. LCA to JQA, March 17, 1815.

29. *Narrative (1)*, 1.

30. Ibid., 30.

31. LCJ to JQA, July 25, 1796; JQA to LCJ, August 6, November 21, 1796, January 31, 1797.

32. JQA to LCJ, June 17, August 13, July 9, 1796.

33. JQA to LCJ, September 12, 1796; for conciliation, see LCJ to JQA, September 13, 1796.

34. LCJ to JQA, November 29, 1796; JQA to LCJ, December 20, 1796.

35. LCJ to JQA, December 13, 1796.

36. The original text of JQA to Joshua Johnson, January 9, 1797, reads "terminate my matrimonial union," which makes little sense and was presumably a slip of the pen; JQA to LCJ, January 10, 1797.

37. LCJ to JQA, January 17, 1797.

38. JQA to LCJ, January 31, 1797.

39. LCJ to JQA, January 31, 1797; JQA to LCJ, February 5, 7, 1797.

40. LCJ to JQA, February 17, 1797; JQA to LCJ, February 12, April 10, 1797.

41. JQA to LCJ, February 12, 1797.

42. LCJ to JQA, February 28, 1797; JQA to LCJ, March 31, 30, February 12, 1797.

43. LCJ to JQA, February 28, April 21, March 27, 7, May 19, 1797; JQA to LCJ, March 14, May 31, March 20, April 10, 1797.

44. April 9, 1797, *Memoirs*, 1:188; JQA to LCJ, April 28, 1797; JA signed the commission for Prussia on June 1, 1797: see Worthington Chauncey Ford, ed., *Writings of John Quincy Adams*, 7 vols. (New York: Macmillan, 1913), 2:173.

45. JQA to Joshua Johnson, December 10, 1800; JQA to LCJ, November 21, 1796.

46. March 5, 1787, Robert J. Taylor et al., eds., *Diary of John Quincy Adams*, 2 vols. (Cambridge, Mass.: Belknap Press of Harvard University Press, 1981), 2:169–71.

47. June 5, 1787, Taylor, *Diary of John Quincy Adams*, 2:233–35.

48. JQA to George Washington Adams and John Adams II, August 21, 1809, *Memoirs*, 2:8–17 (quotations on 9–10).

49. James Johnson, Jr., 1842 letter quoted in Edward S. Delaplaine, *The Life of Thomas Johnson* (New York: Frederick H. Hitchcock, 1927), 351; on appearances, see Joshua Johnson to Wallace and Davidson, February 27, 1772, in Jacob M. Price, ed., *Joshua Johnson's Letterbook, 1771–1774: Letters from a Merchant in London to His Partners in Maryland* (London: London Record Society, 1979), 29; LCA to ABA, March 2, 1834.

50. John Trumbull, *Autobiography, Reminiscences and Letters of John Trumbull, from 1756 to 1841* (New York: Wiley and Putnam, 1841), 184–87 (quotation on 186); *Record*, 71; Frederick Delius to JQA, September 29, 1797. The painter Trumbull, who was the emissary and a Johnson family friend, nowhere mentions Johnson's name in connection with the "Brandy Speculation," but LCA was sure later that her father was involved: see LCA to CFA, January 11, 1842.

51. On his awareness, see April 25, 26, May 10, 21, 1797, JQA Diary; LCJ to JQA, November 29, 1796: "The fates it is true seem to conspire against us, and have I fear destined us to a long separation as my Father is obliged to quit Europe immediately."

52. August 30, September 8, 1797, JQA Diary; Joshua Johnson to JQA, December 1, 1798.

53. *Record*, 70–73; *Nobody*, 4.

54. LCA to AA, May 11, 1806, October 23, 1810; see also LCA to JQA, May 12, 1804: "I brought nothing and therefore have no claim on whatever my life ever has been and ever must remain a life of painful obligation."

55. AA to LCA, January 21, 1811; AA to Catherine Nuth Johnson, May 20, June 9, 1798; LCA to AA, December 19, 1804; Paul C. Nagel, *The Adams Women: Abigail and Louisa Adams, Their Sisters and Daughters* (New York: Oxford University Press, 1987), 173; Price, *Joshua Johnson's Letterbook*, xxvii; JQA to Thomas Baker Johnson, May 27, 1802.

56. *Record*, 72; JQA to Joshua Johnson, October 11, 1797.

57. LCA to Nancy Hellen, September 11, 1798.

58. Joan Ridder Challinor, "Louisa Catherine Johnson Adams: The Price of Ambition" (Ph.D. diss., American University, 1982), 25–26, 74; Price, *Joshua Johnson's Letterbook*, xxvi, 59, 57.

59. Catherine Nuth Johnson to LCA, April 26, 1798; LCA to Joshua Johnson, September 2, 1800; *Record*, 10. It is worth noting that CFA later destroyed many of LCA's letters and Johnson family correspondence may have featured disproportionately in the cull.

60. LCJ to JQA, January 31, 1797; *Record*, 67.

61. JQA to LCJ, February 7, 1797.

62. Paul C. Nagel, *Descent from Glory: Four Generations of the John Adams Family* (New York: Oxford University Press, 1983), 46, 58–59, 76–80, 85–88, 94, 119–22, 178–79.

63. The following discussion of family movements is based on JQA's diary and letters, as well as LCA's memoirs and letters for the period, 1801–15.

64. JQA to LCA, April 9, 1804; AA to LCA, May 21, 1804, January 19, 1806; LCA to JQA, August 12, 1804; LCA to AA, December 6, 1805.

65. LCA to JQA, June 15, 1806; see the chronology in Margaret A. Hogan and C. James Taylor, eds., *My Dearest Friend: Letters of Abigail and John Adams* (Cambridge, Mass.: Belknap Press of Harvard University Press, 2007), 483–88.

66. JQA to LCA, April 9, 1804; LCA to AA, May 13, 1810; November 19, 1811, *Memoirs*, 2:327–28; for the nurse's name, see JQA, Account Book and Miscellaneous Notes, 1810–1814.

67. LCA to JQA, June 10, 1814, January 6, 1815; December 19, 1821, LCA Diary; JQA to AA, May 20, 1812.

68. JQA to LCA, March 9, 1809; August 4, 1809 [*sic*], *Nobody*, 228.

69. July 6, 23, 1809, JQA Diary; July 5, 1809, *Memoirs*, 1:549. *Nobody*, 228, says, mistakenly, that she heard about their commitment to the Russian ministry on August 4, but this was only a day before they sailed.

70. August 18, 1839, LCA Diary.

71. LCA, *The Metropolitan Kaleidoscope*, 12–18.

72. November 22, 1795, January 19, 1796, JQA Diary; Elizabeth Donnan, ed., *Papers of James A. Bayard, 1796–1815*, in *Annual Report of the American Historical Association for the Year 1913: Vol. II* (Washington, D.C.: American Historical Association, 1915), 427; JQA to LCA, August 11, 1821; November 18, 1831, *Memoirs*, 8:427.

73. LCA, *The Metropolitan Kaleidoscope*, 14; September 6, 1824, Donald, *Diary of Charles Francis Adams*, 1:315; October 26, 1827, July 19, 1831, *Memoirs*, 7:346, 8:382.

74. June 4, 1819, *Memoirs*, 4:387–88.

75. LCA to JQA, December 28, 1806.

76. JQA to LCA, January 6, 1807.

77. AA to LCA, December 8, 1804; LCA to CFA, December 21, 1845.

78. November 1, 2, 3, 1818, *Memoirs*, 4:155–57; JQA, "Mrs. Abigail Adams," in *The National Portrait Gallery of Distinguished Americans*, ed. James B. Longacre and James Herring (Philadelphia: James B. Longacre, 1839), 40. For evidence of repression, see November 7, 1830, *Memoirs*, 8:246: "No one knows, and few conceive, the agony of mind that I have suffered from the time that I was made by circumstances, and not by my own volition, a candidate for the Presidency till I was dismissed from that station by the failure of my re-election. They were feelings to be suppressed; and they were suppressed. No human being has ever heard me complain."

79. LCA, *The Metropolitan Kaleidoscope*, 16–18; JQA to AA, April 14, 1801.

80. September 30, 1833, September 20, 1824, in *Memoirs*, 9:18, 6:417–18; see also the diary entry for July 22, 1826, when in Quincy after JA's death, JQA was examining old family wills: "These papers awaken again an ardent curiosity to know more of these forefathers, who lived and died in obscure and humble life, but every one of whom, from the first settlement of the country, raised numerous families of children, and had something to leave by will. There could indeed be nothing found of them but 'the short and simple annals of the poor'": *Memoirs*, 6:134.

81. August 5, 1829, *Memoirs*, 8:155; LCA to JQA, August 12, 1839.

82. *Nobody*, 166, 69; May 14, 1836, March 5, 1821, LCA Diary; on LCA and republicanism, see Michael O'Brien, *Henry Adams and the Southern Question* (Athens: University of Georgia Press, 2005), 32–33.

83. LCA, *The Metropolitan Kaleidoscope*, 12; *Nobody*, 38.

84. July 26, 1811, *Memoirs*, 2:282–83.

85. LCA, *The Metropolitan Kaleidoscope*, 16.

86. JQA to LCA, August 26, 1804; *Nobody*, 156.

87. *Nobody*, 189, 36; LCA to JQA, May 14, 1845.

88. JQA to LCA, May 10, 1806, October 8, 1801, July 23, 1822; LCA to JQA, December 30, 1814, July 27, 1822.

89. *Nobody*, 282–86.

90. Ibid., 261; May 23, 25, 29, 1811, JQA Diary.

91. July 13, 1811, JQA Diary; *Nobody*, 265–66.

92. *Nobody*, 267–68.

93. AA to JQA, November 17, 1811; January 29, 1812, JQA Diary; January 29, 31, February 11, 1812, *Nobody*, 269–70.

94. August 13–31, 1812, JQA Diary; for Polana's name, see "Monthly Payments for June 1812," in JQA, Account Book and Miscellaneous Notes, 1810–1814.

95. September 1–11, 1812, JQA Diary.

96. September 12–14, 1812, JQA Diary; "Emplastum Meloes Vesicatorii Composi-
tum," *Encyclopedia Britannica: Volume XII*, 6th ed. (Edinburgh: Archibald Constable, 1823), 739; "The Physician.—No. VII. Of the Tooth-Ache," *New Monthly
Magazine and Literary Journal* 5 (June 1823): 535.

97. September 15–17, 1812, JQA Diary; the Lutheran Cemetery was sometimes
known as the Strangers Burying Ground: see George Green, *An Original Journal
from London to St. Petersburg, by Way of Sweden; and, Proceeding from Thence, to
Moscow, Riga, Mittau, and Berlin* (London: T. Boosey and J. Hatchard, 1813), 45.

98. September 17, 20, 1812, JQA Diary.

99. JQA to AA, September 21, 1812.

100. September 30, 1812, JQA Diary.

101. February 7, 1814, LCA Diary.

102. *Nobody*, 293; the number on the final line is unclear in the original text and may
read "12," though the child died on September 15.

103. AA to LCA, January 13, 1813.

104. JA to JQA, March 13, 1813; I am grateful to Richard Lounsbury for noticing the
allusion: Quintilian had intended his *Institutio Oratoria* for the education of his
sons, who died before the book was finished, and the sixth book begins with a
famous eulogy to his lost children and spouse.

105. JQA to AA, October 24, 1812.

106. October 22–24, 1812, LCA Diary; LCA to AA, April 4, 1813.

107. October 22, 23, November 6, December 5, 29, 1812, LCA Diary.

108. November 11, 1812, LCA Diary.

109. October 25, 1812, LCA Diary; October 25, 1812, JQA Diary.

110. November 27, December 23, 1812, LCA Diary.

111. LCA to JQA, July 4, 1796, August 12, 1804, June 15, 1806.

112. On the miscarriage, see January 16, 1813, JQA Diary; August 14, 1813, LCA
Diary.

113. August 14, 1813, February 7, 1814, LCA Diary.

6. FROM FRANKFURT TO PARIS

1. LCA to CFA, April 21, 1846.

2. LCA to CFA, December 8, 1837; JQA, Personal Financial Record, 1802–22
["Waste Book and Journal"]; *Narrative (2)*, 33.

3. The two versions of the *Narrative* are contradictory. *Narrative (2)* has: "I was to
start in the afternoon of the ensuing day. When he came again he brought a
Prussian lad of fourteen, the only creature he could find willing to go and, after
arranging my money matters, he put me into the carriage and directed the
postilions as to the route which we were to take, and parted with me with

the kindest wishes." This suggests that Bethmann did not return until a day after the first interview and hence she left on the afternoon of March 18. *Narrative (1)* has: "I was to start at four o clock in the afternoon—He returned in a short time with a boy of fourteen, the only creature he could find willing to go; and after arranging my money accounts, he put me into the Carriage and directed the Postillions as to the route to be taken." This suggests a departure on the afternoon of March 17. Since her Prussian passport was stamped in Karlsruhe on March 18, and Karlsruhe is about ninety miles from Frankfurt, it seems very unlikely that she left on March 18.

4. *Narrative (1)*, 32.

5. A. Schreiber, *The Traveller's Guide Down the Rhine, Exhibiting the Course of That River from Schaffhausen to Holland, and Describing the Moselle from Coblenz to Treves* (Paris: A. and W. Galignani, 1825), 6, 574, describes both routes, though the latter (via Heidelberg) was the route recommended by Reichard and others: see *Abregé du guide des voyageurs en Europe avec l'itinéraire des routes des postes et la carte itinéraire de l'Europe* (Paris: Les Marchands de Nouveautes, 1803), 142; Heinrich August Ottokar Reichard, *Itinéraire de l'Allemagne et des Pays-Bas*, 4th ed. (Paris: Hyacinthe Langlois, 1824), 186; and E. Poppele, *Manuel des postes pour l'Allemagne et les routes principales de l'Europe*, 4th ed. (Frankfurt: Frédéric Wilmans, 1831), 47.

6. Charles Edward Dodd, *An Autumn on the Rhine; or, Sketches of Courts, Society, Scenery, &c. in Some of the German States Bordering on the Rhine* (London: Longman, Hurst, Rees, Orme, and Brown, 1818), 14; Augustus von Kotzebue, *Travels from Berlin, Through Switzerland, to Paris, in the Year 1804*, 3 vols. (London: Richard Phillips, 1804), 1:21; Sir John Carr, *A Tour Through Holland, Along the Rhine and Left Banks of the Rhine, to the South of Germany, in the Summer and Autumn of 1806* (London: Richard Phillips, 1807), 459; Geoffrey Hindley, *The History of Roads* (London: Peter Davies, 1971), 78; John Pinkerton, *Modern Geography: A Description of the Empires, Kingdoms, States, and Colonies*, 2 vols. (Philadelphia: J. Conrad, 1804), 1:451; Jean-Pierre-Guillaume Catteau-Calville, *Voyage en Allemagne et en Suède, contenant des observations sur les phénomènes, les institutions, les arts et les moeurs*, 3 vols. (Paris: J. G. Dentu, 1810), 1:228–29; Wilhelm Render, *A Tour Through Germany; Particularly Along the Banks of the Rhine, Mayne, &c. and That Part of the Palatinate, Rhingaw, &c. Usually Termed the Garden of Germany*, 2 vols. (London: A. Strahan, 1801), 1:20–21.

7. Hindley, *History of Roads*, 74–76 (quotation on 76); for a self-congratulatory history, see Sébastian-Michel Courtin, *Travaux des ponts-et-chaussées, depuis 1800, ou tableau des constructions neuves* (Paris: Goeury, 1812), 1–15.

8. Carr, *Tour Through Holland*, 459–60; Dodd, *Autumn on the Rhine*, 15–16, 125–26, 256; Thomas Raffles, *Letters During a Tour Through Some Parts of France,*

Savoy, Switzerland, Germany, and the Netherlands, in the Summer of 1817 (New York: Kirk and Mercein, 1818), 278; John Russell, *A Tour in Germany, and Some of the Southern Provinces of the Austrian Empire, in the Years 1820, 1821, 1822*, 3rd ed., 2 vols. (Edinburgh: Archibald Constable, 1825), 1:35, 17–18, 32; Poppele, *Manuel des postes*, 83; Edward Augustus Domeier, *A Descriptive Road-Book of Germany* (London: Samuel Leigh, 1830), 73; Reichard, *Itinéraire de l'Allemagne*, 187; H. W. Williams, *Travels in Italy, Greece, and the Ionian Islands, in a Series of Letters Descriptive of Manners, Scenery, and the Fine Arts*, 2 vols. (Edinburgh: Archibald Constable, 1820), 1:30; *The Journal of an Exile*, 2 vols. (London: Saunders and Otley, 1825), 2:140; Charles Tennant, *A Tour Through Parts of the Netherlands, Holland, Germany, Switzerland, Savoy, and France, in the Year 1821–2*, 2 vols. (London: Longman, Hurst, Rees, Orme, Brown, and Green, 1824), 1:355–56.

9. Domeier, *Road-Book of Germany*, 74; Reichard, *Itinéraire de l'Allemagne*, 108, though Schreiber, *Traveller's Guide*, 10, gives a slightly different account of Karlsruhe hostelries; Domeier, *Road-Book of Germany*, 74; Russell, *Tour in Germany*, 1:24; Dodd, *Autumn on the Rhine*, 165; Tennant, *Tour Through Parts*, 1:368, 370. William Bingley, *Travels in North Europe: From Modern Writers, with Remarks and Observations; Exhibiting a Connected View of the Geography and Present State of That Division of the Globe* (London: Harvey and Darton, 1822), 114, says there were thirty-two rural alleys in Karlsruhe, but Tennant, *Tour Through Parts*, 1:369, counts twenty-four, and Daniel Wilson, *Letters from an Absent Brother, Containing Some Account of a Tour Through Parts of the Netherlands, Switzerland, Northern Italy, and France, in the Summer of 1823*, 4th ed., 2 vols. (London: George Wilson, 1824), 1:70, has yet another version.

10. *Narrative (1)*, 32; Nicolas d'Ydewalle, *Monseigneur de Soultz: de l'Alsace à Saint-Pétersbourg, 1775–1812: correspondance et mémoires de la Baronne Mary de Bode* (Gerpinnes: Quorum, 1999), 300; Dodd, *Autumn on the Rhine*, 179–80.

11. *Narrative (1)*, 32; Dodd, *Autumn on the Rhine*, 186; Frank McLynn, *Napoleon: A Biography* (London: Pimlico, 1997), 318–19; James J. Sheehan, *German History, 1770–1866* (Oxford: Oxford University Press, 1989), 272.

12. Wilson, *Absent Brother*, 1:71; John Milford, *Observations, Moral, Literary, and Antiquarian: Made During a Tour Through the Pyrennees, South of France, Switzerland, the Whole of Italy and the Netherlands in the Years 1814 and 1815* (London: Longman, Hurst, Rees, Orme, and Brown, 1818), 208; *Narrative (1)*, 32–33.

13. Thomas Frognall Dibdin, *A Bibliographical, Antiquarian and Picturesque Tour in France and Germany*, 3 vols. (London: Shakespeare Press, 1821), 3:101; *Narrative (1)*, 33.

14. Russell, *Tour in Germany*, 1:15; *Narrative (1)*, 34; Tennant, *Tour Through Parts*, 1:419–20; Mariana Starke, *Travels on the Continent, Written for the Use and Par-*

ticular Information of Travellers (London: John Murray, 1820), 64; Poppele, *Manuel des postes*, 288. The Hotel de l'Esprit was used by Thomas Dibdin in 1818; Dibdin, *Picturesque Tour*, 3:1.

15. Edme Theodore Bourg Saint-Edme, *Itinéraire complet de l'empire Française, de l'Italie, et des provinces Illyriennes*, 3rd ed., 3 vols. (Paris: H. Langlois, 1812), 1:5; Heinrich August Ottokar Reichard, *A Descriptive Road-Book of France*, new ed. (London: Samuel Leigh, 1829), 21; *Narrative (1)*, 34–35.

16. Helen Maria Williams, *A Narrative of the Events Which Have Taken Place in France* (London: John Murray, 1815), 50; Alan Schom, *One Hundred Days: Napoleon's Road to Waterloo* (1993; London: Penguin, 1994), 50–55; Cyprien Désmarais, *Éphémérides historiques et politiques du régne de Louis XVIII depuis la restauration* (Paris: F. M. Maurice, 1825), 37.

17. *Narrative (1)*, 35–36.

18. Russell, *Tour in Germany*, 1:6–7, 10–14; Dibdin, *Picturesque Tour*, 3:92–93, 11, 31, 43–45; *Narrative (1)*, 36; M. Audin, *Guide classique du voyageur en France* (Paris: Audin, 1831), 91; Tennant, *Tour Through Parts*, 1:421–25; An Oxonian, *A Trimester in France and Switzerland* (London: William Clarke, 1821), 53.

19. *Narrative (1)*, 36–37.

20. Ibid., 36, 34.

21. Ibid., 37–46; *Narrative (2)*, 39–48.

22. March 23, 1815, *Memoirs*, 3:178.

23. From Strasbourg to Paris, LCA followed the post roads outlined, among other texts, in Saint-Edme, *Itinéraire Complet*, 2:24–34, 553–59; *État général des postes du royaume de France, avec les routes qui conduisent aux principales villes de l'Europe, dressé par ordre du Conseil d'Administration* (Paris: De L'Imprimerie Royale, 1814), 134–35; Starke, *Travels on the Continent*, 61–63; and Dibdin, *Picturesque Tour*, 2:521–55. The same route was used by Thomas Jefferson in 1788: see Thomas Jefferson Randolph, ed., *Memoir, Correspondence, and Miscellanies, from the Papers of Thomas Jefferson*, 4 vols. (London: Henry Colburn and Richard Bentley, 1829), 1:72.

24. Audin, *Guide classique*, 84, 83, 89; Henri Heitz, *Le Chateau de Saverne: guide historique* (Saverne: Societé d'Histoire et d'Archeologie de Saverne et Environs, 1996), 23–24; Dibdin, *Picturesque Tour*, 2:545–55; "Extract from a Tour Through France, During the Summer of 1818," *Blackwood's Magazine*, February 1819, 595.

25. *Narrative (1)*, 38. On Nancy, see Phillippe Martin and François Pupil, *Nancy from the Middle Ages to the 21st Century* (Metz: Editions Serpenoise, 2005), 6–65, especially 48–65; and Michel Caffier, *Place Stanislaus, Nancy: trois siècles d'art et d'histoire* (Strasbourg: La Nuée Bleue, 2005), 9–76.

26. Williams, *Narrative of the Events*, 45; Schom, *Hundred Days*, 54–56; Désmarais, *Éphémérides historiques*, 37.

27. *Narrative (1)*, 37–38.

28. Marianne Baillie, *First Impressions on a Tour of the Continent in the Summer of 1818, Through Parts of France, Italy, Switzerland, the Borders of Germany, and a Part of French Flanders* (London: John Murray, 1819), 332–36; Saint-Edme, *Itinéraire complet*, 2:34, 3:360; Dibdin, *Picturesque Tour*, 2:535; Un Vieil Amateur, *Almanach des gourmands, servant de guide dans les moyens, de faire excellent chère* (Paris: Maradan, 1808), 189–90; F.-B. Hoffman, *Oeuvres de F.-B. Hoffman: critique, tome II* (Paris: Lefebvre, 1828), 248.

29. Baillie, *First Impressions*, 339; Audin, *Guide classique*, 74, 87; Starke, *Travels on the Continent*, 62; Saint-Edme, *Itinéraire complet*, 2:31; *Narrative (1)*, 38–39.

30. *Narrative (1)*, 39; Dibdin, *Picturesque Tour*, 2:530; Saint-Edme, *Itinéraire complet*, 2:30; *État general (1814)*, 208; Richard Smith, *Notes Made During a Tour* (London: C. and J. Rivington, 1827), 445; Reichard, *Road-Book of France*, 220–21; Charles Dupin, *Forces productives et commerciales de la France* (Paris: Bachalier, 1827), 2:120–21.

31. On champagne in Russia, see George Matthews Jones, *Travels in Norway, Sweden, Finland, Russia and Turkey, Also on the Coasts of the Sea of Azof and of the Black Sea*, 2 vols. (London: John Murray, 1827), 1:419; James Holman, *Travels Through Russia, Siberia, Poland, Austria, Saxony, Prussia, Hanover, & c. & c., Undertaken During the Years 1822, 1823 and 1824, While Suffering from Total Blindness*, 2 vols. (London: George B. Whittaker, 1825), 1:105; Augustus Bozzi Granville, *St. Petersburgh: A Journal of Travels to and from That Capital; Through Flanders, the Rhenich Provinces, Prussia, Russia, Poland, Silesia, Saxony, the Federated States of Germany, and France*, 2nd ed., 2 vols. (London: Henry Colburn, 1829), 2:357; February 20, 1811, *Nobody*, 261.

32. John R. Hailman, *Thomas Jefferson on Wine* (Jackson: University Press of Mississippi, 2006), 256, 179, 231; "List of Wines in the Cellar, 1812," JQA, Account Book and Miscellaneous Notes, 1810–14; Major-General Lord Blayney, *Narrative of a Forced Journey Through Spain and France as a Prisoner of War in the Years 1810 to 1814*, 2 vols. (London: E. Kerby, 1814), 2:302–305 (quotation on 305); *Narrative (1)*, 39.

33. *Narrative (1)*, 39–40.

34. Ibid.; J. T. Headley, *The Imperial Guard of Napoleon: From Marengo to Waterloo* (New York: Charles Scribner, 1852), 45.

35. *Narrative (1)*, 40–41.

36. Johann Christian Ferdinand Hoefer, ed., *Nouvelle biographie générale depuis les temps les plus reculés jusqu'à nos temps: tome trente-cinquième* (Paris: Firmin Didot Frères, 1861), 375–76; Max Roche and Michel Vernus, *Dictionnaire biographique du département du Jura* (Lons le Saunier: Arts et Littérature, 1996), 360, and http://www.napoleon-series.org/military/organization/frenchguard/

c_guardinf3.html (accessed March 31, 2008); Claude Brelot, *Grand notables du premier empire: notices de biographie sociale: 4: Jura, Haute-Saône, Doubs* (Paris: Centre National de la Recherche Scientifique, 1979), 45. The remark is rightly attributed to Michel by Headley, *Imperial Guard*, 248–49, and wrongly to General Pierre Cambronne, who also served at Waterloo, by Victor Hugo in *Les Misérables*.

37. *Narrative (1)*, 41.

38. Ibid., 41–42. However, Bellune had been in Toul a year earlier, when he had been involved in defending France against the Allied Powers, so it is possible that Mrs. Adams misunderstood or misremembered a reminiscence of Michel's: see Charles Theodore Beauvais de Preau, *Victoires, conquêtes, désastres, revers et guerres civiles des Français de 1792 à 1815: tome vingt-troisième* (Paris: C.L.F. Planckouke, 1821), 32.

39. *Narrative (1)*, 43.

40. The following account comes from http://www.familysearch.org (accessed November 11, 2007), which offers information on the Larangot genealogy, and from a chapter entitled "La Poste de Port à Binson et nos maîtres de poste," part of Jean Godart's history of the town, a manuscript copy of which is in the *mairie* of Mareuil-le-Port. On trade in Port-à-Binson, see James Munro Forbes, "Liberation from Verdun," in *The New Annual Register, or General Repository of History, Politics, and Literature for the Year 1806* (London: John Stockdale, 1807), 198, which is an excerpt from James Munro Forbes, *Letters from France Written in the Years 1803 and 1804: Including a Particular Account of Verdun, and the Situation of the British Captives in That City* (London: J. White, 1806).

41. Cf. William Jacob, *A View of the Agriculture, Manufactures, Statistics, and State of Society, of Germany, and Parts of Holland and France: Taken During a Journey Through Those Countries, in 1819* (London: John Murray, 1820), 369: "In the small towns of Saxe Weimar, the post-masters are generally the largest farmers in the district."

42. *Narrative (1)*, 42–43.

43. Ibid., 46–47, 42–43.

44. Ibid., 43.

45. H. M. Garnesson, *Histoire de la ville d'Epernai*, 2 vols. (Epernai: Frères Warin, 1800), 1:104; Michelle Pidoire-Ploix and Françoise Schwartz-Le Jan, *Du haut de la colline de Châtillon* (Châtillon-sur-Marne: M. Pidoire-Ploix, 1993); *Narrative (1)*, 44–45.

46. *Narrative (1)*, 45; *Narrative (2)*, 47, has "Princess Stephanie" written in LCA's hand above the phrase "one of Napoleons Sisters," but Napoleon had no sister called Stephanie: LCA was probably thinking of Stéphanie Beauharnais, the Grand Duchess of Baden, discussed above.

47. Schom, *Hundred Days*, 209; Christopher Hibbert, *Napoleon: His Wives and Women* (London: HarperCollins, 2002), 166–70; Pierson Dixon, *Pauline: Napoleon's Favourite Sister* (London: Collins, 1964), 188–89, 192; Joan Bear, *Caroline Murat: A Biography* (London: Collins, 1972), 255–65.

48. Heinrich August Ottokar Reichard, *Guide des voyageurs en France*, 8th ed. (Weimar: Bureau d'Industrie, 1818), 215; *Narrative (1)*, 45.

49. There are many accounts, but see Jean Baptiste Bullet, *Dissertations sur la mythologie Françoise, et sur plusieurs points curieux de l'histoire de France* (Paris: N. L. Moutard, 1771), 64–92; and, in a travel guide, Régis-Jean-François Vaysse de Villiers, *Description routière et géographique de l'empire Français divisé en quatre régions: première partie: région du sud* (Paris: Potey, 1813), 120.

50. "The Theatres," *La Belle Assemblée: Being Bell's Court and Fashionable Magazine*, October 1814, 183; John Genest, *Some Account of the English Stage from the Restoration in 1660 to 1830*, 10 vols. (Bath: H. E. Carrington, 1832), 8:473–74.

51. Alexander Chalmers, *The Projector; a Collection of Essays, in the Manner of the Spectator, Originally Published Monthly, from Jan. 1802 to Nov. 1809*, 3rd ed., revised and corrected, 3 vols. (London: Longman, Hurst, Rees, Orme, and Brown, 1817), 2:48; *Narrative (1)*, 45–46.

52. Saint-Edme, *Itinéraire complet*, 2:25; Charles William Vane, Marquis of Londonderry, *Narrative of the War in Germany and France, in 1813 and 1814* (London: Henry Colburn and Richard Bentley, 1830), 297–98; Jean-Louise-Henriette Campan, *Memoirs of the Private Life of Marie Antoinette, Queen of France and Navarre*, 2 vols. (London: Henry Colburn, 1823), 2:333–38; duchesse de Angoulême, *Royal Memoirs of the French Revolution* (London: John Murray, 1823), 13–30; Désmarais, *Éphémérides historiques*, 38.

53. *The History of Paris from the Earliest Period to the Present Day*, 3 vols. (Paris: A. and W. Galignani, 1825), 3:95; Pierre Villiers, *Manuel du voyageur à Paris, ou Paris ancien et moderne*, nouvelle ed. (Paris: Delaunay, 1814), 12; Saint-Edme, *Itinéraire complet*, 2:24.

54. March 23, 1815, *Memoirs*, 3:177–78; on the theater, Villiers, *Voyageur à Paris*, 217.

55. *Narrative (1)*, 46.

ACKNOWLEDGMENTS

FOR HELP WITH THE RESEARCH for this book, I am under an obligation to the staff of the Manuscripts Reading Room of the Cambridge University Library, where I examined the microfilm edition of the Adams Papers; to Claude Texier, mayor of Mareuil-le-Port, for making available materials relevant to the history of Port-à-Binson; and, most important, to the editorial team of the Adams Papers at the Massachusetts Historical Society. Margaret A. Hogan, Judith Graham, and Mary T. Claffey not only allowed me to work on Louisa Catherine Adams's papers in their offices, where I was treated with exceptional kindness and courtesy, but subsequently subjected my draft manuscript to their expert scrutiny, a service of especial value for a newcomer to matters northeastern. For subsequent help with illustrations in the gift of the Society, I need also to thank C. James Taylor, Peter Drummey, and Elaine Grublin.

For bringing this book to the attention of its eventual publisher, I am in debt to my agent, Andrew Wylie, who helped to fashion the initial proposal, offered prompt advice when needed, and perused a penultimate draft. At Farrar, Straus and Giroux, Eric Chinski gave the manuscript the sort of close reading that I had heard was no longer available from New York editors; he noticed and corrected my bad literary habits, encouraged my better ones, expunged what was superfluous, and sought to clarify what was overly allusive. His editorial assistant, Eugenie Cha, put up with a frustrating pursuit of illustrations, as well as the logistics of production, with remarkable patience and efficiency.

Since *Mrs. Adams in Winter* is a literary experiment and covers more societies than is rational, it was prudent to seek out critics and readers with expertises different from my own. Fortunately, the University of Cambridge has in its byzantine structure people who know most things, often things worth knowing, and attracts those who live elsewhere, even as far away as Philadelphia and Duxford. Chris Clark, Lizzie Collingham, Marion Kant, Mary Laven, Patricia O'Brien, and Jonathan Steinberg all read the manuscript, corrected my mistakes, directed me to scholarship of which I was unaware, and offered cogent advice on structure and style, much of which I took. As usual, Richard Lounsbury undertook a thorough examination of my work and, in particular, saved me from blunders about the Bourbons.

Lastly, I would like to thank the Bogliasco Foundation, which in the spring of 2008 granted me a monthlong fellowship at the Liguria Study Center; there I benefited from the patronage of Anna Maria Quaiat, the center's director, and of Ivana Folle and Alessandra Natale, its associate directors. I learned much from the other fellows (Barbara Allen, Nina Davenport, Vicenzo Fontana, Martyn Lyons, and Andrew Waggoner) about modern music, New Orleans, the autobiographical documentary, literacy among Italian soldiers, Italian landscape architecture, and, from almost everyone else, much about the rich peculiarities of Italian regional cooking, the frustrations of Italian railways, and the oddities of the Italian academy. But I learned most from Kathryn Kramer and Eva Marie Thüne, who took an interest in how Mrs. Adams was faring in her journey and who cared about narrative.

INDEX

Academia Gustaviana, 83

Adams, Abigail, xiii, xvi, 121, 172–74, 176, 207, 213, 227, 233, 239, 259; biographical sketch by JQA of, 41–42; bluestockings and, 86; correspondence of JQA and, 215, 241, 242, 252–55; correspondence of LCA and, 255–57; death of, 240; grandchildren and, 228–31; Johnson family and, 222; European travels of, 47, 176; marriage of John and, 226; parental philosophy of, 177

Adams, Charles, 227

Adams, Charles Francis, 4–5, 24, 28, 87, 108, 193, 233, 234, 250, 262, 271, 277, 279, 285, 288; Annette Krehmer and, 32–33; at Apothecary's Island dacha, 248; arrival in Paris of, 295; birth of, 229; and carriage breakdown, 126, 127; departure from Saint Petersburg of, 8, 306n2; on father's character, 236–37; and father's departure from Russia, 60; linguistic difficulties of, 5, 231–32; on mother's character, 95; preservation of family history by, 242; religious education of, 258; response to sight of sea of, 112, 116; silver cup presented as keepsake to, 96; at sister's funeral, 252; tsarina and, 20

Adams, George Washington, 152, 172–73, 228, 229, 231, 233, 234, 248, 249, 262

Adams, Henry, xiv

Adams, John, xiii, 172–76, 207, 212–13, 226–27, 231, 233, 236, 245, 318n42; correspondence of JQA and, 215, 241, 255–56; death of, 170, 342n80; in diplomatic postings of, 40, 47, 175; marriage of Abigail and, 226; openness of character of, 239; parental philosophy of, 176–77; papers of, 242; presidency of, 144, 175, 225, 295

Adams, John, II, 228, 229, 231, 233, 234, 248, 249, 262

Adams, John Quincy, xiii–xvi, 9, 51, 95, 125, 134, 168–69, 179, 183, 205, 207, 217, 248, 262, 290; and AA's death, 240–41; anti-Semitism of, 103; bankers of, 117, 186; in Berlin, 138, 140, 143, 149, 153–56, 178, 228; character of, 236–40; correspondence of LCA and, 7, 90–91, 112, 165, 173–74, 246–47, 334n62; and daughter's death, 249–56; departure from Saint Petersburg of, 29, 53, 60; engagement of LCA and, 77–79, 174, 207–15, 219, 224, 226–27; indifference to family history of, 241–42; instability of family life of, 228–34; and JA's death, 170, 342n80; and LCA's arrival in Paris, xiii, 295; literary tastes of, 188, 235–36; marriage of LCA and, xiv–xv, 214–16, 218–47, 258–61; and Napoleon's return from Elba, 199–200; political ambition of, 233, 259–60; presidency of,

Adams, John Quincy (*continued*)
235, 295; religion of, 181–82; journey from
Saint Petersburg to Reval of, 56, 80; in
Saint Petersburg, 13, 27, 29–31, 36, 39–42,
89, 109, 168; as secretary of state, 37, 92,
168, 237–38, 243; in Senate, xvi, 123, 128,
153, 228–30, 238; theatergoing by, 93–94;
upbringing of, 176–78
Adams, Louisa Catherine (née Johnson);
Adamses and, xiii–xiv, 169–70, 172–75;
arrival in Paris of, xiii, 262–63, 293,
295–96; in Berlin, xiv, 119, 121, 138,
140–65; births of children of, 152–53,
172, 229, 247–48; character of, 5–6,
94–95, 121; childhood of, xiv, 84, 169;
correspondence of JQA and, 7, 90–91,
112, 165, 173–74, 246–47, 334n62; and
daughter's death, 249–62; departure from
Saint Petersburg of, 3–4, 7–9, 42–43, 60,
88, 96, 124, 194–95, 228, 262; education of,
84–86; engagement of JQA and, 77–79,
174, 207–15, 219, 224, 226–27; family
background of, 75–76, 218–19; feminine
attitudes of, 86–87; instability of family
life of, 228–34; Jews and, 100–103;
journey of, xiv, 44–45, 55–60 (*see also
names of specific places on route*); marriage
of JQA and, xiv–xv, 214–16, 218–47,
258–61; migratory existence of, 168–69,
178; miscarriages of, xv, 138, 140, 153, 225,
228, 241, 260, 293; militarism mistrusted
by, 134–36; physical appearance of, 5;
portraits of, *2, 139, 294*; religious views of,
181–83; in Saint Petersburg, xiv, 12–42;
servants viewed as social inferiors by,
127–29; superstitiousness of, 109–12;
theatergoing of, 92–94; on voyage from
Boston to Russia, 9–12; writing of, 47,
49–50, 53, 86
Adams, Louisa Catherine (daughter), 248–57,
262
Adams, Nabby, *see* Smith, Abigail "Nabby"
Adams
Adams, Thomas Boylston, 138, 140, 227
Alexander I, Tsar, 4, 9, 15–19, 21, 27, 60, 62,
124, 135, 194, 309n32; Catherine Johnson
pursued by, 22–23; diplomatic relations
with United States established by, 41;
Duchy of Warsaw annexed by, 166;
foreigners in service to, 89; Holy Alliance
of, 93; Jews and, 100; marital infidelities
of, 37–38, 202; in peace negotiations with

Napoleon, 123; property purchased by, 29,
248; prying by, 23–24; Spanish regiment
outfitted by, 35
All Hallows Barking (London), *206*, 207
Allied Powers, 194, 278, 348n38; Armies of,
184, 200, 202, 293
Ambrose, metropolitan of Saint Petersburg
and Novgorod, 13
American Revolution, 123, 172, 175, 225
Amsterdam, 117, 214
Anglicans, 35, 69, 75, 181–82, 209, 252
Anna Pavlovna, Grand Duchess, 19
anti-Semitism, 100, 103
Apraxin, Countess Ekaterina Vladimirovna
(née Princess Galitzin), 194–95
Apraxin, Fydor, 194
Apraxin, Count Stepan Stepanovich, 194
Armée du Nord, 284
Atkinson Academy, 229
Attila the Hun, 136
Auerstedt, battle of, 118
Augusta, Princess, 72
Augustus Frederick, Prince, 152, 156–57
Austria, 10, 13, 199

Babet, Madame, 3, 87, 95, 108, 126, 193, 263,
272, 277, 281, 288, 295, 306n2
Bacciochi, Elisa Bonaparte, 290
Bach, Johann Sebastian, 185
Baden, 167, 265–68
Baedecker, Karl, 50
Bagration, Princess, 38
Bancroft, George and Sarah, 246
Baptiste, 3, 96, 105–108, 125–27, 200, 202,
306n2
Bar-le-Duc, 278
Barzy-sur-Marne, 290
Bath, Earl of, 72
Bavaria, 196, 197
Bayard, James, 63, 66, 81–82, 89–91, 199, 236
Beauharnais, Stéphanie, Grand Duchess, 267,
348n46
Beckford, Benjamin, 10
Beelitz, 180
Before the Storm (Fontane), 146
Beggars Surrounding a Carriage, Epernay
(Lewis), *281*
Belgium, 10
Bellune, Claude Victor-Perrin, duc de, 285,
348n38
Belport, B. de, *283*

Bénaménil, 275

Berka, 195

Berlin, xiv, 19, 46, 86, 121, 125, 127, 132–33, 140–68, 173, 179, 191, 198, 262, 269, 327n47, 329n4, 332n37; Anglican church in, 181–82; bourgeois lifestyle in, 143–44; Congress of, 330n16; design of, 69, 141–43; French occupation of, 118; growth of, 140–41; guidebooks for travel from, 51; Jews in, 101, 103; JQA in, 138, 140, 143, 149, 153–56, 178, 228; to Leipzig, 179; letter to JQA from, 202; narrative of LCA's years in, 47; Prussian court in, 119, 124, 146–55; retreat of royal family from, 137; Schönlanke to, 133; servants in, 128; social circle in, 92–93, 144–46, 155–60, 165; superstitions in, 110

Bétancourt, General Augustin de, 35, 39

Bethmann, Louise Henriette von, 202

Bethmann, Simon Moritz von, 202, 203, 204–206, 263, 338n24, 344n3

Beuharnais, Alexandre, vicomte de, 267

Bezzara, Chevalier, 252

Bible, the, 235

Biron, Ernst, Duke of Kurland, 98

Bischoffsheim, 268

Bischoffwerder family, 110, 111, 156, 159

Bismarck, Otto von, 330n16

Black Ball, The (Adams), 103

Blamont, 275

Blome, Baron Otto, 38

Blücher, Field Marshal Gebhard Leberecht von, 293

Bode, Charles Auguste Louis Frederick de Bode, baron de, 33–34, 66

Bode, Fréderica, 267

Bode, Mary Kynnersley, baroness de, 33–34, 66

Bode-Kynnersley, Marie de, see Colombi, Condesa Marie de Bode-Kynnersley de

Bonaparte, Pauline, 290

Bondy, 54, 273, 292–93; forest of, 291–92

Boston, 9, 86, 128, 169, 174–76, 228–31, 238

Boswell, James, 323n14

Botticelli, Sandro, 27

Bourbons, 99, 165, 270, 276, 285

Brandenburg, 125, 127, 129; Memel to, 122

Brandenburg Gate (Berlin), xiv, 118, 120, 142–43, 146, 163

Braunsberg, 125, 327n47; to Graudenz, 125

Bray, François Gabriel Bray, comte de, 38–39

Bromberg, 131

Brotze, Johann Christophe, 63, 82, 99

Brown, William, and family, 110, 144–45, 152, 155–57, 172

Bruhl family, 156, 159

Brummell, George "Beau," 76, 156

Brummell, William, 156

Bruxner, George Augustus, 8

Buchanan, Andrew, 249, 252

Buchanan, Caroline Johnson, 211, 249

Bussche Hunnefeldt, Baron de, 96

Calau, F. A., 164

Cambridge, Duke of, 151

Cambronne, General Pierre, 348n36

Caraman, Victor Louis Charles de Riquet, duc de, 165, 269

Carlyle, Thomas, 132

Carr, John, 45–46, 50, 67, 69–70, 90

Casanova, Giacomo, 98

Castle of Otranto, The (Walpole), 110

Castlereagh, Lady, 151

Catherine, Grand Duchess, 38

Catherine II (the Great), Tsarina, 12, 13, 15, 18, 25, 26, 32, 34, 40, 74, 83

Caulaincourt, Armand Augustine Louis de, duc de Vicenza, 27, 161–62, 277

Châlons-sur-Marne, 278–79, 293; to Paris, 279; Strasbourg to, 274

Charles V, King of France, 291

Charles XII, King of Sweden, 66

Charleston, College of, 222

Charlottenburg Palace (Berlin), 146, 163

Chartèves, 290

Château Thierry, 273, 274, 287, 290

Châtillon-sur-Marne, 273, 274, 287, 289–90

Cherkovitza, 61, 63

Chevallier, Madame, 38

Chien de Montargis, Le (Pixérécourt), 291–92

Christianity, 70, 182–83; conversion of Jews to, 100, 103

Chudleigh, 71, 74, 80

Chudleigh, Elizabeth, 71–75, 77, 318n42

Churchill, Charles, 72

Cicero, 235

Claude Lorrain, 27

Claye, 54, 291, 292

Cohen, Ephraim and Pessel, 103, 155

Coleridge, Samuel Taylor, 191

Colombi, Condesa Marie de Bode-Kynnersley de, xvi, 33–35, 39, 109–10, 104, 267, 324n20
Colombi y Payet, Conde Antonio, 33, 39, 109–10, 324n20
Condé, Prince de, 34
Confederation of the Rhine (Rheinbund), 10, 166, 202
Congregationalists, 181
Consentius, Kauffman, 118
Constantine, Grand Duke, 23–24, 60, 65, 309n37
Continental Congress, 40
Continental System, 11
Cooper, William, 10
Copenhagen, 28, 92
Copernicus, Nicolaus, 129
Copley, John Singleton, 217
Corps Royal de Chasseurs, 284
Corsica, 10
Cossacks, 115, 136, 200, 278
Cosway, Maria, 74, 318n48
Cour de l'Angleterre, La (Frankfurt), 201
Cour de Darmstadt, La (Karlsruhe), 266
Cranch, Mary Smith, 228–29, 249, 252
Cranch, Richard, 249, 252
Croatia, 10
Croix, La (Karlsruhe), 266
Culm, 125, 130
Cumberland, Duke of, 151
Czartoryski, Prince Adam, 17

Dalmatia, 10
Dana, Francis, 40, 125
Darmstadt, 264, 265
Darmstadt, Duchess of, 153
De l'Allemagne (Staël), 141
Delphine (Staël), 188
Denmark, 9–11, 70
Desaix, General Louis Charles Antoine, 269
Dessau, Prince of, 183
Deutsches Haus (Königsberg), 124
Dick, John Adam, 201
Dickens, Charles, 188
Dietrich, F. C., 164
Disbrowe, Anne, 47
Diziani, Gaspare, 14
Doblen, 97, 105, 112
Dombasle, 275
Domkirche (Riga), 88

Dönhoff, Sophie Juliane, Countess von, 330n14
Dorpat, 81–84, 87–88, 91; Narva to, 79; to Riga, 88
Dorpat Stone Bridge, The (Brotze), 82
Dresden, 19, 156, 179, 191
Drogen, 113
Duben, 183
Dupin, Monsieur, 272, 277, 290, 292, 293, 295

Eisenach, 186, 189, 190, 191–95, 197, 199; to Frankfurt, 196; Leipzig to, 186
Elba, 124, 194, 198–99, 284, 290
Elbing, 125, 129
Eleanor of Aquitaine, 119
Elgin, Earl of, 157
Élisabeth, Princess, 293
Elizabeth, Queen of Bohemia, 266
Elizabeth Alexievna, Tsarina, 4, 8, 12, 13, 16–18, 20–21, 27–28, 267, 308n22, 309n32
Elliott, Charles B., 324n29
Enghien, duc d', 99
England, 10–12, 127, 142, 145, 161, 169, 175, 254; French wars with, 134; imports from France to, 219; quasi-war between United States and, 123; Russia and, 16, 166; treaties between United States and, 9, 63, 77; see also London
English Factory Church (Saint Petersburg), 252
Enlightenment, 101
Epernay, 205, 279–81, 281
Episcopalians, 181; see also Anglicans
Eppes (maid), 128, 175
Erfurt, 166–68, 194
Essai critique sur l'histoire de la livonie (Bray), 39
Esterhazy-Roisin, Countess, 38
Estland, 70, 80
Estonians, 70, 71, 83
État général des postes du royaume de France, 51, 53, 54
Ettlingen, 268
Everett, Alexander, 9
Eylau, battle of, 160

Farren, Elizabeth, 94
Fatalot family, 278

Federalists, 134, 175, 243
Ferdinand, Prince, 145, 149, 329n9, 330n16
Filehne, 131
Finland, 26, 70, 90
Fisher, Miers, Jr., 32
Fontane, Theodor, 146
Fordon, 125, 131
France, xiii, xv, 9–11, 16, 33, 92, 126, 127, 169, 175, 181, 202; border crossing from Germany into, 268–69; cuisine of, 271; German wars with, 118, 130, 133, 134, 158–63, 183–87, 197, 200, 202, 284, 293, 348n38; imports to Britain from, 219; Napoleon's return from Elba to, 198–200, 204; peace between Austria and, 13; road system and travel in, 53–56, 265; Russia invaded by, 21, 89, 98, 100, 123, 131, 135, 136, 191, 193, 200, 254, 264, 280, 284; see also specific cities and towns
Francis I, Emperor of Austria, 199
Frankenstein (Shelley), 110
Frankfurt am Main, 54, 102, 166–68, 179, 186, 189, 201–203, 205–206, 247, 262, 344n3; Eisenach to, 196; to Kehl, 263
Frauenberg, 129
Frederica, Princess Louis of Prussia, 119, 148, 150–51, 153
Frederica Luise, Queen Dowager of Prussia, 148, 155
Frederica Sophia Wilhelmina, Princess, 148
Frederick, Prince, 146
Frederick II (the Great), King of Prussia, 118, 130, 133–34, 136, 141, 145, 146, 148, 323n14, 324n22
Frederick Adolphus, Prince, 156
Frederick Augustus, King of Saxony, 131, 166
Frederick William I, King of Prussia, 133
Frederick William II, King of Prussia, 119, 145, 148, 330n14
Frederick William III, King of Prussia, 16, 118, 119, 123, 124, 146, 148, 150–54, 159, 163, 164, 166, 179, 202, 326n38
Frege, Christian Gottlob, 186
French Revolution, 10, 33, 40, 161, 243, 274, 288
Friedlander, David, 101
Fulda, 166, 192, 195
Fulling, John, 3, 107, 126, 200, 202, 306n2

Gallatin, Albert, 82, 89–90
Galloway, Dr., 249–51, 255
Gaon of Vilna, 101
Garde Impériale, 281, 284, 285
Garlike, Hauptmann, 156
Gelnhausen, 195–96
Genlis, Madame de, 86
George II, King of England, 72
George III, King of England, 127, 156
Georgel, Abbé, 65
Germany, xiii, 10, 33, 34, 69, 92, 93, 100; cuisine of, 271; road system and travel in, 53, 54; superstitions in, 110–11; theaters in, 91; see also Prussia; specific cities and towns
Ghent, 9, 123; Treaty of, 295
Gibbes, Dr., 250–51
Gibbon, Edward, 78, 118
Gisborne, Thomas, 32
Gisborne, Thomas John, 32, 33
Godart, Jean, 348n40
Godfrey, Martha, 10, 23–24
Goethe, Johann Wolfgang von, 142, 185, 187, 188
Golden Hind (Kustrin), 134
Goldsmith, Oliver, 94
Golofkin family, 143, 156, 159
Gostiny Dvor (Saint Petersburg), 32
Gotha, 189
Grand Tour, 156
Grande Armée, 184, 191, 281, 282
Granville, Augustus Bossi, 62, 81, 324n29
Graudenz, 125, 130, 131; Braunsberg to, 125; to Schönlanke, 130
Gray, Francis C., 9, 69, 70, 89
Great Northern War, 66, 70
Green, George, 46, 68, 88, 313n3
Gregorofskii, Helen, 32
Grenoble, 199
Grenville, Elizabeth, Lady Carysfort, 110, 157
Grimké, Sarah, 86
Grimms' fairy tales, 111–12
Gustavus Adolphus, King of Sweden, 187

Hague, The, 40, 178, 208, 209
Hamburg, 69, 127, 156, 172
Hamilton, James, sixth duke of, 72
Hamlet (Shakespeare), 94
Hanau, 196, 198, 200; battle of, 197, 200, 263
Hanover, 156

Hanseatic League, 69
Harpe, Jean François de la, 62–63
Harris, Levett, 35–36, 41, 89, 90, 165, 252, 312*n63*
Harvard College, 215, 218, 222, 233
Hasidim, 101
Headley, J. T., 348*n36*
Heidelberg, 264, 266
Hellen, Nancy (née Johnson), 5, 75, 77, 207, 211, 214, 224, 230, 231, 238–39, 248, 252, 258
Hellen, Walter, 231, 237
Helm, Juliana, 232
Héming, 275
Henry, Prince, 148–49
Heppenheim, 264, 265
Herder, Johann Gottfried von, 188
Hermitage (Saint Petersburg), 20, 25, 30
Hervey, Lieutenant Augustus, 72, 73
Hesse, 168, 198
Hesse-Cassel, 265
Hesse-Darmstadt, 167, 265
Hilkensfer, 87–88
Hogarth, William, 75
Hohenzollerns, 118, 141, 149, 159
Hommarting, 275
Horace (ship), 9–12
Hotel du Cygne (Bar-le-Duc), 278
Hotel de l'Esprit (Strasbourg), 269, 346*n14*
Hotel de Londres (Saint Petersburg), 28, 32
Hotel du Nord (Paris), 295
Hôtel des Postes (Paris), 270
Hotel de Russie (Berlin), 138, 144, 158
Hotel de Russie (Memel), 117
Hotel Saint Petersburgh (Mitau), 99, 105
Hotel Saint Petersburgh (Riga), 89–90, 95
Hotel de Saxe (Leipzig), 185
Hotel de la Ville de Bourdeaux (Saint Petersburg), 28, 310*n49*
Hubbard, William James, *293*
Hugo, Victor, 348*n36*
Huguenots, 124, 141
Humboldt, Wilhelm von, 150
Hunefeld, 195
Hunter, Elizabeth Orby, 158

Iggafor, 81
Imperial Bolshoi Theatre in St. Petersburg (Pattersen), *43, 58*
Imperial University (Dorpat), 83–84
Inconstant, L' (ship), 198

Italy, 10, 26, 92
Ittenheim, 274
Ivan III, Tsar, 65
Ivangorod, 65–66

Jacob, William, 55
Jacobinism, 134
Jacquet family, 276
Jay Treaty, 77
Jefferson, Thomas, 41, 74, 175, 188, 201, 280, 318*n48*, 346*n23*
Jena, 191; battle of, 118, 163
Jerusalem Delivered (Tasso), 152
Jewe, 80
Jewett, Noah, 10
Jews, 32, 89, 100–103, 105, 114, 124, 131, 141, 155, 252, 324*n29*, 325*n31*
Johnson, Caroline (LCA's sister), *see* Buchanan, Caroline Johnson
Johnson, Catherine (LCA's sister), 9, 22–23, 28, 33, 38, 109, 214, 250, 251, 253
Johnson, Catherine Nuth (LCA's mother), 5, 75, 94, 222, 224, 225, 231, 248, 249, 252
Johnson, John, 10
Johnson, Joshua (LCA's father), 75, 77, 84, 85, 94, 119, 172, 181, 208–10, 214, 218–25, 231, 340*n50*
Johnson, Nancy (LCA's sister), *see* Hellen, Nancy Johnson
Johnson, Thomas (LCA's brother), 222
Johnson, Thomas (LCA's uncle), 225
Johnston, Alexander Keith, *198*
Johnston, Robert, 126, 132
Jones, George, 64
Joseph II, Holy Roman Emperor, 264–65
Joséphine, Empress, 160, 267

Kaiserslautern, 205
Kant, Immanuel, 101, 125
Karamzin, Nikolai, 45, 89, 102, 131, 144, 187
Karl Ludwig Friedrich, Grand Duke of Baden, 266
Karlsruhe, 264, 266–68, 344*n3*
Katharine Amalie Christiane Luise, Princess, 266–67
Katte, Hans Hermann von, 133–34
Kaucminde Castle (Kurland), 104
Kazan Cathedral (Saint Petersburg), 30
Kehl, 263, 268, 273; Frankfurt to, *263*
Keller, Fräulein von, 329*n9*

Kemberg, 183
Kemble, Fanny, 94
Kiepena, 61
Kleinpungern, 80
Klemme, La (Eisenach), 193
Klopstock, Freidrich Gottlieb, 91, 188
Koblenz, 50
Kohl, Johann Georg, 80
Königsberg, 8, 101, 112, 114, 118, 124–26, 129, 132, 137, 160; Memel to, 121–23
Koskova, 61
Kotzebue, August von, 45, 92, 122, 183, 188, 320n78
Kozodavlev, Osip Petrovich, 4, 114
Krause, Johann, 83
Krehmer, Annette, 32–33, 39, 250–52
Krehmer, Sebastian, 33, 39, 311n54
Krensitz, 183
Kristiansand, 11
Kronstadt, 10, 11, 28, 32, 74
Kropstadt, 180
Krüdener, Burchard Alexis Constantine, Baron von, 92–93
Krüdener, Julie von, 92–93
Kurland, 70, 89, 90, 97, 100, 104, 113, 206; Society of Literature and Art, 99
Kustrin, 125, 132–33, 135–36, 200, 327n47

La Chaussée, 278
Laighton, John, 10
Lambert, Elizabeth, 76
Lamothe-Langon, Étienne Léon, 199
Larangot family, 287–89, 348n40
Laurens, J. D., 164
Laye, 278
Leigh, Samuel, 50
Leipzig, 50, 165–67, 181, 183, 185–86, 189, 191, 199; battle of, 131, 161, 163, 164, 183–85, 193; Berlin to, 178–80, 179; to Eisenach, 186
Leslie, Charles Robert, 2
Leszczynski, Stanislaus, 276
Letters on the Equality of the Sexes and the Condition of Woman (Grimké), 86
Letters Written During a Short Residence in Sweden, Norway, and Denmark (Wollstonecraft), 46
Lewald, Fanny, 146, 330n10
Lewis, George, 281
Lewis, W. D., 37
Lieven, Countess Charlotte von, 19

Ligny, 278
Lisbon, 208, 214, 219
Litta, Count Giulio Renato de, 13
Litta, Countess Ekaterina Vassilevna, 12–13, 15, 17, 19
Livland, 70, 80, 89, 97
Livonian Brothers of the Sword, 70
London, xiv, xv, 19, 50, 140, 156, 229, 236; Abigail Adams in, 176; John Adams in, 47, 226; Johnson family in, 75–77, 84–85, 94, 127, 128, 172–74, 207, 214–16, 218–21, 225; medievalism of, 69
Longchamp, 278
Lopukhina, Anna (Princess Gagarina), 38
Lose, Johann Jakob de, 203
Louder, George, 10
Louis, Prince, 150
Louis, XIV, King of France, 25, 259
Louis XV, King of France, 161, 276
Louis XVI, King of France, 33, 127, 161, 293
Louis XVIII, King of France, 4, 98, 99, 198, 270, 277, 284, 285, 293
Louis Charles, dauphin, 293
Lubavitchers, 101
Luise, Princess Ferdinand of Prussia, 148–50, 155, 159, 329n9
Luise, Queen of Prussia, xvi, 117–19, 120, 121, 123, 137, 144, 146–47, 150–55, 157, 161, 163, 179, 202, 326n38; mausoleum of, 163–65, 164
Luneville, 275
Lustgarten (Berlin), 142
Luther, Martin, 181, 191
Lutherans, 81, 102, 124, 152, 181, 252
Lützen, 187, 192, 196
Lyttelton, Sarah, see Spencer, Sarah, Lady Lyttelton

Macaire, Chevalier, 291
Madison, Dolley, 86, 121
Madison, James, 84, 232, 233
Maimon, Solomon, 101
Maimonides, Moses, 101
Maison Rouge (Frankfurt), 201
Maison Rouge (Strasbourg), 269
Maisonneuve, Commandeur de, 12
Maistre, Joseph de, 39, 40, 89, 188
Malcom, E., 171
Malplaquet, battle of, 147
Malta, Order of, 13, 38

Maria Federovna (empress mother), 12, 13, 17–19, 21

Marie Antoinette, Queen of France, 293

Marie Louise, Princess, 23, 270

Marie Thérèse Charlotte, dauphine, 293

Marienburg, 125, 129–30

Marienwerder, 125, 130

Marlborough, John Churchill, first duke of, 147

Marshall, John, 41, 188

Mary (ship), 219

Mary I, Queen of England, 152

Maryland, 208, 219, 225; Legislative Assembly, 172

Mason, John, 85

Mayence, 202, 205, 263

Meaux, 273, 291

Medem, Maria, Countess von, 104

Memel, 90, 91, 112, 117–18, 121, 136, 145, 160; to Brandenburg, *122*; letter to JQA from, 202; lighthouse at, *116*

Mendelssohn, Felix, 185

Mengs, Countess, 104

Mennonites, 124

Messelière, comte de, 45

Metropolitan Kaleidoscope, The (Adams), 234–35, 239

Metternich, Klemens Wenzel, Prince von, 167, 199, 202

Metz, 205

Meyer, John Christoph, 8

Michel, General Claude Étienne, *283*, 284–85, 288, 293, 348*n36, 38*

Michelangelo, 25

Milton, John, 85, 235

Misnagdim, 101

Mitau, 97–102, 104–107, 112–14, 320*n78*

Mitchell, John, 320*n76*

Moët, Jean Remy, 280

Monroe, James, 42

Montague, Elizabeth, 72

Montagu, Lady Mary Wortley, 47

Montdidier, Aubri de, 291

Moore, Thomas, 188

Morel, Louis Jean, 99–100, 104–107

Moscow, 123, 194, 254, 264, 280

Munich, 161, 267

Murat, Caroline Bonaparte, 290

Murat, Joachim, 198

Murray, Augusta, 156

Murray, John, 50

Nainal, 80

Nancy, 273–78

Nantes, 68, 69, 84, 172, 219

Naples, 13

Napoleon, Emperor of France, xvi, 10, 11, 16, 19, 21, 22, 35, 53, 93, 100, 105, 118, 123, 124, 131, 133–37, 160, 161, 166, 184, 186–87, 191–200, 202, 204, 254, 262, 264, 267–70, 277, 281, 282, 284, 285, 293, 326*n38*

Narbonne-Lara, Louis Marie Jacques Amalric, comte de, 161–62

Narva, 60, 63, 65–66, 67, 68–69, 74, 80; battle of, 66; to Dorpat, *79*; Saint Petersburg to, *61*

Naryshkina, Maria Dmitrievna, 37

Naumburg, 187

Néale, Ferdinand, Count von, 145, 160

Néale, Josephine, Countess von, 145, 160

Néale, Pauline, xvi, 110, 111, 145–46, 150, 159, 160, 165, 329*n9*, 330*n10*

Nelson (JQA's servant), 10

Netherlands, 9, 10, 18, 40, 77, 78, 83, 117, 118, 148, 207–11, 214, 224, 225

New Jersey, College of, 84

Nikon, Patriarch of Moscow, 81

Noailles, Antonin Claude Dominique Just de, 269

Norman, Captain, 165

Northern Summer, A (Carr), 45, 46, 50, 67

Norway, 10, 11

Ober Bartau, 113

Oberman Gate (Frankfurt), 201

Octa, 29, 33

Opolie, 61

Original Journal from London to St. Petersburgh (Green), 46

Ortelsburg, 118

Osborne's Hotel (London), 223

Ostrometz, 130

Pahlen, Count Peter von, 104

Pahlen, Fedor, 41

Paradise Lost (Milton), 85

Paradise Regained (Milton), 85

Paris, xiv, xvi, 7–9, 19, 25, 140, 191, 199, 206, 263, 273–75, 279, 284, 287, 288, 346*n23*; Abigail Adams in, 176; assault of Allied Powers on, 293; arrival in, 295; Elizabeth

Chudleigh in, 74; guidebooks for travel from, 51; John Adams in, 47, 175; John Quincy Adams in, 90, 93, 173–74, 202, 235, 295; mail between Saint Petersburg and, 53; Napoleon's return to, 269–70, 277, 281, 282, 284, 290, 293; Prussian troops in, 161

Patterssen, Benjamin, *43, 58*

Paul, Tsar, 15–16, 19, 34, 83, 100, 104

Paulucci, Marquis Filippo, 89–91

Paulucci, Marquise Wilhelmina, 90, 91

Pavlovsk (Saint Petersburg), 20

Peabody, Elizabeth Shaw, 229

Peasant Wagons in Estland (Brotze), *99*

Peter I (the Great), Tsar, 13, 25–26, 31, 66, 81, 194, 310*n42*

Peterhof (Saint Petersburg), 20, 25

Phalsbourg, 275

Philadelphia, 172, 176, 228

Philip II, King of Spain, 152, 157

Philippine, Landgravine of Hesse-Cassel, 150

Phillis, Mademoiselle, 38

Pierrepont, Evelyn, Duke of Kingston-upon-Hull, 72, 73

Pitt, Reverend, 252

Pixérécourt, René Charles Guilbert de, 291–92

Plantagenets, 236

Poinsett, Joel R., 30

Polana, Maria, 250

Poland, 18, 26, 70, 100, 112; partitioning of, 70, 113–14, 131

Poland, Nathan, 10

Polangen, 114

Polish-Lithuanian commonwealth, 276

Poltava, battle of, 66

Port-à-Binson, *286*, 287–90, 348*n40*

Porter, Robert Ker, 45

Portugal, 208, 214

Potemkin, Prince Grigori Alexandrovitch, 12

Potsdam, 146, 168, 179

Poussin, Nicolas, 27

Pride and Prejudice (Austen), 145

Prince Louis Ferdinand (Lewald), 146

Proby, John Joshua, first earl of Carysfort, 157

Protestants, 187; *see also specific denominations*

Prussia, xv, 4, 10, 68, 112, 117, 121, 124–26, 131–32, 141, 166, 169, 188, 198, 214, 269; court of, 119, 145–47, 151–55; currency of,

167; French wars with, 118, 130, 133, 134, 158–63, 191, 284, 293; militarism of, 142; road system in, 54, 183; Russia and, 16, 114–16, 136, 264; *see also specific cities and towns*

Puritans, 182

Pushkin, Alexander, 30, 64

Quakers, 35, 121

Quarenghi, Giacomo, 15

Queen Luise as Hebe in Front of the Brandenburg Gate (Wach), *120*

Queen of Spades, The (Pushkin), 30

Quincy, xiii, xiv, 128, 134, 169, 170, *171*, 176, 227–28, 233, 241, 242

Quintilian, 256, 343*n104*

Quinzard, Jean Pierre, 29–30

Radziwill, Prince Anton, 101, 150, 159

Radziwill, Princess Luise, 118, 148, 150, 157, 159–62

Radziwill, Wilhelm, 160

Raskolniki, 81

Ranapungern, 80

Rastadt, 268

Rastrelli, Francesco Bartolemeo, 14, 15, 98

Rauch, Christian Daniel, 165

Reformation, 69, 181

Reichard, Heinrich August Ottokar, 50, 265, 344*n5*

Rembrandt van Rijn, 25

Render, Wilhelm, 201

Report on Weights and Measures (Adams), 168

Reval, 66, 80

Riga, 37, 58, 68, 87–93, 95, 96, 98, 102, 107, 112, 202, 320*nn76, 78*; Dorpat to, *88*; to Memel, *97*; to Saint Petersburg, *52*

Ritchie, Leitch, 102

Roches-Baritaud, Claude de Beauharnais, comte de, 267

Roman Catholics, 39, 69, 114, 152, 181, 183, 187

Roman Empire, 50, 118

Romanovs, 16, 121

Romanticism, 266

Rothschilds, 202, 338*n24*

Royal Marriages Act, British, 156

Royal Navy, British, 117

Royal Opera House (Berlin), 142

Rumiantsev, Nikolai Petrovich, 12, 13, 41

Russia and Russian Empire, xv, xvi, 8, 40, 70, 142, 161, 166, 169, 269; Baltic provinces of, 70, 71, 80–81; banking in, 186; in coalition against France, 11; court of, 14–22, 155; Department of Ceremonies, 14; diplomatic relations of United States with, 40–41; Elizabeth Chudleigh in, 74; foreign policy of, 16; in Great Northern War, 66; household size in, 30; John Quincy's trip to Ghent from, 9; Napoleon's campaign in, 21, 89, 98, 100, 123, 131, 135, 136, 191, 193, 200, 254, 264, 280, 284; narratives of travel to and from, 45–47, *48*, 49; Poland and, 114; Prussian boarder with, 114–16; ranking of aristocrats in, 31; road system and travel in, 53–57; State Board of Foreign Affairs, 3; superstitions in, 109–10; trade between United States and, 41–42; voyage from Boston to, 9–12; *see also specific cities and towns*

Russian Orthodox Church, 13

Rutzau, 113

Saalfeld, battle of, 160

Sade, Marquis de, 160

Sadowa, battle of, 163

Saint Aubin, 278

Saint Dizier, 278

Saint-Domingue, 284

St. George, Melesina, 158

Saint-Jean d'Angély, Comte Regnaud de, 199

Saint John Palace (Berlin), 149, 330*n16*

Saint Julien, Count, 38

Saint Petersburg, xiii, xiv, xvi, 3–43, 56, 132, 137, 144, 165, 168, 178, 206, 229, 231–32, 235, 267, 295, 309*n32*; Anglican church in, 35, 181; aristocratic lifestyle in, 26–28; arrival in, 12; birth and death of daughter in, 247–55, 262; carriage building in, 57; climate of, 24, 42, 309*n38*; departure to Paris from, 3–4, 7–9, 42–43, 60, 88, 96, 124, 194–95, 228, 262; design of, 25–26, 69, 141, 266; diplomats in, 38–40, 233; Elizabeth Chudleigh in, 74; French spoken in, 68; German Balts in, 71; guidebooks for travel to and from, 51–53; Julie von Krüdener in, 93; Germaine de Staël in, 188; imperial court in, 12–24; living expenses in,

28–30; mail between Paris and, 53, 202; markers of distance from, 87, 114; during Napoleonic invasion, 123, 135; to Narva, *61*, 63; population of, 31–32, 140; sexual customs of aristocracy in, 37–38; social circle in, 32–36, 104, 155; superstitiousness in, 109–10; theater in, 20, 91, 93, 292; voyage from Boston to, 9–12; wine in, 280

St. Petersburg Dialogues (Maistre), 39

Sanford, Mrs., 156

Sardinia, 40

Sarrebourg, 275

Saudrupt, 278

Savage, Edward, *139*

Saverne, 274–75

Saxe-Coburg, Duke of, 166–67

Saxe-Weimar, Duke of, 166

Saxony, 162, 166–67, 180, 183, 284

Schadow, Johann Gottfried, 119, 164–65

Schickler Brothers banking firm (Berlin), 103, 155, 165, 323*n14*

Schiller, Friedrich, 91, 118, 185, 187, 188

Schink and Koch, Messrs., 8

Schinkel, Karl Friedrich, 142

Schlegel, August Wilhelm von, 91

Schlosskirche (Wittenberg), 180, 181

Schneur-Zalmen, 101

Schönlanke, 125, 126; to Berlin, *133*; Graudenz to, *125*

Schreiber, A., 344*n5*

Schwarzenberg, Johann von, 81

Schwedenstein (Lützen), 187

Scott, Walter, 185, 325*n35*

Sedan, battle of, 163

Self-Knowledge (Mason), 85

Semigallians, 105

Sens, 273

Seume, Johann Gottfried, 19, 45, 91, 309*n37*

Seven Years' War, 148

Shakespeare, William, 91, 94, 118

Sheremetev Palace (Saint Petersburg), 30

Siddons, Sarah, 76, 94

Silesia, 102, 131, 179, 225

Simpson, Dr., 250, 255

Sirène, La (Meaux), 291

Skavronsky, Count Paul Martinovitch, 13

Slovenia, 10

Smith, Abigail "Nabby" Adams, 227–28, 249

Smith, Joseph Allen, 25

Smith, William Stephens, 227–28

Smith, William Steuben, 9, 23, 109, 252, 253
Socrates, 246
Soleil, Le (Heppenheim), 266
Solms-Braunfels, Prince of, 151
South Sea Bubble, 72
Spain, 10, 35, 284
Spencer, Sarah, Lady Lyttelton, 12, 98, 114, 135, 308n22
Sporting Magazine, 76–77
Stadtkirche St. Marien (Wittenberg), 180
Stadtschloss (Berlin), 142, 146
Staël, Germaine de, 141, 161, 188, 235
Starke, Mariana, 59
Stollhofen, 268
Strasbourg, 99, 205, 268–75, 346n23
Strelna, 43, 60, 65, 179
Stroganoff Palace (Saint Petersburg), 26–27
Sullivan, Martha, 86
Sweden, 9, 10, 26, 42, 69; Baltic region and, 70, 71, 83; in Great Northern War, 66, 317n34
Switzerland, 10, 92, 93

Tacitus, Cornelius, 235
Tadliken, 113
Talleyrand-Périgord, Charles Maurice de, 18
Talmudic study, 101
Tamerlane, 136
Tapiau, 123
Taproom in Inn (Brotze), *63*
Tartuffe (Molière), 94
Tasso, Torquato, 152
Teutonic Knights, 129; Livonian Order of, 66, 70
Thirty Years' War, 187
Thuringia, 181
Tiergarten (Berlin), 140, 142, 149
Tilsit, 123–24, 160, 326n38, 43; Treaty of, 16, 131
Titian, 25
Tolstoy, Leo, 194
Torgau, siege of, 162
Torma, 81
Toul, 278, 285
Tour Through Part of Germany, Poland, Russia, Sweden, Denmark, &c, A (Seume), 45, 309n37
Tourzel, marquise de, 293
Toussaint L'Ouverture, François-Dominique, 284

Travelling Sketches in Russia and Sweden (Porter), 45
Travels from Moscow (Karamzin), 45
Treaty of Paris (1783), 84
Tree, Ellen, 94
Trésaguet, Pierre, 265
Treuenbrietzen, 180
Trieste, 161
Trumbull, John, 340n50
Truntz, 129
Tuileries (Paris), 25, 267, 270, 277, 290, 293

Ukraine, 34, 66, 101
Unitarians, 181, 182
United States, 169, 186, 254; Congress, 168, 177, 229, 295; House of Representatives, 242; diplomatic relations of Russia with, 40–41; quasi-war betwen England and, 123; Senate, xvi, 123, 128, 153, 228–30, 238; State Department, 42, 237, 243; Supreme Court, 225, 229; trade between Russia and, 41–42; treaties between England and, 9, 63, 77; wine in, 280; *see also specific cities and towns*
Uppsala, University of, 83
Urban II, Pope, 290
Uxkull, Baron Boris, 66

Vach, 195
Vaivara, 71
Valk, 87
Van Dyck, Anthony, 27
Van Halen, Juan, 324n29
Varennes, 293
Vauban, Marquis de, 275
Velaine, 274
Venice, 92
Verdun, 205
Verneuil, 290
Veronese, Paolo, 25
Versailles, 25, 161
Victoria, Princess, 146
Victoria, Queen of England, 146
Vienna, 156, 161, 199, 267; Congress of, 38, 124, 159, 163
Vietinghoff, Baron Otto Herman von, 92
Vigée Le Brun, Élisabeth, 27
Vikings, 70
Ville de Lyon (Strasbourg), 269
Vilnus, 123

Vincelles, 290
Vitry-sur-Marne, 278
Vlodeck, Madame de, 38
Void, 278
Volmar, 87
Voss, John Ernest von, 147
Voss, Sophie Marie, Countess von, 147, 153
Voss, Julie Amalie Elisabeth von, 330n14
Voyage á Pétersbourg (Messelière), 45

Wach, Karl Wilhelm, *120*
Wag or Just from College, The (Adams), 84
Wagram, battle of, 197
Wales, 110
Walpole, Horace, 110
War of 1812, 123
War and Peace (Tolstoy), 194
Warren, Mercy Otis, 86
Warsaw, Duchy of, 112, 131, 166
Wartburg, *190*
Washington, D.C., xiv, 32, 47, 121, 128, 169, 170, 178, 228–29, 248, 295; church attendance in, 181; design of, 69, 266; Dickens in, 189; Hellen residence in, 229–31; Russian diplomats in, 40, 41; salon in, 188
Washington, George, 40, 41, 175
Washington, Martha, 147
Wasselone, 274
Waterloo, battle of, 163, 284, 348n36
Watteau, Jean-Antoine, 27
Weimar, 50, 166, 187–89

Weissenfels, 187
Wellington, Arthur Wellesley, first duke of, 284
Westmoreland, Priscilla, Countess of, 146
Whichelo, C.J.M., *206*
Whitcomb (valet), 128, 174
Wieland, Christoph, 187–88
Wilhelmina, Princess Henry of Prussia, 148, 149, 155
Willink & Van Staphorst, 117
Wilmot, Catherine, 309n28
Wilson, William Rae, 101, 132
Winter Palace (Saint Petersburg), 14, 20, 22, 23, 25, 28, 98, 247; Great Church of, 13
Wittenberg, 180–81, 183
Wollstonecraft, Mary, 46
Wrede, Marshal Karl, 197
Wright, Constance, 326n38
Württemberg, 18

Xantippe, 246

Yamburg, 61, 63, 65
Young, Mary, 75

Zähringen, house of, 267
Zala Castle (Mitau), 104
Zalman, Elijah ben Judah Solomon, 101
Zehlendorf, 179